Dialogue for Development

About the Editors

Janak Pandey a Ph.D. of Kansas State University is currently Vice-Chancellor of Central University of Bihar. Earlier served as Vice-Chancellor of Allahabad University and Director, Govind Ballabh Pant Social Science Institute, Allahabad. He is a past president and a Fellow of the International Association for Cross-Cultural Psychology and also of National Academy of Psychology-India. He is a recipient of the Professor V.K.R.V. Rao award, Fulbright and Commonwealth fellowships. He has published on social influence and contemporary issues like poverty and environment. He edited Perspectives on Experimental Social Psychology in India and the six-volumes of research of Psychology in India: The state-of-art based on two rounds of ICSSR survey of Psychology research. He has also co-edited Asian contributions to Cross-Cultural Psychology and Handbook of Cross-Cultural Psychology. In the late sixties, he collaborated with Prof. J.B.P. Sinha on a number of research studies on social motivation.

T.N. Sinha first Ph.D. awardee under Prof. J.B.P. Sinha from Patna University, is an honorary Professor of Human Resource Management at ASSERT Institute of Management Studies, Patna. Recently, Dr. Sinha retired as Professor and Head of the Psychology Department from B.S. College Danapur, Patna (MU). He worked with Prof. Jai B.P. Sinha on a number of research projects and published few research papers jointly with him. He has to his credit around 25 research papers and a number of research reports published in national and international journals of repute. Prof. Sinha has participated in seminars, workshops and conferences in India and abroad and served as Resource person in Training programmes in the field of Education, Health and Management. Prof. Sinha is the founding and life member of ASSERT and presently serving the organization (ASSERT) as Secretary.

Arvind K. Sinha currently a Professor of Psychology at the Department of Humanities and Social Sciences, Indian Institute of Technology, Kanpur worked under supervision of Dr. Jai B.P. Sinha and earned his Ph.D. degree from the Patna University in 1981. He specializes in Organizational Behaviour and he has authored and co-authored over fifty published articles and conference papers in India and abroad. He has served on several academic administrative positions. Earlier he was associated with the A.N.S. Institute of Social Studies, Patna, and the Department of Psychology, University of Allahabad, Allahabad before joining the Indian Institute of Technology Kanpur in 1981. He has been the Convener of the OB Division, and the President (2009) of the National Academy of Psychology (India). He is widely respected for his teaching, research, mentoring, and administrative capabilities and contributions.

DIALOGUE FOR DEVELOPMENT

Festschrift dedicated to Professor Jai B.P. Sinha

Edited by

JANAK PANDEY
T.N. SINHA
ARVIND K SINHA

CONCEPT PUBLISHING COMPANY PVT. LTD.
NEW DELHI-110059

ISBN-13: 978-81-8069-757-9

First Published 2011

Published and Printed by

Since 1974

Concept Publishing Company Pvt. Ltd.
Regd. Office:
A/15-16, Commercial Block, Mohan Garden
New Delhi-110059 (India)
Phones : 25351460, 25351794, *Fax* : 091-11-25357109
Email : publishing@conceptpub.com,
Website: www.conceptpub.com

Editorial Office:
H-13, Bali Nagar, New Delhi-110 015, India.

Cataloging in Publication Data--Courtesy: D.K. Agencies (P) Ltd. <docinfo@dkagencies.com>

National Academy of Psychology (India). Congress (16th : 2006 : Mumbai, India)
Dialogue for development : festschrift dedicated to Professor Jai B.P. Sinha / edited by Janak Pandey, T.N. Sinha, Arvind K. Sinha.
p. cm.
Includes bibliographical references.
ISBN 9788180697579

1. Sinha, Jai B. P. (Jai Ballabha Prasad), 1936- --Friends and associates--Congresses. 2. Social psychology--India--Congresses. 3. Organizational change--India--Congresses. 4. Social change--India--Congresses. I. Sinha, Jai B. P. (Jai Ballabha Prasad), 1936- II. Pandey, Janak, 1945- III. Sinha, T. N. IV. Sinha, Arvind K. V. Title.

DDC 302.0954 22

Professor J.B.P. Sinha (1936-)
Mrs. Geeta Sinha (1942-)

FOREWORD

I am pleased to write a foreword for this book published in honour of Prof. J.B.P. Sinha by his students and colleagues. The book is very appropriately titled "Dialogue for Development" which expresses contents of chapters in the book. The book contains papers covering a number of areas like organizational behaviour; organizational development and change; values and development, institution building, and on professional and social aspects of Prof. J.B.P. Sinha. I myself got greatly impressed in the 1960s by his research on role of human motivation particularly need for achievement on economic development. I witnessed in those days that his work impressed an eminent Economist Prof. A.K. Dasgupta then Director of the A.N. Sinha, Institute of Social Studies. Prof. Dasgupta was well known for his doubts regarding any possible role of psychology in understanding and facilitating development and change. Under the leadership of Prof. J.B.P. Sinha, social-psychology division of A.N. Sinha Institute of Social Studies excelled in quality research, Ph.D. thesis, and training opportunities for young researchers leading to rightful recognition of psychology in understanding and resolving issues related to social and economic development.

This book, which covers range of issues related to development, is recognition of work done by Prof. J.B.P. Sinha and his associates. I wish very active, happy and productive life to Prof. J.B.P. Sinha.

Saanta Sahi
Cuttak-753001
January 14, 2010

Prof. Radhanath Rath
Former Head
Department of Psychology and Co-ordinator,
Centre of Advance Study in Psychology
Utkal University, Bhubaneswar

PREFACE

This festschrift dedicated to Prof. Jai B.P. Sinha is for his seminal contributions to the field of Psychology. Prof. Sinha, after teaching for a few years in Ranchi University, joined the doctoral programme at the Ohio State University in the early sixties and returned to Ranchi in 1965, after obtaining his Doctoral Degree. Soon after, he was offered a position at the A.N. Sinha Institute of Social Studies, Patna, where he established a vibrant research programme focusing Social-Organizational Issues of Development. Prof. Sinha's work received recognition leading to his nomination to various committees of ICSSR, UGC, and NCERT and also to the Board of the International Association of Applied Psychology and to the Executive Committee of the International Association for Cross-Cultural Psychology. He is a recipient of Senior Fulbright Fellowship. He was honoured as a National Fellow by the Indian Council of Social Science Research. In all these positions, he has established a niche for himself that made him distinguished scholar of ideas to promote socio-cultural context sensitive and relevant psychological science.

High quality of Prof. Sinha's research publications in reputed journals and books did not go unnoticed and he received recognition in several ways such as invitation to address plenary sessions and chair symposia in international conferences like International Congresses of Applied Psychology (at Montreal, 1974; Munich, 1978; Edinburgh, 1982; Jerusalem, 1986; Osaka, 1990; Madrid, 1994), International Congresses of Psychology (Acapulco, 1984; Brussels, 1992; Montreal, 1996), and International Congresses of the International Association for Cross-Cultural Psychology (Bhubaneswar, 1980; Acapulco, 1984; Istanbul, 1986). He was also invited to be a visiting Professor in institutions like McGill University, Wake-Forest University, and Hunter College. Since 1982 he continues to be the Vice-President of the World Association for Dynamic Psychiatry.

Departing substantially from the traditional brands and methodology, Prof. Jai B.P. Sinha opted for a more relevant and applied oriented approach. This brought Psychology more close to the reality covering social issues which govern our day-to-day life. His sustained efforts through his research programmes focusing psychology as a policy science expanding its role in national development and his consistent concern for understanding social organization issues using quantitative and qualitative methods with emphasis on indigenous approach has been globally acknowledged. For decades, he has been a leading influence from developing countries to the discipline of Psychology excelling it to the position of enviable prominence. Almost for five decades Prof. Jai B.P. Sinha has been a role model and mentor for a number of students, scholars, colleagues and friends in India and abroad. His continued dedication to research and receptivity to new ideas will keep motivating the future generations as well. Inspired by his work on a wide range of topics, e.g. social motivation and values, leadership and power, organizational culture and development, psychology and development policies, many who came in his contact including contributors of this volume carried his work forward covering new sectors with extention in the realm of community psychology, rural development, health and education, to name a few. Most of the contributors of this volume are indebted to him as doctoral students, co-workers in research and as colleagues and friends. His influence on students and his colleagues and to the next generation of students constitutes a legacy of scientific pursuits, hard work, professional ethics and building a culture of nurturance and support. This book partly gives a glimpse of what has been done to all these years by those who identify with him and consider him as their role model. The book is a token of their appreciation.

In honour of Prof. Sinha a special session on "Dialogue for Development" was organised in the Annual Conference of National Academy of Psychology at I.I.T., Mumbai, in the year 2006. The idea to publish an edited volume of the selected papers reflecting research legacy of Prof. Sinha received momentum. The papers cover a wide ranging themes, i.e. value and culture for social development, leadership for development, institution building and human development. Some papers are on aspects of biography of Prof. Sinha, his work and professional experiences. Altogether nineteen papers and some brief notes on Prof. J.B.P. Sinha are organized into four sections.

Section 1 presents a brief account of how Prof. Sinha ascended to the enviable height from a modest family background of North Bihar to the global platform of academia. Based on in-depth interview with Prof. Sinha, two chapters offer a humble view of his life style together with his academic journey spanning over 50 years. Section 2 addresses the issues which make organizations effective and high performing. The chapters of this section discuss meaning of work, leadership, organizational climate, emotional intelligence, and organizational justice. Section 3 deals with social development. It has a paper on social policy followed by chapter suggesting self-evolving institutions for sustainable development. Another chapter describes an interesting cross-social categorization experiment that has some important implications for social development followed by chapters on social values, collectivist orientation of Indian culture and issues of social justice. Section 4 presents brief notes of Prof. Sinha's associates, friends and colleagues expressing their personal experiences with him. Readers will know more about Prof. Jai B.P. Sinha as he has been known to his associates.

This book has been essentially a team work of colleagues and friends. Dr. Arif Hussan, Dr. Rajeshwar Mishra, Dr. Suman Kumar Singh, Dr. Sudha Rani Sinha, Dr. Jyoti Verma, Dr. Shashi Jain Gupta, and Dr. J.M. Deo have been active members of this team. We recognize their efforts and involvement. We have received valuable help of Dr. R.B.N. Sinha who provided logistic support. His editorial assistance is appreciated. We are specially grateful to Prof. Ramadhar Singh for his support. We thank all the contributors. Mr. Manoj Kumar Verma deserves our special thanks for his secretarial assistance.

Lastly, the editors would like to express their gratitude for the institutional support provided by the ASSERT, Patna; Department of Psychology, Allahabad University; and Department of Humanities and Social Sciences, I.I.T. Kanpur.

Janak Pandey
T. N. Sinha
Arvind K Sinha

CONTENTS

SECTION-2
ORGANIZATIONAL DEVELOPMENT

SECTION-3
SOCIAL DEVELOPMENT

SECTION-4
PROF. JAI B.P. SINHA: AS KNOWN TO US

List of Contributors

Sadanand Singh, Former Faculty, The Ohio State University, USA.

Rajeshwar Mishra, Currently on the Faculty of the Central University of Bihar, also the Founder Secretary and Faculty of ASSERT, Patna, and founder of Centre for the Development of Human Initiatives (CDHI) Jalpaiguri-735 501 (West Bengal) India. E-mail:rajeshwarmishra789@rediffmail.com.

J.M. Deo, PG Centre of Psychology, College of Commerce, Patna, India. E-mail: drjmdeo@gmail.com

Arvind K Sinha, Department of Humanities and Social Sciences, Indian Institute of Technology, Kanpur-208016, India E-mail: aks@iitk.ac.in

Girishwar Misra, Professor, Department of Psychology, University of Delhi, Delhi-110007. E-mail: misragirishwar@gmail.com

Janak Pandey, Vice-Chancellor of Central University of Bihar. E-mail: janakpandey@cbcs.ac.in

Shailendra Singh, Professor, HRM Group, IIM, Lucknow-226 013. E-mail: shail@iiml.ac.in

V.P. Singh, Faculty, J.D. College, Faizabad (UP), E-mail:vpsvijay@yahoo.com

Sunita Singh-Sengupta, Professor in Organizational Behaviour, Faculty of Management Studies, University of Delhi, Delhi-110 007. E-mail: sssengupta@fms.du.ac.in

Dharm P.S. Bhawuk, Professor of Management and Culture and Community Psychology, Shidler College of Business, University of Hawaii at Manoa, 2404 Maile Way, Honolulu, HI 96826, E-mail: bhawuk@hawaii.edu

Arif Hassan, Professor and Deputy Director, Graduate School of Management, International Islamic University, Malaysia. E-mail: arifh@iiu.edu.my

Kailash B.L. Srivastava, Professor, Department of Humanities and Social Sciences, Indian Institute of Technology, IIT-Kharagpur, Kharagpur-721302, West Bengal, India. E-mail: kbls@hss.iitkgp.ernet.in

Soumendu Biswas, Assistant Professor, Management Development Institute, Gurgaon. E-mail: sbiswas@mdi.ac.in

Ajay K Jain, Associate Professor, Department of Organizational Behaviour, Management Development Institute, Gurgaon-122 001, India. E-mail: akjain@mdi.ac.in

Sweta Srivastava Malla, Assistant Professor in Organizational Behaviour Area, Indian Institute of Foreign Trade B-21, Qutab Institutional Area New Delhi-110 016 India. E-mail: swetasriv@yahoo.com

R. Barry Ruback, Professor of Crime, Law and Justice and Sociology at Pennsylvania State University.

T.N. Sinha, Professor of Human Resource Management, ASSERT Institute of Management Studies, Patna, Bihar. E-mail: tnsinha3@gmail.com

Ramadhar Singh, Indian Institute of Management, Bangalore.

Jyoti Verma, University Professor of Psychology, Patna University, Patna, Bihar, India. E-mail: jyotiverma_us@yahoo.com

R.B.N. Sinha, Head, Department of Psychology, B.S. College, Danapur, Patna-800 012 and an honorary faculty, ASSERT Institute of Management Studies, 143 D; S.K. Puri, Patna-800001 (India), Email: rbns2@rediffmail.com

Purnima Singh, Department of Humanities and Social Science, I.I.T., Delhi. E-mail: purnima125@hotmail.com

SECTION-1

JOURNEY OF A SCHOLAR: A SOURCE OF INSPIRATION

Professor Jai B.P. Sinha (hereafter mentioned as JBPS) is a renowned and internationally acknowledged Psychologist from India. He is known for his seminal contribution to Psychology and allied areas in general. Further, his involvement in making the discipline an endogenous, contextual and socially relevant science cannot be undermined. His work, spanning nearly half a century, has influenced the academic as much as it has the practicing professionals. His students and colleagues revere and emulate him for his structured approach, clarity of focus, and commitment to the profession. This section presents a recollection of his journey from a village school to global institutions that established him a distinguished scholar of international repute.

The first chapter authored by Sadanand Singh, a close long time family friend of JBPS, gives a narrative, based on a highly personal recollection of the closest continuing relationship he has had, that spans over half a century. The string of influences JBPS has had over him since his college days have been a perennial source of inspiration throughout his (Dr. Singh) academic career and personal life. The chapter does make a revelation that JBPS preferred academic profession over glamorous Indian administrative job as it would enable him to foster intellectual growth leading to a long term impact on the field of psychology.

In the next chapter, Rajeshwar Mishra, a student of JBPS gives a brief description of the dynamics that shaped a Psychologist in him. The chapter opens with the presentation of JBPS's background. Coming from a modest family of freedom fighters of North Bihar, how JBPS has ascended to enviable position of an internationally acclaimed psychologist traversing from the non-descriptive small village school to American universities and international professional organizations. This has been beautifully depicted in the edited transcripts of the interactive interview with JBPS.

Based on an in-depth interview with JBPS, the presentation of J.M. Deo, another student of JBPS offers a brief account of the facts of his career together with implications of much of his own work with regard to making of a socially relevant psychology in India. It is the result of an exercise that mainly aimed to tease out the significance of JBPS's motivations, experiences, and insights for making Psychology a dominant voice in the discourse on societal and national development *vis-à-vis* the role of academic departments, research institutions, professional associations and above all, the new generation of young and upcoming psychologists in India today. JBPS makes, through this interview, a strong case for developing a psychology that not only is grounded well in the larger historic-socio-cultural context of our milieu but also flows from the development related issues and problems of our times.

In the fourth chapter "Life in the shadow of OB: A travellers accounts of the caravan", Arvind K Sinha, a Ph.D. student of JBPS gives a personalized account of his professional journey for about thirty years. It all began in the year 1975 when he was introduced to JBPS by his (JBPS) batch mate (Late) Dr. Guru Prasad Choudhary. He was so much impressed with the modest but elegant life style of JBPS and the academic, social and personal support he has provided during his Ph.D. research, that he decided to explore, extend and expand the work in OB area further. This chapter presents a brief account of his exploration in the organizational dynamics over a period in collaboration with ten of his own associates, and others.

In the subsequent chapter Girishwar Mishra showers appreciation on Professor Jai B.P. Sinha for his vision, scholarship, and concern for developing a culturally relevant psychology in India. He is one of the rare psychologists who combine in them the rigour of intellectual analysis with cultural sensibility, reflexivity and creativity. During the last three decades, Prof. Sinha has been a source for inspiration, guidance, and encouragement to the academic fraternities. For this reason author takes an opportunity to submit some reflections on the changing images of psychology brought about by Prof. Sinha.

In the last chapter of this section Janak Pandey, briefly reviews work on social motivations of Prof. J.B.P. Sinha. Prof. Sinha was initially impressed by McClelland's theory and he also studied extensively need for achievement and dependency. However, soon he realised that without societal and organizational change, it would not be possible to achieve faster rate of development. The paper narrates a shift in Prof. Sinha research and intervention strategies for development.

The six chapters taken together gradually unfold the reflexive saga of making of the person, making the person into a professional, relating the person with others, and others getting influenced by the person maturing into a source of academic potential and motivation for others to emulate and choose their own course of journey towards a meaningful life.

CHAPTER ONE

In Honour of Jai Sinha

Sadanand Singh

I wish to thank the editors of this volume for giving me the opportunity to open my heart in describing my long and happy relationship with Jai Jee. I have been waiting for this moment to place on record the story of two people and the influence one can have on another by pure selflessness and generosity. Late summer, 1956 brought about the most blessed moment of my life. I was standing at the window of the Bihar University's Duke Hostel in Muzaffarpur, side by side with my newly introduced colleague, Jai Jee. We were both at the beginning of our Master's programme: he in psychology, and I in Hindi literature. I still remember, fifty years on, the first conversation I had with him on the subject of our BA Honours degree—he had been in first place in his field and I was third in mine, and the results we were comparing spanned all colleges (except colleges under Patna University) in Bihar University. The window we stood at was in a room shared by four students, of whom I was one. We left and walked to his room, a single, especially for Prefects. There, we sat and talked incessantly about our families, our future and our enthusiasm for the two years' study that lay ahead.

I soon learned that he came from a family of high standing in Bihar. His granduncle, Mr. Mathura Sinha, was a leader in the Indian independence movement, a well respected freedom fighter, a member of the Legislative Assembly of the state of Bihar and, to give an indication of his status, was closely connected to Rajendra Prasad, President of the newly liberated India. I clearly recall accompanying Jai Jee a few miles from the Hostel to visit Mr. Sinha at his Sarayaganj residence during his convalescence from a long illness. Jai Jee's father, Mr. Sukdeo Sinha, whom we called Kaka (uncle), would also travel some 20 miles from the family home in Gangya to visit his ailing uncle, before travelling on to reside with us in the hostel. Many dignitaries, including, the President, visited Mathura Baboo. Jai Jee's family background naturally endowed him with a refined view of what was, and is good for the still-young democracy of India. His father always wore *khadi* (clothing made from home-spun threads and fabrics) an outward statement and symbol of the fact that he was a member of the Congress Party—India's first governing party, under Nehru, since independence in 1947.

As time passed, Jai Jee and I became as one, and his pattern of life began to influence my own. A clear thinker, his studies kept him at the top of his class for the two years leading to his graduation, in 1958, culminating in a gold medal award.

One of Jai Jee's first tasks after our first meeting was to use his influence and newly gained status with the Hostel Superintendent, Prof. Mitra, helping me relocate to a single room, next to and not dissimilar to his own. While this seems trivial now, in the context of that moment in time this was a demonstration of significant largesse. As his new neighbour, I sought to emulate his study regime and life style habit, both of which were clear of clutter. His vision was linked to a highly focused and well-defined goal, from which he rarely digressed: academic excellence. Duke Hostel was considered the most prestigious student residence, and only a select few were considered for accommodation there. In this luxurious (so I thought) environment, with *verandahs*, gardens adorned with flowers and seating all around, we residents would drink tea and collectively (and heatedly!) discuss current events. The burning issue of the day was 'Ghandi-ism' *versus* communism.

Jai Jee's position was firmly entrenched in the former: a nationalistic, caring stance. Another student, Shobha Jee, a highly articulate student of English Literature, was the main proponent of communism. The exchanges between the two became legendary, with other members of the hostel joining in, but while these discussions were lively, they were always civil. I recall one occasion when Shobha Jee, citing a quotation from a supposed authentic source, was challenged by Jai Jee. His assertion was that it was a trait of the Communists to cite references without access to the original or verifiable source and that this repetition of *mantra* was typically a Communist characteristic. Such debates were a constant and stimulating feature of our two-year stay.

As Jai Jee was the Prefect at the Duke Hostel, he spoke on behalf of the residents with the Superintendent, Prof. Mitra. He always knew what was feasible and Mitra invariably listened his good advice. From food quality, through study hours, right down to the hygiene in the hostel's lavatories, Jai Jee's diplomatic manner carried the day. This prefectural status also bore us other benefits. Our evening routines were legendary; we would walk in a group to the Mess where we were granted special favours and treatment by the Mess Manager. Following dinner, at which Jai Jee and I always ate together, the group would walk, sometimes hand-in-hand and lightly discuss numerous issues, not least the various idiosyncrasies of the Professors.

There is so much to write about our two years at Graduate School. For instance, we regularly travelled to each other's villages, (where I was thrilled to know that in spite of their political connections their feet were as firmly on the ground as the residents of my own village, Saropatty) and the bond formed during this time extended to encompass our entire families. My younger brothers called him Jai Bhaiya (elder brother) and respected him (and respect him still) with the utmost intensity. This bond also was the kernel of my own career development.

During our college days it was clear that Jai Jee would again be the first class gold medallist, and when this occurred, he was assured of a lecturership which manifested at B.S. College, Danapur, Patna, and subsequently at Ranchi University where his teaching extended to postgraduate classes. This was a pivotal time for him as the career path for graduates generally bifurcated, with professional careers on one hand and academic on the other. Then, Indian Administrative Services jobs had immense glamour and, frankly speaking, the potential for riches. After deep deliberation, Jai Jee rejected the opportunities afforded by this superficial glamour, remaining in the professorial position. He reasoned (rightly) that this would enable him to foster intellectual growth, leading to a long-term and sustainable contribution to the field of Psychology.

In a short space of time, his own career had reached a plateau; in Ranchi University, he was comfortably situated in a two-bedroom duplex with his wife, Geeta, in a respectable position. Many would be content with this, but for Jai Jee it was time for a new challenge. In this, I was witness to the clear thinking and methodical approach mentioned before, which came to bear in his seeking and gaining a Fellowship and admission to one of the most highly regarded Doctoral programmes in the United States.

I followed Jai Jee to Ranchi University a year later, in 1960. Ranchi University began its own era of independence and once again, Jai Jee was by my side. For the first few months of my employment I was Jai Jee's house guest, where I resumed creative writing, after early efforts at Khagaria. Some of these were published in reputed magazines as short stories. Being so close to Jai Jee and his wife, Geeta, I took to drawing on them and those around them for characters in my writings. For instance, in *Sukhbir*, published in the magazine *Saptahik Hindustan*, the story draws on a Punjabi family with three young daughters staying near to Jai Jee. Often the father and his girls would show up at tea time in the afternoon and one of them was named Sukhbir.

Jai Jee was a well-liked and respected member of the Psychology Department where the focus of his specialization was group dynamics, but he was an expert in applying statistical methods to various unlikely situations—for instance in the study of aesthetics. While in Ranchi, Jai Jee encouraged me to register for a Ph.D. degree under Professor Devendra Nath Sharma, Department Head and subsequently Vice-Chancellor at Patna University. Jai Jee and I had long discussions over the subject of my thesis. One thing that we were convinced was that I should not work on thesis topics that are highly localized and subjects that have been milked to death: 'do something truly innovative' he said. He brought his deep understanding of experimental design to play in my work. He was convinced that an appreciation of art is not arbitrary, but is guided by man's refined ability to choose from 'beautiful' to 'not beautiful' and this decision-making was not one of either/or, or yes or no, but on a gradual scale. His idea helped me to design an experiment wherein short paragraphs of the most desirable poems by famous poets were given to subjects who were students in Hindi classes and were asked to rate each paragraph on a seven point scale, where 1 was the most appealing and 7, the least. He helped me run factor analyses using some of the known measures of poetic sensibility and was able to discern that the process of appreciating poetry has a parametric base. Thirty years later, I found myself applying Multi-Dimensional Scaling to discern dimensionality underlying the production and perception of speech. For the first time ever, the results of my experiments in the late 1960s to early 1970s were able to demonstrate how the sounds of speech clustered at the X, Y, and Z axes, exhibiting unambiguously the affinity and distances among the sounds of speech.

In no time, Jai Jee had achieved admission to the Psychology Department at Ohio State University with a Fellowship, supplemented with a travel grant from the Fulbright Foundation. His bright star shone ever more brightly at Ohio: He graduated with a four point average while taking challenging courses in statistics in the University's Mathematics department, and more.

As luck would have it, a new Vice-Chancellor was appointed at Ranchi University. He was none other than Sharangdhar Sinha, a past Vice-Chancellor at Patna University, and an Ex-Parliamentary Secretary serving in the Cabinet of the Nehru Government. Sharangdhar Sinha was a friend of Mathura Sinha (Jai Jee's granduncle) and had family ties with Jai Jee's village, Gangya. Indeed, many members of this village worked at the prestigious publishing house, Khargvilas Press, owned by the new Vice-Chancellor.

One of the first things the new Vice-Chancellor learned was that while Jai Jee had already procured a Fellowship and Fulbright travel grant at the Ohio State University, the Registrar of Ranchi University, rejected his application for a leave of absence from Ranchi for his studies abroad. Jai Jee, fully aware of his family ties with the Vice-Chancellor, approached him with a request to overturn the Registrar's decision, and thus it happened. I was with Jai Jee during his meeting with the Vice-Chancellor; not only did he grant the leave of absence, he also heartily congratulated Jai Jee for his exceptional achievement, and granted him the leave with pay!

Sharangdhar Babu's appointment and Jai Jee's relocation, resulted in my becoming a go-between for the two, and the resultant increase in my profile with the Vice-Chancellor's led to recognition and a flood of opportunities arose for me as a result. But the prospect of me following Jai Jee to the USA was bleak, given that no university in the US would accept Hindi as a qualifying degree. That, however, was not going to stop Jai Jee lending a hand.

Jai Jee was enrolled in a multi-departmental and high-level factor analysis course with a statistical wizard, a Professor of Psychology, Dr. Wherry, one of the leading Professors at Ohio State. Wherry's colleague, friend and neighbour was John W. Black—head of the Speech and Hearing department. Black taught Phonetics, which seemed to have some connections with Hindi. Jai Jee's high-level performance in Wherry's class had made him a favoured student and he was sympathetic to Jai Jee's aim of assisting in my coming to the US. While that was going on my connections through Jai Jee led Sharangdhar Sinha to grant me a travel scholarship to Columbus, Ohio. Throughout, Jai Jee had been coaching me in the links between phonetics and speech/language and once in Ohio I was able to meet with John Black. The rest is history: Wherry spoke to Black, and his introduction, together with Jai Jee's recommendation, resulted in Ohio offering me a two-year Fellowship. One year later, in 1963, and now installed at Ohio, I was about to face my demon: Statistics was insurmountable to me. My confidence was not enhanced during a conversation with Wherry, during which he told me he had never had an Indian student fail in Statistics. He told me to 'tutor with Sinha, he's the best of the lot'. Jai Jee not only taught me how to gain a pass but, more importantly, inspired me to love statistics and to realize its amazing beauty.

So, if one traces Jai Jee's career from the early days of his education one will clearly see that he is a product of his own genius and he is truly a self-made man. Along the way, he has helped to shape my own career. From our student days to the present, there is not a day when I do not think of him or am not influenced in some way by his guidance. The kernel he planted in several dimensions is now a fully fledged tree with many branches. And although from time to time there may have cracks in our bond, the strength and depth of the roots of that bond were so deeply implanted that such cracks were merely superficial.

In a humble way, I wish to connect my major achievements to his guidance I received over the years following that encounter in the hostel. When I received the highest Honours of the American Speech-Hearing Association in 2006 and, subsequently, an Honorary Doctorate in Law from Ohio University, our first meeting with Professor John W. Black came to mind. Jai Jee was with me to help interpret my broken English. Black asked me a question. To this day, I do not know what that question was. I guessed that he had asked me to outline my educational goal while at Ohio. I spoke uninterrupted for ten minutes after which Black turned to Jai Jee and, with a smirk, asked 'What did he say?'

This narrative is based on a highly personal recollection of the closest continuing relationship I have ever had, one that spans half a century. The string of influences Jai Jee has had over my career and my life have been indelibly etched in me since our two-year stay at Muzaffarpur (1956-1958), followed by our time at Ranchi University and the Ohio State University, have been a perennial source of inspiration throughout my academic and publishing careers. I have not attempted to write of his academic achievement and leadership roles, even though they are nothing less than exemplary. While time has clouded some of my memory for dates and times, the essence of his goodness can never be erased. He is my best friend.

CHAPTER TWO

Prof. J.B.P. Sinha: Values that Shaped the Psychologist in Him

Rajeshwar Mishra

The present article attempts to outline a profile of Professor Jai B.P. Sinha based on by the author on the basis of personal interview with him. The effort is to delineate and present the set of values that seem to have shaped the Psychologist in him. Apparently, values are not created out of the blue. The what, when, and how questions of life at various life stages have a role to play in evolving the values. The factors that might go in the making of the values might include the family and social mooring, early childhood experiences, early professional innings, ideological issues, and the meanderings of the professional journey at large. With this view in mind, an attempt is made to present a meaningful college out of the large collection of information made available through personal interactions with Prof. Sinha.

FAMILY AND SOCIAL MOORINGS

Prof. J.B.P. Sinha's tryst with knowledge and scholarship can be traced right from his birth. In the aftermath of the devastating earthquake of 1934, the family lost its home and took shelter in the nearby primary school. It was at this temple of learning that JBP was born on 1st of June 1936. His father, late Sukdeo Prasad Sinha, was a freedom fighter with acknowledged nationalist credentials. Always on the run, his father never had time to take special care of his only son. Even otherwise, in the joint family tradition in which he was reared, his father would never put special care to his son—all 15 children in the family were to be treated at par. Even during occasional visits, JBP used to be the **'last kid in the queue'** to receive the sweets and other gifts his father would bring some time. His subdued complaints to his mother never had any significant impact in his favour. However, JBP was adored for his being studious and sober.

Aware of his son's political overtures, JBP's grandpa has always been careful in offering him (JBP) the kind of training and orentation which could help him develop into a wholesome and autonomous individual. JBP was the darling of his grandpa and had the privilege to stay with him in his room. A highly structured person his grandpa would often ask him to explore his cupboard and take out medicines from one of the inner most shelves/boxes. He used to give him the graphic details of where the small tablet was kept. Grandpa was also much disciplined and always demanded healthy ways of living; **'early to bed and early to rise'** was something his grandpa would like to be followed. He wanted JBP to develop into a **determined and confident individual** and be ready to face the turbulent world ahead of him. JBP never grumbled and protested—he religiously followed the prescriptions. This helped him develop system, structure and confidence. JBP confirms that he has great impact of his grandfather on his life. All the structure and system he follows today has greatly been shaped by his grandfather.

Those were the days of freedom movement. Being a nationalist family, his home was always visited by the national leaders like Dr. Rajendra Prasad, Dr. Srikrishna Singh, Chabbinath Pandey and others. There was always discussion hinging around Nehru, Gandhi and freedom movement. This generated, in him, great interest in politics and political affairs. The simplicity of the nationalist leaders also had profound impact on the family including JBP who always maintained simplicity in his behaviour. He recalls how one of his cousins would frown upon the quality of rice whereas he would always relish eating whatever was offered to him.

Because his father was always busy in the political activities, he was also staying with his maternal uncle. They were real Zamindars enjoying life of luxury and fun. There were servants and attendants always available. This offered opportunity to closely watch the power dynamics and hierarchies coming in full play. He never enjoyed the luxurious environment. Influence from the national leaders and naked exposition of exploitation by his maternal uncle might have generated strong feeling against exploitation and discrimination in him.

EARLY CHILDHOOD

JBP went to the local primary school and then to the high school. He was a brilliant student since his childhood and all the teachers were quite impressed with his behaviour as well as with his performance in the classroom. He liked football and was an active player in his village. However, studies were his prime concern and no compromise was ever possible. An incidence during his schooling would be worth mentioning:

> *JBP would always stand first in his class. Once in class eight, he could not maintain his record and fell to the third position. He was demoralized and sad. He made up his mind to reverse the result. He gave up playing football that he was fond of and got detached from all the activities the children would have. People in the family, including, the grandpa were concerned. At the end of the year (class 9th), JBP broke his previous record and obtained all time high marks in all the subjects. He was offered special award for his academic feat.*

He reached high school with very good marks. During the high school, he was impressed with one of the Hindi teachers Mr. Ghayal. He was always encouraging the students and when he spotted JBP he offered all his love and support. He possessed series of books on Hindi poetry and literature which he offered to share with JBP. The books were treasure of scholarly writings and expression by renowned poets like Mahadevi Verma, Jayshankar Prasad, Ramdhari Singh Dinkar, and others. JBP not only relished reading them but also started developing literary knack. During his matriculation examination he got very high score in mathematics. Seeing his brilliance, everybody including his father suggested him to go for the science stream. He was adamant to go for Hindi literature. As a non-interfering father, he agreed with the son and encouraged to pursue the field he felt strongly about.

JBP was all set to join college when the joint family got divided. As a freedom fighter, the father was left with financial scarcity. There was problem for JBP in getting admitted to college. His father had a religious mentor (Maharaj Jee) who used to keep his savings with his father. When his father approached Maharaj Jee for blessing his son for college education, Maharaj Jee, knowing the financial condition of the family, asked JBP's father to take loan from the money he has kept with him. Although this was not a practical solution, this was the last resort. JBP was admitted to the college for his Intermediate in Arts (IA) course. College was not strange as two of his cousins were already in the college. JBP was admitted in the same hostel where his cousins were living. At the college he devoted all his time in studies and even on special occasions seldom visited his home. His cousins, on the other hand, would regularly visit home to see their wives. Occasionally JBP was also persuaded to accompany them, as a moral shield for their frequent visits. However, study for JBP was an article of faith and commitment.

As an Intermediate class student, one day JBP learnt of his marriage having been fixed. He was upset with the decision of his father. 'I was annoyed with my father's religiosity and fatalism but had to obey him as a son, shared JBP. Because of his religious beliefs his father always trusted his religious mentor (Maharaj Jee) and had the conviction that everything, in the end, would be alright. When the marriage was fixed, he (his father) went to visit Maharaj Jee where he fell ill and stayed there for some time. He returned ill and everything related to the marriage was left to JBP who had to organize and manage the event. The marriage was solemnized as per the tradition. JBP was a married person as an intermediate student.

FORAY INTO PSYCHOLOGY

All that happened during his IA studies had its fall out. JBP had to contend with a second class—which was never the case in his career. Considering his keen interest in Hindi literature and good score at the IA examination in Hindi, he opted for Honours in Hindi with Psychology as the optional paper. At this point of time one of his friends, Guru Prasad Chaudhary, proved a great catalyst in shifting JBP from Hindi to Psychology.

As it happened JBP was visiting his psychology laboratory to enquire about the practical classes where he met Mr. Jagdanand Pandey, then a laboratory assistant. He asked him why he did not opt for Psychology for the Honours degree as a subject. JBP was further persuaded to see Prof. Anandi Hazari, who was the Head of the department. Prof. Hazari could very well read the potential in the boy and offered all logic in favour of shifting to Psychology. Guru Prasad Chaudhary, Jagadanand Pandey and above all Prof. Hazari, together, were enough to change his decisions—he made a shift to Psychology. He maintained his academic excellence at both the BA Honours and MA examinations standing first class first. During his graduation, and post-graduation he had a lasting impact of two of his teachers Prof. Azimur Rehman and Prof. S.N. Mazumdar who were always helping him. Talking about Prof. Rehman, JBP describes him as a very structured scholar of statistics whose style was so lucid that made Statistics quite enjoyable. He used the life structure of his grandfather and style of Prof. Azimur Rehman in learning and using Statistics. The two together made learning of Statistics interesting and enjoyable. Prof. Hazari used to be like a patron.

IDEOLOGICAL CONFLICTS

The life at Duke Hostel of the L.S. College in Bihar University, where J.B.P. was a Bachelor and Master student was quite exciting. Guru Babu resided at the house of Mr. Devendra Prasad Singh, a person with strong socialist leaning. He used to visit Jai Praksh Narayan and was greatly influenced by his socialist ideologies. JBP's father had left politics and was devoting much of his time in religious activities. Jai Prakash Narayan was defeated during 1952 general elections and had become indifferent to politics. J.B.P. considered J.P.'s leaving the politics as a 'defeatist' stance. He worked for Mahamaya Babu against Mahesh Prasad Singh—a person belonging to his own caste. All these events created serious conflict in J.B.P. who was already bitter about the way his father and *Maharaj Jee* were taking life into religious rituals and exalted feeling about them being the panacea of all the miseries. However, he was impressed with the sense of independence his father was allowing to him.

THE PROFESSIONAL JOURNEY

There are some important incidences which helped JBP decide on his future career. First was the visit of Prof. S.M. Mohsin to the department of Psychology to conduct practical examinations. Prof. Mohsin was revered, no doubt, but his visit used to send tremors among the students who were aware of his deep knowledge and strict nature. JBP was asked several questions during the examination and was able to impress Prof. Mohsin with his answers. While leaving, Prof. Mohsin patted him and asked to visit him whenever in Patna. This was a great acknowledgement which made JBP impressed with him and created longing for delving deeper into psychology. Another incidence was related to the visit of Prof. Devendra Prasad Singh to the USA for two months. Hearing detailed descriptions of life and society in the USA from Prof. Devendra Prasad created lasting impact on JBP. JBP developed curiosity and longing to have similar exposure in the U.S.A.

Having stood first class first, JBP received a gold medal and rupees 200 as cash award. He went to buy books and one of the first acquisitions was Reizman's famous book the 'Lonely Crowd'. He enjoyed reading the same and at the same time was contemplating his future plans. When he was waiting for the result to come out he was suggested by Sri Sagar Prasad Singh, a very well known academician of that time, to visit Begusarai College which he did and joined as lecturer. The principal Sachidanad was a typical Zamindar who ran the college as he wished. The general environment of the college was also not very pleasant where the students would display all the rusticity they could.

He was strict and was able to point out even little proxy attendance. His flowery Hindi also helped him establish as a capable teacher. Meanwhile there were two vacancies announced for Rajendra College, Chapara and B.S. College, Danapur. Because his result was not yet published, Chapara refused him to consider his candidature.

Danapur is an interesting story. JBP came to Patna and stayed with some of his villagers who were staying in the local Khadgvilash Press. When he informed them that he was going to appear for an interview, he was told that since the college was established and dominated by a dominant caste group, he did not stand a fair chance. He, however, appeared in the interview and was selected on the condition that he would get a higher score than all the other applicants. He achieved this feat. Later, he went back to Begusarai to get himself relieved but the principal was not favourably disposed to the idea. He offered him all the carrots but when he did not relent he came out with the rudest stick-you would not get your salary for the period you have taught. JBP did not mind forgoing the salary. He joined B.S. College, Danapur, Patna in 1958 and was enjoying life with his colleagues and the students. The college environment was not very good as the students were rude and unruly. He imposed some norms to himself—he would not do invigilation for example, and concentrate more in academics. He joined a car pool of three other teachers who were travelling from Patna to Danapur. Back to Patna they would enjoy the delicacies at the then famous Soda Foundation. Life seemed to have acquired a smooth run.

JBP, however, was not some body to stop at this. Soon, there were two vacancies announced by the Bihar Public Service Commission. One of them was for Patna University and the other was for Ranchi University. JBP got selected and subsequently joined Ranchi University in the year1959.

AMERICA CALLING

Nice stories about America from Devendra Babu and pats from Prof. Mohsin during his student days had already fired imagination of JBP to explore all possibilities for higher studies in America. He wanted to undertake quality research and prove himself to be a good psychologist. Under guidance of Prof. Mohsin during his B.S. College days, he had already started going through important journals and even published a couple of articles in the contemporary Indian journals.

After settling down in Ranchi, he started communication with the American Universities and soon was selected for admission at the Ohio State University. USEFI offered him travel support. He was very happy at the prospect of reaching the destination he aspired for. He applied for leave to the Registrar of the University who was very much annoyed with his independently communicating with the American Universities without informing the University. Instead of granting leave, he asked for an explanation as to why he did not take permission before applying to the Ohio State University. He told him, in no uncertain words, that it was not possible to allow him leave. JBP was devastated. He informed the USEFI that he would not be able to avail the scholarship. He, then, learnt that Sarangdhar Babu, whom he knew well as his family friend, had taken over as the Ranchi University Vice-Chancellor. As a last resort, he decided to see him and seek his intervention. He saw him and apprised him of the situation. Sarangadhar Babu disapproved the action of the Registrar and immediately called him. He ordered him to allow leave and also issue a bearer cheque for Rs. 15,000 to support travel and other initial expenses. JBP was asked to proceed with his plans and contact USEFI requesting them to reconsider his case which the USEFI did. This was a critical point which worked in shaping the career and he left for the USA.

LIFE IN USA

JBP joined Ohio State University and started working with Prof. Milton Rosenberg in Social Psychology. Milton had tiff with the local people who behaved shabbily with him. His house was stoned and the university expelled him from the university service. JBP lost his mentor just during the first quarter of the first academic year. He went to the chairperson of the department, Professor Robert J. Wherry, Sr. He encouraged him to shift his specialization from social to industrial. He suggested him to specialize in Factor Analysis (methods). There was yet another reputed professor, James Naylor who was very structured and encouraging. Both the professors were very supportive. Professor Robert J. Wherry, Sr. was very high in his level and seldom appreciated the performance of the students. Once JBP confronted him with—**"I do not understand your statistics".** He said "don't worry; you will get to learn everything soon". The initial months were indeed very stressful. There was another Indian, in Psychology, Devendra Singh, who had taken the statistics course with JBP. They went to Usha Kumar who was senior by a year and appeared very comfortable with her courses. Usha Kumar sermoned them to study hard and not to hang around with each other, rather to mix with American students and get used to American culture. JBP had no choice but to work hard on his own. In the next quarter JBP did extremely well and received all the appreciation.

From the second year onwards, he needed stipend to continue his Ph. D. research. Professor Robert J. Wherry, Sr. asked him to see Professor Salomon Rettig who had some projects and who needed students. He was working with the Institute of Psychiatry. He was working on norm-violating behaviour and asked JBP to go through his and others reprints and come out with proposal. JBP went through the reprints and prepared a proposal and shared with Prof. Rettig. 'You are hired from now'—said Prof. Rettig and he had a job. 'What should I do now that I have a job with you,—asked JBP. 'Focus on your course work and come to work on your proposal that you have developed when you are free,—replied Prof. Rettig.

RESPONSE TO AMERICAN REALITIES—WHITHER INDIAN PSYCHOLOGY

As he was completing his Ph.D. JBP started thinking about what he would do back home. He started consulting works being done in India. He wrote to McClelland and contested his theory on Need for Achievement and suggested that it was not relevant in the Indian context. He was invited by McClelland to Harvard University where he had the opportunity to debate with him for two days. It was at this point of time that contesting with American theories took shape. He found that dissonance theory was not relevant to the Indian context. This was the first occasion he asserted his views and got determined to look at the psychological research from an Indian perspective.

Even in his personal behaviour JBP started asserting his own ways. He would visit night clubs but would not jump and dance. He would eat meat usually forbidden for the Indian Hindus. He realized that America was not for him and he did not belong to America. However, he wanted his family to join him in America and see for themselves what America has to offer to Indians and also to get exposed to the American society. After obtaining Ph.D. he returned back to India in 1965 and joined his lecturer position in Ranchi.

THE INDIAN REALITIES

After he came back, he applied for the post of Reader in Psychology in Bhagalpur University. Three years of foreign experience was not added to his total experience whereas three years of foreign stay of another competing candidate was considered as working experience. JBP, thus, was rejected on technical ground. He got the job whereas JBP was denied the same. This incident exposed him with the realities at the Universities and the world of academia. After some time he received a note from Prof. Mohsin asking him to see him. He was asked to apply for the post of Reader at A.N.S. Institute of Social Studies (ANSISS), Patna. He was not sure what he would do at the institute. He was told that it was a changed place now and lot of academic innovations were being tried under the leadership of Prof. A.K. Das Gupta the then Director. He applied and was selected for the job which he joined in the year 1966.

LIFE AT ANSISS AND QUEST FOR INDIAN PSYCHOLOGY

Fully equipped with the methodological rigour, JBP started pursuing his own research interests. Prof. A.K. Dasgupta was quite supportive and offered him all that was needed to follow his academic pursuits. He would debate with Prof. Dasgupta and would get his points through. Prof. Dasgupta realized for the first time, that psychology was quite relevant, but it (psychology) needed an Indian face. JBP already was exploring Indian face of Psychology and was constantly looking into the contemporary Indian works. A.N. Sinha Institute offered the right environment and support to enable him pursue his professional aspirations and goals, offering psychology an endogenous face.

He attended the Indian Science Congress in Chandigarh and was greatly impressed with the presidential address of Professor Durganand Sinha. His views on poverty, national development and achievement motivation were impressive and relevant to the Indian context. JBP, himself being agitated to look for Indian psychology, found D. Sinha as the person he was looking for. Later, this was followed by Prof. D. Sinha's visit to the institute. Another scholar who impressed JBP was Prof. Radhanath Rath who was also invited for special lecture at the institute. Impressed with the work of JBP, Prof. Dasgupta offered him four advance increments.

JBP's original thinking, commitment and work started attracting people from various centres. Prof. Dharani Sinha invited him to join IIM Kolkata. Prof. Becker wanted him to join IIT Kanpur. All these did not go unnoticed by Prof. Dasgupta who did not want to lose him. A post of professor was created at ANSISS. JBP was selected as professor of psychology who was perhaps the youngest professor of Psychology at that point of time—the year, 1969.

With comfortably saddled in the professorial position, JBP started putting his thoughts into concrete research perspective. He was already itching to find an answer to the need for achievement and hunched that the deep-seated dependency among the Indians could be one of the aspects to be studied. He planned and carried out series of studies in which several of his students also joined. They published their results with convincing explanations which helped Prof. Sinha establish himself as a researcher with independent thinking.

In 1970 Prof. Rettig from Hunter College, USA, offered Prof. Sinha visiting professorship at the Hunter College. Prof. Dasgupta did not allow him to join considering his probation period as professor. After confirmation in 1971 he was allowed to join Hunter College. JBP, however, had a clear time frame. He was to return and join ANSISS on May 25, 1973. JBP realized that ANSISS was the best place to work where he could get the needed support and natural setting to relate his research with. Patna being close to his native place was also convenient to take care of his ageing parents as their only son. He was firm in his decision to stay in Patna and ignored all the offers elsewhere. This proved a stimulating centre and cozy cradle to play with ideas and prove what he thought must be proved—an endogenous framework for the study in psychology dealing with societal issues and concerns.

VALUES THAT SHAPED PSYCHOLOGIST IN HIM

What makes JBP what he is now? A psychologist in him, that he is today, has evolved through an interesting dynamics. A crucial shift happened at the entry point itself. From Hindi literature to psychology must not have been an easy and casual decision. His decision to shift from Begusarai (seemingly a conducive place to grow considering the caste and social formation of the place) to Danapur (an alien and socially incompatible configuration) needs to be understood carefully. His shift to Ranchi University and then to the USA must have been difficult decisions considering the leave vacancy position with Ranchi University and an equally complex and hostile bureaucratic environment. Coping with the socio-cultural terrain of a non-conformist nature, early days in the USA was challenging. Equally challenging was making a niche for himself in the American dominated psychology and carving out a culturally compatible and indigenous framework. What made JBP steer through the difficult and turbulent socio-cultural and academic environment? How could he manage a balance between the high demand of professional excellence and family and social responsibilities? To attempt a convincing answer, one would have to look for a set of value systems, preferences and priorities that JBP assigned for himself, his profession and the family. In order to capture the dynamics, the simplest way is to pick up critical incidences from his life trajectory and try to make inferences and relate them with each other.

His birth, in the aftermath of the devastating 1934 earthquake, seems critical to the birth of an instinct to survive in a harsh and turbulent environment marked by scarcity and conflict of competing demands and interest. Yet, equally important aspect has been the family value of sharing of whatever resources were available within the family fold. A large family with a nationalistic fervour must have taught and helped imbibe the values of equality, justice and collectivism. Growing under the shadow of his grandfather—highly affectionate and at the same time hard in pursuing goals—must have taught him and led to development of leadership focused on task with careful guidance and nurturance. His father with highest level of idealism turned religious afterwards. Although 'the only son of his father', he never enjoyed his undivided favour—the favour was to be uniformly distributed among all the joint family children lest people didn't criticize for his partiality. Combined this with his father's growing religiosity and fatalism must have created ambivalence and subdued resentment. Faced with a weak resource base, he must have developed sense of autonomy and independence to take care of his affairs. Influence of the fiery leaders created a need for establishing niche credentials and that could be one of the factors to have driven him to establish a niche for himself.

In aggregate, the total environment—social, family and physical—shaped a value of resolve and determination to survive and excel even under most challenging circumstances. The impact of national patriots and teachers induced a sense of fair play and justice and the religious and fatalism of his father drove him to be resolute and firm in challenging the orthodoxies and rituals. Life under the shadow of his grandfather taught him the marvel of nurturance and fatherly discipline in developing leadership. An environment of freedom and autonomy offered by the contemporary psychologists like Prof. S.M. Mohsin, Prof. R. Rath and Prof. D. Sinha must have reinforced his convictions about what he valued and preferred to follow throughout his professional journey.

HOW THESE VALUES SHAPED THE PSYCHOLOGIST IN HIM?

The influences, that JBP created on psychology, can be analyzed and interpreted using different perspectives. One of the ways could be to take the analysis on temporal strand using different phases. Yet, another could be in terms of shifts in approaches he evolved and created. Yet another could be in terms of methodological innovations he attempted. A common thread, attached to all the above, is an evolving dynamics which he uniformly maintained in identifying the subject, approach and methods. All have evolved closely with the milieu he related to (Sinha, 2008).

As a non-conformist, he questioned the relevance of research he was doing at the Ohio State and reasoned whether churning out publications could be the goal that he should keep pursuing. His quest for looking around alternatives brought him close to David McClelland who was training the Indian managers for improving their need for achievement (n-Ach.) which he acclaimed to have stronger potential for economic development of India (McClelland, 1961; McClelland and Winter, 1969). He (JBP) was sceptical about the assumptions and findings of David McClelland and based on his childhood experiences of sharing from the limited resources as a strategy for survival conducted experiments which established that the high n-Ach subjects achieve better in unlimited resource scenario. In a limited resource condition, they fail to realize maximum achievement, show less liking for the task and give negative feedback of the competing person (Sinha, 1968: 234). This was a major breakthrough in carving out an independent and equally robust world view on a theme which was, then, an undisputed domain of the American psychologists. His formulations were based on the hunches he derived out of his real life experiences and convictions that he had.

The question regarding India's slow pace of development, however, kept ringing in his mind and he picked up an equally important attribute of Indians. He argued to himself that Indians were more dependent than the Americans. Based on a series of studies (Sinha, 1970; Saha and Sinha, 1973; Sinha and Pandey, 1970a, 1970b, 1971a, 1971b, 1975), he found that dependency was detrimental to initiative and development.

Following closely from his entrenched engagement with social realities and milieu he has lived in, he was curious to unravel the social and cultural realities that influenced development and human initiative. He was enthusiastic to make amends with the existing tools and methods in exploring the realities and suggest necessary changes. He was prepared to contest and refute the Western and American worldview and inject an Indian flavour into psychological research (Sinha, 2008). His extensive studies that followed brought in social values as determinant of development. There were dysfunctional values like *aaram* (rest and relaxation) rather than hard work and personalized relationship rather than contractual relationship that mediated development (Sinha and Sinha, 1974).

An important reflection of JBP's discomfort with the Western worldview on development and quality of life can be seen in his refuting the concept of quality of life in terms of autonomy and freedom. He argued that in a resource constricted environment achievement of basics of life would come first before higher concerns like autonomy may make sense (Sinha, 1977b). He further refuted a purely economic basis of human development. He strongly believed and argued that extreme poverty dehumanizes a person while excessive material affluence desensitizes him to others—both being detrimental to human development. Moderation in economic achievement and inclusion of human values were proposed as the essence of human development. This formulation of human development paradigm can be considered as a bold attempt towards carving out a relevant space for Indianness in psychology. He was supported, in his bold exposition, by contemporary psychologists like Prof. Durganand Sinha.

In contrast to the traditional discourse on leadership, JBP sought to contextualize leadership effectiveness with Indian realities. The Western view on participative leadership, as being more effective, was contested by JBP who found them weak (Sinha, 1980). Meade's recommendation (Meade, 1967) of an authoritarian leadership being effective in an authoritarian culture like India was not acceptable to him who found them weak and less liked by the subordinates. Picking up from Indian realities of a nurturant superior being more effective (Kakar, 1971), JBP paid his ears to the prescriptions from the Indian scriptures, often discussed among the elders in the family, suggesting nurturant support strategies suitable for the growth of the child. He extended his search and looked beyond what Indian scholars were recommending as the condition for effective leadership. Contrary to an ideal Indian prescription that a leader should extend affection and care to his subordinates unconditionally (Chakraborty, 1987, 1993; Singh and Paul, 1985). JBP argued in favour of the principle of reinforcement where nurturance was instrumental in leveraging subordinates to work hard sincerely. The nurturant type of leadership, as formulated by JBP, speaks of his own conviction derived from his early rearing by family members and his teachers who would often offer him encouragement and par with tangible (books/pens) and intangible reinforcements.

Picking up from his collective moorings where the resources—including knowledge—and opportunities were collectively generated and shared, JBP conceptualized the potentials for utilizing the collective social energy for development (Sinha, 1984). Following the model for economic development by Triandis (1984) and others (Inkeles and Smith, 1974) postulating a positive correlation of individualism with development, JBP chose to take a different position. His own experience of growing up in a large Indian family with dozen of siblings, he attributed development to a collective orientation to

Indians. He asserted that a country like India needs to utilize people's collective orientation for its growth. To support his position he observed: "One is struck by the over lasting consultations among the farmers about the sowing time, seeds, cropping pattern, use of fertilizer, etc. In fact, not a single decision, whether it concerns farming or family issues such as marriage of sons and daughters, is made individually" (pp. 172-173).

Having proved what he wanted to prove, JBP decided to expand the range of his studies on organizational culture to framing them within the large Indian societal culture. This included collaborative research explorations in a cross-cultural perspective spanning over different states in India. A comprehensive analysis of the research findings is summarized as follows "Indians are hierarchically oriented; they are conscious and concerned about their power and position in the society. They judge success in terms of power, respect and obey powerful persons, try to gain power, and use it to protect friends and families—even the corrupt ones and exploit the week ones. Further, Indian prioritizes family over work commitments and meets social obligations while work would suffer. They prefer personalized to contractual relationships. People profess ideals but behave in selfish ways and do not keep their promises. Corruption is perceived to be rampant, particularly at high places allowing powerful persons to get away with any corrupt practice (Sinha, 2008). There has been an important regional variation depending upon the socio-cultural and economic contour and frame of reference."

The study on culture and values reflect an entrenched understanding of the social dynamics which he seems to have acquired because of his familiar social moorings and evolving quest for linking psychological research with human well-being. The outcome of the analysis has important implication for the development and organizational effectiveness. The employees' hedging their real intentions while showing extra respect to the boss offers understanding of the potentials of the hedged intentions in eliciting favour from the boss. This also has implication for designing incentive structure based on fair assessment.

KEEPING THE CALL EVOLVING

As a concluding remark I would like to use a summary of a 'virtual academic travelogue' that he wrote and which reads as—"It has been an expedition that was full of pains and pleasures, and above all a sense of calling to keep going on. I hope to continue on till I fade away" (Sinha, 2008). One can read several things between the lines. For me it appears to be the beginning of new calling for the next genre of psychologists. In his prologue to 'Living and Doing Psychology' JBP posited—"I did not start my research with any grand plan nor did I set any high destination to keep calling me. I focused on what I sensed as the most compelling social issues at a particular time point, examined them with the methods that seemed to be the most appropriate, and continued doing so till my research compelled me to move on to a more inclusive frame for a better understanding of Indian social reality"(Sinha, 2008). Implicit in what he said is the inevitable role of psychology in addressing poignant social issues, Indian society is faced with. And he did not end with mere rhetoric with missing structure and plans to carry forward the perspective he evolved, nurtured and moved on.

JBP carefully planned for the next genre of psychologists to be adequately equipped and prepared for the challenges ahead of them. This was done quite subtly and a vast multitude of his students are testimony to this. He did not impose his preference. He helped to create an enabling environment and allowed the students to evolve their plans and destinations. A frequently used refrain from JBP would often say 'everybody has a distinct growth path to follow and they must follow what they value most. They should be encouraged to follow their unique evolving paths and create and synergize diversity.' Today, he enjoys having three generation of students spread over the entire globe. The range of their chosen fields and orientation include psychologists maintaining strict methodological rigour, to practitioners of psychological principles in the fields of community development, education and health management and so forth. There is common thread, however, characterized by an evolving framework and contextual relevance. All of them carry strands of his values and purpose in different measure.

To offer an institutional anchorage to the social scientists founding of ASSERT (Association for Social Engineering Research and Training) has been a timely initiative which he supported and encouraged. This is a forum of individuals who are willing to contribute to the building of a knowledge mass to be used for engineering social change. Following an interdisciplinary framework ASSERT has today, a large membership of psychologists and other social scientists are committed to using their knowledge to engineer social change and human well-being. The weekly discussion brings scholars from all levels—research scholars, faculty members from the University and independent researchers. JBP offers due nurturance and support in an environment of mutual sharing and support. Financially, this endeavour may not appear to be feasible but this forum has done immensely to bring together people to evolve and synergize their efforts and create a credible position for psychology as a discipline with rich potentials for change and attempt a paradigm shift in studying human behaviour and social reality that govern it.

CONCLUSIONS

The academic journey that JBP embarked upon has been long and evolving. First, he strove to outgrow the American shadow and started probing the ground social reality, it was the reality that guided him throughout the journey that was made possible first with the active participation of his companions at home, and then from all over the country and abroad. The large evolving team of professionals characterizes a caravan in search of meaning and essence in endogenous psychology. He moved from dependence-proneness through nurturant-task leadership and *sneh-shradhha* (affection-deference) mode of power relationship to soft-synergetic work culture that he saw as embedded in the societal culture drawing its essence from the ancient psycho-philosophical thoughts. Of course, he retained the scientific temper; but had to re-define what was thought to be scientific in terms of the methods and the procedures that seemed most helpful in understanding and unfolding of increasingly complex social reality. In the process, the baggage of tools was unfolded and added to the existing tool kit.

JBP has been able to attract fellow travellers willing to sail with or alongside him in his evolving journey. Most of them proved to be valued companions sharing their diversities and innovations. The journey continues and evolves further with JBP still offering the needed direction to sail through.

REFERENCES

Chakraborty, S.K. (1987). *Managerial effectiveness and quality of work life: Indian insights*. New Delhi: Tata McGraw Hill.

Chakraborty, S.K. (1993). *Managerial transformation by values: A corporate pilgrimage*. New Delhi: Sage.

Inkeles, A. and Smith, D.H. (1974). *Becoming modern*. London: Heinemann.

Kakar, S. (1971). Authority patterns of subordinates behaviour in Indian organizations. *Administrative Science Quarterly*, 16, 298-307.

McClelland, D.C. (1961). *The achieving society*. New York: Van Nostrand.

McClelland, D.C. and Winter, D.G. (1969). *Motivating economic development*. New York: Free Press.

Meade, R.D. (1967). An experimental study of leadership in India. *Journal of Social Psychology*, 72, 35-43.

Saha, S. and Sinha, J.B.P. (1973). The transfer of model effects on dependence proneness. *Indian Journal of Psychology*, 48, 23-29.

Singh, N.K. and Paul, O. (1985). *Corporate soul: Dynamics of effective man-management*. New Delhi: Vikas.

Sinha, J.B.P. (1967). Ethical risk and censure avoiding behaviour. *Journal of Social Psychology*, 71, 267-275.

Sinha, J.B.P. (1968). The nAch/nCooperation under limited/unlimited resource conditions. *Journal of Experimental Social Psychology*, 4, 233-248.

Sinha, J.B.P. (1970). *Development through behaviour modification*. Bombay: Allied Publishers.

Sinha, J.B.P. (1973). Organizational climate and problems of management in India. *International Review of Applied Psychology*, 22, 55-64.

Sinha, J.B.P. (1976). Outgrowing the alien frame: A review article. *Vikalpa*, 1, 63-67.

Sinha, J.B.P. (1977b). The quality of working life in the Indian setting. *Journal of Social and Economic Studies*, 5, 235-248.

Sinha, J.B.P. (1980). *The Nurturant Task Leader*. New Delhi: Concept Publishing Company Pvt. Ltd.

Sinha, J.B.P. (1984). Towards partnership for relevant research in the third world. *International Journal of Psychology*, 19, 169-178.

Sinha, J.B.P. (1988a). Collectivism, social energy, and mental health. *Dynamic Psychiatry*, 21, 110-115.

Sinha, J.B.P. (2008). *Living and Doing Psychology*, Unpublished research monograph, prepared for a symposium on Indian Psychology: Theory Methods and Trends during the NAOP conference at the IIT, Guwahati on December 14-17,2008.

Sinha, J.B.P. and Sinha, M. (1974). Middle class values in organizational perspective. *Journal of Social and Economic Studies*, 1, 95-114.

Sinha, J.B.P. and Pandey, J. (1970a). Strategies of high nAch persons. *Psychologia*, 13, 210-216.

Sinha, J.B.P. and Pandey, J. (1970b). Retention of experimentally induced change in dependence proneness as a function of social support. *Indian Journal of Experimental Psychology*, 4, 60-63.

Sinha, J.B.P. and Pandey, J. (1971a). Dependence prone persons under congruent and incongruent expectations. *Indian Journal of Psychology*, 46, 13-29.

Sinha, J.B.P. and Pandey, J. (1971b). The process of decision making in dependence prone persons. *Journal of Psychological Research*, 46, 36-37.

Sinha, J.B.P. and Pandey, J. (1975). Reinforcement and model's efficiency as factors in decision making of dependence prone persons. *Indian Journal of Psychology*, 50, 49-57.

Triandis, H.C. (1984). Toward a psychological theory of economic growth. *International Journal of Psychology*, 19, 79-96.

CHAPTER THREE

On Making of a Socially Relevant Psychology in India: Some Excerpts from Interviews with Professor Jai B.P. Sinha

J.M. Deo

Both as an innovative researcher and prolific writer, Professor Jai B.P. Sinha's globally acknowledged acumen for socially relevant research is deeply characterized by profound social consciousness (Gelfand, Erez and Aycan, 2007; Gupta, 2007). He was indoctrinated to the world of academic research in psychology during his graduate work in the USA in the mid-sixties with heavy doses of quantitative methods, multi-variate analyses, and experimental designs (Rettig and Sinha, 1966; Sinha, 1967). Upon his return to India, he, however, soon realized the inadequacy of experimental designs in course of his work on need for achievement (Sinha, 1968, Sinha and Pandey, 1970). His search for alternative avenues and domains made him explore a number of societal problems, such as, dependence-proneness (Sinha, 1970), *aram* culture, poverty syndrome, preference for personalized relationships, problems of public sector organizations etc. (Sinha, 1973).

In one such study, it was serendipitously found that dependence-prone persons took greater initiative and higher risk than low-dependence persons when they were placed under a leader who expected them to do so (Saha and Sinha, 1973). This resulted in a series of studies on leadership wherein a number of culture-specific findings challenged the dichotomy of leadership styles in the Western literature (Sinha, 1980). It was reported that whereas participative leaders were perceived as weak, and authoritarian leaders were disliked as well as ineffective, it was a blend of nurturance and task (NT) orientation that rendered a leader effective *vis-à-vis* subordinates who preferred dependency and personalized relationships, and accepted the superiority of the leader. As such, the model of N-T leadership as developed by Professor Sinha drew substantially from the Indian ethos of nurturance (Kakar, 1971), dependency, personalized relationships, and task orientation (Ganguly, 1964) even though it simultaneously adopted the contingency approach and the principle of reinforcement from the western literature. Professor Sinha, by then, had fully outgrown the alien framework of sophisticated experimental designs and quantitative analyses. Instead, he started believing that his research must reflect such a symbiotic interdependence with his social milieu that the two must impact each other (Sinha, 1981; 1997). Professor Sinha later affirmed that a truly meaningful research springs from the encounters of a researchers with his/her context and that the process of doing such research is unsustainable unless the researcher draws on the ideas, concepts, theories, and methods of compatriots who share the same context and the same heritage and are engaged in similar ventures (Sinha, 1994a: 239).

A leader with the best style cannot, however, be effective if he does not have power to use his style. Professor Sinha realized this during his interactions with the managers of the organizations where he studied leadership. Hence, the study of dynamics of emerging power patterns in work organizations (Singh, 1985; Singh-Sengupta, 1989; Sinha, 1986; 1994b, Sinha and Singh-Sengupta, 1991), wherein Professor Sinha and his associates not only used *Hindi* expressions such as *apna-paraya* (ingroup-outgroup), *sneh-shradha* (affection-deference), and *kripa* (blessings) etc. but also techniques such as graphic scales and vignettes/word-pictures with a view to capture the social reality with all its finer nuances.

Professor Sinha's search for a more holistic picture of complex realities took him far away from simulations, manipulations, and sophisticated quantifications. He gradually moved towards supplementing quantitative data with qualitative observations, secondary sources data, and critical incidents (cf. Sinha, 2008a). It is important to note here that but for one experiment on leadership (Sinha and Sinha, 1984), no simulation/manipulation study has been conducted after 1980 by Professor Sinha in his research career that has since witnessed remarkable methodological shifts ranging from conceptual through structured surveys and interviews to informal discussions, e-mail interviews, and corroboration through secondary source data quite in sync with his expanding research interests, e.g., the *Hindu* identity (Sinha, 1982), planning strategies (Sinha, 1985a), the Indian concept of health and healing (Sinha, 1985b), work culture (Sinha, 1990; 2000), development of psychology as a policy science (Sinha,1992), cultural embededness of industrial organizations (Sinha, 1994c), context sensitivity in Indian organizational behaviour (Sinha and Kanungo, 1997), cross-cultural management (Sinha, 2000; 2004), and the socio-cultural embeddedness of behaviour within and of the Indian organizations (Sinha, 1994a; Sinha, Gupta, Singh, Srinivas and Vijaykumar, 2001; Sinha, Sinha, Bhupatkar, Anand, Gupta, Gupta, Panda, Singh, Singh-Sengupta and Srinivas, 2004; Sinha and Pandey, 2007) etc.

Based on his conviction that indigenization of organizational behaviour (OB) research in India must be an integrative process of growing from within, retaining the cultural heritage, and yet being open to relevant concepts, methods, and theories irrespective of their places of origin (Sinha, 1994), Professor Jai B.P. Sinha, in his latest book entitled *Culture and Organizational Behaviour*, presents the basic knowledge about OB as it has developed in the West as also situates it in the Indian cultural perspective (Sinha, 2008b: xviii). The book not only covers all the topics that routinely form part of OB courses in major universities and management institutes in India but also seeks to raise new issues that emanate from the interface of Indian culture and organizational behaviour for further deliberations. It contains a number of concerns (e.g., focus on larger context, socio-cultural heritage, developmental goals, indigenization, integration etc.) that are common to almost all his earlier writings and can, thus, be regarded as the denouement of Professor Sinha's vision of teaching, research, and practice of psychology as a non-ethnocentric, truly universal and socially relevant science of behaviour with the potential to enable individuals, societies, and nations across cultures to overcome the constraints that thwart their well-being and development.

It is against this backdrop that an attempt has been made in the present chapter to learn from Professor Sinha as to (a) why he did the kind of psychology that he did in his time? and (b) what was the experience like? The following text is based on edited transcripts of a series of interviews and interactions with Professor Jai B.P. Sinha the first of which was conducted in his office at ASSERT, Patna in September 2006 in the wake of *NAOP* symposium on *Dialogue for Development.* In the text that follows JBP refers to Professor Jai B.P. Sinha and JMD refers to J.M. Deo.

JMD: You have said that you drifted into psychology by a sheer chance and soon found yourself enjoying it. What was this enjoyment like? Any memories of a special friend or any particular teacher who first took you into psychology and then made it enjoyable to you?

JBP: My first love was *Hindi* literature .... I wanted to do my graduation with *Hindi* literature as my major subject and psychology as a side subject, the idea being that knowledge of people's ways of thinking would facilitate me in writing creative literature. But ... a very dear friend of mine, late Guru Prasad Choudhary, wanted me to opt for psychology as a major subject. He prevailed upon me to accept that having a knowledge of people's mind is the most appropriate way to enter into creative literature. My teachers Professor Jagdanand Pandey and Professor Anandi Hazari were quite encouraging and supportive. Accordingly, I soon developed a liking for the subject. I was fascinated by the theories and concepts that I was introduced to by my teachers. The best teacher I ever had was Professor Azimur Rahman. I owe a lot to him for my interest in statistics which served me well when I worked for my Ph.D. at Ohio State University (USA) under Professor Robert J. Wherry Sr.

JMD: Your ticket to Ohio was like a dream come true, even as your concern for socially relevant research in psychology does not seem to have allowed much space to your training in methodological elegance in your later work. How important do you think is international exposure/linkage for the professional growth and advancement of an Indian psychologist?

JBP: Ph.D. work sharpened my capability to conduct research. I employed this capability to do the kind of research that I wanted because of my concern for social relevance. I am often inclined to let my research problems decide the contents as well as the methods to study them and yet I find quantitative methods such as factor analysis and regression analysis quite useful in my attempts to comprehend a complex social situation. It is not that my American training turned into an appendage or it was not useful. Exposure to the Western culture made me a more open person, willing to view things from different perspectives. Earlier I was quite rigid and orthodox in my world-view ... but thanks to my on campus training as well as off campus exposure and day to day interactions there in the USA, I realized that you may view things from a position that differs vastly from my perspective and yet we both can be equally right. This was a great help in my professional growth. It was this sense of openness and receptivity to the multiplicities of reality around oneself that attracted me towards research that was contextually embedded although I later found it increasingly difficult to get such works published in foreign journals. They found all sorts of flaws; variables besides being unfamiliar to their readers were also said to have been inadequately operationalised, whereas the Indian journals were over receptive. This tough-abroad and easy-home combination further encouraged me to outgrow the alien framework by focusing more on pressing social problems.

JMD: Both as a researcher and a writer you always focus on larger context, folklore, colonial legacy, developmental goals, indigenization, and integration etc. To what do you attribute this sensitivity to immediate milieu as well as larger context?

JBP: I was attracted to the idea of social relevance right from my childhood. I was born into a family of freedom fighters under strong Gandhian influence. I think ... I owe it to my family environment and especially to my father who always wanted to do so much for this land of ours and our fellow countrymen. Later, when I came in contact with Professor Durganand Sinha whose approach to life in general and psychological research in particular has a deep influence on me. My fascination for social relevance got fine tuned into our (common) concern for problem oriented research for societal and national development.

JMD: What has been your comfort/satisfaction level as a psychologist living and working in the so-called backwaters of India known as Patna? Any trouble with regard to funds or facilities?

JBP: Working in and from Bihar ... especially at the A.N. Sinha Institute of Social Studies in Patna, was a very satisfying experience to me both personally and professionally. It was the best place to work for me ... all possible facilities were available there for research without any undue teaching load or obligations, although I loved teaching and taught post-graduate students twice a week in Patna University for well over two decades. It was at Patna that I was offered a full professorship at the relatively young age of 33. Professor Radhanath Rath ... I still recall ... very fondly used to refer to me as the youngest full professor of Social Psychology in India. The liberty to do my own thing, at my own pace, is what I valued most. I found the entire system at the A.N. Sinha Institute in Patna highly supportive, co-operative and conducive in this regard.

JMD: You have said in a paper in 1994 that your research has been largely *emic*. Could you please elaborate?

JBP: My research on real-life issues that pertained to societal problems has been quite absorbing to me, even though it made collaboration with my international colleagues and counterparts increasingly difficult. I now realize that we all have our own islands with their own psycho-historical and cultural contexts and unless bridges are built for communicating and sharing, none of us can have the benefits of a universal psychology. It has also been difficult to conduct collaborative research with Indian psychologists despite the fact that I extensively borrowed from them.

JMD: Is that why you strongly advocated for multi-location, multi-author studies by psychologists in India?

JBP: This is one route that I have always wanted psychologists working in India to take so that individualized, fragmented and sporadic forays are replaced by a comprehensive and sustained engagement for culturally embedded and socially relevant body of psychological knowledge. The legacy of working with small samples of individuals and groups with standardized tests and sophisticated experimental designs has for quite long prevented psychologists from generating an aggregate data base that can help us theorize in a large, heterogeneous country like India. My earlier attempts in this direction were made through systematic correspondence with my network of peers and students. It used to be quite slow and time taking at that time but with availability of e-mail I now find the idea and practice of multi-locational, multi-authorship studies hugely beneficial on two counts. In view of the diversity of culture and my own location at one of the most backward places in the country, I think that by undertaking such studies we become truly pan-Indian in our researches as also successfully supplement what many of us may otherwise lack at the local level in terms of intellectual stimulation and interaction or other such resources.

JMD: What remains to be done for making psychology a dominant voice in the discourse on development?

JBP: Our science is in a very deplorable state in our country as of now. Many from amongst us do not venture into research that is required to be historically grounded or related to the developmental needs of the country. A host of systemic forces, such as, poor societal demand for quality, lack of resources etc. induce our friends in academia to resort to short-cuts to personal benefits. We certainly need to have such resource and training centres that are equipped with all the required facilities as also put a premium on psychological research for social and national development ...but our first and foremost requirement relates to psychologists' consciousness of, and receptivity to, social problems. Only socially conscious and responsible psychologists can be expected to come forward for socially relevant researches.

JMD: What could be the role of research institutions and professional associations in this regard?

JBP: We have not been able to create and promote conditions in which younger people feel encouraged to come forward for socially relevant research in psychology. ICSSR (Indian Council of Social Science Research, New Delhi) is one such agency that readily funds this type of research. Where are the others?

NAOP (National Academy of Psychology, India), I think ... has a definite role to play in this regard; it must strive to create such an enabling environment that gives impetus to innovations like auto-updating of syllabi ... say, every five years ... or peer or self-evaluation of teachers as also a scheme for young, up-coming psychologists to join together for collaborative research, and they need to have liberal access to senior psychologists through NAOP for undertaking socially relevant research.

JMD: What is your message to the young as well as not so young psychologists in India?

JBP: If you keep on applying Western concepts and models and go on blindly following the dictates of the methodology, you cannot hope to make a meaningful, worthwhile contribution. Our regard for reliability, validity and control etc. must not be allowed to distort or dilute our concern to conduct creative and innovative researches. In order to be able to comprehend the reality we all must start to ask ourselves: What do we want to study? Why do we want to study it? How do we want to study it? Questions such as these become all the more important because our task is to acquire a holistic understanding of problems specific to our socio-cultural contexts, its historicity, and macro and micro features. It is only by contextualizing psychology in the Indian reality that we can hope to make it socially relevant.

JMD: Thank you very much Sir for sharing your experiences, thoughts and views on making of a socially relevant psychology in India.

REFERENCES

Ganguly, H.C. (1964). *Structure and Process of Organisation*. Bombay: Asia Publishing House.

Gelfand, M.J., Erez, M. and Aycan, Z. (2007). Cross-cultural Organizational Behaviour. *Annual Review of Psychology*, 58, 479-514.

Gupta, R.K. (2007). Global mindsets, Indian roots. *Great Lakes Herald*, 1(1), 71-77.

Kakar, S. (1971). Authority patterns of subordinate behaviour in Indian organisations. *Administrative Science Quarterly*, 16 (3), 298-307.

Rettig, S. and Sinha, J.B.P. (1966). Bad faith and ethical risk hypothesis. *Journal of Personality*, 34, 275-286.

Saha, S. and Sinha, J.B.P. (1973). The transfer of model effects on dependence proneness. *Indian Journal of Psychology*, 48, 23-29.

Singh, C.B.P. (1985). Behaviour strategies in power relationship. *Unpublished Ph.D. Thesis,* Patna University, Patna.

Singh-Sengupta, S. (1989). Changing patterns of power distribution in banking organisations. *Management and Labour Studies*, 14, 183-193.

Sinha, J.B.P. (1967). Ethical risk and censure avoiding behaviour. *Journal of Social Psychology*, 71, 267-275.

Sinha, J.B.P. (1968). The nAch/nCooperation under limited/unlimited resource condition. *Journal of Experimental Social Psychology*, 4, 233-248.

Sinha, J.B.P. (1970). *Development through Behaviour Modification*. Bombay: Allied Publishers.

Sinha, J.B.P. (1973). *Some Problems of Public Sector Organisations*. New Delhi: Concept.

Sinha, J.B.P. (1980). *The Nurturant Task leader*. New Delhi: Concept.

Sinha, J.B.P. (1981). In search of research identity. In J. Pandey (Ed.), *Perspectives on Experimental Social Psychology in India* (pp. 241-252). New Delhi: Concept.

Sinha, J.B.P. (1982). The *Hindu* (Indian) identity. *Dynamic Psychiatry*, 15, 148-160.

Sinha, J.B.P. (1985a). Planning strategies in a developing country. In R. Diaz-Guerrero (Ed.), *Cross-Cultural and National Studies in Social Psychology* (Vol. 2). Amsterdam: North-Holland; pp. 399-410.

Sinha, J.B.P. (1985b). Concept of health and healing in India. *Dynamic Psychiatry*, 18, 30-39.

Sinha, J.B.P. (1986). Emerging power patterns in work organisations. *Management and Labour Studies*, 11, 86-96.

Sinha, J.B.P. (1990). *Work Culture in the Indian Context*. New Delhi: Sage.

Sinha, J.B.P. (1992). A key address on developing psychology as a policy science: Problems and prospects. In B. Wilpert, H. Motoaki, and J. Misumi (Eds.), *General psychology and environmental psychology: proceedings of the 22nd International Congress of Applied Psychology* (Vol. 2, pp. 403-418). Hove (UK) and Hillsdale (USA): Lawrence Erlbaum.

Sinha, J.B.P. (1994a). Indigenisation of OB research in India: A subjective view. *Indian Journal of Social Work*, 55 (2), 238-242.

Sinha, J.B.P. (1994b). Power dynamics in Indian Organisations. In R.N. Kanungo and M. Mendonca (Eds.), *Motivation Models for Developing Countries*. New Delhi: Sage; pp. 213-229.

Sinha, J.B.P. (1994c). Cultural embeddedness and developmental role of industrial organisations in India. In H.C. Triandis, M.D. Dunnete and Leaetta M. Hough (Eds.) *Handbook of Industrial and Organizational Psychology*, (Vol. 4; 2nd ed.), Paulo Alto, C.A.: Consulting Psychology Press.

Sinha, J.B.P. (1997). In search of my *Brahman*. In M. Bond (Ed.), *Working at the interface of cultures: 20 lives in social science (pp. 77-84)*. London: Rutledge.

Sinha, J.B.P. (2000). (Ed.) *Managing cultural diversity for productivity: the Asian ways*. Tokyo: Asian Productivity Organization.

Sinha, J.B.P. (2004). *Multinationals in India: Managing the interface of cultures*. New Delhi: Sage.

Sinha, J.B.P. (2008a). Creating enabling conditions for human development. *The Social Engineer*, 11 (2), 8-25.

Sinha, J.B.P. (2008b). *Culture and Organisational Behaviour*. New Delhi: Sage.

Sinha, J.B.P., Gupta, P., Singh, S., Srinivas, E.S., and Vijaykumar, V.S.R. (2001). Societal beliefs, organizational climate, and managers' self-perception. *Vikalpa*, 26 (1), 33-47.

Sinha, J.B.P. and Kanungo, R.N. (1997). Context sensitivity and balancing in Indian organizational behaviour. *International Journal of Psychology*, 32 (2), 93-105.

Sinha, J.B.P. and Pandey, A. (2007). Indians' mindsets and the conditions that evoke them. *Psychological Studies*, 52 (1), 1-13.

Sinha, J.B.P. and Pandey, J. (1970). Strategies of high aAch persons. *Psychologia*, 13, 210-216.

Sinha, J.B.P. and Singh-Sengupta, S. (1991). Relationship between manager's power and the perception of their non-manager's behaviour. *Indian Journal of Industrial Relations*, 26, 341-351.

Sinha, J.B.P., Sinha, R.B.N.; Bhupatkar, A.P.; Anand; Gupta, P., Gupta, R., Panda, A., Singh, S., Singh-Sengupta, S., and Srinivas, E.S. (2004). Facets of Societal and Organizational Cultures and Managers' Work Related Thoughts and Feelings. *Psychology and Developing Society*, 16 (1), 1-25.

Sinha, J.B.P. and Sinha, T.N. (1984). Stress as a factor of shift in leadership styles. *Journal of Social and Economic Studies*, 12, 224-252.

CHAPTER FOUR

Life in the Shadow of OB: A Traveller's Account of the Caravan

Arvind K Sinha

Life is a handful of short stories, pretending to be a novel.

—*Anonymous*

This paper is attempted to be crafted in the tradition of reflexive *auto ethnography* (e.g., Dyson, 2007; Hayano, 1979; Holt, 2003), a very different piece of presentation compared to my other outputs so far and I wish it remains so, a singularly unique and a peculiar one in my personal career profile. Autoethnography is a genre of writing and research that connects the personal to the cultural, placing the self within a social context (Reed-Danahay, 1997). Reflexivity refers to the researcher's scrutiny of his or her research experience, decisions, and interpretations in ways that bring the researcher into the process and allow the reader to assess how and to what extent the researcher's interests, positions, and assumptions influenced inquiry. A reflexive stance informs how the researcher conducts his or her research, relates to the research participants, and represents them in written reports (Charmaz, 2006: 188-189). Ethnography means recording the life of a particular group and thus entails sustained participation in their milieu, community, or social world. It means more than participant observation alone because an ethnographic study covers the round of life occurring within the given milieu (x) and often includes supplementary data .... The goal of such ethnography is to gain an insider's depiction of the studied world (Charmaz, 2006: 21). Ethnography and its subtle variants have emerged as a valid method of bringing into life the interactive coexistence of the observer and the observed, the researcher and the researched, the journey and the traveller, and ramification thereof. An increased number of social science scholars are acknowledging its value over hard-core quantification, e.g., Brison (1997), Bryman (2001), Frank (2000), Hammersley and Atkinson (2007), Srivastava (1991), and Vahali (2003). However, from the research participants' standpoint, the ironic outcome may be an outsider's report (Pollner & Emerson, 2001). I do not deny, and apologize for such a possible outcome of the present endeavour at the outset itself. From a conventional stance of evaluation, this piece may have a lot of redundancy contained into it, however, looked at from a different perspective, it contains a personalized account of a rather lonely journey of the author for about thirty years, though paradoxically the loneliness has always had a company or two of sorts as co-travelers who walked some of the distance together.

According to Bruner (1986) there are two modes of cognitive functioning—two modes of thought, each providing distinctive ways of ordering experience, or constructing reality" (p. 11). Argument and story (narrative) are distinctive ways of ordering thought, experiences, or constructing a reality. As such, although they are both "ways of knowing", they vary greatly in the procedures used for verification. To Bruner what each seeks to convince us about is fundamentally different. An argument convinces us about what is truth based with an appeal to particular procedures, which have been used to establish formal and empirical truth. On the other hand, a good story convinces us because of its lifelikeness. Metaphor can be seen as one part of storytelling that does just this, i.e., it produces lifelikeness. A good story does not establish truth, like an argument, but presents verisimilitude (Dyson, 2007).

THE BEGINNING

It all began in the year 1975 when the providence had "planned" a meeting of mine with Professor Jai B.P. Sinha (Jai Ballabh Prasad Sinha for full, hereto after referred as JBPS). By that time I had already spoilt about 5 years of my life time due to my semi-politico-activist orientation and delayed examination schedule of the University; else I would have had my Master's degree by 1971. I had already had about 6-7 job offers of various denominations and had to leave them for family reasons apparently linked to my status of the only child of my parents. The idea of getting a Ph.D. degree "somehow" and getting into a nearby academic joint "anyhow" would have served the purpose of my senior family members splendidly. One of my very revered teachers (Late) Dr. Guru Prasad Choudhary had developed some affection for me during an earlier educational tour, which sustained, and offered to introduce me to one of his batch mates, JBPS, as due to some local considerations it was not possible for me to get enrolled for Ph.D. in my own university. I was ushered in what appeared to me then the immaculate drawing room of JBPS on a morning following a very stormy previous evening, which had forced us to spend the night in a dingy hotel. I had kept awake in drenched clothes for the night, had not had a bath, could not have a shave, and had not even combed my hair as I did not have any comb, clothes were crushed and shoes were soggy and muddy with flooding rain water spread all over from the previous night rains! I could clearly see that JBPS was none too pleased with the sight of the creature accompanying his batch-mate and touted as a bright student, and if the appearance was any indicator of the content, the prospects of my upper story and future career in general genuinely must have looked very dismal to him. But friendship is a wonderful thing; as later on I discovered it for myself ! For the sake of friendship with his batch mate, it must have been that I suppose, JBPS did not show me the door immediately. He put me on some kind of a trial of my academic prowess for three days, and must not have had to work hard to discover that I had not had much, instead what he probably *discovered* was my desire, commitment, and dare I say authenticity, with which I gracefully acknowledged all my foolish attempts at proving my academic worth. I guess he also got somewhat *convinced* of these qualities in me to some extent. By that time, I had also discovered that I had many deficits that I shared with him and probably none of the positive and desirable qualities, which he had possessed. In terms of commonality, I came from a somewhat similar socio-economic-geographical territory, studied at the same college, and had been taught by a couple of same teachers. Perhaps we had gone through some similar shocks of college life experiences in the hands of the authorities. On positive side, he had almost everything that I did not have, style, panache, and stature—so much so that I had a difficult time understanding why on earth this person has to "read" any more? Understated elegant existence and *humility* has been his hall mark of life style, so far as I understood, and he started providing me the inputs, academic, social, and personal in his own style. It took me quite a while to appreciate his *vision*. I started to work with him, had applied for UGC Junior Fellowship, got it one day. The forenoon was a happy one—I would be assured of financial assistance and would not be a burden on my family. The evening brought different news though, the same day. I had lost my father!

To borrow an expression, my life seemed overwhelmed with death and loss—why would I spend time...life seemed too short (Holman Jones, 2004: 47). It took me a good three months to decide the course of action of my future. Vulnerability seeks support and emotions are a scarce commodity in work domain. I took a hard decision; I came back to JBPS to continue my work. Something stuck in my psyche that day: *one must move on, the show must go on; the journey has to go on regardless*! The much needed *social and emotional support* came not so much from my familial sources but from two earlier students of JBPS, namely, Professor Tribhuvan N. Sinha, and Professor Sudha R. Sinha, which made me sustain and we still remain a family though not dependent on reaffirmation and confirmatory acts of reliability tests of relationships. Practically, I stayed with JBPS at the A.N.S. Institute of Social Studies (ANSISS), Patna, for a little over two years between 1976 and 1978. I wanted to stay at the ANSISS, applied for a position twice, but for different reasons each time, I could not get into the faculty cadre over there. As a child of destiny, I had to undergo a premature *weaning* experience (the first encounter with a Freudian trauma), and soon I found myself in the Department of Psychology, University of Allahabad, standing with shaking legs and pounding heart and a mind fogged with anticipatory fears in front of one of the greatest stalwarts in the Indian history of Psychology, Professor Durganand Sinha, a truly towering personality in more than one sense. That was my second encounter with Freudian trauma (the *toilet training!*). That was the year 1978. The time between the years 1978 and 1981 was truly a *learning experience* of great importance to me. The learning showed up when I had to leave the Allahabad University in 1981; the dominant feeling then was not of weaning but that of zeal of a explorer. The joys, sorrows, struggles, accomplishments, and the friends that I earned have always remained my cherished treasures. Later on, I learnt that two influences had been common between me and JBPS. After having stood first in the first class, Professor Anandi Hazari, our Head of the department at the University, out of personal goodwill had *dissuaded* both of us from taking up the academic career as he wanted us to do well in life, and Professor Durganand Sinha had been a motivating force both in JBPS's as well as my life. Now it can be told that Professor Durganand Sinha had desired that I remain in his department. It was I, who in a sense "betrayed" him, for personal reasons, and chose to come to the Department of Humanities and Social Sciences, at the Indian Institute of Technology, Kanpur, in 1981. It took me a while to settle down, and decide the course of action for my days to come. By that time I had personal encounters with several "powerful" models of human existence.

One such model was that of Professor Lal Bachan Tripathi, who, in his own words, "discovered" me in a conference of the Uttar Pradesh Psychological Association at Kashi Vidya Peeth, Varanasi. He kindly nurtured my career *through support from a distance*. Close support came from three wonderful friends, namely, Professor Anand Prakash, Professor Prem Sagar Nath Tiwari, and Professor Yoganand Sinha who is more popularly known as Raghu Sinha. From these wonderful friends I could learn *the immense value, pleasure, and strength of sharing*. What I realized early in my career is that *no model of a person need be emulated in totality and if anyone copies someone completely, (s)he still remains a copy*. I also realized that *one must contribute to the society at large and that there is no one single best way of contribution*. One might as well take several aspects of various models and create a virtual model for oneself and then try to concretize that virtual model, and that there would be costs involved. It has been a privilege to be in person with JBPS for some time and mentally and emotionally all this while. It has been wonderful learning to walk from him, having walked with him for some time, and then having taken a separate path for my personal journey ahead. JBPS has been doubtlessly one of the key figures in advancing the area of Social Psychology in India, and paving the ground for inception and growth of organizational behaviour from the academic side of it. It was fortunate to have come into his contact and thereby perhaps becoming one of the firsts in this country who truly worked in organizational behaviour area to earn their Ph.D. degree. Obviously my first encounter with serious academics had been during my own Ph.D. work. As is true with most research scholars, I also dabbled with several topics. It was at that time that I learned *the value of doing a piece of research with which one can personally relate*. I came from an academic system that was a source of more pain than pleasure, and the only visualization of organizations that I had had in the beginning was that of the academic system. Mainly inspired by the working style of our own Head of the department Professor Anandi Hazari, who has had influenced the lives of both JBPS and mine, and looking at JBPS as a sharp contrast, I ventured to work on "The effect of headship styles on quality of education". During the course of my Ph.D. work itself I had to leave JBPS and come over to the Department of Psychology, University of Allahabad, which was my first encounter with work-life. I submitted my Ph.D. thesis while working at Allahabad. Those were the days of no e-mails, and no immediate-connection phones in India, so by and large I worked for livelihood, and also for my thesis in absence of any close supervision, away from my family. *The quest for the emotional support kept on looming large.*

TREADING THE MEANDERING PATH TO UNKNOWN WITH THE CO-TRAVELLERS

At the University of Allahabad, I had the chance to meet Professor Janak

Pandey, who turned out very supportive to me and provided much needed socio-emotional support and also academic guidance whenever he could. From Professor Janak Pandey I learnt *the value of "structural-equation" management, time management, and perseverance of the highest order under very adverse circumstances.* Working in absence of my direct supervisor JBPS gave me the opportunity of *learning to work alone,* and coming out of his very charming personality influence and imbibe some of the characteristics of other role models whom I admired for various reasons. Well, I earned my Ph.D. degree (Sinha, 1980) and shifted to the Indian Institute of Technology, Kanpur, in 1981. That was my first encounter with the realities of working with total strangers and yet having to prove myself. The wise counsel of Professor Janak Pandey came in very handy, he always used to confide with me: *nobody loves me; they only care for my work.*

Within a year or two, there was a research scholar admitted in the Ph.D. programme of our department, who is now a well known name, Professor Shailendra Singh. It was a coincidence that he had done his Masters from the University of Allahabad, and I had had some interaction with him earlier. He chose to work with me for his Ph.D. He was a very hard working person, and in those deprived days working on mainframe computer with dummy terminal and only one permitted printed output in 24 hours schedule for students maintained by the computer centre, he produced a landmark research document of his time. In fact, half of the time got wasted as he had started working on a problem (strategic management) of which he was not convinced at that time, so practically he did his work in two years only as against seemingly four and a half years.

Singh (1990 a; 1990 b) studied the stress phenomena among the male executives from seven private and three public sector organizations. The results indicated that the executive stress may be better understood as a composite of three constituents, namely stressor, stress, and strain; that the stress experience was of a different nature in junior level management cadre than the upper level management cadre and finally that some of the factors that could reduce the level of stressful transaction and enhance the level of positive outcomes would include: climates of warmth, trust, and professionalism. Although the area of stress research was not entirely a virgin area even at that time, with remarkable zeal and perseverance, Shailendra Singh could fathom out some of the findings in a rather conclusive manner, which were rather new at that time, in Indian setting. His major findings were that: (i) of the ten dimensions of stress, inadequacy of role authority and experience of inequity were top two in that order. (ii) Experience of inequity was a major contributor in the variance of job satisfaction (21.38%) and organizational commitment (12.36%). (iii) Nurturant Task (NT) leadership significantly contributed to job performance and job satisfaction. (iv) He further identified a factor named "Happy Work Life" (HWL) consisting of organizational commitment, job satisfaction, personal effectiveness, sense of power; negative loading of alienation and intent to leave. (v) A linear combination of 12 variables explained 87 per cent of variance in Happy Work Life. (vi) All stress dimensions: experience of inequity, role ambiguity, and lack of leadership support contributed negatively to HWL while Work Oriented Coping, Advancement Opportunities, and Decentralized Decision Making contributed positively to it. (vii) Indian executives were found to have a mixed locus of control in contrast to many popular models of locus of control advocating the existence of only two or three factors. Factor analysis of Locus of control scale responses revealed 8 significant factors instead of three dimensions as proposed by Levension. (viii) Stress dimensions had by and large negative linear relationship instead of inverted-U type relationship as commonly suggested in several pieces of literature.

In sum, the organizational stress dimensions negatively influenced commitment, performance, and satisfaction, and triggered strain responses. It was asserted that fair play or perception of equity is a necessary condition for commitment and satisfaction.

During my interactions with Shailendra Singh, I learned *the value of close supervision, hard work, learning by doing, participative functioning, mutual sharing, and flexible time schedule*; I still remember him ringing my door bell at 4 AM and both of us riding (actually he riding the pillion and me pulling!) the same bicycle to computer centre to debug a computer programme! I benefited immensely in terms of personal growth, and perhaps he did too. Currently he is Professor at the Indian Institute of Management, Lucknow.

The next companion in my journey was a lady Archana Shukla who is also Professor at the Indian Institute of Management, Lucknow. I am pretty sure that those of us, who had seen her only in her student days, will not be able to recognize her now. From a very docile existence in those days she has transformed herself into a tigress of sorts and is widely acknowledged as one of the best trainers around the country.

Shukla (1988) explored the constructs of creativity, competence, and excellence in work organizational setting. Additionally, 21 other variables were also included. Based on a sample of 290 executives from six public and four private sector work organizations of north India, the author suggested that creativity, competence, and excellence were the salient variables in organizational dynamics. She could also identify some variables that were associated to those three variables.

With Archana Shukla, I could learn the *value of personalized support, and implantation, as also going away from the direct influence of the primary mentor*. I guess moving away from IIT, Kanpur to University of Allahabad, to Centre for Organizational Development, Hyderabad, to Xavier Institute of Management, Bhubaneshwar, and finally to the IIM, Lucknow had instilled into her a rich brew of varied experience, and capabilities.

Soon after Archana Shukla, Kailash Bihari Lal Srivastava, currently Professor at the Indian Institute of Technology, Kharagpur, had joined me. Srivastava (1990) conducted a study using a sample of 270 lower and upper level male executives from six public and private organizations of north and western India in an exploratory framework and focused on the relationship between the variables divided into two categories labelled as the antecedents and consequence or resultant. The former comprised the entrepreneurial orientation of the role incumbents, leadership style, climate, structure, and quality of work life. The latter category comprised the variables of organizational effectiveness, personal effectiveness, job satisfaction and organizational commitment. The results suggested that variables included in the study could be treated as important in organizational dynamics. An important insight obtained was that a multidimensional perspective and Western findings may not necessarily be usable in Indian setting.

My interactions with Kailash had been as intense as that with my first associate Shailendra Singh. Both of them stayed very close to each other, but they were quite a material for study in individual contrast. The hall-mark of Kailash had been, according to me, *allowing oneself to move with the "flow" and remain contented, while working only as hard as you comfortably can*. It has served him well. One of the finest persons at heart, he now even looks prosperous and has contributed significantly to profession and other people's lives as far as I know.

Next, I happened to work with Parvinder Gupta *nee* Parvinder Kaur, who is currently a Professor at the Indian Institute of Management, Ahmedabad. She was introduced to the department partly as a result of the social resurrection effort by one of our senior colleagues, Professor Usha Kumar (herself a witness to the India-Pakistan divide and the personal level fallouts thereof), who had met her in a temporary shelter where members of the *Sikh* community were kept for protection against the backlash of killing of the Prime Minister Indira Gandhi, which had given rise to unprecedented carnage and riots in the city of Kanpur as also elsewhere in the country. Having recently escaped what could have turned into a major personal trauma; Parvinder came with a bruised psyche and dogged determination to me to seek help in moving further on in life. I dare say that I am yet to see another person who had invested so much of hard manual labour and serious effort in compiling the only two-volume thesis that the Humanities and Social Sciences Department of the IIT, Kanpur has so far produced during the days of rather impoverished infrastructural facilities.

Kaur (1992) attempted to understand in depth the concept of success and its various ramifications in the organizational setting. The author could identify the seven major constituents of a construct called idealized success. It was suggested that for enhancing motivation the management attempts should take into consideration role incumbents' very specific and personal conception of success and that a motivation management strategy based on a consonant idealized success conception of the role incumbent, combined with some structural consideration such as industrial categorization, hierarchical level; and the organizational strategic orientation may help the organizational designers and the top management to make the organization move towards high tech. or prospector strategic orientation.

Again in her company, both from her work, and her stance in life I learnt *the values of die hard attitude towards work, uncompromising quality, comprehensiveness, and self-sacrifices in favour of work accomplishment, and that it is much more worthwhile to pursue your own definition of success rather than a conception of success thrust upon you by traditions and outmoded or societal structures that may be distanced from self.*

Sonal Kumar *nee* Sonal Khare, currently an Organizational Development Specialist (ODS), Education and Employee Relations Department, Dartmouth Hitchcock Medical Center, Lebanon, New Hampshire, USA, was another of my associates. Kumar (1995) studied the concept of quality human resource in 14 work organizations. The results suggested that the construct of quality human resource could be important in organization dynamics. The top management orientation and disposition also emerged as important constructs contributing to organizational effectiveness. The component of quality HR called *interpersonal effectiveness and innovations*, and the component of structural and climate factors called *task standardization* emerged as the most salient predictors of the operationalized construct of organizational effectiveness.

Sonal Kumar was *a rare combination of goal oriented behaviour, hard working when she chose to work, careful future planning, personalized relationships, and "carefully careless" attitude.* She has been able to travel quite a distance in life, thus I guess that the qualities she possessed must be a good recipe in that combination. I remain quite impressed with her social accomplishments.

Manjari Srivastava, another of my associates, currently an Associate Professor at the Narsee Monjee Institute of Management and Higher Studies, Mumbai came from a family of academicians, had all the good qualities of personal nature. However, her personal circumstances did not allow her *to be at work for the entire stretch of time allotted* to her, which apparently affected the quality and total time consumed by her work. Nonetheless, she had probably produced one of the most comprehensive documents that took into account the individual, group and the organizational aspects of effectiveness into account simultaneously. She also had the admirable *quality of goal directedness, humaneness, and personal sacrifices.* It is heartening to see that she is trying to be back to full time profession after a time lag owing to personal circumstances.

Srivastava (1996) explored the concept of effectiveness at the individual, work group and organization level, in detail. The study included a number of other variables also in the categories of: (a) Individual characteristics, (b) The contingency variables at individual levels, (c) Group characteristics, and (d) Contingency variables at group levels. Results based on a sample of 250 middle level executives from seven public and six private sector work organizations suggested that there is a need to understand the construct of effectiveness not only as a whole but in terms of three, though mutually related sub-categories, namely individual, group, and organizational levels. Further, the study could specify the nature of precise relationship among the dimensions of the variables, which according to the author could be used to enhance quality of decisions regarding personal management and overall organizational management.

Sumita Rai, currently an Associate Professor at the Management Development Institute, Gurgaon has been one of my closest associates at personal level. The wonderful aspect of her relationship with mine is that it is difficult to give a definite name to our relationship. Beginning from a total stranger to a close family member like relationship and again getting distanced as a matter of natural events and *sharing a vast range of feelings and emotions* were the qualities of mutual existence that make this associate of mine stand out from my other associates. I would not be grossly wrong to acknowledge that much like a potter, who had no experience of dealing with exactly this kind of clay, I decided to create one of the more distinctive *objet d'art* if I could. It was very difficult for me, for her, and I guess for others around on the periphery of the process. It took a lot of *beating from inside and patting and supporting from outside, and in the process at times, mud slinging on both parties, while almost continuously spinning on the potter's wheel.* Both of us attempted to achieve the unachievable; given our rather limited mutual technical and human expertise and skills. By the grace of God the enterprise did see a culmination that might be treated as satisfactory.

Rai (2000) attempted a novel approach to understand the structure and dynamics of a construct identified as the Organizational Worth. It was postulated that an organization is worthwhile if it consists of a good proportion of worthwhile persons, especially the persons occupying management level roles. The work was conceptualized around the concept of social equity theory, and executed in an exploratory framework. It was argued that persons who are able to maximize some particular kinds of value realizations in their lives could be expected to be more worthwhile. Sample consisted of two hundred and sixty-one male, managerial level executives of banking organizations. The results showed that the concept of Organizational Worth is a meaningful concept in organizational dynamics. The dimensions of worth at individual level could be identified and their relationships with several outcome variables of organizational importance could be shown.

Ajay Kumar Jain, currently an Associate Professor at the Management Development Institute, Gurgaon, had been the last of the male students of mine so far, who was trying to get ahead of his female batch-mates through sheer hard work and initiative. A personalized pleasant relationship maintenance effort from his side at least was his other admirable quality. His experiences of working with Amity Business School, Indian School of Business, and Management Development Institute, Gurgaon have given him training and confidence to grow into fine academics.

Kumar (2002) attempted to understand the dynamics of the construct of Organizational Citizenship Behaviour (OCB) within the framework of organizational behaviour. Another objective of the work was to discriminate the OCB from other seemingly similar kind of behaviours for instance, impression management and Ingratiation etc. The thrust variables included were OCB, *In-Role Behaviour* (IRB), *Emotional Intelligence, Self-Management,* and *Impression Management.* The auxiliary variables included in the research were: The *Individual Level Variables,* including Background Variables, Work Locus of Control, Social Power, and Ingratiation. The *Organizational Level Variables,* including Organizational Structure, Organizational Size, Organizational Units, International Collaborative Venture Status, Organizational Support, and Psychological Contract. The *Individual Level Outcome Variables,* including Job Satisfaction, Career Orientation, Personal Effectiveness, Organizational Commitment, Work Recognition, Reputational Effectiveness, General Health,

Perceived Job Mobility, Turnover Intention, and Vertical Trust. The *Organizational Level Outcome Variables,* including Organizational Effectiveness, and Organizational Productivity. Twenty-one research questions were identified. The sample consisted of 250 male middle-level executives of six two-wheeler manufacturing units from north India. Major findings were that OCB as well as Job Performance (IRB and OCB) were the significant predictors of the organizationally relevant outcome variables. OCB and Impression Management were not the similar concepts. Self-management was a better significant positive predictor of Job Performance than Impression Management. Emotional Intelligence was a significant negative as well as positive moderator of the relationship between Self-Management and Job Performance. All major thrust variables, namely Emotional Intelligence, Self-Management and Organizational Citizenship Behaviour were found to be the significant positive predictors of the organizationally relevant outcome variables like personal effectiveness, job satisfaction, organizational commitment, general health, interpersonal trust, organizational effectiveness etc. Organizational Citizenship Behaviour and Impression Management were not found to be the similar concepts. However, both were found to be related to some extent. Emotional Intelligence was found to be a significant negative moderator of the relationship between Self-Management and Job Performance (IRB & OCB). At most places, Emotional Intelligence and Self-Management both were found to be the positive predictors of Job Performance except with *Altruism and Sportsman Spirit* dimensions of OCB. In case of Altruism and Sportsman Spirit dimension of OCB, Emotional Intelligence acted as a positive moderator and to some extent with Organizational Pride, Social and Functional Participation and Individual Initiative also. Most interesting results pertaining to OCB was found in relation to the concept of Social Power. On one hand, *Referent Power, Legitimate Power, Expert Power* and *Intra-Work Reward Power* were found to be the significant positive predictors of organizationally relevant outcome variables, whereas Information, Coercive, and Extra-Work Reward Power were found to be less significant predictors and even negative predictors at some places. On the other hand, OCB was found to be the significant positive predictor of *Intra-Work Reward Power, Expert Power* and *Referent Power.* OCB predicted Coercive and Legitimate Power negatively, and had shown no relationship with Extra-Work Reward Power and Information Power. Collaborated Small organizations were found to be highly effective in comparison to Collaborated Large, Uncollaborated Small and Uncollaborated Large Organizations. Uncollaborated Organizations were found to be high in terms of OCB activities, whereas Collaborated Organizations were found to be high in terms of self-management practices with a few exceptions (e.g., Generalized Compliance, dimension of OCB was found high in Collaborated Organizations, whereas Planning Practice, dimension of self-management was found to be high in Uncollaborated Organizations. The qualitative analyses showed that an ideal organizational role incumbent had OCB related traits to a large extent. The theoretical and applied implications, limitations of the study, and suggestions for future research were advanced.

Neelu S. Bhullar, *nee* Neelu Sarai, currently Associate Professor at the Management Development Institute, Gurgaon, was already in job when she started looking for opportunities of adding to her qualifications. Her location in the Management School of CSJM, Kanpur University, which is situated at a short distance from IIT, Kanpur made her visit IIT, Kanpur for utilization of its comparatively vast academic reserves like library and chances of interaction with qualified faculty members. She has always impressed me *with a rather immensely balanced personality, extremely hardworking, razor sharp intellect, a flaming tendency to enjoy work for work itself, and a blazing desire to excel in whatever she takes up; one of the finest specimens of utmost belief in personal worth, dignity, and authenticity.*

Sarai (2005) attempted to understand the role of service climate in sustenance and enhancement of effective performance of the role incumbents in hospitality industry. It was posited that composite effectiveness would be reflected in organizational productivity, organizational effectiveness, and personal effectiveness. Further, it was postulated that in addition to service climate some other variables would also contribute to the effective performance. These were identified as organizational structure, perceived organizational support, work recognition and reward, and trust. Effective performance would either depend upon or get reflected into general health of the role incumbents, role efficacy, role satisfaction, job satisfaction, organizational commitment, self-esteem, level of depression, intent to quit, feeling of loneliness, doubt about trustworthiness of others, career orientation, and perceived job mobility. The background and the values of the role incumbents would also contribute to effectiveness considerations. Sixteen major hypotheses, eight auxiliary hypotheses, and six research questions were identified. The sample consisted of 227 lower and middle level respondents from 12 hospitality organization units located in northern and western India. Data were analyzed using correlations, factor analysis, regression analysis, canonical correlation, *t*-test, multivariate analysis of variance, discriminate analysis, and path analysis. Major findings were that service climate conducive to internal customers, organizational structure, work rewards, perceived organizational support, trust in work group, and trust in organization contribute to important person level and organization level outcome variables. The theoretical and applied implication, limitations of the study and suggestions for future research were advanced.

By the time Sweta Srivastava, currently an Assistant Professor at the Indian Institute of Foreign Trade, New Delhi, came to me, owing to my personal compulsions I had almost determinedly told myself that I am not going to personally supervise any more Ph.D. students. However, *the studied patient stance, a highly cultured demeanour, and personal appeal with a backdrop of past connection* to the Department of Psychology, University of Allahabad she had obtained her Master's degree from, a place to which I owe much of my personal collection of credit points, or shall I term it as *idiosyncratic debts*, Sweta was successful in superseding my personal compulsions.

Srivastava (2005) attempted to understand the role of organizational justice, and the parameters of organizational support mechanisms in sustenance and enhancement of psychological well-being, which in turn was postulated to contribute to a number of organizationally relevant outcome variables, with a focus upon the target group (N = 270 males) of a security-service organization personels. The specific variables included were organizational justice, well-being, political interference, perceived organizational support, supervisors' support, ego-resilience, internal motivation, organizational commitment, organizational citizenship behaviour, happiness, job satisfaction, personal effectiveness, and effectiveness on conceived roles. Also included in the research were brief aspects of personal and organizational values, and biographical information. Major findings were that internal motivation, ego-resilience, well-being, and organizational justice were significant positive predictors of organizationally relevant outcome variables. Two rather unexpected findings were attained. The results show that *Internal Motivation* turned out to be a positive significant predictor for the entire set of organizationally relevant outcome variables, which included Organizational Commitment, Effectiveness in Active Role Implementation, Effectiveness in Preventive/Maintenance Roles, Organizational Citizenship Behaviour, Happiness, Effective Dealing with Individuals, Effectiveness in Dealing with Group, Environment and Human Growth Issues, Personally Important Job Accomplishment, and Job Satisfaction. Additionally, it was discovered that the dimensions of *well-being*, namely Continuous Learning and Growth in Life, and Personal Growth and Satisfying Self-Concept, were significant positive predictors of internal motivation. Further, organizational justice and organizational support were found to be positive contributors to well-being, which apparently were needed to alleviate the sense of a lack of psychological well-being that seemed to prevail among the respondents. *It is heartening to note that the variables of internal motivation, and ego-resilience have showed up as matters of importance not only in dissertation but also in her personal life*!

CULMINATION OF THE VOYAGE

As if the wheel had taken one full rotation, I sort of formally began my career at Allahabad University, and Sweta, my last Ph.D. student so far, came from the same place. The story that began in the hands of Professor Jai B.P. Sinha way back in 1975 seemed to take a halt with him being recommended by the IIT, Kanpur to conduct the oral examination, which he did in 2005. The cosmic clock had clocked a full span of thirty years by then.

I thought it was time to have a little sigh of relief. All my personally undertaken academic responsibilities, by and large, had been successfully and satisfactorily been taken care of. Personal problems on family front were mounting by now. I was sitting alone in my office, and visualizing the fleeting images of all my associates entering in and going away the doors. It was also time to look back, take a stock and try to reorient myself, in absence of my trusted associates. I found myself lonely. But the show has to go on, the journey must continue.

The account of the journey would not be complete without making mention of the two names that have not been mentioned so far. The first is that of Professor Girishwar Misra, currently Professor of Psychology at the University of Delhi, one of the finest academicians that the country has produced so far; a long time associate and a guiding force since my Allahabad days of 1978, he has been able to coax me to churn out some useful work from time to time, and has kept me alive in the process. I remain indebted to him for his intellectual and social stimulation value. Like the *Gestalt*, his contributions to my life cannot be described through its elemental building blocks. The second person is the one whom I had noticed for a much longer time than I have known and actually "felt", Professor Dharm P.S. Bhawuk, Professor of Management and Culture and Community Psychology at the Shidler College of Business, University of Hawaii at Manoa, Honolulu, USA.

I had started recollecting myself and with the help of some of my undergraduate students' course work started to weave some ideas. Taking cues from some of the ideas of JBPS appearing in his books and writings all this while again, I could create a bit of information assimilation that got accepted for presentation in the IACCP, Athens, 2006 conference, however, I was not able to get visa in time due to my engagements with the family problems. Nonetheless, just prior to the present article going to press I had an opportunity to participate in conference of the International Academy of Intercultural Research (August 15-19, 2009) Honolulu, Hawaii, USA, where a modified version of the article originally planned for the Athens conference was presented (Sinha, 2009, August). The study attempted to understand the relevance of some cultural factors as contingencies for leadership effectiveness. Data were obtained through structured questionnaires from 100 male managers of banks located in two different regions of India on the variables of (a) prevailing work culture, (b) leadership style, and (c) perceived performance. Different geographical locations in India offered a possibility of comparison and contrast as it is a large country with diverse and localized cultural influences. Emphases on status consciousness, initiative taking, and commitment were the focal components of cultural comparison between the two regions. Results based on regression analysis and *F*-test showed that in organizations enveloped by a culture strong in status consciousness but poor in initiative taking and commitment, a leadership marked by fierce resolve and humility combined with a strategist approach was conducive to better performance as compared to a simple participative leadership. By comparison, in organizations enveloped by a culture relatively low in status consciousness but strong in initiative taking and commitment, a participative leadership showed performance results as good as leadership marked by fierce resolve and humility combined with a strategist approach. Implications for conflict resolution between and within internal and external customers were noted. Further, a suggestion was made towards a contingency approach for leadership effectiveness based on a need to consider values and culture as the contingency variables.

Academic inputs and outcomes apart, this was the occasion that gave me an opportunity to feel the content of the person whom I had known before but not quite, Professor Dharm P.S. Bhawuk, which I shall always cherish as of immense personal value to me, and the full nuance of which is difficult to described at this moment. There is only one word for me to describe him to myself—*awesome*!

THE PERSONAL INSIGHTS

So what have I learnt, a person engaged in the study of Organizational Behaviour during my personal journey in life through the profession the providence gave me as my *karma*? By way of summary, *I learnt the value* of all those things that have been presented in italics above in the main body of this writing. Let's take an overview.

1. Humility is a great virtue and force.
2. Vision.
3. One must move on, the show must go on; the journey has to go on regardless.
4. Giving social and emotional support is important.
5. A worthwhile experience is a learning experience.
6. It does not matter if you are dissuaded by a figure of authority; give it a try by yourself.
7. Support, even from a distance, has a value.
8. Sharing is priceless. There is immense value, pleasure, and strength generated through mutual sharing.
9. One must contribute to the society at large and that there is no one single best way of contribution.
10. The value of doing a piece of research with which one can personally relate.
11. The value of "structural-equation" management, time management, and perseverance of the highest order under very adverse circumstances.
12. Learning to work alone.
13. Remember, nobody loves me; they only care for my work.
14. The value of close supervision, hard work, learning by doing, participative functioning, mutual sharing, and flexible time schedule.
15. Value of personalized support, and implantation, as also going away from the direct influence of the primary mentor.
16. Allowing oneself to move with the "flow" and remain contended, while working only as hard as you comfortably can.
17. The values of die hard attitude towards work, uncompromising quality, comprehensiveness, and self-sacrifices in favour of work accomplishment, and that it is much more worthwhile to pursue your own definition of success rather than a conception of success thrust upon you by traditions and outmoded societal structures.
18. Interpersonal effectiveness and innovations.
19. The value of task standardization.
20. Value of a combination of goal oriented behaviour, hard working when one chose to work, careful future planning, personalized relationships, and "carefully careless" attitude.

21. To be at work for the entire stretch of time allotted, or available.
22. Quality of goal directedness, humaneness, and personal sacrifices.
23. Sharing a vast range of feelings and emotions.
24. Beating from inside and patting and supporting from outside, and in the process at times, mud slinging on both parties, while almost continuously spinning on the potter's wheel.
25. Sheer hard work and initiative.
26. Personalized pleasant relationship-maintenance efforts.
27. Intra-Work Reward Power, Expert Power and Referent Power, and Organizational Citizenship Behaviour.
28. Capacity to enjoy work for work itself, and a blazing desire to excel in whatever one takes up combined with utmost belief in personal worth, dignity, and authenticity.
29. A studied patient stance, a highly cultured demeanour, and personal appeal with a backdrop of past connection to a common set of people and places, internal motivation, and ego-resilience.
30. Idiosyncratic debts.
31. Maintenance of internal motivation may be of paramount importance.
32. Subjective well-being ought to be maintained.

The collection of these nuggets of realizations is the treasure for me to preserve, to work with, to remain with and to move on. Only time can and will tell me how useful has been the collection for me and for my co-travellers.

THE PROFESSIONAL REALIZATIONS

The personal journey has taken me through a tour of not only personal feelings, emotions, sensibilities and a quest for eternal compatibility, but also through a trek of hard core research based realizations in the broad area of the Organizational Behaviour. Some insights as wrap-around are described in order to have the glimpse of the other side of the journey as well. The full account has been presented by the author elsewhere (Sinha, 2009); the concluding remarks are presented here.

The overall quantum of research produced by the Indian researchers in the period covered seems to be impressive on surface. However, if one tries to delve deeper below the surface, the research endeavours undertaken in an area-wise manner, appear to be rather small in number, which sometimes suffer from theoretical and methodological rigours, making not very potent statements, and following a time tested and comfortable approach. Perhaps there is a need to locate the role of OB research and practice in social construction and *vice versa.*

In terms of the *emerging focal areas* (i) the cultural and cross-cultural concerns seem to have gained popularity and prominence, also there is a visible shift from variable based research to the issues of relevance based research in works of a few researchers in the area. (ii) Competencies, and various aspects of HRM including training, too seem to have gained ground. (iii) Old favourites like leadership, climate, stress, satisfaction, involvement, and commitment seem to retain their popularity. The *areas that are emerging but are yet-to-make-bold-statement* include: (a) Psychological well-being, Service Organizations, and Organizational Citizenship Behaviour; (b) Qualitative research; and (c) Small organizational set-up research including the IT units and the NGOs. *Areas of deficiency needing attention* include: (a) Theory building, theory testing through rigorous methods, such as structural equation modelling. Learned use of time series or longitudinal data, and clinical approach to organizational behaviour is lacking too. (b) Strictly applied research with clear-cut and direct applicability seems to be scant as well. "What does it take—how to do it—what does it mean" type but high level professional standard research is badly needed to help in making Social-Psychology based OB professionally viable. (c) Action research, and acceptance of intensive and careful case studies, may be with a very small number of respondents or even a single but potentially worthwhile case, on an equal footing compared to a moderately large number of respondents based research design. (d) By a similar token of concern, very large systems, giant corporations, their genesis, sustenance, management, growth and development, the short-term and long-term vision behind them, the founders and their successors; and the impact such large systems make on the other organizations and the constituents of the society, has been a relatively little explored area in sustained OB research. (e) Rigorously planned and executed experimental, quasi-experimental, and field experimental research is almost an extinct species, and one would be delighted to see its resurrection. (f) Precious little attempts seem to have been made to explore the *systemic* properties of the organizational endeavours and to provide a guideline for future explorations. Research on *intangibles* should be the focus of research in coming days. (g) Interventions and applications should form a valid agenda for the future research and practice attempts in the OB area, rather than just understanding, explorations, and theoretical enunciations. (h) Finally, a clear understanding of the human person in crucial roles, in various capacities within the totality of the organizational efforts and beyond, and his/her location in the galactic expanse of organizational structures and processes need to be relocated and repositioned. The near future science and practice of OB would need to act with a rapid response to the demands arising out of globalization and open competitive environment. Some of the major issues would include culture, ethics, and values at work place; effective leadership at various levels of organizational activity; inter-culturally competent workforce; establishing synergy with global MNCs; and workforce diversity including repositioning of gender issues. An area of neglect that is closer to gender issues but important in its own right is that of security. Security at physical, emotional, and now virtual level can be an involving area of OB research. The individual and group level OB research ought to make concerted efforts to meet the need of the hour in order to make its mark. The individual is entitled to the status of a Global citizenship, and the science of OB ought to provide the tools, techniques, trainings, and the armours for survival and growth. In the days to come, the difference between an athlete and a champion would be minimal in terms of structural prerequisites. The real difference will be marked by the differential in passion!

EPILOGUE

The closing years of life are like the end of a masquerade party, when the masks are dropped.
—Arthur Schoenhauer

As Dyson (2007) carefully noted, there are risks involved in telling personal and professional stories and seldom can the whole story ever be told. Although there are parts that should, or can, never be shared on moral and ethical grounds; what is told, is told from my perspective with my filters engaged. Some of the stories that were related to me during my research cannot be shared because to do so would jeopardise the privacy of the individuals involved (Dyson, 2007: 44). Ellis and Bochner (2000) also place a key responsibility on the authors "who made themselves and their experience, a central focus of their research" (p. 734). They believe that recently there has been "a wave of interest in personal, intimate, and embodied writing" (p. 734). Personal feelings and thoughts should be included, but not in such a manner as to bring harm to others. Although I was the person collecting the evidence, I was also one of the participants engaged in the process and in the product. What I, as an individual does, affect others and I am also affected by others because we live within an interdependent ecosystem. Ellis (1997) claims that in her early forays into narrative writing she experienced intimidation, or a fear of personal exposure. It wasn't until she achieved increased status as an academic and experienced personal grief, which demanded expression, that she was prepared enough to give it a go. "Now it felt less risky to write something other than traditional social science, something that would be engaging, therapeutic and sociologically useful" (p. 126). I share a similar feeling and stance in life at this stage.

While many confessional tales have as their goal the reassurance of the reader that their findings are "uncontaminated" and hence "scientific" and "valid" (Van Maanen, 1988), I have as my goal the opposite: to reassure the reader that my findings are thoroughly contaminated. This contamination with my own lived experiences results in a rich, complex understanding of ... my own experience (Ellingson, 2001: 54).

I will be happy if I see myself as a person having travelled together and also alone, having contributed to those lives who came in direct contact with me, and also to other's through some of those, and attained sufficient courage to forgive those who did not come up to my expectations, and that would certainly include I, me, and myself. Existence is always a bi-directional if not multi-directional process; I can already see so many foot prints and imprints of the actual and vicarious co-travellers on my psyche. I would also prefer to attain my extinction or *moksha* into the oblivion where the sun sets for me and I seek my slumber in the misty full-moon nights; and then the sun rises but for others and I smile from the veil of clouds; and I seek blessings from my teacher on every *Ashadha Poornima* (a full-moon night of a particular month called *Ashadha* somewhere near June, not particularly clear and bright, usually heralding the onset of rainy season in north India, but a date earmarked when the disciples of Indian tradition would try to meet or seek blessings of their "the teacher" or the *Guru*, no matter what) for eternity in favour of the continuance of the *Guru-shishya parampara* (a tradition of the teacher-disciple relationship). I prefer that no one remembers me, yet the smoke curls and fragrance of *Anamita* (namelessness) keep lingering even as the newer mentors move the potter's wheel and the creative force of the nature just cannot help but *maybe cherish it too, I will keep on drifting happily...with the flow.*

> *"There is no such thing as a 'self-made' man. We are made up of thousands of others. Everyone who has ever done a kind deed for us, or spoken one word of encouragement to us, has entered into the make-up of our character and of our thoughts."*
>
> —Adams, George Matthew

Note: In contrast with the regular tradition of Psychological literature, the identities of the persons, works and places have not been suppressed or disguised to facilitate the reflexivity and ethnographic details. The narrative is based on informed consent of the persons whose names appear in the text.

REFERENCES

Brison, S.J. (1997). Outlining oneself: Trauma, memory, and personal identity. In D.T. Meyers (Ed.), *Feminists rethink the self* (pp. 12-39). Boulder, CO: Westview Press.

Bruner, J. (1986). *Actual minds, possible worlds*. Cambridge, Massachusetts and London, England: Harvard University Press.

Bryman, A. (2001). Introduction: A review of ethnography. In A. Bryman (Ed.), *Ethnography*, Vol. I (pp. IX-XXXIX). London: Sage Publications Ltd.

Charmaz, C. (2006). *Constructing grounded theory: A practical guide through qualitative analysis*. New Delhi: Sage Publications India Pvt. Ltd.

Dyson, M. (2007). My story in a profession of stories: Autoethnography—an empowering methodology for educators. *Australian Journal of Teacher Education*, 32 (1), 36-48. Retrieved September 8, 2009, from http://ajte.education.ecu.edu.au/issues/PDF/321/Dyson.pdf

Ellingson, L.L. (2001). "Then you know how I feel": Empathy, identification, and reflexivity in fieldwork. In A. Bryman (Ed.), *Ethnography* (vol. IV, pp. 52-74). London: Sage Publications Ltd.

Ellis, C. (1997). Evocative autoethnography. In W.G. Tierney and Y. Lincoln (Eds.), *Representation and the text: Re-framing the narrative voice* (pp. 115-139). Albany: State University of New York Press.

Ellis, C. and Bochner, A. (2000). Auto-ethnography, personal narrative, reflexivity. In K. Denzin and Y. Lincoln (Eds.), *The Handbook of Qualitative Research* (2nd ed., pp. 733-767). Thousand Oaks, California: Sage Publications.

Frank, A. (2000). The standpoint of a storyteller. *Qualitative Health Research*, 10(3), 354-365.

Hammersley, M. and Atkinson, P. (2007). *Ethnography: Principles in practice*. (3rd ed.). London: Routledge.

Hayano, D.M. (1979). Auto-ethnography: Paradigms, problems, and prospects. *Human Organization*, 38, 113-120.

Holman Jones, S. (2004). Building connections in qualitative research. Carolyn Ellis and Art Bochner in conversation with Stacy Holman Jones [113 paragraphs]. *Forum Qualitative Sozialforschung/Forum: Qualitative Social Research*, 5 (3), Art. 28. Retrieved September 8, 2009, from http://www.qualitativeresearch.net/index.php/fqs/article/viewArticle/552/1194.

Holt, N.L. (2003). Representation, legitimation, and autoethnography: An ethnographic writing story. *International Journal of Qualitative Methods*. 2 (1), 1-22.

Kaur, P. (1992). *Success: Options and Organizational Dynamics*. New Delhi: Segment Books.

Kumar, A. (2002). *Essence and consequence of organizational citizenship behaviour: The role of self-management, emotional intelligence, and impression management*. Unpublished doctoral dissertation, Indian Institute of Technology, Kanpur, India.

Kumar, S. (1995). *Quality Human Resource: The Pivotal Link between Top Management and Organizational Effectiveness*. Unpublished doctoral dissertation, Indian Institute of Technology, Kanpur, India.

Pollner, M. and Emerson, R.M. (2001). Ethnomethodology and ethnography. In P. Atkinson, A. Coffey, S. Delamont, J. Lofland, and L.H. Lofland (Eds.), *Handbook of ethnography* (pp. 118-135). London: Sage Publications Ltd.

Rai, S. (2000). *Organizational Worth: A Social Equity Perspective,* Unpublished doctoral dissertation, Indian Institute of Technology, Kanpur, India.

Reed-Danahay, D. (1997). *Auto-Ethnography*. New York: Berg.

Sarai, N. (2005). *Organizational behaviour perspective on hospitality industry: The service climate imperative.* Unpublished doctoral dissertation, Indian Institute of Technology, Kanpur, India.

Shukla, A. (1988). *Creativity, Competence, and Excellence: Work Organization Scenario.* Unpublished doctoral dissertation, Indian Institute of Technology, Kanpur, India.

Singh, S. (1990 a). *Executive under Stress: Explorations in the Structure and Dynamics*. New Delhi: Classical Publishing Company.

Singh, S. (1990 b). *Organizational Stress and Executive Behaviour*. New Delhi: Sri Ram Centre for Industrial Relations.

Sinha, A.K. (1980). *The effects of headship styles on the quality of education*. Unpublished doctoral dissertation. Patna University, Patna.

Sinha, A.K. (2009). Individual and group-level processes in organizations. In G. Misra (Ed.), *Psychology in India Volume II: Social and Organizational Processes* (pp. 105-214). Delhi: Indian Council of Social Science Research/Longman imprint of Pearson.

Sinha, A.K. (2009, August). *Culture as a contingency variable for leadership effectiveness: Conflict resolution in service organizations*. Paper presented at the 6th Bienniel Conference of International Academy of Intercultural Research, Honolulu, Hawaii, USA.

Srivastava, K.B.L. (1990). *Exploration of Certain Work Organization Dynamics: An Indian Experience.* Unpublished doctoral dissertation, Indian Institute of Technology, Kanpur-208016, India.

Srivastava, M. (1996). *Effectiveness: Considerations Appertaining to Individuals, Groups, and Organizations*. Unpublished doctoral dissertation, Indian Institute of Technology, Kanpur, India.

Srivastava, S. (2005). *Organizational Justice and Psychological Well-being: Explorations in a Security-service Organization*. Unpublished doctoral dissertation, Indian Institute of Technology, Kanpur, India.

Srivastava, V.K. (1991). The ethnographer and the people: Reflections on the fieldwork. *Economic and Political Weekly,* (June 1-8), 1408-1414.

Vahali, H.O. (2003). From a researcher's notebook: Scattered thoughts on research and researching. *Psychological Studies,* 48, 28-37.

Van Maanen, J. (1988). *Tales of the Field: On writing Ethnography*. Chicago: University of Chicago Press.

CHAPTER FIVE

Psychology through the Works of Professor Jai B.P. Sinha: Some Reflections

Girishwar Misra

THE CONSTRUCTION OF MODERN PSYCHOLOGY

In the history of human knowledge, modern social sciences are latecomers. Most of them developed in twentieth century as a part of the enlightenment project in the Western world. Shaped under the historical, political, and ecological circumstances, they assumed specific roles and functions *vis-à-vis* distinctive societal challenges and existing knowledge structures in philosophy and physical sciences. They institutionalized the study of human phenomena, which were human creations and therefore, culturally fashioned rather than natural things, as was the case with investigations in the physical sciences. Convinced by the positivist notion of science, the study of human behaviour was also brought within the sphere of rational and scientific inquiry by imitating and adapting to the ways and means of physical sciences. In this effort, psychologists created social and psychological objects and invented tools that were subjected to the methodological practices at par with physical sciences. Under the impact of physical sciences, the emphasis was on detailed scrutiny of the different facets of psychological reality in ways compatible and specific to the vocabulary and communication modes prevalent in the physical sciences. Inevitably this had constraining consequences for creating concepts, methods, and criteria for understanding that was sharable by the members of psychological community and broader society.

While psychological issues are part of lived reality of humans, the strategy adopted by psychologists had two effects. It made the *Shastra* of psychology inaccessible and obscure to the common man and ensured the validity claims through the practices accepted by the in-group of their colleagues. In this process, psychological theories and principles became independent entities and people and their lives became mere sources of data or sites of exploration, used for the purpose of testing, and application of those ideas. In brief, a new scheme of knowledge construction and dissemination was put in place which created a gulf between the reality as it was lived and its objectified form or representation which was to be investigated and communicated to the scientific community and society. The knowledge was 'packaged' in a manner that was accessible to only a small fraction of the society which had special training and acquaintance with that system. The understanding thus emanating from disciplinary practices led to many distortions, which were entrenched so deep that one had difficult time escaping the same.

THE JOURNEY OF PSYCHOLOGY IN INDIA

Upon reflection, one realizes that the discipline of psychology is faced with several ontological and epistemological questions which are quite disturbing. The problems are further compounded in a tradition-rich country like India. Historically, modern psychology travelled from Europe and transplanted in India, which differed from the discipline's parental society, in terms of knowledge traditions, life style, and ecological characteristics. However, the British rule, pursuing its agenda of colonization, deliberately distanced the academic pursuits in India from its cultural moorings. The new learning, however, was projected as scientific and a dependable source of knowledge and therefore, cultural relevance became a non-issue. For many of us, psychology was and is distinguished from sister disciplines such as sociology, social work, anthropology, in terms of its greater emphasis on scientific methodology, use of sophisticated statistical techniques, and a microscopic orientation in viewing things in isolation. It is in this spirit that psychology textbooks and teaching programmes emphasized on experiments, practical work, and statistics as the key features and took pride in declaring psychology a 'science'. This reminds us of recent discussions in several groups of Indian psychologists questioning about the 'core' of psychology. Concerns have been voiced about the need to transform an imported psychology into a discipline that would be relevant and appropriate to the Indian culture. There is a need to shape the discipline of psychology to the needs of the local culture. Therefore, today psychologists find it difficult to identify the core of psychology except that it has methodology which in fact cannot be called psychological in nature. The spirit of scientism is so strong and aspirations for making psychology an exact science are so deeply entrenched that teaching and research programmes are ready to sacrifice psychological understanding in favour of empiricist and quantitative methodology.

The circumstances were such that the methodology and instrument centric view of the discipline prevailed and the academic community adapted to it. Being a 'science', psychology was expected to become universal in its constitution and application. Its spirit, as reflected in contents, methodology, and ideology, maintained a stance that expected formulation of uniform laws of psychological science. Society and its psyche were constituted as the object of study but had no role in the structuring of the discipline. This provided strong impetus to establish experimental psychology and psychometry and apparently culture-free measurements and analyses. The tools of psychological inquiry were initially created by psychologists in Germany, England, and United States. However, being projected as universal, they were treated as readily transferable to other cultures. The transfer of knowledge had many advantages and disadvantages. The Indian psychologists had at their disposal imported ready-made ideas, concepts and tools. This acceptance has created a gap on the plane of concepts and methods between Western psychologists and their Indian counterparts. The passive dependence on the Western scholars continues till today. But more crucial is the possibility of distortion in the construction, representation, and interpretation of psychological reality caused by the imposition of imported conceptual categories. The various conceptual categories having culture-specific roots cannot fit the reality equally well everywhere. The problem of translating categories/concepts across cultures has often proved to be a complex problem.

TOWARDS A CULTURALLY RELEVANT PSYCHOLOGY: THE STRUGGLES AND CONTRIBUTIONS OF PROFESSOR JAI B.P. SINHA

The state of affairs in the discipline of psychology in India have been analyzed and reviewed by several scholars. In the last three decades, interaction with cross-cultural psychologists and subsequent efforts to develop cultural and indigenous psychologies has influenced the research agenda of Indian psychologists. The general trend is still confined to the Western tradition. A critical concern, however, is emerging. A close perusal of reviews of research of psychology in India brings into focus many gaps and challenges along with few accomplishments. In general there seems to be denial and avoidance, but creative response has been rare. Prof. Jai B.P. Sinha has shown skill in drawing from the reservoir of concepts and methods, adapting them to the requirements of reality and even developing new tools of enquiry and analysis. His autobiographical essay entitled 'In Search of My Brahman' (Sinha, 1997) provides an account of the transformation in Indian psychologists. He has organized it in four sections, i.e. *Yatra, Neti neti, Asthir chitta,* and *Swantah sukhae* and has shared the way he moved in his academic journey towards a culturally rooted psychology for India. This account is very instructive and helps deciphering the formative influences instrumental in shaping the academic engagements of Indian psychologists.

Prof. Sinha completed the Master's course in India and moved to the United States (US) for higher studies in Psychology. His training in Ohio State University in the US led him to attend the issues of social development. He became interested in the study of achievement motivation (Sinha, 1968a) and experimentally showed that under limited resource conditions the groups of high nAch individuals are unable to maximize their collective outputs and developed interpersonal dislike for group members. This finding did not go well with McClelland's ideas (see for details Sinha, 1981). It was followed by another study (Sinha & Pandey, 1970) which demonstrated that high nAch people maximize achievement by any means and are less concerned about the justifiability of the means used. On the other hand, altruistically oriented persons use resources less selfishly but are not able to maximize their individual outputs. These initial studies exemplify an academic engagement with cultural sensibility and demonstrate constructive and productive conceptual interchange.

Like many or perhaps most of us, Prof. Sinha was faced with a dilemma 'discomfort—to stay with methods' and 'study only those fragments of Indian reality which the methods could cope with or to explore the bigger chunk of real life issues which seemed to be more relevant but less amenable to the straitjacketed methodology he had employed so far' (Sinha, 1997: 79). The most prevalent practice among the Indian psychologists has been and still continues is to respect the method and compromise with the choice of the facet of reality to be studied. They have faith in the rituals of scientific method as the boundary condition of knowledge and therefore, reality, as considered in the study, gets adapted to the method. This kind of method/instrument dependence has led to proliferation of innumerable studies, which hardly tell anything substantial about the reality being studied.

Prof. Sinha notes that he wanted to find most viable entry point in the interplay of the complex growth process in India. He zeroed in on 'dependence-proneness', a concept that drew his attention earlier (Sinha, 1968b, 1970). He thought that 'dependence-proneness needs to be changed if India has to grow'. During the 1970s, he became interested in grasping the nuances of real life problems into small researchable pieces and to investigate them in sequential order. He talked about *Aram* culture, poverty syndrome and the need to outgrow the alien framework. While working out the details of the psychology of dependence-proneness he noticed that highly dependent people, if placed under a leader who expected them to do well, perform at a higher level. He noted a pattern of interaction that was a blend of nurturing and task oriented (NT), that makes a leader effective (Sinha, 1980). In essence, the NT model of leadership 'drew on the Indian ethos of nurturance, dependency, personalized relationship, and status consciousness. Simultaneously, it adopted the contingency approach and the principle of reinforcement from Western literature (see Sinha, 1997: 81). The model was a blend of the East and West. The NT model of leadership is considered as a significant contribution to field of leadership studies. It has been put to practice in understanding and changing the reality of organizations.

The observations of Prof. Sinha on the relevance of culture-specific research are very pertinent. He observes that such studies were 'recognized by compatriots as well as international colleagues'. This observation is very significant. It brings into focus the contextual sensitivity as the core issue in the construction, representation and use of knowledge. In today's world, societal demands are found critical to the process of knowledge production. A large section of the community of Indian psychologists has been concerned more with the 'context for justification' rather than the 'context of discovery'. They have been engaged and preoccupied with testing Western theories on Indian samples. This emphasis partly explains the preoccupation of methods and instruments that are problematic. In order to relate to social reality, we need to develop relevant methods and tools (see Sinha, 1973).

The limitations of prevalent methodology led Prof. Sinha to rethink and expand the conceptual and methodological tool kit. In order to get a holistic picture, he moved to the use of observation, secondary data, group interviews and critical events. These efforts allowed him to understand Indian social reality better. In this context I would like to refer the notion of collectivism. His insightful analysis (Sinha, 1982a, 1982b) showed that the Indian collectivism is different in terms of permeable ego-boundaries and clearly demarcated and meticulously protected boundaries of the social groups; the struggle for power due to scarce resources leads to narrowly drawn in-group boundaries, hierarchical in-group structure, tolerance for deviations from group norms, and orientation to cultivate social networks of friends and relatives and safeguard each others interest. He also drew attention to the concept of 'social energy' (Sinha, 1985). It is an experience of being aroused or activated because of the social groups and collectives. The reflections of Prof. Sinha are critical for the positioning of psychologists in socially relevant research process (see Sinha, 1982a, 1985).

Prof. Sinha notes that his experience in the US showed that the researcher is 'a part of the worldview where the life styles and the types of research were interrelated and supported each other' (Sinha, 1997: 78). The same does not happen when one applies the Western constructs to the Indian setting. On his return to India, he posed many questions regarding the relationship between research, knowledge, and methodology. Instead of being overwhelmed by the impressive array of Western studies and imitating, replicating or extending the same he decided 'to distinguish substance from superficialities' (Sinha, 1997: 78) and ventured for undertaking culturally relevant research that may attend to the problems of national development (Sinha, 1990b). He did not allow his concern for alternatives to interfere with the pursuit of work.

In general, Indian psychological research in its modern form has ignored the Indian tradition. Apart from other reasons, the contemporarity of psychological investigations and rigid adherence to psychological constructs interferes with the understanding of present in relation to collective past. The Indian situation owing to its richness, depth and continuity makes it even more difficult. According to Prof. Sinha, an understanding of Indian culture requires a holistic and multi-method approach integrating both etics and emics (2004a). This aspect has often been ignored in formulating the approach to problems. The result is that while number of researchers and publications has grown yet the quality of research has not improved to the same degree (Sinha, 1993).

Usually, our studies focus on immediate circumstances and least attention is paid to the historical context. Prof. Sinha has taken a serious note of the cultural context and has argued in favour of indigenization of psychological researches, with reference to theory and methodology (Sinha, 1997a, 2000, 2002). In view of the significance of *Desh* (Space), *Kal* (Time) and *Patra* (Person) and centrality of relationship, Sinha and Kanungo (1997) have considered context sensitivity and balancing as key factors in shaping organizational behaviour. More recently, Prof. Sinha has ventured into understanding the Indian mind-set and has revealed how Indians manifest diverse mind-sets in different contexts. One of the empirical studies (Sinha & A. Pandey, 2007) yielded evidence showing that Indians manifest a materialist mind-set in multinational organizations, dependence-prone or collectivist mind-set in family owned, bureaucratic, and or traditional organizations, depending on whether they valued either easygoing life or stable relationships respectively. Indians are holistic in terms of combining excellence in work, personalized relationships, abstract thinking, emotionality, rationality and spirituality in those organizations that valued both performance and people. Materialistic mind-set was associated with manipulative behaviour and the holistic mind-set with a proactive stance that manifested in innovative and extra-ordinary performance under inspiring superiors; both materialistic and holistic mindsets were instrumental to success at work, in different organizational contexts. Culture emerged as a powerful context related to person's behaviour. Mind-set varies depending on the context.

Prof. Sinha's critique, reflection, reconstruction and integration is visible in his reviews, monographs and volumes pertaining to work culture, leadership, values and other prominent concerns in the area of organizational behaviour (Sinha, 1990a, 1994, 1995, 1997a, 2000, 2004b, 2008; J.B.P. Sinha and D. Sinha, 1990) and indicates an evolution in his thinking, a desire to address different audiences, and constructive engagement with contemporaneous societal challenges. He has dealt with issues of partnership with colleagues across developed and developing countries and taken steps to organize multicentric studies (Sinha *et al.,* 1994) to understand the cultural patterns of behaviour. In this way he has taken lead in organizing fellow colleagues and engaging with them in planning and conducting studies.

In the work of Prof. Sinha one finds richness in terms of breadth of scope as well as depth of concerns. He is confident that authentic cultural or indigenous research is an appropriate research modality. He observes:

'I do not have the need to carry the cross of someone's theory or approach; nor do I have resources to try mine in some other cultures. My hunch is that even if I try, I will be imposing my emic under the delusion of realizing an etic. May be the best I can do is to try to be a cultural rather than cross-cultural psychologist. May be the route to universal science of psychology is through many indigenous psychologies forming overarching patterns (Sinha, 1997: 83). We all have our own islands—psycho-historically and culturally determined. They form clusters, some being closer while others are more distant. It is unrealistic to think that some day the clusters will join to form one big monolithic mass. All we can do is to explore our own islands and build bridges to communicate and share' (p. 83).

I have described selectively, rather than exhaustively, some of the issues through whose analysis and investigation Prof. Sinha has embarked upon his academic pursuit. The impulse to make psychology socially relevant has led

Prof. Sinha to explore various facets of the Indian psyche. His work indicates a patient, methodical, and unremitting effort to relate to the social reality. His contributions offer a sound basis on which one can build research and intervention.

REFERENCES

Sinha, J.B.P. (1968a). The nAch/cooperation under limited/unlimited resource conditions. *Journal of Experimental Social Psychology*, 4, 233-248.

Sinha, J.B.P. (1968b). The construct of dependence proneness. *Journal of Psychology*, 70, 129-131.

Sinha, J.B.P. (1970). *Development through Behaviour Modification*. Bombay: Allied Publishers.

Sinha, J.B.P. (1973). Methodology of problem-oriented research in India. *Journal of Social and Economic Studies*, 1, 93-110.

Sinha, J.B.P. (1980). *The nurturant task leader: A model of the effective executive*. New Delhi: Concept.

Sinha, J.B.P. (1981). In search of research identity. In J. Pandey (Ed.) *Perspectives on experimental social psychology* (pp. 241-252). New Delhi: Concept.

Sinha, J.B.P. (1982a). The Hindu identity. *Dynamic psychiatry*, 19, 148-160.

Sinha, J.B.P. (1982b) Power structure, perceptual frame and behavioural strategies in a dynamic relationship. In R. Rath *et al.* (Eds.) *Diversity and unity in cross cultural psychology*. Lisse: Swetes and Zeitlingrer.

Sinha, J.B.P. (1985). Collectivism, social energy and development in India. In Isabel Reys Lagunes and Ype H. Poortinga (Eds.). *From a different perspective: Studies of behaviour across cultures* (pp. 109-119). Lisse: Swetes and Zeitlingrer.

Sinha, J.B.P. (1990a). *Work culture in the Indian context*. New Delhi: Sage.

Sinha, J.B.P. (1990b). Role of psychology in national development. In G. Misra (Ed.), *Applied Social Psychology in India* (pp. 171-199). New Delhi: Sage Publications.

Sinha, J.B.P. (1993). The front and the bulk of Indian psychology. *Psychology and Developing Societies*, 5, 135-150.

Sinha, J.B.P. (1994). Cultural embeddedness and the developmental role of industrial organizations in India. In H.C. Triandis, M.D. Dunnette, and L.M. Hough (Eds.), *Handbook of industrial and organizational psychology*, 4 (pp. 727-764), US: Consulting Psychologists Press.

Sinha, J.B.P. (1995). *The cultural context of leadership and power*. New Delhi: Sage Publications.

Sinha, J.B.P. (1997a). A cultural perspective on organizational behaviour in India. In P.C. Early and M. Erez (Eds.), *New perspectives on international industrial/organizational psychology* (pp. 53-74). San Francisco, CA, US: The New Lexington Press/Jossey-Bass Inc.

Sinha, J.B.P. (1997b). In search of my Brahman. In M.H. Bond (Ed.). *Working at the interface of cultures: Eighteen lives in social science* (pp. 77-84). London: Routledge.

Sinha, J.B.P. (2000a). Integrative indigenization of management in India: practices and prospects. *Indian Journal of Industrial Relations*, 35 (4), 439-460.

Sinha, J.B.P. (2000b). *Patterns of Work Culture: Cases and Strategies for Culture Building*. New Delhi: Sage.

Sinha, J.B.P. (2002). Towards indigenization of psychology in India. In G. Misra, and A.K. Mohanty (Eds.) (2002). *Perspectives on Indigenous Psychology* (pp. 440-457). New Delhi: Concept.

Sinha, J.B.P. and Kumar, R. (2004a). Methodology for understanding Indian culture. *The Copenhagen Journal of Asian Studies*, 19, 89-104.

Sinha, J.B.P. (2004b). *Multinationals in India: Managing the Interface of Cultures*. New Delhi: Sage.

Sinha, J.B.P. (2008). *Culture and Organizational Behaviour*. New Delhi: Sage.

Sinha, J.B.P. and Pandey, J. (1970). Strategies of high nAch persons. *Psychologia*, 13, 210-216.

Sinha, J.B.P. and Sinha, D. (1990). Role of social values in Indian organizations. *International Journal of Psychology*, 25, 705-714.

Sinha, J.B.P., Daftuar, C.N., Gupta, R.K, Misra., R.C. Jayeetha, R., Jha, S.S., Verma, J., and Vijayakumar, V.S.R. (1994). Regional similarities and differences in people's beliefs, practices, and preferences. *Psychology and Developing Societies*, 6, 131-150.

Sinha, J.B.P. and Kanungo, R.N. (1997). Context sensitivity and balancing in organizational behaviour. *International Journal of Psychology*, 32, 93-105.

Sinha, J.B.P., and Pandey, Ashish (2007). Indians' mindsets and the conditions that evoke them. *Psychological Studies*, 52, 1-13.

CHAPTER SIX

Social Motivations Research: Enthusiasm of the Sixties to Present Indifference

Janak Pandey

Professor J.B.P. Sinha had unique opportunity in early years of socialization in his family which was a centre of freedom movement activities and later after independence of India in 1947, a place of intense debate on problems associated with nation building. Intrinsically motivated for research, young Prof. Sinha in his search for best possible training opportunity succeeded in getting admission with fellowship in the Doctoral Programme of the Ohio State University (OSU). Award of a Fulbright travel grant further facilitated his cherished mission to have best possible doctoral level research in a prestigious university of USA. At OSU, young Sinha was not only impressed by theories and scientific methods including rigour of statistical analysis, he excelled in all courses and demonstrated it by publishing empirical work in top journals.

The Second World War was followed by accelerated independence movements leading to end of colonial rules and emergence of new nation states including India. The independent India under the charismatic leadership of Jawaharlal Nehru, the first Prime Minister opted for all-round planned development of the nation. India launched its ambitious five-year plans with well-defined targets to be achieved in each plan period. The Planning Commission was established and mostly economists and bureaucrats were involved as its experts and other social scientists were ignored as they were considered of not much relevance. A well trained social psychologist, Prof. Sinha strongly believed in strength of psychology in understanding human nature and shaping it for development. He also realized that it was almost non-utilized in development processes and nation building either at individual or at societal level. Prof. Sinha's exposure to debates on issues of national importance kept a fire alive in him and he felt necessity of scientific study of behaviour in social context in a way that findings of research have some utility in solution of problems of librated nations particularly of India facilitating development process.

Among the social sciences, psychology was seen with least importance in understanding development. Prof. Sinha was uncomfortable due to this unfair status to psychology. Interface of his training in psychology and concern for the development, led Prof. Sinha to formulate new perspective for understanding social reality and strategic role of social psychology for development. In his Foreword of Prof. Sinha's first book (Sinha,1970) presenting findings of series of experimental and survey research on social motivation completed under his leadership, then Director of A.N. Sinha Institute of Social Studies, A.K. Dasgupta, a reputed economist accepted human motivation as critical aspect of economic development. He argued that human motivation had not received the attention it deserved. Dasgupta lamented that "one of the chief obstacles to economic development is lack of aspiration of people" and he recognized that problem was not only technological, it was psychological and related to human factor. Prof. Sinha's systematic research programme on human motivation answers to some of these observations. Sinha studied how fatalism, religious ritualism, and resistance to mobility and acceptance of innovation, led to inefficiency and slow decision making and in turn retarded economic development.

Though as a doctoral fellow at OSU, Prof. Sinha matured as a top grade social psychologist, he did not have much opportunity to examine possibilities of use of psychology in development process in real social context. Certainly, he did not want to get into rat race of churning out research papers following certain paradigms of his *gurus* at OSU. In search of alternatives, he got attracted to David McClelland who had launched a training programme for Indian managers at Kakinada and Vellore for enhancing their need for achievement (n-Ach) which in turn would facilitate economic development. McClelland's book, *The Achieving Society* (1961) had gained some popularity in development discourse. McClelland's argument that need for achievement promotes entrepreneurship and that in turn positively determines economic development was based on a series of studies. Prof. Sinha responded positively to McClelland (1961) achievement motivation proposition as a critical input to accelerate economic growth. Intensive interactions with McClelland in a two-day seminar at Harvard prior to returning to India did not convert Prof. Sinha as a his follower. Prof. Sinha actually became his critic. McClelland also respected work of Prof. Sinha and utilized it in his theorization. Sinha argued that enhancement of achievement motive at individual level may not be the best thing to do for economic development in a situation of limited resources. He experimentally demonstrated that high n-Ach led to more resource creation and better performance but this was also combined with grabbing resources and putting others to disadvantages. In comparison to selfish, altruistic orientation in n-Ach participants led to less misuse and creation of resources but also led to less achievement (Sinha,1970). The findings and conclusions drawn based on these studies were questioned in terms of external validity in real complex world.

Achievement motivation, however, is a critical human factor for economic development and social change. As a true believer in application of social science knowledge in resolution of problems, Prof. Sinha engaged himself with two approaches in an evolutionary way. First, he was impressed by individualistic psychology approach and tried to bring change using all possible methods in individual's motivation leading to reduction in dependence proneness and raising initiative and achievement motivation. According to this approach, a large number of individuals with high achievement motive will impact positively development process. As a keen and critical observer, Prof. Sinha identified another motivational-behavioural disposition typical of Indians and he called it dependence-proneness (DP). Uncalled for dependence-proneness slowed down work and productivity. He defined dependence-proneness in terms of a set of behavioural pattern such as uncalled for attention, guidance, support, and help seeking behaviour in making decisions and taking actions in situations where individuals could act on their own. In more than a dozen of studies and doctoral theses of his students, he and his associates found that dependence-proneness was correlated, with religious ritualism, fatalism, superstition, obedience, apathy, passivity, and many similar behavioural dispositions. This led Prof. Sinha to conclude that DP causes resistance in acceptance of innovation, mobility and risk taking. Sinha's analysis suggests that motivational and behavioural dispositions, however, are inculcated and maintained by conducive family and larger societal structures and by ongoing processes. So, bringing change in individual's motivation and behaviours at a large scale may not be practical and even possible. Sinha clearly concluded that dependence proneness is maintained mostly by the social support, that is reinforcements emanating from social structure (Sinha,1970). Prof. Sinha realized limitations of training programmes at individuals level to change motivation and behaviour and therefore, a shift took place in his approach.

Based on his work, Prof. Sinha got convinced to the fact that changing individuals with hope that they will change organization and society would not work on a large scale. Therefore, he moved towards other approach related to changes in organizations and system in a manner that influence induction of growth-conducive behaviours like initiative, decision making, performance, excellence and quality in work of the individuals who constitute organizations and make the larger society. Generally, psychologists are comfortable with the first approach which led to development of science of behaviour modification. Prof. Sinha realized that individuals fail to sustain initiative in the larger system and organizational structures which encourage dependency, indecision, and lethargy. He argued that structural changes in organizations, values and culture of the larger societal system may change individuals and these changes may be sustained. He advocated for modifying the structural aspects of organizations and aligning social values with development processes.

Organizations and social systems may create and nurture pro-development motivation, values and expectations in individuals. Social engineering is therefore required to shape social organizations and institutions which in turn nurture appropriately motivational-behavioural dispositions facilitating economic and social development. Thus, it is possible to shape and make individuals behave in conducive way for rapid economic growth by "changing the social expectancies which support and maintain dependence proneness". This shift in approach is evolutionary and is based on commitment of Prof. Sinha to make psychology relevant for the societal development rather than some changes at individual level which may not last if organizations and societies are not structured to sustain those changes.

Prof. Sinha argued in favour of introducing change for development through change in organizational structure. Any society is a cluster of overlapping organizations and groups with each having its norms and pattern of functioning. Individuals in organizations behave not in vacuum but with reference to organizational demands. It was a well founded paradigmatic shift in approach from changing individual's motivation to changing organizations for development. He argued "manipulate the organizational structure so as to put specific demands to the individuals—what they ought to do and what they ought not to do" (Sinha, 1970: 69). He accepted crucial role of a leader in any organization. A leader has to function in a socio-cultural context and therefore, efficient and effective leadership has to be culturally appropriate. The shift from study of social motivation (n-Ach, dependency, affiliation, social anxiety, etc.) to organizational structure, climate and change was based on research and commitment to explore new strategies facilitating change at individual and institutional level for development. So, we find that Prof. Sinha moved forward and by the mid-1970s, he was fully involved in study of organizational cultures and their roots in societal cultures. So, for nearly four decades using multi-methods his emic studies have focused on larger Indian societal culture and its organizations and institutions. Prof. Sinha's psycho-philosophical thoughts have evolved over the years with greater emphasis on the larger society to understand individual's cognition and conduct. He continues to be creative, insightful and refreshing in terms of his research output as his thoughts grow with his age.

REFERENCES

McClelland, D.C. (1961) *The Achieving Society*. Princton, N.J.: Van Nostrand.

Sinha, J.B.P. (1970) *Development Through Behaviour Modifications*. Bombay: Allied Publishers.

SECTION-2

ORGANIZATIONAL DEVELOPMENT

Organizations have crucial role to play in the development process in most democratic societies. High performing organizations seem to accelerate the pace of development. Research in the area has proved beyond doubt that the factors operating within the organization have much bearing on performance of the organization. The chapters of this section focus on some of the organization level factors that make significant contribution to development of the organization.

The seventh chapter, authored by Shailendra Singh and V.P. Singh addresses the issue as to what makes an organization high performing and what differentiates it from average and not so high performing organization. These questions may not be new, but they arouse the interest of academics and practitioners alike. Answer to these questions may be of practical value to all concerns. A case has been made here that intangible assets—organizational culture including HR policies, practices and strategy positively contribute to organizational performance.

In the next chapter, Sunita Singh-Sengupta makes a paradigm shift in the conceptualization of meaning of work and its psychological and spiritual implications in the organizational context for optimal performance. The discussion centres around the issue whether work is a 'mean' or an 'end'. The author takes the stand of promoting work as an end for better integration of individual and work. The chapter provides a comparison with respect to the conceptualization of meaning of work in Western and Eastern context. The perspective on work in the West seems to be 'exteriorized'; however, it seems to be 'interiorized' in the Eastern context. She emphasizes the need to move towards the 'interiorized' meaning of work as it helps in integrating the different selves of an individual leading to perfection and attainment of enjoyment at work place.

The chapter "Beyond conflict violence and retaliation: Gandhijee as an exemplar of indigenous approach to leadership education" by Dharm P.S. Bhawuk presents an indigenous approach to leadership. By showing eight selected clips from the famous actor and director Attenborough's film *Gandhi,* the author has tried to demonstrate that leadership concept can be derived from indigenous perspectives. The clips show Gandhi's value-based service oriented leadership style, which though grounded in indigenous cultural values, is still generalizable across cultures. He is an "exemplar" in his thought, speech and action. The author has been using the clips for leadership education and is not shy of making a claim that in a short span of just about two and a half hour, students get inspired to emulate Gandhi.

The next chapter, authored by Arif Hassan emphasizes the ethical and moral aspects of leader and defines leadership that includes element of trust, besides skill and competencies. The essential components that build subordinates' trust in leadership seem to include integrity, competence, loyalty and openness. The author argues that perceived trust in the leader will perhaps lead to higher level of leader's authenticity as perceived by followers that makes the leader effective.

In the era of neo-liberalization, Indian organizations have been exposed to multinational cultures, where new management thoughts and ideas have been made accessible to them. In this light, the eleventh chapter by K.B.L. Srivastava and Soumendu Biswas examines the impact of changed perception about the organizational climate on job satisfaction.

Ajay K. Jain, in the next chapter, "The Impact of emotional intelligence on self-rated performance and self-efficiency perception", postulates that emotional intelligence will have positive influence on the development of self-confidence and self-efficacy, which provide potential for self-management behaviour that may further lead to higher satisfaction both in life and at work place. If so, there can be a strategy for enhancing emotionally intelligent behaviour in organizations through training to develop one's faith in his/her ability to take up challenging jobs.

Effectiveness is considered as one of the most important underlying phenomena for sustaining the organization and its growth. The last chapter of this section by Sweta Srivastava Malla addresses to this issue. Through the study conducted in a security-service organization, the author has attempted to examine the construct of organizational effectiveness at three levels: (a) effectiveness on conceived roles, (b) personal effectiveness, and (c) job accomplishment. Internal motivation, lesser politics in organization, leader's support and perceived organizational justice emerged as key variables for organizational effectiveness at the three levels.

CHAPTER SEVEN

Performance of Health Care Organizations: Can Organizational Culture Make Difference?

Shailendra Singh and V.P. Singh

INTRODUCTION

Traditionally, national development used to be equated with economic development (Sinha, 1984); measured in terms of per capita gross domestic product (Sinha, 2008). While balancing the definition of human development, United Nations Development Programme (UNDP) has put 'human being' at the centre of development. The UNDP report emphasized that Human Development is a development paradigm that is much more than just the rise or fall of national incomes. Human Development has been defined in the following words:

> *"It is about creating an environment in which people can develop their full potential and lead productive, creative lives in accord with their needs and interests. People are the real wealth of nations. Development is thus about expanding the choices people have to lead lives that they value. And it is thus about much more than economic growth, which is only a means—if a very important one—of enlarging people's choices. Fundamental to enlarging these choices is building human capabilities—the range of things that people can do or be in life. The most basic capabilities for human development are to lead long and healthy lives, to be knowledgeable, to have access to the resources needed for a decent standard of living and to be able to participate in the life of the community."*
>
> (Human Development Report, 2002)

Human Development Index (HDI) is the normalized measure of life expectancy, literacy, education, standard of living and GDP per capita for countries worldwide. Mahbub ul Haq emphasized that the basic aim of development is to enhance people's choice. It may be unlimited and can be varied overtime. It may include: greater access to knowledge, better nutrition and health services, more secure livelihoods, security against crime and physical violence, satisfying leisure hours, political and cultural freedoms and sense of participation in community activities. He further clarified that the objective of development is to create facilitating environment so that people can enjoy long healthy and creative lives.

Sinha (1968; 1970; 1980; 1984; 2008) and his associates (Sinha & Pandey, 1970; Sinha *et al.*, 1999) have been keenly interested in development issues. Social relevance, cultural embeddedness, and development have been the common thread in the works of Jai B.P. Sinha. This paper is also addressing a development issue—performance of health care organizations. Creating, managing and sustaining high performance in organizations is the concern of one and all. Be it researchers, management practitioners, entrepreneurs, politicians, health professionals, or social workers, everyone wants his/her enterprise to be high performing. They may be using different conceptual framework, tools, or other ways and means to achieve the same goal-effective and efficient performance (Singh, 2002). This research in its modest way has addressed the same problem as to what makes an organization high performing and what differentiates a high performance organization from average ones or not so high performing organizations? These questions may not be new, but they arouse the interest of academics and practitioners alike and answers to these questions may be of practical value to all concerned.

A case has been made here that intangible assets—organizational culture including HR policies and practices and strategy positively influence organizational performance.

There has been growing interest in service-sector organizations due to its positive contribution in the economy of the country. Within service-sector, health care industry is getting prominence for two reasons. First, the health care services are most critical and development of any nation is assessed based on indicators of health status. Secondly, the demands for health care services are so high that public health care system is not able to cater the requirements of its people. Keeping the importance of health care services in mind, we have tried to profile what constitutes a high performance health care service organization and how it differs from its counter parts in low performance group.

The performance of health care organizations is receiving increasing attention in most countries. Both quantitative systems (e.g. report cards, league tables and other rating systems (Smith, 2002a, b) and qualitative assessments (e.g. through accreditation visits and inspections (Walshe, 2003) have grown up at increasing levels of sophistication and intrusiveness. Now, greater attention is being paid to the "softer" aspects of organizations and professional practice: the deep-seated assumptions, values and working practices that have been affirmed over decades and woven into the fabric of health care delivery. These assumptions and patterns of behaviour within an organization are often referred to as "organisational culture"—and there is considerable effort towards changing of organizational culture under health reforms. Yet, evidence from the research literature for a link between the culture of an organization and performance including the quality and safety of the care are relatively scant (Scott *et al.*, 2003).

ORGANIZATIONAL PERFORMANCE AND ITS KEY DRIVERS

In this section we have defined organizational effectiveness and have presented brief overview of key drivers of performance. The terms high performance organization, excellent organization, effective organization have been used interchangeably in the literature to refer to high performance organizations. The concept of effectiveness is very broad in nature and commonly understood by everybody but difficult to define. From amongst several approaches, we have taken "competing values perspective" in defining effectiveness/high performance. Following Quinn and Rohrbaugh (1983), we have used a two dimensional framework: internal *vs.* external focus, stability *vs.* flexibility in structure. Based on the combination of two dimensions, we have internal focus and flexible structure leading to human relations emphasis, external focus and flexible structure leading to open system emphasis. A combination of internal focus and stable structure lead to internal process emphasis while stable structure and external focus lead to rational goal emphasis. In real organizations, these competing values can be seen co-existing together. Each of the four approaches represents different management values with respect to focus and structure. It suggests that multiple goals: output goals, acquisition and human resource development goals are simultaneously pursued by organizations. Further, it suggests that effectiveness criteria are managements' values and how opposing values can coexist. Managers need to decide which value they would like to accord high priority compared to others.

Operationally, we defined organizational performance in terms of achievement of multiple objectives and satisfaction of multiple stakeholders. We have used a measure of organizational performance consisting of 15 items representing competing value perspective. Items included: innovativeness, operating efficiency, morale of employees, growth rate of revenue/activity, adaptability, stability of performance from one year to another, financial strength, learning and growth of employees, public image and goodwill, employer-employee relationship, and impact on industry and sector, quality of services, level of patient recovery and satisfaction, social responsibility and business ethics. A single item measure of overall performance was also used.

ORGANIZATIONAL CULTURE

Participants within a formal organizational structure generate shared patterns of beliefs, assumptions, values and expectations, collectively termed 'organizational culture' (Deal & Kennedy, 1982; Schein, 1990). These beliefs and expectations produce norms or commitments—informal rules for behaviour—which provide a context within which individuals in an organization can interpret and approach their work (Khademian, 2002). Organizational culture has been termed as 'Corporate Soul' (Singh and Paul,1985) and "the spirit and the ethos" (Pareek, 2004). Sinha (2009) defined organizational culture as the totality of assumptions, values, norms, and behaviour of employees that create physical and social artefacts of an organization. He (Sinha, 1990) also talked about five layers of organizational culture:

1. Organizational mission, vision, goals and objectives and underlying philosophy of management.
2. Organizational structure, systems, work, technology, nature of capital, and other hardware of an organization.
3. Group attributes like nature of power and authority relationship, group dynamics, leadership, work relationship etc.
4. Work and non-work policies and practices.
5. Beliefs, values, and norms of work and non-work areas including family, community and religious spheres.

Sinha (1990, 1999) observed three distinct pattern of organizational culture: (a) Soft culture, (b) Technocratic culture, and (c) Work centric nurturant culture. Soft culture organizations are characterized by restricted autonomy and centralization of power. Management feels restricted in initiating actions that would facilitate organizations to maintain high productivity. Employees believe that hard and sincere effort is less important than meeting social and personal obligations. A technocratic culture is characterized by effort to provide highest possible quality of product, use of latest technology, new system of managerial practice, innovation, penetrating new markets etc. Work Centric Nurturant Culture (WCNC) is similar to technocratic culture as far as emphasis of work is concerned. In WCNC, employees believe that management rewards hard work, recognizes merit, set clear standards of performance. Employees' needs and expectations are met. Superiors take personal interest in career progression and well-being of the subordinates. As the subordinates mature, they are encouraged to assume greater responsibilities. Such culture helps in generating and sustaining high performance.

The organizational culture model used in this study is based on four cultural traits that have been shown in the literature to have an influence on organizational performance: involvement, consistency, adaptability, and mission (Denison, 1990; Denison and Mishra, 1995; Gordon and DiTomaso, 1992; Kotter and Heskett, 1992). These traits actually captured vision, mission, goals and objectives, HR policies and practices and strategy. Each of four traits is measured with three component indexes. We have provided the brief overview of organizational model as proposed by Denison and colleagues.

INVOLVEMENT

Empowerment: Individuals perceive to have the authority, initiative, and ability to manage their own work. This inculcates a sense of ownership and responsibility towards the organization.

Team Orientation: People perceive that working cooperatively towards common goals is valued which generates a feeling of mutual accountability among employees.

Capability Development: The organization continually invests in the development of employee's skills in order to stay competitive and meet on-going business needs.

CONSISTENCY

Core Values: Members of the organization share a set of values which create a sense of identity and a clear set of expectations.

Agreement: Members of the organization are able to reach agreement on critical issues. This includes both the underlying level of agreement and the ability to reconcile differences when they occur.

Coordination and Integration: Different functions and units of the organization are able to work together well to achieve common objectives. Organizational boundaries do not interfere with getting work done.

ADAPTABILITY

Creating Change: The organization develops capacity and methodology to meet changing needs. It is able to read the business environment, react quickly to current trends, and anticipate future changes.

Customer Focus: The organization understands and responds to their customers and anticipates their future needs. It reflects the degree to which the organization is driven by a concern to satisfy their customers.

Organizational Learning: The organization receives, translates, and interprets data from the environment into opportunities for encouraging innovation, gaining knowledge, and developing capabilities.

MISSION

Strategic Direction and Intent: Clear strategic intentions convey the organization's purpose and make it clear how everyone can contribute and "make their mark" on the industry.

Goal and Objectives: A clear set of goals and objectives can be linked to the mission, vision, and strategy, and provide everyone with a clear direction in their work.

Vision: The organization has a shared view of a desired future state. It enshrines core values and captures the hearts and minds of the organization's people, while providing guidance and direction.

Denison's Organizational Culture model suggests that twelve factors are positively related with organizational effectiveness and organizational performance (Dension, 1990; Dension & Misra, 1995). Not adequate empirical evidence is available in Indian setting regarding the relationship between dimensions of organizational culture and organizational performance, thus worth pursuing. Keeping the results of Western studies in mind, we expect that high performance organizations will have relatively better organizational culture.

THE STUDY

The results reported in this paper are a part of large on-going study 'High performance organizations'. In the present paper we have used the data from

50 health care organizations in private sector from north India whose administrators and medical officers agreed to participate in the study. These organizations were providing general and emergency health care, specialty health care and super-specialty health care. We collected two responses from each organization, one from administrator and other from medical officer. The two responses of each organization were aggregated and a composite mean was generated for each variable. Thus, data presented here have used organization as unit of analysis.

MEASURES

Organizational Performance: Organizational performance was measured using 15 items of which 12 items were adopted from Khandwalla (2003) and remaining three items were constructed specifically for this study. All items were on a five-point Likert-type scale ranging from 1 to 5, where '1' measures very low performance of the organization as compared to other similarly placed institutions in the area, industry, country, and '5' measures very high performance. Overall performance of organizations was also measured by a single item on a 5-point scale where 5 means very high overall performance whereas 1 means very low overall performance.

Organizational Culture: Modified version of 60-item scale of Denison *et. al.* (2006) was used to measure 12 constructs of organizational culture. Each of the 12 constructs was measured using five items on the questionnaire. All questions were on a five-point Likert-type scale ranging from 1 to 5 where 1 means strong disagreement with the statement and 5 means strong agreement. For reversed worded items, scoring was also reversed.

MULTI-DIMENSIONAL NATURE OF ORGANIZATIONAL PERFORMANCE

Organizational performance data were subjected to factor analysis with varimax rotation and a criterion of extraction of factors till the Eigenvalues reached to 1. Data revealed two factors and together explained 67.77 per cent of variance. Decision was made to include the item in the factor where it had the highest loading. The first factor consisted of 11 items and explained 43.62 per cent of variance. Items included in the factor are: innovativeness, operating efficiency, morale of employees, growth rate of revenue/activity, adaptability, stability of performance from one year to another, financial strength, learning and growth of employees, public image and goodwill, employer-employee relationship, and impact on industry and sector. Based on loading composition, we called it generic performance. Alpha reliability of the factor was .95.

The second factor consisted of four items and explained 24.15 per cent of variance. This factor has items related to quality of services, level of patient recovery and satisfaction, social responsibility and business ethics. We named this factor as Performance in Quality and governance areas. Alpha reliability of the factor was 0.79.

Overall Performance: Overall performance was assessed through a single item on a 5-point scale ranging from very low (1) to very high (5) performer. Distribution of overall performance data revealed a mean score of 3.2 on a five point scale (Mean = 3.20, SD = 0.76). The data suggest that respondents on average have rated their hospitals and nursing homes as moderate performers. Of the total hospitals studied, 10 per cent have been rated either low or very low performers. Similarly, 12 per cent hospitals have been rated as low to average performers while 34 per cent of the hospitals have been rated as average performers. In total, 56 per cent hospitals were rated between average and low performers. Incidentally, Median and Mode of overall performance are also 3. Only 44 per cent of the hospitals in the sample were rated very high to between average and high. In order to examine differences between high and low performance hospitals, criteria of median split was used. Hospitals falling between Median score and below on overall performance were treated as Low performance group while hospitals falling above the median score formed the part of High performance group. High performance group consisted of 44 per cent of the cases while Low performance group included 56 per cent of the cases.

Difference Across High and Low Performance Organizations: Based on Median split, we created two groups. Organizations scoring higher than median value on overall performance were included in high performance group. The other half-median and below scoring organizations were formed part of low performance group. Such splitting did not create equal group. Forty-four per cent of the organizations were classified in high performance group while 56 per cent organizations were in low performance group. We used t-test with unequal cell frequency to examine group differences. In order to examine our proposition we examined difference between high and low performance organizations across organizational culture dimensions. A clear trend is visible that high performance group on average has a higher score on organizational culture dimensions than its counterparts in low performance group. It can be safely said that high performance organizations are perceived to have better organizational culture than its low performance counterpart. For all the dimensions of organizational culture, high performance group had a higher score than its counterparts. However, if we closely examine the differences, we find that high performance group has done significantly better, on nine dimensions of the twelve ($p < .05$). On two dimensions, namely, agreement and strategic direction and intent, high performance group scored higher but the difference was marginally significant ($p < .10$).

We observed that t-value was highest for creating change suggesting ($t = 3.21$, $df = 48$, $p < .01$) that high performance group had a better system for creating and managing change than their counterparts. The finding is in expected direction, as it is quite intuitive to observe organizations anticipating change and plan ahead for managing challenges in the environment likely to do better than organizations which do not have system to create and manage change. The second highest observed difference was on customer focus ($t = 3.15$; $df = 48$; $p < .01$). The trend suggested that organizations which concentrated on satisfying their customers would likely to do better than those who ignore or did not focus on satisfying their customers. This finding again lends support to our hypothesis. Interpretation of the finding is straightforward, concentrate on satisfying customer needs, they will serve as agents of organizations. Satisfied customers give repeat business and give reference to others, thus volume of business increases which eventually leads to high performance in terms organizational outcomes.

Team orientation was found to be higher in high performance group as compared to low performance group ($t = 3.01$; $df = 48$; $p < .01$). Results supported the first hypothesis. Providing health care services is not the job of one person. It requires concerted effort of the whole team of role incumbents including ward attendants, nurses, paramedical staff, doctors, laboratory technicians, cleaning staff etc. It is quite obvious to find relatively higher team orientation in high performing hospitals.

Goal and objectives, vision, and empowerment were also rated to be relatively higher in high performance organizations. Goals and objectives have always provided motivational force to people to perform better. Similarly, vision provides long term course of action and sense of purpose to aspire for superior performance. Both goals and objectives form part of the mission in Densions's organizational culture framework. Several researchers (Hamel & Prahalad, 1994; Selznick, 1957) have emphasized that successful organizations have clear sense of purpose and direction that defines organizational goals and strategic objectives and a vision to shape the future of organization. Empowerment again is a positive factor for enhancing performance by enabling the role holder to take initiative, sense of responsibility, and ownership of the job, thus expanding high effort for high attainment.

Organizational learning, core values and coordination and integration were also relatively high in high performance group but the magnitude of difference was relatively weak ($p < .05$). Results suggest that sticking to their core values, tendency to continuously learn and upgrade oneself and good coordination and integration help in improving organizational performance. Hospitals' learning paradigm is to learn from their own experience as well as from the best practices in the industry. When various sections, groups, and departments have competing goals, there is always need for coordination and integration. Organizations having effective coordination and integration function deter their members to function for cross-purposes, and work for building synergy. Sticking to core values shared across organizations builds identity of organizations which eventually help organizations in improving their image as brand.

Predictors of Organizational Performance: We used stepwise regression analysis to identify critical predictor of performance. The two dimensions of performance and overall performance were used as dependent variables while 12 organizational culture dimensions were used as independent variables. Results suggested that team orientation was the most important variable in the entire performance dynamics as it emerged a significant contributor in all the three regression equations ($p < .01$). In the case of generic performance, only team orientation emerged as significant variable and explained 47 per cent of variance (R^2=.47; F (1,48) = 42.78; $p < .01$). In service industry, team orientation is being emphasized as the goal of the organization—providing excellent health care services is quite interdependent, thus collaboration of professionals and others employees is a must. For performance in quality and governance areas, creating change along with team orientation have accounted for 75.7 per cent of variance (R^2=.76; F (2, 47) = 73.18; $p < .01$). Between the two, team orientation is relatively stronger predictor (β = .55; $\underline{t}$ (df = 47) = 4.07; $p < .01$). Creating change (β = .40; $\underline{t}$ (df = 47) = 3.21; $p < .01$) variable incorporates organizations' capacity and methodology to meet changing needs. Organizations high on this dimension of organizational culture are able to read the business environment, react quickly to current trends, and anticipate future changes. Thus, a positive contribution to quality performance and governance is an expected result.

Team orientation also emerged as a lone significant predictor of overall performance. It explained approximately 37 per cent of variance (R^2=.37; F (1, 48) = 28.27; $p < .01$). This result has again reinforced the importance of cooperation and collaboration, cohesiveness, and trust among teams at work in achieving overall performance. Results by and large have supported the hypotheses, that high performance organizations are perceived to have better organizational culture as compared to their counterparts in low performance groups. Team orientation has emerged as a critical factor in predicting generic performance, performance in quality and governance areas, and overall performance. The findings support the contention of Sinha (1998, 1999), that synergistic work culture or WCNC characterized by philosophy of self-reliance, strong work norms, and humane practices help produce performance. Theory of organizational culture by Denison and Mishra (1995) also got support.

HIGH PERFORMANCE IN HEALTH CARE ORGANIZATIONS AND DEVELOPMENT

The HDI is a simple composite measure of the overall achievement of a region in terms of three basic dimensions of human development—a long and healthy life, knowledge and a decent standard of living. For achieving any kind of development including development defined in HDI, we require high performance organizations. Health care organizations play a vital role in influencing the health status of people in the regions as they play both preventive and curative roles. The government sector in India is finding it very difficult to provide quality health care services to its people on its own, and there is a need to develop partnership with private sector health care organizations on urgent basis. What factors do make private sector health care organizations high performing has been studied under this context.

The study examined the differences between high and low performance hospitals on organizational culture, high and low performance groups were identified through their scores on overall performance. Organizations scoring above median point were treated as high performance organizations while organizations scoring on median and below were treated as low performance organizations. High performance group scored higher on organizational culture dimensions, suggesting that high score on positive organizational dimensions lead to better performance. Regression analysis revealed that team orientation and creating change were critical factors in determining various dimensions of performance. The findings have clear implications for development in health sector. If the administrators, policy-makers and leaders are keen to enhance performance of their organizations, they should focus on organizational culture including HR policies and PI strategy. However, to begin with, they should focus on organizational culture and HR policy particularly on team orientation and ability to deal with uncertainties and reward commitment and loyalty by following commitment to team orientation.

A word of caution is due; as these conclusions are drawn from cross-sectional data on hospitals in private sector. More studies with larger samples and in larger hospitals may reveal clearer picture. Moreover, future studies may also focus on other service industry to understand dynamics of high performance. This study has captured only linear relationship between performance and organizational culture within cross-sectional design. Such design may not be good for establishing causal relationship. Future studies may use more complex model of organizational performance examining causal relationship between organizational performance and its antecedents.

REFERENCES

Deal, T.E.; and Kennedy, A.A. (1982). *Corporate Cultures: The Rites and Rituals of Corporate Life*. Addison-Wesley, Reading.

Denison, D. (1990). *Corporate culture and organizational effectiveness*. New York: John Wiley & Sons.

Denison, D.R., Janovics, J., and Yong, J. (2006). *Diagnosing organizational culture: Validating a model and method*. Working Paper, Denison Consulting.

Denison, D.; and Mishra, A. (1995). Toward a theory of organizational culture and effectiveness. *Organizational Science*, 6(2), 204-223.

Gordon, G.; and DiTomaso, N. (1992). Predicting corporate performance from organizational culture. *Journal of Management Studies*, 29(6), 783-798.

Hamel, G.; and Prahalad, C.K. (1994). *Competing for the future*. Boston, MA: Harvard Business School Press.

Human Development Report (2002). United Nations Development Programme (UNDP). New York: Oxford University Press.

Khademian, A.M. (2002). *Working with culture: The way the job gets done in Public Programmes*. Washington, DC: CQ Press.

Khandwalla, P.N. (2003). *Corporate Creativity*. New Delhi: Tata McGraw Hill.

Kotter, J.; and Heskett, J. (1992). *Corporate culture and performance*. New York: Free Press.

Pareek, U. (2004). *Understanding organizational behaviour*. New Delhi: Oxford University Press.

Quinn, R.E. and Rohrbaugh, J. (1983). A spatial model of effectiveness criteria: Towards competing values approach to organizational analysis. *Management Science* 29, 363-77.

Schein, E.H. (1990). Organizational culture. *American Psychologist*, 45, 109-119.

Scott, T., Mannion, R., Marshall, M. and Davies, H. (2003b). Does organisational culture influence health care performance? A review of the evidence. *Journal of Health Services Research and Policy*, 8 (2), 105-17.

Selznick, P. (1957). *Leadership in administration*. Evanston, IL: Row and Peterson.

Singh, N.K., Paul, O. (1985). *Corporate Soul: Dynamics of Effective Management*. New Delhi: FORE Publications.

Singh, S. (2002). *High Performance Organizations: Key Issues and Strategic Alternatives*. New Delhi: New Age.

Sinha, J.B.P. (1968). The nAch/nCooperation under limited/unlimited resource conditions. *Journal of Experimental Social Psychology*, 19, 233-248.

Sinha, J.B.P. (1970). *Development through Behaviour Modification*. Bombay: Allied Publisher.

Sinha, J.B.P. (1980). *The Nurturant Task Leader*. New Delhi: Concept.

Sinha, J.B.P. (1984). Towards partnership for relevant research in the third world. *International Journal of Psychology*, 19, 169-177.

Sinha, J.B.P. (1990). *Work Culture in Indian Context*. New Delhi: Sage.

Sinha, J.B.P. (1998). Work culture in a developing country: the case of India (pp. 333-349). In Adair, J.G., Belanger, D., and Dion, K.L. (Eds.), *Advances in Psychological Sciences Vol. I: Social, personal and cultural aspects*. Hove England: Psychology Press.

Sinha, J.B.P. (1999). Confluence of cultural and managerial influences. A new paradigm for Organizational Behaviour. *Indian Journal Industrial Relations*, 35(1), 27-42.

Sinha, J.B.P. (2000). *Patterns of Work Culture: Cases and Strategies of Culture Building*. New Delhi: Sage.

Sinha, J.B.P. (2008). Creating and enabling conditions of human development. *Social Engineer*, 11(2), 8-25.

Sinha, J.B.P. (2009). *Culture and Organizational Behaviour*. New Delhi: Sage.

Sinha, J.B.P.; and Pandey, J. (1970). Strategies of high nAch persons. *Psychologia*, 13, 210-216.

Sinha, J.B.P., Kumar, A., Singh, B.B., and Singh, S. (1999). Voluntary organizations in Bihar: Trapped in opportunity structure and handicapped by structural deficiencies. *Social Engineer*, 8, 35-45.

Smith, P. (2002a). *Measuring Up: Improving Health System Performance in OECD Countries*, OECD, Paris.

Smith, P. (2002b). Performance management in British health care: will it deliver? *Health Affairs*, 21(3),103-5.

Walshe, K. (2003). *Regulating Healthcare: A Prescription for Improvement?* Open University Press, Bukingham.

CHAPTER EIGHT

Re-conceptualizing the Meaning of Work: From Work as a Mean to Work as an End

Sunita Singh-Sengupta

Without work all life goes rotten—but when work is Soulless, life stifles and dies
—Albert Camus

The Concise Oxford Dictionary defines 'work' as "expenditure of energy, striving, application of effort or exertion to a purpose." The late Victorian economist Alfred Marshall said that labour was 'any exertion of mind or body undergone partly or wholly with a view to some good other than the pleasure derived directly from the work'. The definition emphasizes on the output derived out of physical and mental labour. It does not give much importance to the pleasure derived directly from the work. Keith Thomas (1999) expanded the meaning of this definition, "...Work has an end beyond itself, being designed to produce or achieve something, it involves a degree of obligation or necessity, being a task that others set us or that we set ourselves; and it is arduous, involving effort and persistence beyond the point at which the task ceases to be wholly pleasurable" (p. xiv).

The literature suggests two different streams of thought on 'work'. On the one hand, work has, since time immemorial, been seen as a curse, a result of the Fall and a punishment for Sin. It was something that, it was assumed, everyone would naturally try to avoid. On the other hand, work was widely admired as a divine activity, practiced by God during the creation of the World and by Adam and Eve in Eden. It was sacred duty and the source of all human comforts, creating wealth and making civilization possible. It was a cure for boredom and melancholy and remedy for vice. It was the only sure route to human happiness, bringing health, contentment and personal fulfilment.

The classical economists took the first of these two views. Adam Smith agreed with Dr. Johnson that every man was naturally an idler. It was axiomatic that human beings preferred leisure to work. The object of working was to acquire wealth, and the object of wealth was to avoid having to work. The labouring classes, it was said, worked only out of necessity: to avoid starvation or to acquire additional goods that they coveted for their practical utility or as a means of keeping ahead of their neighbours without either stick or carrot, the inertial force of human indolence would be sure to reassert itself. The native people in the overseas colonies were cited as further proof of this natural inclination to idleness. John Stuart Mill shares, "...laziness was an innate and deep-seated urge, to which, without the most strenuous application, the human animal would invariably succumb" (Thomas, 1999: xviii). In the twelfth and thirteenth centuries European theologians gave work a more positive status, stressing its social and moral benefits and representing St. Benedict's observation that idleness was the enemy of the soul. But they did not represent work as innately satisfying. For the Puritans in England and America, work was praiseworthy because St. Paul had said that those who did not work should not eat; because work fostered a spirit of renunciation and was good for the character; because it made people healthier; and because society functioned more smoothly when everyone had a lawful calling. However, the Puritans said very little about the intrinsic satisfactions that work might bring with it. For them, it was a divine command; and its main advantage was that it kept people out of mischief and enabled them to provide for themselves.

For all this emphasis on moral duty, there were plenty of people who demonstrably enjoyed the tasks they were paid to perform. Scholars like Keith Thomas (1999) hold the opinion that if labour were enjoyable, then it could not be counted as work. As Sir Dudley North (1641-1691) put it: 'If it was agreeable to do anything called work, it was not really so but pleasure...It is incident to the true nature of work not to delight in it' (Thomas, 1999: xviii).

In the Industrial Age, Karl Marx promoted a theory of work in which man, through the advances of technology, would be able to engage in free productive activity and control the world. Workers would contemplate themselves in the work of their own hands. The reality of the industrial age, during Marx's time, was that workers suffered long, hard work hours. They worked for mere survival rather than self-realization. The harshness of the work environment drove Marx to promote the rise of the working class to revolt and eliminate the cause of their hardships—private ownership of the means of production. After the revolution, workers would be free to express themselves in productive activity and be in total control of the world, somewhat like God.

A contemporary theory of work comes from the analysis of Sigmund Freud. Freud believed we are primarily pleasure-seeking creatures. Thus, Freud mandated that every human man needs leben und arbeiten ("to love and to work"), and the hymnist wrote, "Awake, awake to love and work." However, this primary nature is in direct conflict with the requirements of work. Therefore, the modern worker is merely postponing immediate gratification of their desires. They work so that they may earn enough money to subsequently enjoy the benefits of the modern society. We live our lives in conflict: the benefits of work are self-preservation and enjoyment, but the immediate reality of work is self-denial (Hardy, 1990).

WHY DO WE WORK?

Work shapes our life and identity. Some of the most profound insights about work and life are found in the famous fables of the ancient story teller Aesop, who wrote about animals who act, think, and talk like human beings. In the well-known fable, "The Grasshopper and the Ant", Aesop locked horns with the question, to work or not to work? He wrote:

> *"The ants were employing a fine winter's day in drying grain collected in the summer time. A grasshopper, perishing with famine, passed by and earnestly begged for a little food. The ants inquired of him, "why did you not treasure up food during the summer?" He replied, "I had not leisure enough. I passed the days in singing", they then said in derision: "If you were foolish enough to sing all the summer, you must dance supper less to bed in winter"* (1924: 16).

This is a cautionary tale. It does not say that a life of work is better than a life of singing, but rather if you want to sing, you have to be willing to pay the price. The issue here is self-sufficiency and fairness—if you don't work, you don't eat and you should not expect others to feed you. Aesop's story gives us a choice. You can lead the brief happy life of the grasshopper or the long prudent life of the ant. Aesop was somewhat ambivalent about industriousness. Greed, miserliness, and covetousness sometimes accompany hard work. In another story, "The Ant", he tells us that the ant was once a farmer who kept a jealous eye on his neighbour and stole some of his produce. Zeus, angry, changed the man into ant, and Aesop wrote, "Although his form has changed, his character has not, for he still goes around the fields gathering up the wheat and barley of others and storing it up for himself." Aesop worried that industriousness, when motivated by envy can lead to theft, avarice and miserliness.

In Aesop's another story "Ant and the Bee" the bee and the ant have a dispute over who is more prudent and industriousness. They appeal to Apollo for a judgement. This god applauds the ant's care, foresight, and independence from the labours of others, but he says, "it is you alone that you benefit; no other creature shares any part of your hoarded riches. Whereas, the bee produces, by his meritorious and ingenious exertions, that which becomes a blessing to the world." Again we see chinks in the moral armour of hard work. It is good to provide for one, but it is even better to contribute a pleasing and "useful product for society." We admire hard work much more if people do it for some purpose that lies beyond pure self-interest. The Buddhist scriptures use the bee as a model of the environmentally responsible businessperson. They tell us, "The wise and moral man shines like a fire on a hill top, making money like a bee, which does not hurt the flower."

APPROACHES TO LIFE

Aesop's stories tell us about three different approaches to life showed by ant, grasshopper and bee:

1. Frugal, acquisitive and hardworking, the antlike worker values security above all else. He spends all his time working at a moderately interesting job, makes cautious career choices, has little involvement in non-work activities, and takes few vacations and fewer chances. Like the ant this sort of person saves for retirement, mortgaging certain enjoyments for 65 years of his or her life in the hopes of making up for it in the last 10 or 20. Ants work for the future, but don't always know what to do when (or if) they reach it. The merit of the ant's life plan is that his frugality saves him from want, prepares him for emergencies and ensures self-sufficiency.
2. In contrast to the ant the grasshopper lives for the present and sacrifices the future. His playing goes nowhere and leaves nothing behind. There is a pleasure in a life of play, but is there meaning?
3. The bee works like an ant but takes pleasure and finds meaning in producing a good and useful product that is appreciated by others.

- The bee symbolizes a life of useful and rewarding work;
- The ant represents a life of work and security.
- While the grasshopper depicts a frivolous life of play and uncertainty.

This story tells us about the different approaches to life. But the question arises, why different people adopt different approaches to life probably because of the different nature of man. The nature of man is determined by his mental state. This can be better understood with the analogy suggested in *The Gospel of Sri Ramakrishna* (1996):

> *This world is like a fishing-net. Men are fishes, and God is the fisherman. When the fish are entangled in the net, some of them try to tear through its meshes in order to get their liberation. They are like the men striving for liberation. But no means all of them escape. Only a few jumps out of the net with a loud splash, and then people say, 'Ah! There goes a big one!' In the like manner, three or four men attain liberation. Again, some fish are so careful by nature that they are never caught in the net; some beings of the ever perfect class. Most of the fish are trapped; but they are not conscious of the net and their imminent death. No sooner are they entangled than they run headlong, net and all, trying to hide them in the mud. They do not make the least effort to get free. On the contrary, they go deeper and deeper into the mud. These fish are like the bound men. They are still inside the net, but they think they are quite safe there.*

The attitude towards work will be different for the four different categories of individuals and this attitude is shaped by the three *gunas*, i.e. *Sattvic*, *Rajasic* and *Tamasic*. The human mind, according to *Sankhya* school of Indian philosophy, is a manifestation of *mula-prakriti* or primordial *prakriti*. One can have a better understanding from Table 8.1.

This analogy very aptly describes the different categories of people and their focus on work. This taxonomy of the individuals is based on their mindsets. The *bound souls* take the transitional perspective of work (work as a means), however, the liberated souls take the transcendental approach to work (work as an end). In between falls the souls aspiring after liberation who if remains focused and practices certain mental exercise to understand the importance of work in his/her life, apart from monetary gain, is moving towards the liberated souls. 'Work' in this perspective is multifaceted.

Table 8.1

Different Souls	*Attitude Towards Work*	*Perspective towards Work*	*Attributes*
The Bound Souls	They value security and spend their time on moderately interesting jobs. They are like silk worms. The worms can cut through cocoons if they want, but having woven the cocoons themselves, they are too much attached to them to leave them. And so they die there.	Transitional Perspective: Work as a Mean	*Tamasic*
Souls Aspiring After Liberation	They try to figure out meaning in their work. They try to practice dispassionate work.	Multifaceted Approach to Work	*Tamasic-Rajasic*
The Liberated Soul	They have transcendental approach to work and life. They are free souls and not attached to monetary incentives rather strive for good life by an inward approach.	Transcendental Approach: Work as an End	*Rajasic-Sattvic*
The Ever-Perfect Soul	These are already awakened soul at work. They practice stern renunciation in whatever they do.	Work for the Work Sake	

DIMENSIONS OF WORK

The Public Agenda Foundation has explored the fundamental question of what people see as their primary motive for working. Three possibilities were examined:

- The first level of motivation sees work primarily as a means of survival.
- A second level of motivation assumes that the basic survival needs have already been met and places a heavy demand on improving one's standard of material well-being.
- A third level takes both survival and increasing standards of living as given and focuses on personal growth and self-development as the primary motive for working (Underdahl, 2000).

The research experiences and observations suggest that a significant number of jobholders now see self-development as their primary motive for working. Srivastava's parable (a) of the traveller dramatizes the importance of "attracting and exciting members of the organization so that they will want to do what need to be done to make the vision a reality":

There is the story of a man travelling through the countryside who came upon three men using sledgehammers to break up a mountain of rocks. 'Why are you doing such work?' the traveller asked the first workman. 'Because my boss told me to,' he replied. The traveller asked the same question to the second man, who replied: 'I am earning a wage so I can feed and shelter my family.' The traveller turned to the third workman and asked: 'why are you doing this work?' And the man replied: 'I am building a cathedral.'

This parable indicates three different attitudes towards work. Work in its primitive form is the order/request from others. It is worth quoting a conversation between Pandit Nehru and a worker:

Pandit Nehru: Why are you doing this work?

Worker on Bhakra Dam: Sahib Bahadur, that man tells me to take those stones over there. At the end of the work he gives me some money. That is why I do it.

From Sunil Khilnani (1960), *The Idea of India,* 1997.

For the second person work is just an economic activity. More work means more wages. One often remembers the lines of D.H. Lawrence:

Wages

The wages of work is cash,
The wages of cash wants more cash.
The wages of want more cash is vicious competition.
The wages of vicious competition is—the world we live in.

D.H. Lawrence (1885-1930), 1929, quoted by Keith, 1999.

It is only the third person who finds meaning in his work. "...a man must work, toil in the sweat of his brow, whoever he may be, for that is meaning and object of his life, his happiness, his enthusiasm..." (Thomas, 1999 : 47).

Sigmund Freud in 'Civilizations and Its Discontents' writes that laying stress upon importance of work has a greater effect than any other technique of living in the direction of binding the individual more closely to reality, in his work he is at least securely attached to a part of reality, the human community. Work is no less valuable for the opportunity it and the human relations connected with it provide for a very considerable discharge of libidinal component impulses, narcissistic, aggressive and even erotic, than because it is indispensable for subsistence and justifies existence in a society (1930).

Thus, we can capture the different perspectives on 'work' in the following diagram.

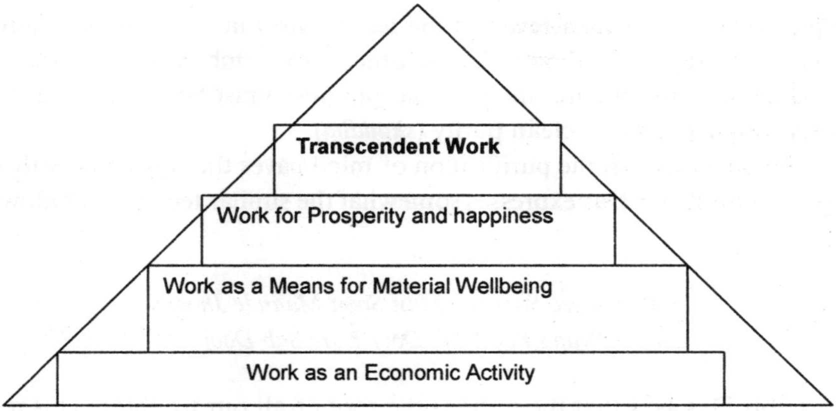

For the rest part of the discussion we will be focusing on 'Transcendent work: Work for work sake'. Enriching the quality of quotidian life, transcendent work surpasses and exceeds consuetudinary connotations of work. One often remembers the lines of Rabbi Eleazar Ben Azariah who writes,

> "...*Great is work, for every craftsman walks out with the implements of his calling, and is proud of them. Thus, the weaver walks out with a shuttle in his ear. The dyer walks out with wool in his ear. The scribe walks out with his pen behind his ear. All are proud of their craft. God speaks of his work.*"
>
> (Keith, 1999: 145).

In transcendent work, the action of working provides stimulation and impetus because through it, the individual becomes all that he is capable of becoming; Terkel Baker epitomizes,

> "*Work is an essential part of being alive. Your work is your identity. It tells you who you are. It's gotten so abstract. People don't work for the sake of working. They're working for a car, a new house, or a vacation. It's not the work itself that's important to them. There's such a joy in doing work well.*"
>
> (Quoted by Underdahl, 2001: 52).

THE INDIAN APPROACH TO TRANSCENDENT WORK

Transcendent Work in Indian context can be well understood by "Pushti Maarg" suggested in Vallabha's philosophy known as Shuddhadvaita Vedanta. The root "push" expresses the action of being "well-fed, nourished, healthy, and prospering". Vallabha revealed the *pushti-marga* in order to help human beings to progress from the one to the other. In its embodied state, the soul (*jiva*) is defiled and impure (*dushta*), and progress must be made towards its real and original state of clean purity (*shuddha*).

This suggests that the purification of mind paves the way of growth and progress. Sant Kabir Das expresses somewhat the similar feelings in following lines:

Kabir Soyee Soorma, Man Soon Maande Jhoojh
Panch Pyada Paari Le, Door Kare Sab Dooj

Kabir Das says that the mind is the root of all our troubles. This mind is what creates a myriad of thoughts that drive us everywhere and do not allow us to rest in peace. Thoughts are instigated, fed and driven by our five sensual desires—Lust, Anger, Intoxication with Pride, Attachment and Greed. He calls these as pawns because they are protecting the true enemy that lies behind—The Mind. Here the game is won only when we go beyond the sensual (pawn-like) pleasures and conquer the Mind who has been running the show.

Swami Vivekananda once said that we must learn not only to attach the mind to one thing exclusively, but also to detach it at a moment's notice and place it upon something else.

Fulfilling Marx's aspiration to "make man into man," into an individual capable of fully realizing his potential, transcendent work challenges and rewards. The individual is able "to have some time at work to experience the laughter of discovery" (Levine, 1986).

> *[Transcendent work is] of high existential rank...autonomously performed by the individual according to his desire for personal actualization [by which]...the individual accomplishes something that in the eyes of other individuals is desirable as an end in itself...High rank activities are not effortless, yet they are intrinsically rewarding.* [emphasis mine] —(Quoted by Underdahl, 2001: 52).

The question arises, what makes work transcendent? What transforms work from stultifying labour into an "intrinsically rewarding" process?

Writing to his brother, Van Gogh articulates the qualities of passion characterizing transcendent work: "We should all have a profession with which we can occupy ourselves. I wish to accomplish something. I find it necessary to work, and to work constantly. I must work—and work hard. I love to paint!" (Underdahl, 2001: 54).

In the book 'My Life and Work' the authors Ford and Crowther (2005) mention that the natural thing to do is to work—to recognize that prosperity and happiness can be obtained only through honest effort.

The Indian religio-philosophical approach to work emphasizes on intense activity but in the midst of eternal calmness—the calmness which cannot be ruffled, the balance of mind which is never disturbed, whatever happens. The best example of 'Man At Work' as described according to Vedanta philosophy in *Gita* is Arjuna. Swami Vivekananda in his lecture delivered in London on 10th November, 1896 on 'Practical Vedanta' says, "...The less passion there is, the better we work. The calmer we are, the better for us, and the more the amount of work we can do. When we let loose our feelings, we waste so much energy, shatter our nerves, disturb our minds, and accomplish very little work. ...The man who gives way to anger, or hatred, or any other passion, cannot work; he only breaks himself to pieces, and does nothing practical. It is the calm, forgiving, equable well-balanced mind that does the greatest amount of work (Complete Works of Swami Vivekananda, Volume 2, 2002: 292-293).

WORK AS AN END

The emphasis of Maslow in Eupsychian Management on "self-actualization *via* a commitment to an important job and to worthwhile work could also be said, then, to be the path to human happiness" [emphasis mine] (1965: 6). Edgar Schein's description of the 'being-in-becoming' orientation, that emphasizes 'self-development, self-actualization, fulfilling one's potential' and focuses upon "the development of all aspects of self as an integrated whole" (1985: 102) highlights the importance and priorities of transcendent work. The integration of individual and organizational development envisioned by Argyris is becoming a reality in today's workplace (Underdahl, 2001: 59).

The Indian approach to work emphasizes the importance of time in work. To quote the lines of Sant Kabir Das,

Kaal Kare So Aaj Kar, Aaj Kare So Aab
Pal Mein Parle Hoyegi Bahuri Karega Kab

The poet says that it is in the NOW, in the spontaneousness that one gets energized to do, to achieve, to realize. As they say, it is NOW or NEVER. This emphasis on present emphasizes on detaching oneself from the past and future and making full use of present time in order to give one's best. In the famous Nachiketa story *Yama* explains the difference between 'perfection' and 'enjoyment'. "...Perfection is one-thing and enjoyment another; these two having different ends, engage men differently. He who chooses perfection becomes pure. He who chooses enjoyment misses his true end. Both perfection and enjoyment present themselves to man; the wise man having examined both distinguishes one from the other. He chooses perfection as being superior to enjoyment, but the foolish man chooses enjoyment for the pleasure of his body" (Complete Works of Swami Vivekananda, Volume 2, 2002: 161).

Therefore, the path to realize work as an end is to focus on 'perfection'. This can be attained by practicing 'discrimination' and 'renunciation'. Discrimination ('not this, not this') helps one reaching the 'real' by discarding the 'unreal'. Renunciation means to work in a dispassionate way. Renunciation can be of two types: strong renunciation and mild renunciation. This can be better understood with the help of a story:

> *At one time there was a drought in a certain part of the country. The farmers began to cut long channels to bring water to their fields. One farmer was stubbornly determined. He took a vow that he would not stop digging until the channel connected his field with the river. He set to work. The time came for his bath, and his wife sent their daughter to him with oil. 'Father', said the girl, 'it is already late. Rub your body with oil and take your bath.' 'Go away!' thundered the farmer. 'I have too much to do now.' It was past mid-day and the farmer was still at work in his field. He didn't even think of his bath. Then his wife came and said: 'Why haven't you taken your bath? The food is getting cold. You overdo everything. You can finish the rest tomorrow or even today after dinner.' The farmer scolded her furiously and ran at her, spade in hand, crying: What? Have you no sense? There is no rain. The crops are dying. What will the children eat? I have taken a vow not to think of bath and food today before I bring water to my field. Through a whole day's back breaking labour the farmer managed by evening to connect his field with the river. Then he sat down and watched the water flowing into his field with a murmuring sound. His mind was filled with piece and joy. He went home, called his wife, and said to her, 'Now give me some oil and prepare me a smoke.' With serene mind he finished his bath and meal, and retired to bed, where he snored to his heart's content.*

The determination he showed is an example of strong renunciation.

> *Now, there was another farmer who was also digging a channel to bring water to his field. His wife, too, came to the field and said to him: 'It's very late. Come home. It isn't necessary to overdo things.' The farmer didn't protest much, but*

put aside his spade and said to his wife, 'Well, I'll go home since you ask me to.' (All laugh). That man never succeeded in irrigating his field.

This is a case of mild renunciation.

What is the differentiating factor in the personality of above mentioned two farmers that is revealed in their different behaviour? The stern renunciation is the 'single-mind devotion' that may lead to perfection in work. The question arises, what lifts up the mild renunciation to stern renunciation. This suggests that work has a spiritual dimension in it. This spiritual dimension of work focuses on 'work for work sake' not for money, not for status and not for anything else. This altogether emphasizes a different attitude towards work where the anchorages are in the inner psyche of the individual that is manifested in his/her work being performed in the external work.

In this backdrop, it becomes important to talk about mood (*bhava*) with respect to work. The work and the worker (here 'worker' means the person performing work) relationship can be one of the following (Swami Nikhilananda, 1996: 115):

1. *Shanta*: The serene attitude and single-mind devotion.
2. *Dasya*: The attitude of a servant towards his master.
3. *Sakhya*: The attitude of friendship.
4. *Vatsalya*: The attitude of mother towards her child.
5. *Madhur*: The attitude of a woman towards her permour.

One need to have one of these attributes. These attributes are the expression of emotions (*bhava*). One should get in love with one's transcendental goals and feel intoxicated. We will discuss each attribute and its relevance one by one. Let us start from the last one.

Madhur

Work should be an integral part of an individual's life. Work and life should not be seen separately. It has to be something like what the great poet Rahim says,

Pritam Chhabi Nayanan Basi, Par Chabbi Kahan Samaya
Bhari Saray Rahim Lakhi, Pathik Aapu Phiri Jaaye

The meaning reveals that just like the attitude of a woman towards her beloved work should be close to one's heart in the form of love in the eyes. This can only happen by a peaceful and pure mind. The impurities should not have any scope for entering into it. This attribute (*bhava*) expands on the central theme of love for love sake.

Vatsalya

The person performing a task should own its responsibility in the same way as a mother owns the responsibility of her child. The mother selflessly with full of affection observes the childlike activities of her child and enjoys it. In *vatsalya bhav*, the mother and the child forget their own selves and become totally absorbed in the other. Being able to forget one's identity is an essential prerequisite in the "*Vishudh-Advaita*" philosophy. Thus, when the individuals start working in a dispassionate way and are able to recognize the happiness while performing it, he is moving towards transcendent work. The mind becomes carefree and there is no material desire involved in it and the individuals work for the work sake.

Sakha

This is attitude of a friend. People who work together at self-selected and fulfilling tasks develop strong attachments, loyalties, warmth, respect and interdependence. Inspired by *dvaita* philosophy, *Sakhaya-bhav* utilises friendship as a medium for relating to God as an equal. As friendship can only exist between equals, God raises the human to His level and becomes one with the soul. As a friend, *sakhas*, look to each others' comforts. The "*Sakhaya-Bhakta*" follows this ideal further by not hurting the Lord and His feelings by words or action. All arguments and friendly tiffs are resolved amicably and quickly. Sudama is an ideal *sakhya-bhakta* who did not ask any favours from his divine friend. The central theme/idea is to have friendship for friendship sake. *Sakha bhakta* see the universe, and all within it, as friends and so works for the universal good without seeking or expecting rewards.

DASYA

Sevak Swami Ek Mati Jo Mati Mein Mati Mili Jaye
Chaturai Rijhe Nahin Rijhe Maan Ke Bhaye

Saint Kabir beautifully narrates the master-servant relationship. The servant immerses himself in the desires of his master. *Dasya-Bhava* centres on serving the Lord without question. Main idea is to serve with love, not servility. *Dasya* also cultivates humility, resilience, capacity for hard work and flexibility. These characteristics are essential for a good devotee as well as a social worker.

The ideal *dasa* should treat the world as the domain of his Lord, and hence serve everyone with love and devotion. *Dasa* should serve selflessly, without seeking rewards or recognition. In recognition of this silent service, the Lord protects his beloved servants with great care. Hanumanji is the ideal *Dasa-Maharaj*. His loving service was rewarded by Rama with such fond words as "I am for ever indebted to you. You are dearer to me than all my relatives, nay; you are more precious than my soul." For a *dasa*, such praises are worth more than all the wealth in the universe.

SHANTA

This attitude (*bhav*) denotes an orientation that is contemplative in nature and is without emotion and free from all personal relationships. The person should try to do his/her duty in a detached way. The maidservant in a rich man's house performs all her duties, but her mind dwells on her home in the country. This is an example of doing duty in a detached way.

The *Gita* says that we have to work, constantly work with all our power; to put our whole mind in the work, whatever, it be, that we are doing. At the same time we must not be drawn away from the work by anything else; still we must be able to quit the work whenever we like.

This attitude towards work can be understood by the lines written by Rahim,

Chaah Gayee Chintaa Mitee Manuvaa Beparvaah
Jisko Kachho Na Chaahiye Ve Saahab Ke Saath

Here the poet says that if you are able to detach yourselves with the desires then you become a liberated soul and this brings you into the *anandamayakosha*.

At this point it is worth quoting Henry Ford's comments,

> *The natural thing to do is to work—to recognize that prosperity and happiness can be obtained only through honest effort. Human ills flow largely from attempting to escape from this natural course...I take it for granted that we must work. All that we have done comes as the result of a certain insistence that since we must work it is better to work intelligently and forehandedly; that the better we do our work the better off we shall be. All of which I conceive to be merely elemental common sense. As we serve our jobs we serve the world* (2005).

Comments such as these indicate that the formula for transcendent work might be stated as follows:

Attitude + Sincerity and Honesty = Transcendent Work

It is the attitude of the individuals that lead towards different orientations towards work. Kabir Das has beautifully said,

Kaam Kaam Sab Koi Kahe, Kaam Na Chinhe Koi
Jeti Man Ki Kalpana, Kaam Kahabe Soi

The meaning implied is that our inner feelings shape our perception of work. However, to search the soul of work is a move towards 'work for the work sake'. We need to have one of the orientations towards work (as mentioned earlier). The scholar believes and advocates the 'devotional path' (*bhakti marg*) where the work rests on the righteousness adopted involuntarily by the individual. To quote from the diary of Beatrice Potter, "…I love my work; that is my salvation; I delight in this slow stepping towards truth…." (17 August, 1889; published in My Apprenticeship, 1926).

This single-minded devotion to one kind of activity can be seen in persons of artistic temperament, i.e. painters, musicians, poets etc., who have strong intrinsic bent towards one activity and nothing can hold them back from it and nothing ever pall the pleasure of the exertion. Therefore, any occupation which satisfies the instinct of emulation has unceasing charm.

Kelley in his book "The Gold-Collar Worker: Harnessing the Brainpower of the New Work Force" writes, "…The work for which people live, of course, must be stimulating, challenging, meaningful and rewarding. They want work that interests them during their day-to-day activities and that gives them a significant level of responsibility" (1985: 47-48).

TOWARDS AN INTEGRATIVE APPROACH TO WORK

Fluctuations in the state of the economy, pressures imposed by the emergence of a global marketplace, and the steady introduction of new technology have wide-ranging implications for the nature and meaning of work from both individual and organizational standpoints. Academic literature in psychology and management demonstrates that values are a key aspect of the work experience and define the meaning of various facets of that experience, including jobs and organizations. For example, personal values are thought to play an important part in both work-related attitudes and behaviour. The increasing emphasis on self-fulfilment and the optimization of human potential for involving the whole individual as pointed out earlier by Maslow (1965) and then by Drucker (1982) suggests that we need to have a re-look on how 'work' is being conceptualized at workplace. We cannot think of self-fulfilment and involving the whole individual at work if the two, i.e. 'individual' and 'work' are perceived as separate entities. The need is to integrate the two. This integrative approach towards work can be achieved if we replace the mind set of 'work as an economic activity' to "work for work sake". There is no contradiction about the fact that human beings work to meet the requirements of basic needs. But why is it that for one money becomes more important and for other meaningful work. The person for whom money becomes more important is one who dwells in *Annamaya Kosha* (The Food Sheath) and is mostly guided by *tamasic* and *tamasic-rajasic* attributes (*gunas*). However, the quest for meaningful work leads towards emotional, psychological and spiritual growth. The individual in this quest comes to *Anandamaya Kosha* (The Blissful Sheath) and is guided by *sattvic* attributes (*gunas*). In order to have an integrative approach towards work we need to move from 'transitional perspective' (work as a mean) to 'transcendental perspective' (work as an end). The latter resonates and brings spirit at work. This spirit (or *bhava*) enables one to focus on 'work for work sake' which is likely to create euphoria. In this 'euphoria at work' the worker is completely immersed into his work through stern renunciation and discrimination and finds the meaning of his life in his meaning of work. *Ek hi saadhe sab sadhe, sab saadhe sab jaaye* (if you follow one thing you will achieve it, but if you want everything, you won't achieve anything). It is apt quoting Swami Vivekananda who says,

> *Take up one idea. Make that one idea your life-think of it, dream of it, live on idea. Let the brain, muscles, nerves, every part of your body, be full of that idea, and just leave every other idea alone. This is the way to success.*

REFERENCES

Drucker, P. (1982). Employing the whole man. In *the Practice of Management* (pp. 262-272). New York: Harper and Row.

Ford, H. and Crowther, S. (2005). My life and work. Project Gutenberg: E text No. 7213. Freud, S. (1930). *Civilization and its discontents*. Germany.

Hardy, L. (1990). *The fabric of this world*. Grand Rapids, Michigan: Eerdman's Publishing Company.

Kelley, R.E. (1985). *The gold collar worker: Harnessing the brainpower of the workforce*. Addision-Wesley Publishing Company Inc.

Khilnani, S. (1997). *The idea of India*. New York: Farrar Straus Giroux.

Maslow, A.H. (1965). *Eupsychian management: A Journal*. Homewood Ill: Richard and Irwin And Dorsey Press.

Schein, E.H. (1985). *Organizational culture and leadership*. San Francisco: Jossey-Bass.

Swami Nikhilananda (1996). *The Gospel of Sri Ramakrishna*. Chennai: Sri Ramakrishna Math Printing Press.

The Complete Works of Swami Vivekananda (2002). Volume 2. Kolkata: Advaita Ashram.

Thomas, K. (1999). *Work*. New York: Oxford University Press.

CHAPTER NINE

Beyond Conflict, Violence, and Retaliation: Gandhi as an Exemplar of Indigenous Approaches to Leadership Education

Dharm P.S. Bhawuk

Marsella (1998) presented the template of "global-community psychology." He entreated researchers to replace the Western cultural traditions by more encompassing multicultural traditions, and reiterated the need to emphasize the cultural determinants of human behaviour (Bhawuk, 2008a, 2008b, 1999; Gergen, Gulerce, Lock, & Mishra, 1996; Pawlik, 1991). He recommended the systems orientation and noted that many indigenous psychologies are well equipped to deal with ascending dimensions of behavioural contexts, from individual to family to society to nature to spirituality (Bhawuk, 2008c, 2005, 2003). He further proposed that qualitative research including such methods as narrative accounts, discourse analysis, and ethnographic analysis should be encouraged. An attempt is made here to show how indigenous models of leadership can enrich our understanding of leadership in the global context.

Leadership education is a challenging task. Much of leadership is an art, though there are some aspects of leadership that can be quantified and learned. People can learn to communicate clearly, but we cannot train people to formulate vision. People can learn about group dynamics and risk analysis, but we cannot train them to make decisions. For example, for every decision that Gandhi made that led him to success, there were well trained people on the side of the British government who failed to make a decision to neutralize Gandhi's strategy. May be truth does win in the end, as an Indian saying goes (*satyameva jayate*), but we do not have a template to train people to recognize truth, and then to pursue a course of action that will lead to the establishment of that truth. And this is further compounded by the very nature of social truths—they are constantly changing.

The indigenous Indian approach to education has always been through story telling. Students ask questions and teachers tell stories to clarify the issues. Often, the stories provide exemplars whose behaviours could be emulated. For example, in the epic *Ramayana*, its author, sage Valmiki, provides Rama as an exemplar of *Maryada* or appropriate behaviour. But there are many others in his epic who are exemplars, and Gandhi himself was inspired by the story of Shravan Kumar, as much as by Rama, as an exemplar of an ideal son dedicated to the service of his parents.

In my teaching I use the film, but other biographies of Gandhi (Bose, 1947; Prabhu & Rao, 1961; Tendulkar, 1951) as well as his autobiography (Gandhi, 1957) can also be used as the source of Gandhi's story. Thus, in this Indian tradition, much like Valmiki's Rama, Gandhi as a person has become an exemplar that people today can learn from and emulate.

The strife that the world faces today requires us all to rise to the occasion at whatever level we may be to bring about changes. Gandhi stands for taking personal responsibility in our community of family, organizations, and society at large, and then taking action in our own rights to make a difference. This indigenous approach is perhaps generalizable across cultures and countries, and that is the advantage of using Gandhi as an exemplar for leadership education. The life of other great leaders could similarly be used to educate people about leadership.

At the risk of some controversy, I propose that the more abstract the educational task is, the easier it is to address it through exemplars, which provide concrete examples to deal with the abstract task in a metaphorical way. How should we deal with change? Gandhi's words and deeds exemplify that we have to be the change that we want to bring about. How should we deal with people who are oppressive and overbearing? Gandhi's message is crystal clear—through *ahimsa* or non-violence. Anger and retaliation has no room in managing differences or conflicts, even with those who are the oppressors. Thus, Gandhi exemplifies an indigenous approach of dealing with conflict, and it is only through *ahimsa* or non-violence that we can deal with it. Retaliating violence with violence by following the adage an eye for an eye would make us all blind, said Gandhi. When violence is confronted with love, violence melts away. The war on terrorism that the United States has been waging since September 11, 2001, is clearly the path that will leave us all blind, which is becoming quite transparent today in Iraq and Afghanistan, and many other parts of the world that is literally being destroyed by violence and war.

It is also relevant to note here that the model of Nurturant Task Leader proposed by Professor Jai Ballabh Prasad Sinha (Sinha, 1980) is exemplified by Gandhi, and showing the clips facilitates a discussion of various leadership models in the class. On the surface, one could argue that Sinha's model is quite similar to the popular Western models developed at Ohio State University (Fleishman, 1953, Fleishman, Harris, & Burt, 1955) and University of Michigan (Bowers & Seashore, 1966; Likert, 1961, 1967) in the 1950s and 1960s in that it captures the two key aspects of leadership, focusing on task *versus* focusing on people. However, the similarity stops there as the model is different in both its philosophy and practice. As the model proposes, leaders in India are people oriented first, and they achieve the tasks through people by nurturing them and inspiring them to perform, not at the cost of or by sacrificing people. The interest of their subordinates is always paramount in the minds of Indian leaders, who are relational in their orientation (Bhawuk, 1997; Bhawuk & Munusamy, 2006). And in that sense it is an indigenous model that captures the process of leadership.

Gandhi paid the utmost consideration for people's welfare, and any disregard of people's welfare would be tantamount to violence and go against the tenets of *ahimsa* or non-violence, an important indigenous value. Thus, sacrificing people for the task would be a form of violence unacceptable to Gandhi. The Western model of leadership assumes that it is OK to sacrifice people for achieving organizational or national goals, and this is characterized by a leadership style low on consideration and high on structure (Bhawuk, 2004). This is also likely to go against another philosophy that Gandhi championed,—it is as important that our means are right as is the end we are pursuing[1] . Thus, by showing the film clips we can discuss not only indigenous

1. Sissela Bok in his Foreword to Gandhi's *Autobiography* (written in April 1993) notes that not only did Gandhi contributed to the "shaping of a new path to collective resistance to injustice," but also left three legacies that he exemplified through his life. According to him, Gandhi's first legacy was "his strong belief that all people can shape and guide their lives according to the highest ideals, no matter how insignificant and powerless they might feel themselves to be." Gandhi's second legacy, to quote Bok, "Evil means, he [Gandhi] insisted, corrupt and degrade not only the purposes for which they are undertaken but also the persons who stoop to such means. Overcoming the urge to resort to such means is hardest when one aims to rectify past injustices. It is because 'hate the sin and not sinner' is a percept so rarely practiced that the 'poison of hatred spreads in the world' (p. 276)." Bok argued that Gandhi's third legacy is his "insistence

and Western models of leadership but also ethical issues that are pertinent to leadership education.

Released in November 1982, the film Gandhi won 8 Oscars for the best film, actor (Ben Kingsley), director (Richard Attenborough), Art Direction, Cinematography, Costumes, Film Editing, Writing (Original Screenplay), and was received well by people all over the world. Einstein's words about Gandhi, "Generations to come will scarce believe that one such as this ever walked the earth," came to be true when the film was released, and people coming out of the theatre were heard saying that the only other person like Gandhi that they could think of was Jesus. Richard Attenborough was encouraged by Pandit Nehru to make a film on Gandhi, and had said that if Indians made the film they may glorify him so much that the human Gandhi may not come out in the film. Clearly, Attenborough does justice to the human part of Gandhi, and it is in humanness that his greatness shines. Gandhi's life was his message, a clear message that right means need to be used to achieve the goals. Right goals achieved by following the wrong means was not acceptable to Gandhi, and this point comes out quite poignantly in the film, and is a lesson worth sharing with business students.

In what follows, I present eight clips (Briley, 1982) from the film that capture Gandhi's leadership journey quite elegantly, and discuss the indigenous concepts and values that drove Gandhi's actions. By showing these clips, I am able to demonstrate that leadership behaviours can be learned. I present a description of each of the clips, and discuss how I use them to highlight the learning points. It is hoped that learning about Gandhi would help the students become authentic service oriented leaders.

LESSON 1: PEOPLE CAN DEVELOP INTO WHO THEY WANT TO BE (LEADERS ARE NOT BORN)

I show the opening of the film, which serves as a brief introduction to who Gandhi was, and how he was viewed by celebrated people of his time. This may not be necessary while teaching in India, but it may help the students to

---

that personal change and the ability to bring about social change are linked. He warns that it no use striving to implement principles such as non-violence or justice in public affairs so long as one neglects them in one's personal life. And it is wise to begin in small and piecemeal ways. Everyone can carve out, should they so wish, "zones of peace" in their own lives – territories where every effort will be made to banish violence and untruth. By so doing, one will be preparing the ground for "the world of tomorrow." (*Autobiography*, p. xvii)

learn how widely internationally acclaimed Gandhi was in his life time. The first scene shows Gandhi as a lawyer in South Africa. He is dressed in a Western suit, and is seen to be travelling in a first class compartment in a train. A fellow white traveller complains to the conductor that a non-white man was travelling in the first class compartment, and the dialogue between Gandhi and the conductor goes on as follows:

SCENE 1: TRAVELLING FIRST CLASS

CONDUCTOR : Here—coolie, just what are you doing in this car?

(Gandhi is incredulous that he is being addressed in such a manner.)

GANDHI : Why—I—I have a ticket. A First Class ticket.

CONDUCTOR : How did you get hold of it?

GANDHI : I sent for it in the post. I'm an attorney, and I didn't have time to—

(He's taken out the ticket but there is a bit of bluster in his attitude and it is cut off by a cold rebuff from the European.)

EUROPEAN : There are no coloured attorneys in South Africa. Go and sit where you belong.

(He gestures to the back of the train. Gandhi is nonplussed and beginning to feel a little less sure of himself. The porter, wanting to avoid trouble, reaches for Gandhi's suitcases.)

PORTER : I'll take your luggage back, baas.

GANDHI : No, no—just a moment, please.

(He reaches into his waistcoat and produces a card, which he presents to the conductor.)

GANDHI : You see, Mohandas K. Gandhi, Attorney at Law. I am going to Pretoria to conduct a case for an Indian trading firm.

EUROPEAN : Didn't you hear me? There are no coloured attorneys in South Africa!

(Gandhi is still puzzled by his belligerence, but is beginning to react to it, this time with a touch of irony.)

GANDHI : Sir, I was called to the bar in London and enrolled in the High Court of Chancery—I am therefore an attorney, and since I am—in your eyes—coloured—I think we can deduce that there is at least one coloured attorney in South Africa.

(The Porter stares—amazed!)

EUROPEAN : Smart bloody kaffir—throw him out! (He turns and walks out of the compartment.)

CONDUCTOR : You move your damn sammy carcass back to third class or I'll have you thrown off at the next station.

GANDHI (anger, a touch of panic): I always go First Class! I have travelled all over England and I've never.

And at the next station, he is thrown out of the first class compartment with his luggage. He was humiliated and angered, and he looks at the white traveller and ticket collector sneering at him as the train inches away from the station. Getting thrown out from the first class compartment in South Africa marked the beginning of Gandhi's journey as a leader.

In India people believe that you can become who you want to be, and the most famous story is that of Saint Valmiki, the author of *Ramayana.* Valmiki had started his life as a thief and robber, but when he realized that even though he was doing the bad work to support his family, his family members were not going to share the sin with him. Once a wise man brought that to his attention by confronting him, and forcing him to ask his family members if they would be a part of his sinful activities, he decided to transform himself. The wise man asked him to chant the name of the Lord Rama. He was so uneducated and confused that he actually chanted the name in reverse, *Mara,* which means death. But because his intentions were pure, he became a great sage, even by chanting the name in reverse! Thus, personal development is a part of the indigenous culture, and we see this also in the life of Gandhi.

This episode allows me to make the general point that leaders are not born. People become leaders when they choose to serve a cause (or an organization, e.g., military or business). Leaders pick a cause that has a personal meaning for them. Gandhi decided to represent the Indian community in South Africa who were suffering from racial discrimination. That people are not born as leaders but develop into leaders becomes quite transparent as the students see the next episodes.

LESSON 2: SOLUTIONS DERIVED FROM THE CONTEXT (LEADERS USE CREATIVE SYMBOLS)

In India people believe that everything in the nature is in balance and good and bad are the two sides of the same coin. In this worldview, the solutions to problems are also inherently embedded in the same context. We find reflection of this wisdom in many verses in the classical texts. For example, one verse says that one should use the thorn to take out a thorn in ones hand. And we found Gandhi creating solutions from the context both in South Africa and in India. Leaders use symbols to lead, and symbols do not have to be fancy. They can be simple. Gandhi demonstrated this on many occasions. First, in South Africa, his very first *Satyagraha* (or civil disobedience as he called it early on) was based on rejecting the pass that Indians were required to carry with them all the time. He argued that the pass differentiated Indians from Europeans who represented the white colonial power, and by destroying the pass Indians could eliminate that imposed difference. Thus, the pass became a symbol of oppression, and destroying it was a symbolic success, which is captured quite well in the scene described below.

Scene 2: Burning the Pass

Mosque Exterior Day

We see a rather crudely stitched sign: "Indian Congress Party of South Africa." Gandhi, now sporting a moustache, stands with Khan and Singh near a fire that has been started in the open area before the Mosque. A wire basket has been placed on supports over the fire. Before them, a small crowd, mostly Indians (Hindus, Sikhs, Muslims), but with a few Whites drawn by curiosity. Gandhi whispers, trying to ignore the crowd.

Gandhi :	There's the English reporter. I told you he'd come. We see the English reporter waiting skeptically. Near him, trying to be inconspicuous on the edge of the small crowd, are five policemen (one sergeant and four constables). A horse-drawn paddy wagon is drawn up beside them.
Khan :	You also said your article would draw a thousand people. (If the crowd numbers 100, they're lucky.) At least some of the Hindus brought their wives. We see five or six women in *saris* standing together.
Gandhi :	No. I asked my wife to organize that. We feature Gandhi's wife, Ba, standing at the front of the women. She possesses a surprising delicacy of feature, with large expressive eyes and a beautiful mouth—but at this moment, she is ill at ease and uncertain, forcing herself to do that which she would rather not.
Singh (alarmed) :	Some of them are leaving. Gandhi wets his lips nervously. He glances with a little

apprehension at the police, then takes his notes from his pocket and moves to the front of the fire. He holds up his hand for attention. He forces a smile—then starts reading—

GANDHI : Ladies and Gentlemen, we have asked you to gather here to help us proclaim our right to be treated as equal citizens of the Empire.

It is flat and dull, like someone reading a speech to himself or herself, and those in the crowd who had hesitated before wandering off shrug and continue on their way. Gandhi is unnerved by it a little but he struggles on-louder, but just as colourlessly.

GANDHI : We do not seek conflict. We know the strength of the forces arrayed against us, know that because of them we can only use peaceful means—but we are determined that justice will be done!

This last has come more firmly, and he lifts his head to the crowd, as though expecting a reaction. Three or four committed supporters applaud as on cue, but his technique is so inexpert that it draws nothing but blank faces from the bulk of them. He glances nervously at Ba, who is embarrassed for them both now. She wraps her *sari* more closely around her and her expression is a wife's "I told you so"—sufferance, mortification and loyalty, all in one. Gandhi wets his lips again—and takes a square of cardboard from his pocket—his "pass."

GANDHI : The symbol of our status is embodied in this pass—which we must carry at all times, but no European even has to have.

He holds it up. A constable glances at the police sergeant.

GANDHI : And the first step to changing our status is to eliminate this difference between us.

And he turns and drops his pass in the wire basket over the fire. The flames engulf it.

The police sergeant's eyes go wide with disbelief. The crowd murmurs in shock. At last, Gandhi has got a reaction, but the dropping of the card has been as matter-of-fact as his speaking, with none of the drama one might expect from so startling a gesture. Even so, a constable glances at the police sergeant again, "Do we take him?" The sergeant just shakes his head, "Wait."

Khan moves up to Gandhi as the tremour of reaction ripples through the crowd.

KHAN (quietly) : You write brilliantly, but you have much to learn about handling men.

He takes Gandhi's notes from him, and faces the crowd.

KHAN (the reading not fluent, but firm and pointed): We do not want to ignite... the fear or hatred of anyone. But we ask you—Hindu, Muslim and Sikh—to help us light up the sky... and the minds of the British authorities—with our defiance of this injustice.

It is the end of the speech. He looks at the crowd. No one knows quite what to do. Gandhi harrumphs—gesturing to a shallow box Singh holds. Kahn turns back, extemporizing rather lamely.

KHAN : We will now burn the passes of our committee and its supporters. We ask you to put your passes on the fire.

POLICE SERGEANT : Oh, no, you bloody well don't!

He has stepped forward with his constables, who have faced the crowd, halting the tentative movements of the few committed supporters towards the fire.

POLICE SERGEANT : Those passes are government property! And I will arrest the first man who tries to burn one! He is facing the crowd. Behind him, Khan holds himself erect and slowly takes his own card from his pocket. He holds it aloft and then lowers it resolutely into the wire basket. The crowd reacts and the sergeant turns just in time to see it dropped in the flame.

POLICE SERGEANT : Take him away!

He gestures to a constable, who turns from the crowd and marches to Khan, seizing him by the arm and marching him to the paddy wagon. As he passes the sergeant, the sergeant takes his Billy club, and faces the crowd, rapping the club menacingly against his hand.

POLICE SERGEANT : Now—are there any more?—

Behind him, Gandhi wavers indecisively a moment, then takes the box from Singh and moves to the fire. Ba holds her hand to her mouth—terrified. Again, the crowd's reaction turns the sergeant. Gandhi is at the fire. For a second, his eyes lock with the sergeant's—and then nervously, he takes a card and drops it in the wire basket, and another.

POLICE SERGEANT : You little Sammy bastard—I—

He has leapt across the distance between them, knocking the box from Gandhi's hands, sending the cards flying and shoving Gandhi to the ground. He turns and faces the crowd angrily, pointing the Billy club threateningly.

POLICE SERGEANT : You want that kind of trouble—you can have it!

Again, a murmur from the crowd turns him. Gandhi, on his hands and knees, blood trickling from his abraded cheek, has picked up a card from the ground and he leans forward apprehensively, his eyes fearfully on the sergeant, but he drops it defiantly in the basket. The sergeant's fury bursts—and he slams the Billy club down on Gandhi's head. Gandhi sags to the ground. Ba screams. She starts to run to him, but the other women seize her.

BA : Let me go!

She fights loose, but one of the constables takes her firmly. The sergeant turns from the commotion to see that Gandhi, his head oozing blood, has crawled to his knees again and is picking up another card. The crowd watches. The newspaper reporter watches. Ba stares in anguish. Gandhi lifts the card. The sergeant stares at him, angry but his emotions somewhat in control after the first blow.

SERGEANT : Stop!

An instant of hesitation, then Gandhi drops the card into the basket. The sergeant almost stops, but he strikes again. A quiver of distaste at his own act crosses his face as Gandhi sags.

Ba's anguished face is wet with tears. The newspaper reporter stares without making notes. Khan, at the paddy wagon, watches in wonder.

Gandhi, his head bleeding badly now, rises to his knees—a breath and he gropes around the ground for another card. His fingers finally clutch one.

The sergeant stares, his face wracked with uncertainty and confusion.

Gandhi lifts the card and painfully holds it over the fire, then drops it in the basket.

The sergeant slams the Billy club down again—firmly, but with a manifest reluctance. The crowd watches breathlessly, the newspaper reporter stares. The sergeant draws a breath, grasping the club, but he bites his lip as he sees Gandhi lift his head feebly, his shaking hands, stained with his own blood, groping for another card…

Another example of using a creative symbol is found in the Salt March that Gandhi led. The idea behind the protest was simple—To deny the British authority to collect tax on salt, Indians would walk to the Indian Ocean in droves and make salt from the ocean. The creativity of the solution can be seen in the British government ignoring it first, and later regretting it upon discovering how Gandhi was able to mobilize hundreds of thousands of people to participate in this simple protest. This is a long episode, but the film captures it quite well, and even those who do not know about the Salt March do get a good understanding of what it was and how it was carried out.

SCENE 3: SALT MARCH

Featuring Gandhi staring out to sea, his mind locked in reflection, and suddenly his head lifts, his eyes become alert, he is caught by some excitement, which he weighs for a moment, and then he stands, his manner suddenly tingling with optimism.

Walker stares at him, then at what Gandhi seems to be looking at.

His point of view. The waves lapping the shore below them.

Walker turns back to Gandhi, puzzled. But there is no mistaking the sudden glow in Gandhi's face.

WALKER : You know what you're going to do.
Gandhi looks at him, a teasing smile.

GANDHI : It would have been very uncivil of me to let you make such a long trip for nothing.
The grin broadens, and then he starts briskly down the promontory. Walker scrambles up after him.

WALKER : Where are you going?
Gulls fly over them, squawking in the growing light. Gandhi pauses, looking up at the gulls, then back down to the sea.

GANDHI : I'm going back to the *ashram* (then firmly) and then I'm going to prove to the new Viceroy that the King's writ no longer runs in India!
He turns from the sea to Walker, his eyes confident, elated, and then he continues on down the promontory. Still baffled, Walker glances at the sea, at him, and then hurries after.

Lord Irwin's Office. Interior. Day.

Close shot—the Viceroy, a "new one," Lord Irwin.

IRWIN : Salt?

Another angle. He is looking in astonishment at his principal secretary. His ADC, a general, a brigadier, a senior police officer are with him. Like him, they hold the same offices, but are a new team.

PRINCIPAL SECRETARY : Yes, Sir. He is going to march to the sea and make salt.

Irwin looks at him, still trying to penetrate the significance of the act. The senior police officer helps.

SENIOR POLICE OFFICER : There is a Royal Monopoly on the manufacture of salt, sir. It's illegal to make it or sell it without a Government licence.

Irwin has listened; it's beginning to make a little sense.

IRWIN : All right—he's breaking the law. What will he be depriving us of, two rupees of salt tax?

PRINCIPAL SECRETARY : It's not a serious attack on the revenue, sir. Its primary importance is symbolic.

IRWIN : Don't patronize me, Charles.

The principal secretary blanches.

PRINCIPAL SECRETARY : No, Sir. I—in this climate, Sir, nothing lives without water—or salt. Our absolute control of it is a control on the pulse of India.

Irwin looks at his ADC, then paces a bit, pondering it.

IRWIN : And that's the basis of this "Declaration of Independence"?

SENIOR POLICE OFFICER : Yes, Sir. The day he sets off everyone is supposed to raise the flag of "Free India." Then he walks some two hundred and forty miles to the sea and makes salt.

A moment as Irwin considers it, and then it is the general who speaks.

GENERAL : I say ignore it. Let them raise their damn flags, let him make his salt. It's only symbolic if we choose to make it so.

PRINCIPAL SECRETARY (pointedly) : He's going to arrive at the sea on the anniversary of the massacre at Amritsar.

Irwin has turned to him. And this makes up his mind.

IRWIN : General Edgar is right—ignore it. Mr. Gandhi will find it's going to take a great deal more than a pinch of salt to bring down the British Empire.

He is concerned enough to be angry, but certain enough to be dogmatic.

The Ashram. Exterior. Dawn.

It is very early, the light just beginning to break, and we are looking out across the river towards the distant town, and against the pink glow of the sky we can see people in groups wading across the river towards the ashram. And suddenly a mass of people, hidden by the embankment, appear at the top of the steps coming up from the river, and the camera lifts slightly with their movement and we see that they are but the forerunners of a long tendril of humanity that stretches across the river, all the way back to the distant outskirts of the city.

And around the ashram many fires are burning, people are cooking breakfast, some are packing knapsacks for the journey, others are strewing the path from the ashram with leaves.

Gandhi's Bungalow. Interior. Dawn.

Quiet, just the buzz of activity from outside the building. Gandhi lies on a mat and Ba and Mirabehn are massaging him with oil as he checks page proofs, an oil lamp by his side. Nehru sits cross-legged next to him, taking the proofs as Gandhi finishes them. Maulana Azad sits to one side. Behind them Desai is making notes on Gandhi's instructions.

Gandhi (to Nehru):... the real test will come if I am arrested. If there is violence, we lose all our moral advantage. This time it mustn't happen.

He looks at Nehru and Azad solemnly to emphasize the point. Nehru nods; a little smile.

Nehru : We're not beginners anymore. We've been trained by a strict sergeant major.

He means Gandhi of course, and Gandhi accepts the reference, but it is the acceptance of the strict sergeant major: "Don't fail me." Then he looks to Azad.

Gandhi : If I'm taken, Maulana is to lead the march. If he is arrested, Patel, then Kripalani, then yourself.

Nehru nods. Ba moves to massage the top of Gandhi's head.

Ba : You should be relaxing.

Gandhi grins, looking at Mirabehn, who is massaging his legs.

Gandhi : I'm sure I'm fit for at least five hundred miles.

MIRABEHN : You should ride the pony. It is not necessary to walk to prove the point.

Gandhi looks at Nehru, a benign shrug.

GANDHI : I have two of them bossing me now.

Nehru smiles. He stands, having taken the last proof sheet. Azad rises with him.

NEHRU : We must get these to the printer. (He looks down at Gandhi.) I know it will succeed. Even my mother is prepared to march.

Gandhi is pleasurably impressed with that.

GANDHI : And Jinnah?

NEHRU (a beat) : He's waiting. He's not prepared to accept it will mean as much as you think.

GANDHI (smiles confidently): Wait and see... wait and see...

He leans back and closes his eyes. Ba rubs his head soothingly. Nehru bends and squeezes his arm in farewell. Gandhi nods, not opening his eyes. Nehru and Azad smile at Ba and leave.

The Ashram. Later. Exterior. Day.

The sun higher, but still early light. A green, white and saffron flag (the colours of India) is pulled up an uneven pole. The sound of gentle clapping.

Gandhi is off to one side, just in front of the veranda of his bungalow, not paying attention to the ceremony. Ba and Mirabehn watch from the veranda as Pyarelal (Desai's new assistant), with a knapsack over his own shoulders, hands Gandhi his. As Gandhi slips it on, the ashramite boy whom we saw with the goat hands him a long staff. And Gandhi moves around the edge of the bungalow, heading towards the entrance of the ashram.

A long line of ashramites and marchers stretches from opposite the flagpole to the entrance of the ashram. As Gandhi walks briskly along it, they turn, ready to follow him.

When he nears the entrance Gandhi sees Walker standing in front of a collection of newsmen, cameramen, and a newsreel crew. He begins to smile, Walker returns it. Gandhi pauses by him.

GANDHI (of the press): You've done me a great service.

WALKER (a grin, then a play on Gandhi's words to him): It would have been uncivil of me to have let you make such a long trip for nothing.

Gandhi smiles. He turns back towards his bungalow. Ba and Mirabehn stand there watching, Desai with them. Gandhi holds

their gaze a second, then turns and starts forward. Pyarelal takes up a position next to him, the marchers follow.
Featuring Walker. He steps back, letting Gandhi proceed into the range of the cameras on his own. The crowd around the entrance throws flowers in Gandhi's path, some calling out, "Long live Mahatma Gandhi!"
Gandhi passes the cameramen and starts along the trail.

The Path to Gandhi's Ashram. Exterior. Day.

A thinner crowd here, but going all along the path. To one side we see two police cars drawn up, and several policemen (a British officer, a British sergeant, and four Indian constables) lined up near them.

As Gandhi nears them, Walker moves up beside him. Some of the newspaper cameramen trot behind to get the picture of Gandhi's arrest. Among the newsmen we see Collins.

Featuring Gandhi and Walker, Pyarelal just behind them all glancing ahead at the police, who are now quite near.

WALKER : Is it over if they arrest you now?

GANDHI : Not if they arrest me—or a thousand—or ten thousand. (He looks at Walker.) It is not only generals who know how to plan campaigns.
Walker smiles—a little uneasily—for they are now near the police. Gandhi nods to them amiably as he passes along in front of them. Walker is turning, watching for a move from the police but begins to grasp that there may be none. He hurries along closer to Gandhi again, one eye still on the police.

WALKER : What if they don't arrest you? What if they don't react at all?
Gandhi glances at him. Walker too wears a knapsack. Gandhi nods to it, though never breaking his pace.

GANDHI : Do you still have your notebook? (Walker fumbles for it; Gandhi goes right on talking.) The function of a civil resister is to provoke response. And we will continue to provoke until they respond, or they change the law. They are not in control—we are. That is the strength of civil resistance.
He nods politely towards the British police officer at the end of the police line. Walker stops, letting the procession march on by him, looking at the British police officer, then writing busily in his notebook. Collins stops by him.

COLLINS : What'd he say?

WALKER (wryly) : He said he's in charge...

An Indian Village. Exterior. Day.

A dusty approach to a dusty little village. Both sides of the track are lined with peasants holding flower petals and leaves, all gazing expectantly down the road. Behind them the village is strung with the green, white and saffron colours of Independence.

Two large policemen stand arms-akimbo at the front of them all, their postures imposing and threatening, though the impression is somewhat weakened by the children skirting around them.

A little band of drummers and flute players suddenly begins to play. The crowd starts to jump up to see, and the flower petals begin to float in the sky. "Gandhi! Long live Mahatma Gandhi!"

Another angle. Gandhi and the procession of marchers and ashramites stride down the dusty road towards, them.

A newsreel truck and crew ride along about two-thirds of the way back. A car of cameramen and reporters tails at the end. Featuring Gandhi. He looks at Walker, walking along a few paces behind him, at the side of the procession. He is wiping sweat from his face.

GANDHI : Are you going to walk all the way?

WALKER (a weary grin) : My name is Walk-er. And I intend to report it the way it is.

Gandhi smiles and turns back. He shakes his head.

GANDHI (to himself): "My name is Walk-er"...

And grinning at it, he passes by the policemen and into the cheers of the crowd.

Long shot, high. As the procession trails into the village, we see several villagers, knapsacks or bundles strung over their shoulders, run around the police and join the end of the procession.

A Field by the Road. Exterior. Night.

In the dark a large group of students comes stumbling, laughing, across the ditch that separates the road from the field. The student leader gets clear of the ditch and comes upon Pyarelal and Walker. They are standing near a group of American newsmen playing poker by a campfire. He addresses Pyarelal good-naturedly.

STUDENT LEADER : We've come to join the march. What do we do?

PYARELAL (bluntly) : Be sure you're awake in the morning. (It comes from a knowledge of students. He smiles and nods off.) Find a place to sleep.

The student leader follows his gaze and the camera pans off with his glance. We see that the numbers have grown immensely. Fires dot the field and spread and spread and spread. Behind Walker and Pyarelal the newsreel truck and three cars for reporters are spread out around the fires. We identify a couple of Frenchmen and a Japanese. Walker looks at Pyarelal and shakes his head in wonder at it all.

Tree. Exterior. Dawn.

A small Indian boy is high in a dead tree. Below him a couple of bone-thin cattle graze in the early light as he stares off.

Dusty Road. Boy's Point of View. Exterior. Dawn.

The huge procession stretched out along the road.

Resume the boy. He grins as though he is privy to some great secret.

A "Y" Junction of Two Country Roads. Exterior. Day.

A blunt, rotund, powerful-looking woman (Sarojini Naidu) in an outrageously colourful *sari* strides along the dusty road as though she could cover another thousand miles—and means to. The sound of hundreds of marching feet, of cars, some distant singing. The camera lifts and pulls back. We see that Naidu is marching just behind Gandhi, like a determined lieutenant, and that the procession has grown even greater. Two newsreel trucks now, four cars of reporters, some people riding donkeys, some walking with camels trailing, loaded with belongings.

And at the "Y" junctions the newsreel crews suddenly go into action because another enormous procession is waiting to join the first, mingling already, making one immense column of humanity.

And as they pass the camera up close we see an extraordinary variety of participants: old, young, students, peasants, ladies in *saris* and jewels, Muslims, Hindus, Sikhs, Christian nuns, untouchables, merchants, some vigorous and determined, others dishevelled, tired and determined.

Suddenly the sound of waves and gentle wind.

The Beach at Dandi. Exterior. Day.

The camera closing fast (helicopter) as the silhouette of a man appears running up a sand dune, lifting his arms to the sky and the camera sweeps over him and up, revealing a crescent of beach and ocean, and for a second it holds on the sea as it did at Porbandar, then pivots to the truly astronomical crowd thronging the shore, an immense wheel of human beings, and in its hub a gathering around Gandhi. We descend on that centre, recognizing the newsmen, Walker, Pyarelal, Sarojini Naidu, and at last Gandhi picking up a handful of natural salt and lifting it high.

GANDHI'S VOICE-OVER : Man needs salt as he needs air and water. This salt comes from the Indian Ocean. (The salt crystals are added to an urn already partially full. The camera pulls back and Gandhi lifts the urn. All around him the pressing crowd: newsreel cameramen, reporters—Walker, Collins, Naidu, Pyarelal. Firmly.) Let every Indian claim it as his right!

ANNOUNCER'S VOICE-OVER : ... and so once more the man of non-violence has challenged the might of the British Empire. And with that we get the Movietone Music tag and as the film fades, the lights go up on.

Lord Irwin's Office. Interior. Day.

A couple of civil servants move about to raise the window shades while Lord Irwin stares at the blank screen set up in his office. The general, the brigadier, the senior police officer, Irwin's ADC and the principal secretary are all present. The two men who ran the projector are quietly dismantling it.

Finally, Irwin turns to the senior police officer, who fidgets, but answers the implied questions.

SENIOR POLICE OFFICER: They're making it everywhere, Sir—mobs of them—publicly. Congress leaders are selling it on the streets of Delhi.

Irwin sighs.

BRIGADIER : We're being made fools of around the world!

GENERAL : Isn't there any instruction from London?

Irwin nods.

IRWIN : We're required to stop it. (He stands, his mind made up.) And stop it we will. (He looks at the senior police officer.) I don't care if we fill the jails, stop it. Arrest anyone, any rank—except Gandhi. We'll cut his strength from under him. And then we'll deal with the Mahatma.

For the first time he is truly angry.

LESSON 3: LEADERS ARE AUTHENTIC: THEY WALK THE TALK

In the traditional Indian culture authenticity is so valued that people are constantly reminded that they have to practice *ahimsa* or non-violence not only in action but also in their speech and thought. The gap between thought and speech, thought and action, or speech and action must be minimized, and this clearly shows how authenticity is an indigenous value. Gandhi showed courage in the face of physical abuse and harm, which was shown in scenes one (he gets violently thrown off the train at the station) and two (he gets hit with a rod by the police) discussed above. Clearly, leaders demonstrate in their behaviour what they preach, and are often in the trenches with their followers and suffer with them to earn their respect. There is no waving of a magic wand to earn the respect of followers! Leaders work shoulder to shoulder with their followers to earn their respect, and Gandhi demonstrated it again and again in his life. Here it should be noted that Gandhi did not act to impress his collaborators or to earn the respect of his followers. He acted in the way that he thought was appropriate without worrying about what others would think about his actions. Gandhi exemplified authenticity, which could be seen in his practice of non-violence in his daily life, which he preached. It is particularly interesting to note how the preacher, Charlie Andrew, (scene 4 below) thought that the teaching of Jesus ("But I tell you not to resist an evil person. But whoever slaps you on your right cheek, turn the other to him also." Matthew: 5.39) about offering the other cheek was only a metaphor! Gandhi believed in offering the other cheek, literally, if necessary, providing a gold standard for authentic behaviour.

SCENE 4: TURNING THE OTHER CHEEK

Gandhi's House. Johannesburg. Exterior. Morning.

Gandhi comes from the house door. He carries a briefcase and is still dressed in European clothes, though far less elegant than we have seen him in before. His mien, the cut of his hair, all suggest a passage of time. As he turns, he stops because he is face to face with Charlie Andrews, a very tall, thin Englishman, who wears a rumpled white suit and a clerical collar. He has descended from a horse-drawn taxi that carries his luggage. He too has stopped. For a moment they both appraise each other, neither speaking. Then

CHARLIE : You'd be Gandhi—(Gandhi nods.)... I thought you'd be bigger.
GANDHI : I'm sorry.

CHARLIE : I—I mean it's all right. It doesn't matter. (He suddenly steps forward and thrusts out his hand.) I'm—my name is Andrews, Charlie Andrews. I've come from India—I've read a great deal about you.

GANDHI : Some of it good, I hope.

He turns and waves to the parlor window. The three boys are there—all bigger—and Ba holds a new addition; they all wave. And Gandhi turns back, and starts down the long, hilly street.

GANDHI (to Charlie) : Would you care to walk?

He gestures Charlie on and starts walking.

Charlie nods uncertainly. He looks back at the cab in confusion, then signals the driver to follow and hurries on to match strides with Gandhi's brisk pace.

GANDHI (noting Charlie's collar): You're a clergyman.

CHARLIE : Yes. I've—I've met some very remarkable people in India... and—and when I read what you've been doing here, I—I wanted to help. (He looks at Gandhi, then smiles awkwardly.) Does that surprise you?

GANDHI : Not anymore. (And now he smiles.) At first, I was amazed... but when you are fighting in a just cause, people seem to pop up—like you—right out of the pavement. Even when it is dangerous or—

Johannesburg Suburb. Exterior. Morning.

They have come to a turning, nearer to town, the area poorer, run-down. Ahead of them three youths (twenty, twenty-one) in working clothes, carrying lunch boxes, lean indolently against a building directly in their path. They react to the sight of Gandhi—fun. Then stride the pavement menacingly. One of them tosses aside his cigarette.

FIRST YOUTH : Hey—look what's comin'!

SECOND YOUTH : A white shepherd leading a brown Sammy!

CHARLIE : Perhaps I should—

Gandhi restrains him and shakes his head.

GANDHI : Doesn't the New Testament say, "If your enemy strikes you on the right cheek, offer him the left"?

He starts to move forward. Charlie hesitates, then follows nervously, more nervous for Gandhi than himself.

CHARLIE : I think perhaps the phrase was used metaphorically... I don't think our Lord meant—

They are getting closer. The youths laughing, whispering.

GANDHI : I'm not so certain. I have thought about it a great deal. I suspect he meant you must show courage—be willing to take a blow—several blows—to show you will not strike back—nor will you be turned aside... And when—

One youth has flicked his cigarette—hard. It lands at Gandhi's feet. He pauses, looking at the youth.

GANDHI : ... and when you do that it calls upon something in human nature--something that makes his hate for you diminish and his respect increase. I think Christ grasped that and I—I have seen it work.

He starts forward again; he is almost on the youths—clearly frightened, but...

GANDHI : Good morning.

FIRST YOUTH : Get off the pavement, you bloody—

And he reaches forth to haul Gandhi from the pavement, but—-

A WOMAN'S VOICE: Colin! Colin! What are you doing?

A woman is leaning out of an upstairs window, looking down at the fracas disconcertedly. It is the first youth's mother and her presence reduces the pitch of his hostility considerably.

FIRST YOUTH: Nuthing... nuthing. We were just cleaning up the neighbourhood a little.

A snickering response from the other youths—but they are embarrassed by the questioning disapproval of Colin's mother's attitude. There's no note of apology in her cold stare at Gandhi, but she clearly believes her son should not be doing what he is doing.

COLIN'S MOTHER: You're already late for work. I thought you'd gone ten minutes ago.

The moment of crisis has passed. Nothing will happen while she is there. Gandhi steps back on the pavement, addressing the first youth.

GANDHI : You'll find there's room for us both.

And he steps around him, Charlie trailing, as the first youth stares at them sullenly.

As they stride on, Charlie glancing back—

Charlie (relieved): That was lucky.

Gandhi: I thought you were a man of God.

CHARLIE (wittily, but making his point): I am. But I'm not so egotistical as to think He plans His day around my dilemmas.

Gandhi laughs as they turn the corner.

LESSON 4: COMMUNICATING THE VISION OF AHIMSA (LEADERS COMMUNICATE THEIR VISION)

Leaders share their vision clearly, and this can be seen when Gandhi categorically states that he would die for the cause at hand, *But Not Kill for Any Cause*. Gandhi was deeply steeped in the indigenous value of *ahimsa*, and stood by it in every situation. He was emphatic that Civil Disobedience required provoking the oppressors but was adamant that it did not entail hitting or killing them, and he communicated these ideas beyond doubt. Comparing the two scenes (scene 2 and 5) allows the students to see for themselves how even great leaders learn to present their ideas in public and become effective communicators through practice. It is quite clear that Gandhi was not a brilliant speaker to begin with, though he wrote well, but did acquire public speaking skills over the years.

SCENE 5: PREPARED TO DIE BUT NOT KILL

Imperial Theatre. Interior. Night.

The theatre is packed. The front rows near the stage are held by rich Muslim merchants, the back of the stalls with small traders, peddlers, artisans—Muslim, Hindu, Parsee, and Sikh. The gallery is bulging with indentured labourers—largely Hindus. The mood is restless, belligerent.

On the stage, Gandhi moves forward and he holds up his hand for silence. Seated on the stage are Khan, Singh, three more leaders of the Indian community. Charlie Andrews and Herman Kallenbach sit at the very end of the line of chairs. Gandhi looks around the audience and we see the packed house from his point of view, ending with two plain clothes European policemen conspicuous in seats at the end of the front row. A uniformed policeman stands near them.

GANDHI (to the house): I want to welcome you all!

A buzz, then applause—loud and defiant. When is subsides Gandhi looks down at the plainclothes policemen, fixing his gaze on them.

GANDHI : Everyone of you. (Then, still at them) We—have—no—secrets.

And again, the audience bursts into applause. The policemen just sit like stone—confident, sure, immune to rhetoric.

GANDHI : Let us begin by being clear about General Smuts' new law. All Indians must now be fingerprinted—like criminals. Men and women. (A rising, angry response; Gandhi just waits.) No marriage other than a Christian marriage is considered valid. Under this Act our wives and mothers are whores... And every man here a bastard.

In the gallery a rhythmic pounding signals the anger and protest and is taken up around the hall. The police stare imperturbably. Khan leans towards Singh, nodding to Gandhi.

KHAN : He's become quite good at this.

Singh smiles at the understatement. Gandhi holds up his hand, silencing the hall.

GANDHI : And a policeman passing an Indian dwelling—I will not call them homes—may enter and demand the card or any Indian woman, whose dwelling it is.

A VOICE : God damn them!

Gandhi just waits.

GANDHI : Understand! He does not have to stand at the door—he may enter.

Now a violent response—a large, powerful merchant rises in the third row.

MERCHANT : I swear to Allah I will kill the man who offers that insult to my home and my wife! (A guttural cheer; he glares at the police.) And let them hang me!

Another cheer. When it subsides, Tyeb Mohammed rises near the back, where he is seated with a number of other young men.

TYEB MOHAMMED: I say talk means nothing. Kill a few officials before they disgrace one Indian woman—then they might think twice about such laws!

The police half rise to look back at him, but there is a smattering of applause and several stand to look back.

TYEB MOHAMMED'S FRIEND: In that cause, I would be willing to die!

And now there is general applause. Gandhi waits, then.

GANDHI : I praise such courage. I need such courage—because in this cause, I too am prepared to die... (A response; he looks at Tyeb Mohammed). But, my friend, there is no cause for which I am prepared to kill.

He looks at the audience. This is the more sober Gandhi they have come to know.

GANDHI : I have asked you here tonight because despite all their troops and police, I think there is a way to defeat this law. Whatever they do to us we will attack no one, kill no one... But we will not (the climatic point) give our fingerprints—not one of us.

He looks down at the police, making the point stick. There is a tentative reaction from the audience, but uncertain.

GANDHI : They will imprison us, they will fine us. They will seize our possessions. But they cannot take away our self-respect if we do not give it to them.

A VOICE FROM THE GALLERY: Have you been to prison? They'll beat us and torture us! I say—

GANDHI : I am asking you to fight—! (It catches the audience a little, holds them.) To fight against their anger—not to provoke it!

He has their attention now.

GANDHI : We will not strike a blow—but we will receive them. And through our pain we will make them see their injustice (quickly) and it will hurt, as all fighting hurts! (Utter silence.)... But we cannot lose. We cannot. (He looks down at the police.) Because they may torture my body, may break my bones, even kill me... (Up to the house). They will then have my dead body—not my obedience.

And now he gets the response he has wanted. Firm, mature, determined. Gandhi holds up his hand.

GANDHI : We are Hindu and Muslim—children of God, each of us. Let us take a solemn oath in His name that—come what may—we will not submit to this law.

He looks at the audience. A second, then a merchant stands, signifying his pledge. And then another. Then Tyeb Mohammed and the youths about him. Then all over the theatre they begin to stand and on the stage until everyone is standing. It is all done in silence. Gandhi looks at the full theatre—all standing. He takes a step forward.

GANDHI (a coarse singing): God save our gracious King... Long live our (the audience takes it up)... noble King. (And their voices fill the auditorium) God save the King!

The above scene captures Gandhi's philosophy of Satyagraha quite well. Gandhi defined it as the "Force which is born of Truth and Love or non-violence." Satyagraha is to be done through *ahimsa* (or non-violence) without exception, and Gandhi believed that it is not necessary to pursue any cause through violence. The strength of the protesters lies in not submitting to the offensive law or practice, and also from their collective effort. Gandhi was able to demonstrate this again and again in his life. In this case (scene 5 above), General Smuts' law was repealed before it could be implemented.

LESSON 5: LEADERSHIP IS ABOUT *TYAG* OR SACRIFICE (LEADERS MAKE PERSONAL SACRIFICE)

The value of *tyag* or sacrifice is narrated in many Indian stories in the classic and modern texts. In the *Ramayana*, Rama is known to have given up his kingdom to please his father, and Sita decided to give up the comfort of the palace to accompany her husband, Rama, to the forest for fourteen years. Thus, an indigenous value shown by leaders including Gandhi invariably is *tyag* or sacrifice.

Gandhi was in jail many times for long durations, and suffered physical abuses at the hands of the British authority. Perhaps the biggest tragedy of the Indian freedom movement occurred in Punjab when people were celebrating *Baishakhi* (a festival) at the Jaliyanwalah Bagh. Brigadier-General Dyer ordered his troops to fire at people who had gathered in the garden. They fired at people who could not run away from the walled garden, shooting 1,650 bullets to kill 1,516 people! Clearly they fired to kill, and not to disperse the gathering. Such tragedies would test the belief and patience of any leader. Though deeply hurt by this massacre, Gandhi still held fast to his belief in non-violence. He believed that *Satyagraha* alone would lead India to independence. No action was taken against General Dyer, who later retired from the British military. The massacre of Jaliyanwalah Bagh remains as a historic thorn in Indo-British relationship, and the refusal of Queen Elizabeth to offer an apology for this historic brutality further festers the wound.

SCENE 6: THE MASSACRE OF JALLIANWALLAH BAGH

Jallianwallah Bagh. Amritsar. Exterior. Day.

A large public garden, enclosed by a thick, old, crumbling wall. A large crowd is gathered around a speaker on a platform at one side of the park. It is political, but the crowd is mixed. We see Muslims and Hindus, many of them Sikhs, old men, little children, and women with babes in arms. Some donkey carts, a sense of fair-time gaiety.

We close in on the speaker—a Muslim. He clutches a copy (we need not see the title) of Gandhi's journal.

SPEAKER : ... England is so powerful—its army and its navy, all its modern weapons—but when a great power like that strikes defenseless people it shows it brutality, its own weakness! Especially, when those people do not strike back. (He holds aloft the clenched journal.) That is why the Mahatma begs us to take the course of non-violence!

The Entrance of the Jallianwallah Bagh. Exterior. Day.

General Dyer, his armoured car, his sepoys, moving towards the gate. Dyer looks ahead calmly.

His point of view. The Gate of the Bagh. A rickety double gate in the high crumbling wall. On each pillar, poster notices for the meeting: "For Congress—For Gandhi." In the distance the speaker and the assembled crowd. Nearer, a few vendors, loiterers and children. At the sound of the armoured car and marching feet, a few turn in curiosity.

Another angle. The armoured car grinds forward. It won't go through the gates, one fender scraping against the gate post. Dyer gives a quiet order, the car backs away. Dyer jumps down lightly—a man in splendid condition. He walks through the gate and stands quietly in the at-ease position, hands clasping his swagger stick behind his back, looking off at the speaker.

SPEAKER : ... If we riot, if we fight back, we become the vandals and they become the law! If we bear their blows, they are the vandals—God and His law are on our... (He glances up.) side.

Long shot—his point of view. The two platoons of sepoys, rifles at the port, trot smartly through the gate and fan out on either side of the motionless and dominant figure of Dyer. Resume the speaker.

SPEAKER (soldiering on):... We must have the courage to take their anger...

Medium close—the sepoys and Dyer. He issues his commands in a quiet and unemotional voice, as though they were on manoeuvres.

DYER : Port arms, Sergeant Major.

The sergeant major issues the command. The troops port arms.

DYER : Load.

Again, the sergeant major barks the command; the bolts slam back and forth, the magazines clatter.

Featuring the platform and the front of the crowd. They have all turned now to watch, frozen in incredulity and fascination.

The sound of the sergeant major's orders and the sinister rattle of breeches and bolts drifting to them.

SPEAKER (almost to himself as he too is riveted):... Our pain will be our victory.

Their point of view. The distant figures facing them.

Resume the crowd. Numbly they begin to back away, pressing against the speaker's stand, themselves. A man picks up a child.

Their point of view. The small, distant figures of the sepoys again. A word of command. One platoon kneels and takes aim.

Another command. The second platoon, standing behind the first, takes aim.

Featuring Dyer. His ADC approaches. The British police officer stands off to one side.

ADC : Do we issue a warning, sir?

DYER (stiffly): They've had their warning—no meetings. It is final.

Resume the crowd. A ripple of panic now, everyone pressing back, but still they cannot credit what they see. Only one or two have the presence of mind to push clear and seek shelter. It is too late.

Close shot Dyer, still calm.

DYER : Sergeant Major—

SERGEANT MAJOR: Take aim!

Long shot over the sepoys and their sights, the wavering crowd distant.

DYER : Fire!

Flash shot along the line of sepoys; the rifles jerk and bang. The crowd, running, screaming.

SERGEANT MAJOR: Reload!

A dreadful press of panic-stricken people flying towards the walls. And again the crash of rifles. Some fall. Others run off-screen in an aimless, irresistible wave.

Dyer is walking behind his men, telling them, with a view to maximum accuracy, what he has told them on the firing range (it makes him a little irritable to have to repeat it).

DYER : Take your time. Take your time.

He looks off at the crowd. His eyes narrow.

A group of men are hurling themselves at a breach in the top of the wall, hanging there, scrabbling for a purchase, some disappearing, a few heroic individuals astride the wall reaching down to assist their women and children in the swirling crowd below.

DYER : Corporal!

CORPORAL : Sir!

DYER : Over there.

He nods. The corporal looks.

CORPORAL : Sir.

He directs the attention of his neighbours in the firing line towards the new target; they shift their aim.

A man reaching for a child—who is also propelled upward by its mother from below—is hit, falls, so that he and the child crash into the crowd below.

Sepoys firing *ad lib.* Dyer watching the effect, careful and conscientious.

Swift tracking a man running through the staggering crowd, over the litter of bodies, his mouth open, his eyes wild. He arrives at a well, throws down the rope and slides down it. Others seize the idea and in panic throw themselves into the well, dropping out of sight.

Featuring Dyer. Meticulously, he taps a corporal on the shoulder with his swagger stick and indicates the well. The corporal signals his line of men.

At the well. The gathering crowd—men, women—and laced with rifle fire.

From behind the sepoys we see the whole Bagh, littered with dead and dying, a thick rock around the well, the walls hanging with wounded and dying, the firing continuing, loud, loud, louder…

The Armoury Hall. The Fort of Lahore. Interior. Day.

Silence. The camera is close as it crosses a table with legal documents. Gradually we hear a muffled cough, whispers, shuffled papers, and it at last comes to a large close shot of General Dyer.

Another angle. A Commission of Inquiry sits in the large Armoury Hall of the Old Fort. Dyer faces a panel of Commissioners: Lord Hunter, presiding, Mr. Justice Rankin, General Barrow, a British civil servant, and an Indian barrister.

The Commission functions like a public parliamentary committee—little ceremony, no judicial robes, a small group of public and press, who sit on wooden chairs behind a barrier that isolates the Commission's business.

Much of that public is English—fellow officers and civilians.

A Government Advocate (English) turns to face Dyer.

ADVOCATE : General Dyer, is it correct that you ordered your troops to fire at the thickest part of the crowd?

Dyer glances woodenly at the panel—a man in some shock at the consequences of what he assumed was an act worthy of praise.

DYER (righteously): That is so.

The Advocate looks at him with a degree of disbelief—more at his attitude than his statement.

ADVOCATE : One thousand five hundred and sixteen casualties with one thousand six hundred and fifty bullets.

A slight reaction from the public section. Dyer's jaw tightens.

DYER : My intention was to inflict a lesson that would have an impact throughout India.

He stares at the panel like a reasonable man making a reasonable point. The evasiveness, the only half-buried embarrassment of their response only deepens his own withdrawal into himself.

INDIAN BARRISTER : General, had you been able to take in the armoured car, would you have opened fire with the machine gun?

Dyer thinks about it. Then unashamedly—

DYER : I think, probably—yes.

A muted reaction from the public section. The Indian barrister stares at him a moment, then simply lowers his eyes to his notes.

HUNTER : General, did you realize there were children—and women—in the crowd?

DYER (a beat): I did.

For the first time there is the hint of uncertainty in his manner.

ADVOCATE : But that was irrelevant to the point you were making?

DYER : That is correct.

There is just a tremor of distaste quickly suppressed among the panel. Not so quickly in the public section.

ADVOCATE : Could I ask you what provision you made for the wounded?

Dyer looks at him quickly. The question is unexpected, even a little "clever." The officers listening clearly resent it.

DYER (a moment, then firmly): I was ready to help any who applied.

And that answer stops the Advocate. He smiles dryly.

ADVOCATE : General… how does a child shot with a 3-0-3 Enfield "apply" for help?

Dyer faces him stonily, a seed of panic taking root deep in his gut.

Jallianwallah Bagh. Exterior. Day.

Quiet: the same silence as at the Court of Inquiry. The camera is panning slowly along a section of the wall. We are close and see the bullet holes, the patches of splashed blood, the scratches where fingers have dug at the surface of the wall to claw a path to safety... Gandhi, matching that of Dyer, whom we have just left. He is surveying the wall in the now empty park numbly, desolately. Nehru stands a few feet away from him, his mood the same, the same benumbed grief and incredulity.

Resume the wall—Gandhi's point of view. The camera continues its pan—bits of human hair matted in the dried blood, and the bullet-ripped foliage, the well, trampled ground around it, little pieces of clothing. Flies buzz around the debris. Abstractedly, Gandhi touches the bucket rope that lies across the surround. Nehru has moved to the other side of the well. Gandhi lifts his eyes to him.

LESSON 6: SERVING COMMON GOOD (LEADERS CHAMPION FAR REACHING ISSUES USING SIMPLE METHODS)

Service is highly valued in the Indian culture, both in family and community. Children learn to serve their parents from the childhood. Teachers or Gurus receive service from their students or disciples, so much so that the way to make progress on one's spiritual journey is through the service of one's spiritual master. Noble Kings were supposed to serve their subjects even at the expense of making personal sacrifices, and there is the story of King Vikramaditya who took the wrath of Sani, one of the nine planetary gods, upon himself to relieve one of his subjects from the extreme sufferings brought upon him by Sani. Thus, it is expected that leaders would serve people by choosing far-reaching issues, issues that serve the common good. Gandhi fought for the Independence of India, and he also fought for the rights of Untouchables in India. Leaders are creative in that they use simple methods that help mobilize the masses. Burning imported British clothes not only symbolized violating British Power; but also hurt the British economy. Gandhi encouraged people to wear Indian clothes and to use fabric made in India. He not only stopped wearing Western clothes but also started the Khadi movement by dedicating some time everyday to spin cotton for his own clothes. His simple lifestyle made it easy for his followers to identify with him. Clearly, followers find it easy to emulate the leaders when leaders represent the people and live the life they face everyday. As seen in the clip, later on Gandhi became a half-naked fakir (one who lives on alms) to become one with the poor, for most people in India were so poor in his time that they were literally half-naked.

SCENE 7: WEARING KHADI AND BURNING BRITISH CLOTHES

Gandhi fiddles with his glasses, preoccupied; finally he looks out over the crowd and holds up a hand—almost lazily—and gradually, but quite definitely, the crowd stills.

GANDHI : My message tonight is the message I have given to your brothers everywhere. To gain independence we must prove worthy of it.
We intercut with the crowd, listening raptly. Gandhi holds up one finger.

GANDHI : There must be Hindu-Muslim unity—always. (A second finger.) Secondly, no Indian must be treated as the English treat us so we must remove untouchability from our lives, and from our hearts.
Neither of these goals is easy, and the audience reaction shows it. Now Gandhi raises a third finger.

GANDHI : Third—we must defy the British.
And the crowd breaks into stamping and applause. Gandhi lets it run for a time, then stills it with the one small gesture as before.

GANDHI : Not with violence that will inflame their will, but with firmness that will open their eyes.
This has sobered the audience somewhat. Now he looks out across them as though seeking something. Then

GANDHI : English factories make the cloth—that makes our poverty. (*A reaction.*) All those who wish to make the English see, bring me the cloth from Manchester and Leeds that you wear tonight, and we will light a fire that will be seen in Delhi—and London!
There is an excited stir; he silences it.

GANDHI : And if, like me, you are left with only one piece of homespun—wear it with dignity!

Close shot—the ground. As suit coats, shirts, vests, trousers, are flung into a pile. Featuring the two British soldiers—later—on the edge of the crowd, staring off, and their faces now brightly lit by darting flames. Their point of view. A huge triangular pile burns before the platform, an excited half-naked crowd swirling in the shadows around it.

Resume the two British soldiers. They look at each other with a kind of fear a rampant crowd can excite in those who must hold it.

The above scene also allows a discussion of how it is easy to fight the enemies from the outside, especially those who are coming from another country, but difficult to deal with issues emerging from within the country. Indians were able to fight the British successfully to become an independent country overthrowing two hundred years of British rule. However, India is still plagued by Hindu-Muslim violence and riots, and the untouchables are far from getting a decent living or the respect every human being deserves. The same is true in the case of organizations. It is easier to deal with the changes in the external environment than to bring about internal changes. Change management is hardest when it comes to changing organizational culture and practices that have evolved over a long period of time. But great leaders do not shy away from confronting internal issues, and Gandhi contributed a lot to the betterment of the lives of the untouchables in India. There is another scene in the film where Gandhi takes the tray from the servant and serves the Congress leaders beverages to make the point that Indian leaders needed to first reform their own behaviour of not treating other Indians with respect, especially those who performed the menial tasks, before they could fight the British rule.

LESSON 7: LEADERS ARE READY TO DIE FOR THEIR CAUSE

The most noble of all *tyag* or sacrifice is to give up one's life to save another person. Saint Dadhichi is known to have given his life so that his bones could be used by the King of Gods, Indra, to build the weapon *Vajra* or thunder, to help him fight and slay the demon Vritrasur. King Shivi is known to have given his limbs and offered his life to protect a pigeon who sought protection of him from a falcon. In the modern times, King Shahjahan, who built Taj Mahal, was willing to give his life to provide justice to the woman whose husband was killed by his wife when she had gone hunting. There were many occasions when Gandhi risked his life to save the country from catastrophes. For example, he started to fast until death in 1947 to stop the Hindu-Muslim violence in the streets of Calcutta. What the British machinery and the Indian military could not achieve together—managing the riots—Gandhi achieved single-handedly by his *Satyagraha.* Violence stopped in Calcutta as a result of his *Satyagraha*. There is an interesting scene that I find suitable to end the class with, which captures the divine justice that Gandhi proposed to an angry man who had killed an innocent Muslim child as a revenge for the murder of his child by the Muslims. Gandhi suggested to this person that his penance would entail raising an orphan Muslim child as his own, but that the child should be raised as a Muslim!

SCENE 8: DIVINE JUSTICE OR A WAY OUT OF HELL

The Goondas stand. They glance at Suhrawardy; he smiles tautly and they start to leave, but one (Nahari) lingers. Suddenly, he moves violently towards Gandhi, taking a flat piece of Indian bread (*chapati*) from his trousers and tossing it forcefully on Gandhi.

NAHARI : Eat.

Mirabehn and Azad start to move towards him—the man looks immensely strong and immensely unstable. But Gandhi holds up a shaking hand, stopping them. Nahari's face is knotted in emotion, half anger, half almost a child's fear—but there is a wild menace in that instability.

NAHARI : Eat! I am going to hell—but not with your death on my soul.

GANDHI : Only God decides who goes to hell…

NAHARI (stiffening, aggressive): I—I killed a child… (Then an anguished defiance) I smashed his head against a wall.

Gandhi stares at him, breathless.

GANDHI (in a fearful whisper): Why? Why?

It is as though the man has told him of some terrible self-inflicted wound.

NAHARI (tears now—and wrath): They killed my son—my boy!

Almost reflexively he holds his hand out to indicate the height of his son. He glares at Suhrawardy and then back at Gandhi.

NAHARI : The Muslims killed my son… they killed him.

He is sobbing, but in his anger it seems almost as though he means to kill Gandhi in retaliation. A long moment, as Gandhi meets his pain and wrath. Then

GANDHI : I know a way out of hell.

Nahari sneers, but there is just a flicker of desperate curiosity.

GANDHI : Find a child—a child whose mother and father have been killed. A little boy—about this high.

He raises his hand to the height Nahari has indicated as his son's.

GANDHI : ... and raise him—as your own.

Nahari has listened. His face almost cracks—it is a chink of light, but it does not illumine his darkness.

GANDHI : Only be sure... that he is a Muslim. And that you raise him as one.

And now the light falls on Nahari. His face stiffens, he swallows, fighting any show of emotion; and then he turns to go. But he takes only a step and he turns back, going to his knees, the sobs breaking again and again from his heaving body as he holds his head to Gandhi's feet in the traditional greeting of Hindu son to Hindu father. A second, and Gandhi reaches out and touches the top of his head.

Mirabehn watches. The Goondas watch. Suhrawardy watches. Finally

GANDHI (gently, exhaustedly): Go—go. God bless you...

DISCUSSION

When I showed the film Gandhi in an MBA class, as I regularly do, one of the students raised an objection. He said, "What is the point of showing an idealist like Gandhi to business students. We are never going to be like him. It is not possible for us to act like Gandhi." I had raised the same question with the late Mr. Janaki Prasad Singh, an educator and educational leader par excellence, whom I respected for his idealism, wisdom, and what is often referred to in India as being a "dry honest" person—one who refuses to accept even a gift because it may compromise his or her future decisions. This was many years ago when I was still in my twenties. I had asked him—"Why did you people raise us with idealism? All my friends who are not idealistic are riding in Mercedes, and are making a lot of money, whereas I seem to be carrying the burden of idealism travelling in crowded buses, and having a poor middle class life in general." As always he was insightful and profound in his explanation.

"You know, when they have drought (which happens quite often in India), people eat everything they have, but they never touch the seeds. They would much rather die than eat the seeds. You know why? Well, all droughts end, and rain comes sooner or later. When rain comes, you cannot do anything if you don't have seeds. Idealism is the seed of humanity. We plant it in our future generations so that when we need the seeds, it will be there." I have savored that moment with Janaki Babu all my life. With all my foibles, and compromises I have made in life, I still carry the seeds of idealism in me. That is why I personally find Gandhi relevant today, more so for business students who touch the world through their work in organizations.

In the wake of Enron and WorldCom crisis that the business world has seen, if we do not have exemplars like Gandhi, we will be without seeds to plant when rain comes. By discussing about Gandhi in business schools we can plant the seeds of idealism in the future generation of managers. Some will carry it, others will not. But there will be some who would save the seeds for the rainy days. This was my response to that student, and the motivation to write this paper about using Gandhi to discuss leadership in business schools.

To summarize, students learn that leaders are not born, but emerge by championing a cause that is significant for a community they represent. We all have to take personal responsibility for representing a cause. It is not assigned to us. Leadership is about taking the initiative in identifying a cause that is large enough to touch many people, and taking action for the betterment of their lives. Leaders use symbols effectively, and symbols are creatively crafted by them from the context in which the community functions. Often symbols are viewed as something abstract, but by viewing the clips students get to see that symbols are created from little things like passes people have to carry or the tax people have to pay for something as common as salt. Leaders are authentic people and not only talk the talk but also walk the talk. This is clearly something that Gandhi is an exemplar of. Sometimes, the myth created around a leader makes it difficult for people to emulate them. The clips clearly show that leadership skills like creating a vision and clearly communicating it to the followers are acquired over time with effort, even by great leaders like Gandhi. Leadership invariably involves making much personal sacrifice for the cause championed, and it is important to bring this to the attention of students. Leadership is not only about basking in fame, but also about enduring much suffering over a long period of time. Leaders choose far-reaching issues and simple methods. Again, the importance of simple solutions is made transparent in the clips. And, finally, leaders are, and have to be, ready to die if they have to for the cause they champion.

The film clips clearly show Gandhi's value-based leadership style, and students are able to see that a real person practiced these values in rather trying situations. Showing the clips helps emphasize many important aspects of leadership in a relatively short time of about two and one-half hours.

Students are able to see a larger than life leader and invariably get inspired to emulate Gandhi. Gandhi truly stood by what he said: MY LIFE IS MY MESSAGE. And he stands out as an exemplar of authentic leadership style. Gandhi in his life, as well as in the Attenborough film, offers us an opportunity to demonstrate what it means to be an authentic leader, and is a great way to inspire young people in their leadership journey.

Aknowledgement: I am grateful to my student, Maggie McCann, for library research, and to Vijayan P. Munusamy and Keith H. Sakuda for their constructive comments.

REFERENCES

Bhawuk, D.P.S. (2008a). Toward an Indian Organizational Psychology. In K.R. Rao, A.C. Paranjpe, and A.K. Dalal (Eds.), *Handbook of Indian Psychology* (pp. 471-491). New Delhi, India: Cambridge University Press.

Bhawuk, D.P.S. (2008b). Science of Culture and Culture of Science: Worldview and Choice of Conceptual Models and Methodology. *The Social Engineer*, 11 (2), 26-43.

Bhawuk, D.P.S. (2008c) Anchoring Cognition, Emotion, and Behaviour in Desire: A Model from the Bhagavad-Gita." In K.R. Rao, A.C. Paranjpe, and A.K. Dalal (Eds.), *Handbook of Indian Psychology* (pp. 390-413). New Delhi, India: Cambridge University Press.

Bhawuk, D.P.S. (2005). A Model of Self, Work, and Spirituality from the Bhagavad-Gita: Implications for Self-Efficacy, Goal Setting, and Global Psychology. In K. Ramakrishna Rao and Sonali B. Marwaha (eds.), *Towards a Spiritual Psychology: Essays in Indian Psychology*. New Delhi, India: Samvad Indian Foundation.

Bhawuk, D.P.S. (2004). Individualism and collectivism. In the *Encyclopaedia of Leadership*, Volume 2, 706-710. Thousand Oaks, CA: Sage.

Bhawuk, D.P.S. (2003). Culture's Influence on Creativity: The Case of Indian Spirituality. *International Journal of Intercultural Relations*, 27 (1), 1-22.

Bhawuk, D.P.S. (1999). Who Attains Peace: An Indian Model of Personal Harmony. *Indian Psychological Review*, 52 (2 and 3), 40-48.

Bhawuk, D.P.S. (1997). Leadership through Relationship Management: Using the Theory of Individualism and Collectivism. In R.W. Brislin and K. Cushner (Eds.), *Improving Intercultural Interactions: Modules for Cross-cultural training Programmes*, Volume 2, pp. 40-56. Thousand Oaks, CA: Sage.

Bhawuk, D.P.S., and Munusamy, V.P. (2006). Are high achieving Asians individualists? In Edith W. Chen and Glenn Omatsu (Eds.), *Teaching about Asian Pacific Islanders: Effective Activities, Strategies, and Assignments for Classrooms and Workshops* (pp. 95-102), Lanham, MD: AltaMira Press.

Bok, Sissela (1957). Foreword. *The Story of My Experiments with Truth*. Boston, MA: Beacon Press.

Bose, Nirmal K. (1947). *Studies in Gandhiism*. Calcutta: Indian Associated Publishing Co.

Bowers, D.G., and Seashore, S.E. (1966). Predicting organizational effectiveness with a four factor theory of leadership. *Administrative Science Quarterly*, 11, 238-263.

Briley, John (1982). *Gandhi*. (Screen play for the film Gandhi by Sir Richard Attenborough) available at *http://www.gandhiserve.org/video/gandhi_screenplay.html*

Fleishman, E.A. (1953). The description of supervisory behaviour. *Personnel Psychology*, 37, 1-6.

Fleishman, E.A., Harris, E.F., and Burtt, H.E. (1955). *Leadership and supervision in industry*. Columbus, OH: Bureau of Educational Research, Ohio State University.

Gandhi, Mohandas K. (1957). *An Autobiography: The Story of My Experiments with Truth*. Boston, MA: Beacon Press.

Gergen, K., Gulerce, A., Lock, A., and Mishra, G. (1996). Psychological Science in cultural context. *American Psychologist*, 51, 496-503.

Likert, R. (1961). *New patterns of management*. New York,: McGraw-Hill.

Likert, R. (1967). *The human organization*. New York,: McGraw-Hill.

Marsella, A.J. (1998). Toward a "Global-Community Psychology". *American Psychologist*, 53 (12), 1282-1291.

Pawlik, K. (Ed.) (1991). The psychological dimension of global change [Whole Issue]. *International Journal of Psychology*, 20.

Prabhu, R.K., and Rao, U.R. (1961). *The mind of Mahatma Gandhi*. Ahmedabad, India: Navajivan.

Sinha, Jai B.P. (1980). *The nurturant task leader*. New Delhi: Concept.

Tendulkar, D.G. (1951). *Mahatma: Life of Mohandas Karamchand Gandhi* (Volume 1). Government of India: Publications Division.

CHAPTER TEN

Imbued with Integrity and Endowed with Knowledge: Leaders that Build Trust

Arif Hassan

INTRODUCTION

Although studies on leadership in organizations have a long history (Bass, 1960), only recently concerns are shown for ethical aspects of leadership (Robbins & Judge, 2007). Events of recent years from corporate sector reinforce this concern. The most recent financial crisis and the looming dangers of recession in different parts of the world seem to have originated from failed corporate leaders who believed in manipulations of accounts and indulged into blatant unethical corporate practices. The very trusted leaders were found to be corrupt. A check of recent corporate scandals on Wikipedia (http://en.wikipedia.org/wiki/Accounting_scandals) gives a long list of cases involving big names and big companies. For instance, WorldCom faked nearly $ 4 billion in operating cash flow. Enron executives manipulated their financial statements. Tyco International's CEO is charged with cheating on sales taxes. But one name from the most recent past tops them all. He is Bernard Madoff. His investment scandal occurred after the discovery that former NASDAQ chairman Bernard Madoff's asset management business was actually a giant Ponzi scheme. The US federal authorities arrested Madoff on December 11, 2008. On March 12, 2009, Madoff pled guilty to 11 felonies and admitted to operating the largest investor fraud ever committed by an individual. According to a federal criminal complaint, client statements showing $65 billion in stock holdings were fictitious, and no stocks were ever purchased since the scheme began in the 1980s (Wikipedia).

Such cases are not reported only in the US. It is happening in other parts of the world as well. The recent story comes from India. Mr. Raju the Chairman of Satyam, a well known Computer giant, was reported involved in a scandal similar to Enron's where he confessed that he had padded Satyam's accounting books for personal gains. Immediately, the scandal eroded $2.2 billion in shareholder wealth. Satyam's stock fell 41 per cent. The Bombay Stock Exchange removed Satyam from its Benchmark Sensitive Index, a day after the National Stock Exchange dropped the stock from the Nifty.

Advocating need to understand the importance of trust in business, popular management guru Covey (2006), observed that "leaders around the world have made it increasingly evident that speed to market is now the ultimate competitive advantage... Low trust causes friction, whether it is caused by unethical behaviour or by ethical but incompetent behaviour. Low trust is the greatest cost in life and in organizations, including families. Low trust creates hidden agendas, politics, interpersonal conflict, interdepartmental rivalries win-lose thinking, defensive and protective communication. On the other hand trust builds speed (p. xxv).

Arguing forcefully for trust in business Covey (2006) further asserts, "The ability to establish, grow, extend, and restore trust with all the stakeholders—customers, business partners, investors, and coworkers—is the key leadership competency of the new global economy" (p. 21).

Perhaps, there cannot be a better time as well as reason to study leadership from ethical and moral perspective than now. As one author rightly commented, "No one can deny that Adolf Hitler was an effective leader. He led Germany from depression to prosperity and from being a crippled military power to being the most powerful and efficient military machine in the world—all in a few short years. However, most would deny that he was a "good" leader (Drouillard & Kleiner, 1996: 30). Surprisingly, most authors have defined leadership merely as an influence process that leads to the achievement of groups' goal. There is need to define leadership that includes elements of morality, ethical conduct and goodness, besides skills and competencies (Drouillard & Kleiner, 1996).

WHAT IS TRUST?

In common usage trust implies confidence. The opposite of trust—distrust—is suspicion. When we trust people we have confidence in their integrity and abilities. When we distrust people, we are suspicious of them—of their integrity, their agenda, their capability or their track record (Covey, 2006).

Covey further adds to say, "The difference between a high and low-trust relationship is palpable! Take communication. In high-trust relationship, you can say the wrong thing, and people will still get your meaning. In a low-trust-relationship, you can be very measured, even precise, and they'll still misinterpret you" (p. 7).

More specifically, trust may be defined as "a positive expectation that another will not—through words, actions, or decisions—act opportunistically" (Boon & Holmes, 1991). Positive expectation assumes knowledge and familiarity about the other party. Trust is based upon past experience. It takes time to build trust. It would be hard to trust someone immediately when nothing is known about the other person.

The term opportunistically included in the above definition refers to the inherent risk and vulnerability in any trusting relationship. Trust involves making oneself vulnerable as for example, when we keep our valuables with someone for safekeeping or share some intimate information to someone. By its very nature, trust provides opportunity to disappointment or to be taken advantage of. But trust is not taking risk *per se;* rather, it is willingness to take risk (Mayer, Davis, & Schoorman, 1995). This willingness to take risk is common to all trust situations (Johnson-George & Swap, 1982).

The key dimensions of trust include the following: integrity, competence, loyalty, and openness (Schindler & Thomas, 1993). Integrity refers to honesty and truthfulness. It is considered the most important determinant of trust. For example, in a study when employees were given a list of 28 attributes related to leadership, honesty was rated the most important by far (Jones, 2003). Competence encompasses an individual's technical and interpersonal knowledge and skills. It is unlikely that someone will trust a person whose ability is a suspect. Consistency relates to an individual's reliability, predictability, and good judgement in handling situations. Inconsistency between words and actions decrease trust. This is more visible in leadership role. Nothing is noticed more quickly than a discrepancy between the words and actions. Loyalty is the willingness to protect and save face for another person. Finally, trust requires openness meaning one can rely on another person to give full truth and not the half truth.

Generally speaking, trust is referred in relation to the character of an individual who embodies a sincere character and walks the talk. Though character is essential to trusting relationship, it is not the only factor that engenders trust. Equally important factor is the competence. Competence includes capabilities, skills, performance, and past record of achievements.

With the increasing focus on ethics in our society, the character side of the trust is fast becoming the price of entry in the new global economy. However, the differentiating and often ignored side of trust—competence—is equally essential. An airline pilot may be sincere in character yet one would not take the risk of flying with him if he is known to be incompetent or even less competent. Similarly, a person may be highly talented and competent, but if he is not honest, he is not going to be trusted. In short, trust is a function of two things: character and competence (Covey, 2006). These two dimensions of trust is reflected in most of the contemporary theories of leadership using different terms or words to express the idea, "but if you reduce the words to their essence, what emerges is a balancing of character and competence" (Covey, 2006: 31). Let us take the following examples from Covey's (2006) list.

Jack Welch—former CEO of GE—talks about managers being judged on their performance in two dimensions: "Live the values" (Character) and "Deliver results" (competence).

Jim Collins talks about Level 5 leader "having extreme personal humility" (character) and "intense professional will" (competence).

Warren Buffett—CEO of Berkshire Hathaway—prioritizes "integrity" (character) and "intelligence" (competence) as the qualities he looks for in people.

Obviously, building trust is the essence of leadership. In the following sections the author will examine the leadership literature to find out the role of trust in leadership.

LEADERSHIP AND TRUST

Trust is the building block of social exchange and role relationship. Leader-member relationship needs trust. When trust is broken it can have serious adverse effects on a group's performance (Dirks & Ferrin, 2002). When followers trust leader, they are willing to be vulnerable to the leader's action—confident that their rights and interests will not be abused (Hosmer, 1995). Honesty, for instance, consistently ranks at the top of most people's list of characteristics they admire in their leaders. Trust is the foundation for effective communication, employee motivation, intention to stay in the job, and extra-role behaviour. Fairholm (1994) put this rightly by stating that: "If followers consider their leaders trustworthy, they will probably have faith in their orders, instructions, values, and visions. If the necessary trust is lacking, leaders will find it difficult to have their ideas get accepted" (p. 104).

Trust in leaders is discussed in theories concerned with the dyadic relationship between leaders and followers and is acknowledged as an important construct affecting their relationships. For instance, leader-member exchange theory suggests trust reflects a matured relationship between leader and subordinate (Dansereau, Graen & Haga, 1975). Bennis and Naus (1985) posit that earning the respect of followers is a requirement for effective leadership. Sinha (1980) advanced the concept on Nurturant-Task leader which embodies the element of trust based upon personalized relationship with subordinates through nurturance, care, and interest in their well-being.

According to Fairholm (1994), some key elements that build effective trusting relationship between leader and followers include acceptance, assumptions, authentic caring, ethics, individual character, leadership, and predictability.

Acceptance comes from agreement on group goals, intra- and inter-personal control, acknowledgement of differences between others and self, thus reducing fear of personal failure and the negative action of others. Acceptance occurs when an individual perceives that the world is a safe place to live in. In inter-personal relationship when behaviour becomes predictable and caring, trust based on positive assumptions would develop.

Authentic caring is the outcome of being a leader perceived as open, personally interested and worthy of trust. It shows that the leader is interested in the well-being of followers and is willing to meet their needs. Leadership that develops trust also consists of consistency in communication, cooperation, and congruency in words and action. Individual character is the expectancy held by the followers that they can trust and rely on the word, promise, or statement of leaders. Finally, predictability builds trust when the follower can confidently forecast what the leader will do in any given situation.

Mayer *et al.* (1995) have proposed a model to explain the role of leader-followers trust on work outcomes. The follower (Trustor) assesses the ability, benevolence, and integrity of the leader (Trustee) in determining the degree to which trust is a factor in the relationship. Ability is defined as a group of skills, competencies, and characteristics that enable a party to have influence within some specific domain. Benevolence is the degree to which the trustee wants to demonstrate goodwill towards the trustor. Integrity is the degree to which the trustee's behaviours are similarly valued by the trustor. This may include predictability and honesty. This proposed model examines the character of both the trustee as well as the trustor. The outcome of the trust or lack of trust is perceived as a result of ability, benevolence, and integrity the leader either possesses or does not possess. This positive or negative trust outcome may influence future interactions between leader and follower.

Research suggests that leader's effectiveness may be attributed to employees' perceptions that trust is promoted and maintained as an important characteristic in the working relationship (Bass, 1990; Hogan, Curphy & Hogan, 1994). Such emphasis has been found to be an important dimension of leader behaviour (Fleishman & Harris, 1962) and a major component in the transformational leadership model (Kirkpatrick & Locke, 1996).

A leader's effectiveness depends upon the employees' perceptions that leaders possess attributes that promote trust (Bass, 1990; Hogan, Curphy, & Hogan, 1994). It is also understood that "all leaders require trust as a basis for their legitimacy and as the mortar that binds leader to follower" (Nanus, 1989: 101). Such perceptions of authentic trust were found to create source credibility (Butler, 1991). That may contribute to positive reactions in followers. Trust in leader has been found to influence employees' work commitment, intention to stay in the organization, organizational citizenship behaviour, quality of communication, and decision making (Dirks & Ferrin, 2002).

In a recent study quality of relationship based on trust between employees and employers was found to contribute to employees' level of engagement. Also engaged employees were found to have more positive attitudes and intentions towards their organization (Cropanzano & Mitchell, 2005). Harvey, Kelloway, and Duncan-Leiper (2003) found trust in management to be vital 'buffer' helping prevent burnout among employees of large accounting firm. Surprisingly, little attention has been given in the leadership studies to the role of trust in influencing follower's behavioural outcomes. As noted by Atkinson (2004), studies on trust in relationship development have generally focused on romantic relationships rather than the specific features of organizational relationships. As a result, generalizability of trust relationships in other social context is difficult (Fritz, 1997).

Leadership is not value free. The effectiveness of a leader is judged both on the ends and the means to achieve goals as well as the moral contents of those goals. Events of the past few years have resulted in deep distrust for corporate leaders and have led the search for moral and ethical leaders. In this backdrop, the concept of authentic leadership is gaining popularity.

AUTHENTIC LEADERSHIP

Authentic leadership theory has been advanced as an approach to leadership that includes behaviours such as transparency (Avolio *et al.*, 2004), altruistic actions (Michie & Gooty, 2005), and behavioural consistency (Gardner *et al.*, 2005; Eagly, 2005). The topic of authentic leadership is receiving increased attention from practitioners and scholars alike (Avolio, Gardner, Walumbwa, Luthans, & May, 2004; George, 2003; Gardner & Schemerhorn, 2004; Luthans & Avolio, 2003; May, Chan, Hodges, & Avolio, 2003; see also *The Leadership Quarterly,* Volume 16, Number 3, 2005). As pointed out by George (2003), authentic leaders exert influence well beyond bottom line success to influence solving public policies and to address social and organizational problems and issues.

Authentic leadership theory leverages synergies from Avolio's past research on transformational (Bass & Avolio, 1994) and full-range leadership (Avolio *et al.*, 1999; 2002; 2005) and Luthans' past work in positive organizational behaviour, and psychological capital (Luthans *et al.*, 2004; Luthans & Youssef, 2004), and positive approaches to leadership (Luthans, Luthans, Hodgetts, & Luthans, 2001). Rooted in ancient Greek lore and philosophy, the modern concept of authenticity has evolved during the past 80 years (Erickson, 2005). As part of a larger theory of "optimal" self-esteem, Kernis (2003) defines authenticity as "the unobstructed operation of one's true, or core, self in one's daily enterprise." Thus, authenticity is supported and reinforced through how one lives and interacts with others. Kernis (2003) identifies four key components of authenticity: awareness, unbiased processing, action and relational authenticity.

Self-awareness is defined as "having awareness of, and trust in, one's motives, feelings, desires, and self-relevant cognitions." Thus, self-awareness includes an awareness of one's strength and limitation; as well as how he or she feels at the time and the potential effect those emotions have on current beliefs and actions. Self-awareness is a critical component of authentic leadership because one must first be aware of his or her self and also of relevant emotions before he or she can act in accordance with those aspects of the self. The leader must be high in self-awareness so that he or she can first act accordingly, then encourage and support others in the organization to do so as well.

The goal of transparency is achieved through the leader's appropriate self-disclosure, specifically in the areas of values, identity, emotions, and goals/ motives which, in turn, enhance follower trust levels related to the leader. By encouraging organizational members to act according to positive values and emotions, the leader creates an environment around transparent relationships and communications. Unbiased processing was put forth by Kernis (2003) as a factor that is critical for psychological well-being that relates to the manner in which one processes self-relevant information that he or she is presented. Unbiased processing refers to a process where one collects information and feedback in a manner that does not allow for denials or distortions that are more subjective in nature. Thus, the ability to objectively process information related to one's self is critical in order to be truly authentic

In the positive psychology literature, authenticity is defined as owning one's personal experiences, thoughts, and emotions (Harter *et al.*, 2002). However, in addition to owning one's experiences and thoughts, authenticity also involves acting in accordance with those thoughts or that one's actions are congruent with one's beliefs. That is, one's degree of authenticity is based on whether an individual's actions support one's true self *versus* one's actions being based on attempts to gain the approval of others (Luthans & Avolio, 2003; Gardner *et al.*, 2005). However, rather than being purely authentic or inauthentic, Erickson (1995) asserts that people are best described as existing on a continuum from more to less authentic. This view of authenticity as existing on a continuum is parallel to the view taken by Luthans and Avolio (2003). One is not necessarily completely authentic at all times, but is seen as more or less authentic. The more one acts in accord with his or her true self will determine the degree of that individual's level of authenticity. The authentic leader is expected to be a model of transparency for others throughout the organization by first acting in accord with his or her values and by encouraging others in the organization to do so as well. Since followers' perceptions of and trust in the leader are largely based on the leader's behaviours and actions, those actions must be aligned with the leader's espoused values and the behaviour must be consistent to be seen as genuine or authentic behaviours.

Furthermore, leaders who are more open and who self-disclose more would be expected to instill higher levels of trust in their followers (Gardner *et al.*, 2005). Therefore, the leader must consistently act in accordance with his or her espoused values shared transparently with followers and by doing so, the leader acts as a role model for followers who would then be expected to have a higher level of trust in the leader. The last component of authenticity put forth by Kernis (2003) is that of relational authenticity. Relational authenticity involves valuing and achieving openness and transparency (truthfulness) in one's relevant relationships. Relational authenticity involves one showing his or her true self, good or bad to relevant others. By accepting others' points of view and by acting based on appropriate feedback and suggestions, the leader sets the standard for others in the organization to welcome feedback and inputs as well. Thus, transparency is a critical component of authentic relationships that is proposed to strengthen trust levels.

AUTHENTIC *VERSUS* ETHICAL AND MORAL LEADERSHIP

There seems to be a good overlap between authentic and moral/ethical leadership. The philosopher Jean Paul Sartre wrote a lot about authenticity, arguing that to be an authentic person, an individual needs to be honest with oneself and avoid self-deception. Authentic leaders know who they are, know what they believe in and value, and act on those values openly and candidly. Their followers would consider them to be ethical people. According to Rhode (2007), leadership is inescapably value laden. The essence of effective leadership is ethical leadership, which requires morality in means as well as ends.

Authenticity blends the emotional, the subjective, and the intuitive processes that are so critical to guiding us through our lives with the conventionally accepted way of working with objectivity, empiricism and the scientific methods (Elsner, 2000). However, distinctions are made between ethical and moral leadership. Northhouse (2004) makes a distinction based on his work. According to his brief explanation, "ethical" leadership is grounded in the concept of duty and personal responsibility, while "moral" leadership implies the development of virtue or moral character. Northhouse (2004) further conceptualized two domains of ethical leadership theory: theories about leaders' conduct, and theories about leaders' character. Ethical theories are about the actions of leaders and their consequences while ethical leadership is about who such people are as persons.

AUTHENTIC LEADERSHIP AND TRUST

Luthans and Avolio (2003) describe an authentic leader as one who is "genuine, reliable, trustworthy, real, and veritable". Thus, trustworthiness is proposed to be an intrinsic feature of authentic leadership. In this sense, trustworthiness is also viewed as an antecedent to authenticity. That is, those that are trustworthy are seen as more authentic. Therefore, perceived trust in the leader will perhaps lead to higher levels of leader authenticity as perceived by followers.

As noted earlier, Luthans and Avolio (2003) viewed the authentic leader as one who is trustworthy, genuine, real and reliable. Consistency, integrity, openness, promise fulfilment and receptivity to suggestions and input are core components of authenticity. In terms of cognitive trust, people base decisions on what they have deemed trustworthy or untrustworthy behaviour by an individual with whom they have interacted and the consistency of that behaviour. Thus, reliability and dependability are usually seen to be fundamental components contributing to cognitive trust levels (McAllister, 1995).

The issue of reliability and dependability have been central themes to the 'type' of trust that is relevant in transparent and authentic relationships because the authentic leader is based on values-driven behaviour and beliefs which are more stable and more easily adhered to on a consistent basis (Luthans & Avolio, 2003; Avolio *et al.*, 2004; Gardner *et al.*, 2005; Avolio & Luthans, 2006).

Authentic leadership theory proposes that leaders adopt a process of integrating one's inner life with the work that they do (Elsner, 2000) paying attention to what Palmer *et al.* (2000) has referred to as the "inner landscape." It strives to unite inner dreams with external realities and creates a complete, natural "one". Authentic leadership requires introspection, critical self-reviews of values and performance and emotional maturity.

AUTHENTIC *VERSUS* TRANSFORMATIONAL LEADERSHIP

The leadership studies in the past one decade have shifted its focus from the traditional or transactional models to theories that describe leaders who have extraordinary effects on both individuals and organizations (House & Shamir, 1993). Bass (1985) defines transformational leaders as those who motivate followers to perform beyond expectations by focusing attention on the higher order needs, promoting a climate of trust, and suggesting they transcend their own self-interests for that of the organization. The transformation process is accomplished through the promotion of ethics, values, and long-term goals. In general, followers' objectives are assessed, their needs are satisfied, and they are treated as valued employees within an organization. This connection between the leader and followers leads to increase in trust and motivation which in turn leads to increase in effort, creativity, and productivity over time (Bass, 1985).

Transformational leaders exhibit charisma (idealized influence), inspirational motivation, individualized consideration, and intellectual stimulation (Bass, 1985).

Idealized influence occur may leaders become role models to followers and they begin to trust, admire, and respect the leader, and never question their motives. The development of inspirational motivational behaviour occurs when leaders provide meaning and challenge to assign tasks through motivation and inspiration. Followers' enthusiasm and optimism is expressed which increase team spirit. Intellectual stimulation is defined as a behaviour that promotes creative and innovative thinking in any situation or problem by questioning personal and other's perspectives (Bass, 1985). Leaders encourage followers to think "outside the box" when solving problems. Individualized consideration relates to behaviour that promotes a supportive environment in which mentoring and coaching are performed based upon followers need. The leader may also act as a teacher, confidant, and/or facilitator.

In sum, transformational leaders develop relationships with subordinates that promote and inspire them to forgo their own self-interests for the collective good. Strong emphasis is placed upon followers' needs, values, and morals.

TRANSFORMATIONAL LEADERSHIP AND TRUST

Gillespie and Mann (2004) note that "whilst theories of transformational leadership differ in some specific leadership behaviours they identify, all theories posit trust as a central feature of the relationship such leaders have with their followers, and postulate that it is through followers' trust and respect in their leader that they are motivated to perform beyond expectations" (p. 590).

Dirks and Ferrin (2002) conducted a meta analysis of studies examining the relationship between trust and leadership and found a strong relationship between transformational leadership and trust. However, other empirical works on specific transformational leadership behaviour and trust have produced mixed results. Some transformational leadership practices such as providing an appropriate model, individualized support, and fostering group goals, are consistently positively associated with trust in leader (Butler, 1999; MacKenzie *et al.*, 2001, Podsakoff *et al.*, 1996, 1990). However, mixed results have been found for other transformational practices, such as articulating a vision, setting high expectations, and intellectual stimulations. For example, in a study of managers and professionals Podsakoff *et al.* (1996) reported no significant associations of these three variables with trust. In yet another study Podsakoff *et al.* (1996) found that high performance expectations and intellectual stimulation have negative influence on trust. In contrast to these findings, Butler (1999) report is that all six of these transformational leadership practices have a positive impact on trust in the leader in self-directed work teams.

These mixed findings on transformational leadership practices and employees' trust suggest the importance of contextual factors as well as the sample.

Authentic leadership is more similar to transformational leadership than to any other leadership style (Avolio & Gardner, 2005). However, the authentic leadership dimension of transparency does not appear to overlap much with the four behavioural dimensions of transformational leadership, namely idealized influence, inspirational motivation, individualized consideration, and intellectual stimulation. According to Avolio and Gardner (2005), relational transparency may be a focal point of authentic leadership.

AUTHENTIC *VERSUS* TRANSACTIONAL LEADERSHIP

The behavioural dimensions of transactional leadership, including initiating structure and active management-by-exception, do not overlap with the authentic leadership behavioural dimensions of transparency, altruistic action, and behavioural consistency in any way. Authentic leadership does not involve initiating structure or management-by-exception behaviours (Avolio *et al.*, 2004). However, the two approaches do not contradict each other and Avolio and Gardner (2005) suggested that it is possible to have a leader who is both authentic and transactional.

TRANSACTIONAL LEADERSHIP AND TRUST

Transactional leadership provides contingent reward on followers' performance. Unlike transformational leaders, they do not require a high level of trusting relationship with followers (Bass, 1985; Jung and Avolio, 2000). Jung and Avolio (2000) argue that transactional leadership, including contingent reward, is inadequate for building the level of trust to achieve the full potential of a workforce.

However, others (e.g., Shamir, 1995) argue that consistent honouring of transactional agreements characterized by contingent reward, can build team members trust with the leader. In their meta analysis, Dirk and Ferrin (2002) also report a moderate to strong relationship between transactional leadership and trust in leader. In conclusion, there are competing theories and mixed findings on the role of transactional leadership in building followers trust.

AUTHENTIC *VERSUS* LAISSEZ FAIRE LEADERSHIP

Authentic leadership and *laissez faire* leadership do not share any behavioural dimensions. *Laissez faire* leaders do not use transparency, altruistic actions, or behavioural consistency (Bass, 1998). Unlike with transactional or transformational leadership, a leader could not use this approach to leadership and at the same time use authentic leadership. The altruistic actions dimension of authentic leadership would necessitate that the leader take a more active role in leadership than a *laissez faire* leader provides.

HOW TO BUILD TRUST

Covey (2006) provides a list of 13 behaviours of effective leaders who build and maintain trust. They talk straight, show respect, create transparency, right wrongs, show loyalty, deliver results, get better, confront reality, clarify expectation, practice accountability, listen first, keep commitments, and extend trust first. However, these behaviours need to be balanced. For example, talk straight need to be balanced show respect. Any behaviour pushed to the extreme becomes a liability. The job of a leader is to extend trust first—not a blind trust but a smart trust with clear expectations and strong accountability.

One can build trusting relationship with his/her coworkers by practicing authentic leadership which has the elements of transparency, acting consistently on espoused values, and becoming a role model. The leader deals openly with everyone as he/she knows that hidden agendas erode people's trust. Such leader considers all points of view and sees the situation from other person's perspective. He/she may not agree with others point of view but shows respect to others views. Keeping promises is yet another important characteristic that build trust. Such a leader would never say one thing and do another. If the promise cannot be fulfilled the person would explain why and not hide the fact that he/she could not keep his/her words. Finally, such a leader care about his subordinates. A relationship based on care builds trust and the subordinates will try to come to the expectations of the leader.

SUMMING UP

Trust is going down almost everywhere—in our personal relationships and in our culture and organizations. We are experiencing a crisis of confidence in the financial market. The leaders who were trusted turned out to be offenders. Trust means having a confidence in the character and competence of an individual, believing that personal vulnerabilities will not result into losses, and opportunities provided will not be misused. Leadership effectiveness requires subordinates' trust. Of late, leadership literature has recognized the importance of this construct and have emphasized on moral and ethical aspects. The two essential elements that build trust, namely, character and competence have been dealt with in contemporary leadership literature using different terms, the essence of which points to the role of trust in leadership effectiveness.

REFERENCES

Atkinson, S. (2004). Senior management relationship and trust: An exploratory study. *Journal of Managerial Psychology*, 19, 579-587.

Avery, G.C. (2004). *Understanding Leadership*. Thousand Oaks, CA: Sage Publications.

Avolio, B., Bass, B., and Jung, D. (1999). Re-examining the components of transformational and transactional leadership using the Multifactor Leadership Questionnaire. *Journal of Occupational and Organizational Psychology*, 72(4), 441-462.

Avolio, B.J., and Gardner, W.L. (2005). Authentic leadership development: Getting to the root of positive forms of leadership. *Leadership Quarterly*, 16(3), 315-338.

Avolio, B.J., Gardner, W.L., Walumbwa, F.O., Luthans, F., and May, D.R. (2004). Unlocking the mask: A look at the process by which authentic leaders impact follower attitudes and behaviours. *Leadership Quarterly*, 15(6), 801-823.

Avolio, B.J. and Luthans, F. (2006). *The High Impact Leader: Moments Matter in Accelerating Authentic Leadership Development*. McGraw-Hill, New York.

Bass, B.M. (1960). *Leadership, Psychology, and Organizational Behaviour*, New York: Sharper.

Bass, B.M. (1985). Leadership: Good, better, best. *Organizational Dynamics*, 13(3), 26-40.

Bass, B.M. (1990). *Bass and Stogdill's Handbook of Leadership*. New York: Free Press.

Bass, B.M. (1998), *Transformational leadership: Industrial, Military, and Educational Impact*: London: Lawrence Erlbaum Associates Publishers.

Bass, B.M. and Avolio, B.J. (1994). Improving Organizational Effectiveness through Transformational Leadership. Thousand Oaks, CA: Sage.

Bennis, W.G., and Nanus, B. (1985). *Leaders: The Strategies for Taking Charge*. New York: Harper and Row.

Boon, S.D. and Holmes, J.G. (1991). The dynamics of interpersonal trust: Resolving uncertainty in the face of risk. In R.A. Hinde and Groebel (eds.), *Cooperation and Prosocial Behaviour*, Cambrigde UK: Cambridge University Press.

Butler, J.K. (1999). Trust expectations, information sharing, climate of trust, and negotiation effectiveness and efficiency. *Group and Organizational Management*, 24, 217-238.

Covey, S.M.R. (2006). *The Speed of Trust*. New York: Free Press.

Cropanzano, R. and Mitchell, M.S. (2005). Social exchange theory: An interdisciplinary review. *Journal of Management*, 31, 874-900.

Dansereau, F., Graen, G., and Haga, W.J. (1975). A vertical dyad linkage approach to leadership within formal organizations: A longitudinal investigation of the role making process. *Organizational Behaviour and Decision Making Processes*, 13, 46-78.

Dirks, K.T., and Ferrin, D.L. (2002). Trust in leadership: Meta-analytic findings and implications for research and practice. *Journal of Applied Psychology*, 87, 611-628.

Droullard, S.E. and Klieiner, B.H. (1996). Good leadership. *Management Development Review*, 9 (5), 30-33.

Elsner, P.A. (2000). *Authenticity and Leadership: Integrating Our Inner Lives with Our Work*. [On-line]. Available at: www.paulelsner.com March 13, 2001.

Erickson, T.J. (2005). Testimony submitted before the U.S. Senate Committee on Health, Education, Labour and Pensions, May 26. Fairholm, G. (1994). *Leadership and the Culture of Trust*. Westport, CT: Praeger.

Fleishman, E., and Harris, E.F. (1962). Patterns of leadership behaviour related to employee grievances and turnover, *Personnel Psychology*, 15, 43-56.

Fritz, J. (1997). Men's and women's organizational peer relationships: a comparison. *The Journal of Business Communication*, 34, 27-46.

Gardner, W.L., Avolio, B.J., and Walumbwa, F.O. (Eds.) (2005), *Authentic Leadership Theory and Practice: Origins, Effects and Development*. Oxford, UK: Elsevier Science.

Gardner, W.L., and Schermerhorn, J.R. Jr. (2005). Unleashing Individual Potential: Performance gains through positive organizational behaviour and authentic leadership. *Organizational Dynamics*, August.

George, B. (2003). *Authentic leadership: Rediscovering the secrets to creating lasting value*. San Francisco, CA: Jossey-Bass.

Gillespie, N.A. and Mann, L. (2004). Transformational leadership and shared values. *Journal of Managerial Psychology*, 19 (6), 588-607.

Harter, J.K., Schmidt, F.L., and Keyes, C.L. (2002). Well-being in the workplace and its relationship to business outcomes: A review of the Gallup studies. In C.L. Keyes and J. Haidt (Eds.), *Flourishing: The positive person and the good life* (pp. 205-224). Washington, DC: APA.

Harvey, S., Kelloway, E.K., and Duncan-Leiper, L.(2003). Trust in management as a buffer of the relationships between overload and strain. *Journal of Occupational Health Psychology*, 8 (4), 306-315.

Hogan, R., Curphy, G., and Hogan, J. (1994). What we know about leadership: Effectiveness and personality. *American Psychologist*, 49, 493-504.

House, R.J. and Shamir, B. (1993). Towards the integration of transformational, charismatic and visionary theories. In Chemers, M.M. and Ayam, R. (Eds.), *Leadership Theory and Research: Perspectives and Directions*, Sydney: Academic Press.

Hosmer, L.T. (1995). Trust: The connecting link between organizational theory and philosophical ethics. *Academy of Management Review*, April, p. 393.

Johnson-George, C. and Swapt, W. (1982). Measurement of specific interpersonal trust: Construction and validation of a scale to assess trust in specific other. *Journal of Personality and Social Psychology*, p. 1306.

Jones, D. (2003). Do you trust your CEO? *USA Today*, February 12, p. 7B.

Jung, D.I. and Avolio, B.J. (2000). Opening the black box: An experimental investigation of the mediating effects of trust and values congruence on transformational and transactional leadership. *Journal of Organizational Behaviour*, 949-964.

Kilpatric, S.A. and Locke, E.A. (1996). Direct and indirect effects of three core charismatic leadership components on performance and attitudes. *Journal of Applied Psychology*, 81, 36-51.

Kernis, M. (2003). Toward a conceptualization of optimal self-esteem. *Psychological Inquiry*, 14, 1-26.

Luthans, F. and Peterson S.J. (2002). Employee engagement and manager self efficacy: Implications for managerial effectiveness and development. *The Journal of Management Development*, 21(5/6), 376-387.

Luthans, F. and Youssef, C.M. (2004). Human, Social, and Now Positive Psychological Capital Management: Investing in People for Competitive Advantage. *Organizational Dynamics*, 33(2), 143-160.

Luthans, F., and Avolio, B.J. (2003). Authentic leadership development. In K.S. Cameron, J.E. Dutton, and R.E. Quinn (Eds.). *Positive organizational scholarship*: 241-261. San Francisco: Barrett-Koehler.

Luthans, F., Luthans, K.W., Hodgetts, R.M., and Luthans, B.C. (2001). Positive approach to leadership (PAL): Implications for today's organizations. *Journal of Leadership and Organizational Studies*, 8(2), 3-20.

Mackenzie, S.B. Podsakoff, P.M. and Rich, G.A. (2001). Transformational and transactional leadership and salesperson performance, *Journal of the Academy of Marketing Services*, 29 (2), 115-134.

May, D.R., Chan, A., Hodges, T., and Avolio, B.J. (2003). Developing the moral component of authentic leadership. *Organizational Dynamics*, 32: 247-260.

Mayer, R.C., Davis, J.H., and Schoorman, F.D. (1995). An integrative model of organizational trust. *Academy of Management Review*, 20, 709-735.

McAllister, D.J. (1995). Affect and cognition-based trust as foundations for interpersonal cooperation in organisations. *Academy of Management Journal*, 38, 24-59.

Michie, S., and Gooty, J. (2005). Values, emotions, and authenticity: Will the real leader please stand up? *Leadership Quarterly*, 16(3), 441-457.

Nanus, B. (1989). *The Leader's Edge: The Seven Keys to Leadership in a Turbulent World.* Chicago, IL: Contemporary Books.

Northhouse, P.G. (2004). *Leadership: Theory and Practice*, (3rd Ed.), Sage: London.

Palmer, B., Walls, M., Burgess, Z., and Stough, C. (2000). Emotional intelligence and effective leadership. *Leadership and Organizational Development Journal*. 22 (1), 5-10.

Podsakoff, P.M. Mackenzie, S.B. and Bommer, W.H. (1996). Transformational leader behaviour and substitutes for leadership as determinants of employee satisfaction, commitment, trust, and OCB, *Journal of Management*, 22 (2), 259-298.

Podsakoff, P.M., Mackenzie, S.B., Moorman, R.H., and Fetter, R. (1990). Transformational leader Behaviours and their effects on followers' trust in leader, satisfaction, and organizational citizenship behaviours. *Leadership Quarterly*, 1, 107-142.

Rhodes, H.J. (2007). *Confronting the Challenges of Student Engagement: A Case Study of a School-Based Intervention*. Dissertation, Pardee Rand Graduate School.

Robbins, S.P. and Judge T.A. (2007). *Organizational Behaviour* (12th Ed.). Pearson Education, Prentice Hall.

Rousseau, D., Sitkin, S., Burt, R., and Camerer, C. (1998). Not so different after all: A cross-discipline view of trust. *Academy of Management Review*, 23, 393-404.

Schindler, P.L. and Thomas, C.C. (1993). The structure of interpersonal trust in the workplace, *Psychological Reports*, October, pp. 563-573.

Shamir, B. (1995). Social distance and charisma; theoretical notes and an exploratory study, *Leadership Quarterly*, 6 (1), 19-47.

Sinha, J.B.P. (1980). *The Nurturant—Task Leader*, New Delhi: Concept Publishing Company Pvt. Ltd.

CHAPTER ELEVEN

Organizational Commitment and Job Involvement as Moderators of Relationship between Psychological Climate and Job Satisfaction

Kailash B.L. Srivastava and Soumendu Biswas

INTRODUCTION

Organizations in India have been exposed to multinational cultures since the opening up of the economy a decade back. One of the more consistent observers of this globalised influence of the New Economic Policy of 1991 and its consequence with reference to changes in Indian organizations and their management practices has been Jai B.P. Sinha. In a relevant study Sinha (2000) referred to the fact that in the face of trans national influences, Indian organizations while adopting contemporary management techniques and practices retained their salience in terms of organizational culture. Furthermore, Sinha (2001) referred to the idea, which addressed normative issues with reference to Indian organizations and leadership values and practices. These ideas were further reinforced in the study conducted by Sinha (1999).

The basis of the current study is rooted in the studies of Jai B.P. Sinha (Sinha, 1997; Sinha & Singh, 1995) which discuss the various facets of human resource management imperatives and their impact on employees' satisfaction level. With reference to the predictors of job satisfaction of employees in Indian organizations, Sinha and Singh focused on organizational climate while predicting an employee's overall organizational satisfaction. Based on this study, the current paper examined the impact of routine work environment or perceptions about the psychological climate by employees on the extent to which he or she is satisfied with his or her job.

Climate, whether organizational or psychological, has traditionally been operationalized in terms of individual perceptions about organizational attributes (Joyce & Slocum, 1984). Jones and James (1979: 205) have defined psychological climate as "an individual's cognitively based description of the situation involving psychological processing of specific perceptions into more abstract depictions of psychologically meaningful influences in the situation and which tends to be most closely related to situational characteristics that have relatively direct and immediate ties to individual experiences." Thus, it has been conceptualized as an individual's phenomenological experience wherein he or she processes and abstracts situations to cognitive map of their work environment and in doing so they are evaluating the environment and making sense out of such valuation (James, James & Ashe, 1991).

In the context of the current study, the dimensions of psychological climate developed by Brown and Leigh (1996) were found to be appropriate in capturing the relevant facets of psychological climate and relating it to the outcome variables. The dimensions of psychological climate considered are supportive management, role clarity, contribution, recognition, self-expression and challenge (Brown & Leigh, 1996: 367).

Literature related to psychological climate (James, Hater, Gent & Bruni, 1978; Leigh, Lucas & Woodman, 1988) indicates that individual attitudes and behaviour are its important consequences. Some of these consequences are employee attitudes, motivation, and performance (Field & Abelson, 1982; James, Hater, Gent & Bruni, 1978; Lawler, Hall, & Oldham, 1974; Litwin & Stringer, 1968; Payne & Pugh, 1976). Parker, Baltes, Young, Huff, Altmann, Lacost and Roberts (2003) clearly mention that psychological climate as a construct has been found to directly impact numerous individual-related outcomes. Brown and Leigh (1996) have established that at a given level, psychological climate has a direct and significant antecedent effect on job involvement, and organizational commitment.

H1. A favourable psychological climate would predict a greater degree of organizational commitment.

H2. A favourable psychological climate would predict a greater degree of job involvement.

Commitment of an individual at the workplace is reflected in various ways such as commitment to the organization called organizational commitment, commitment to the workgroup, to another individual, to profession or to the union the individual belongs to (Meyer & Allen, 1997). Of particular interest in the context of the present study is the construct of organizational commitment. Organizational commitment finds mention in literature in relation to variables such as personal characteristics of the employee such as job attachment and other role-related factors, job characteristics, professional behaviour and other work experiences (Hrebiank & Alutto, 1972; Koch & Steers, 1978; Morris & Koch, 1979; Steers, 1977; Welsch & La Van, 1981). A recurring criterion of organizational commitment appears to be job satisfaction. Based on the findings from literature, we posit the following hypothesis:

H3: Higher the level of an employee's organizational commitment more would he or she be satisfied with his or her job.

Job involvement is an attitudinal variable that depends on interactions of individual differences of perceptions of work environment and personality characteristics (Ruh, White & Wood, 1975). Conceptualized thus, job involvement appears to be a construct that follows directly from the way individuals are affected by their work environment and interpersonal relationships at work (Ruh, White & Wood, 1975) and thus it may be theoretically conceivable that job involvement affects job satisfaction.

H4: Higher the level of an employee's job involvement more would he or she be satisfied with his or her job.

Job satisfaction is a multidimensional construct manifesting the emotional evaluation of individuals regarding their expectations and how well they have been met. Schnake (1983) conceptualized three dimensions of job satisfaction representing intrinsic, extrinsic and social aspects of job satisfaction. In effect, Schnake's dimensions of job satisfaction cover cognitive and affective responses made by individuals in connection to their work environment.

METHOD

SAMPLE

357 individuals from various firms in India representing the manufacturing as well as the service sector provided responses to a standardized questionnaire

dealing with psychological climate, organizational commitment, job involvement and job satisfaction. Ratings were made by the respondents.

MEASURES

Psychological climate was measured using the psychological climate measure reported by Brown and Leigh (1996) comprising 6 factors, namely supportive management, role clarity, contribution, recognition, self-expression and challenge.

Organizational commitment was measured using the 23-item organizational commitment scale as developed and reported by Meyer and Allen (1997) taking into account affective, continuance and normative commitment.

Job involvement was measured using 6 items of the Job Attitude Scale as developed and reported by Lawler and Hall (1970).

Job satisfaction was measured using the 11-item Job Satisfaction Instrument as reported by Schnake (1983). The scale reported three dimensions of job satisfaction, namely extrinsic satisfaction, intrinsic satisfaction and social satisfaction.

RESULTS

The data were analyzed to examine the mean, SD, and inter-correlation among the relevant constructs. First, the Cronbach alpha values for the scales used for measuring the various constructs reflect a high score on the reliability quotient. Correlations among the relevant constructs are also representative of a high level of significance, with all of them displaying correlations at levels equal to or above the 99 per cent level.

PATH ANALYSIS

Path analysis applying structural equation methods were conducted using AMOS 4.0 (Arbuckle & Wothke, 1999). Since the data used for analysis in this study were univariately normal, maximum likelihood estimation (MLE) algorithm was used to determine the fit indices.

The fit-indices used for analyzing the current data were the goodness-of-fit index (GFI), the Adjusted goodness-of-fit index (AGFI), the normed chi-square (normed χ^2), the Tucker-Lewis Index (TLI), and the root mean square error of approximation (RMSEA). This was because they were found to be most relevant for the current study. According to Hair, Andersen, Tatham and Black (1998) the recommended fit value for GFI AGFI and TLI are equal to or greater than .90. With regard to RMSEA a value of .00 indicates perfect fit and values below .08 are considered good fits. Finally, AMOS 4.0 reports normed χ^2 as CMIN/d.f. While Hair, Andersen, Tatham and Black (1998) recommend a value of $1.0 \leq$ normed $\chi^2 \leq 3.0$, the current paper finds the analyzed normed χ^2 well within the recommended range.

For the proposed model as depicted in Figure 11.1 the normed χ^2 value is 1.84 indicating a value well within the acceptable range. The GFI being .96, AGFI value at .92 and the TLI value at .96 indicate an excellent model fit. In the same lines, the RMSEA was found to be .05, well below the acceptable range of .08.

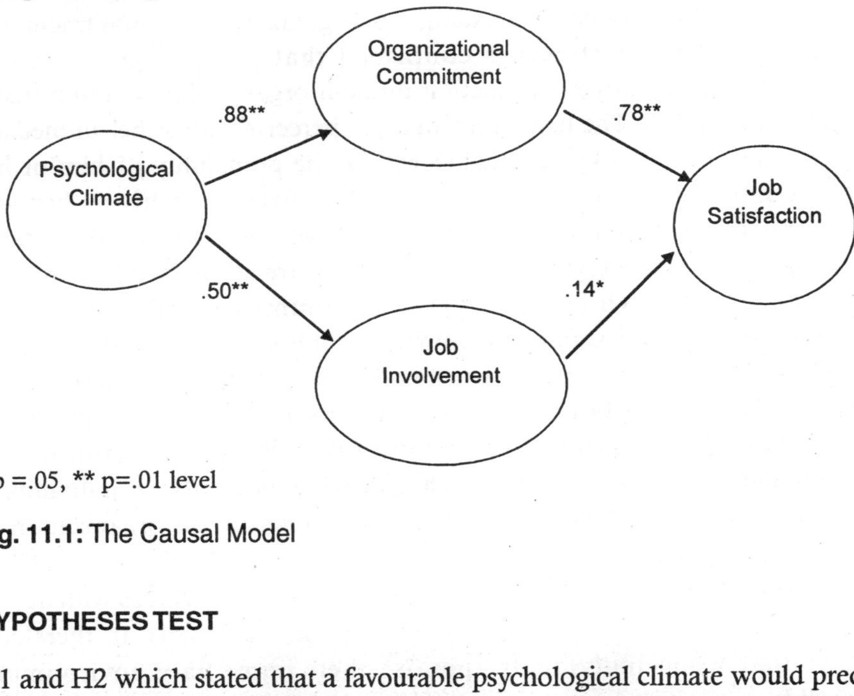

* p =.05, ** p=.01 level

Fig. 11.1: The Causal Model

HYPOTHESES TEST

H1 and H2 which stated that a favourable psychological climate would predict a greater degree of organizational commitment and a favourable psychological climate would predict a greater degree of job involvement were found to be acceptable based on the standardized regression estimates which predicted that both organizational commitment (Standardized $\beta = .88$, $p \leq .01$) and job involvement (Standardized $\beta = .50$, $p \leq .01$) were significantly associated with psychological climate. The acceptance of this hypothesis states that an individual's perception of his/her day-to-day work environment has a significant bearing on the involvement and commitment to the organization. Psychological climate is an individual level variable which defer from individual to individual depending upon how he or she perceives the work environment.

H3 stated that higher the level of an employee's organizational commitment more would he or she be satisfied with his or her job (Standardized $\beta = .88$, $p \leq .01$) and H4 which stated that a higher level of an employee's job involvement would lead to greater level of his or her job satisfaction was also justified based on the standardized regression estimates which were .78 ($p \leq .01$) and .14 ($p \leq .05$) respectively.

DISCUSSION

The current study focused upon examining the impact of psychological climate on job satisfaction through the mediation of organizational commitment and job involvement. The findings confirmed that psychological climate significantly influences job satisfaction through organizational commitment and job involvement. The better an employee perceives his or her immediate environment at the workplace, higher will be the probability of him or her being committed to the organization and involved with his or her job. Organizations can, therefore, help provide employees with a more comfortable and congenial working environment so that they are at ease while at work.

Significantly, while organizational commitment as well as job involvement both had significant impact on job satisfaction, the level of significance of job involvement was found to be lesser than organizational commitment. This may be because while job involvement is essentially related to how motivated a person is to perform his or her task, organizational commitment is a broader construct that includes not only an individual's attachment to his or her daily chore, but also to others in the organization as a social behaviour. Thus, the results implies that line management and HR department should work in tandem in order to provide employees with day to day environment that is viewed favourably by the individuals. It, therefore, follows that when individuals appraise their immediate environment favourably, a positive impact is created on their interest in their jobs and dedication to the organization. Employees then come to work voluntarily with appropriate level of enthusiasm. Incidences of absenteeism, loitering, and social loafing gets reduced to a large extent.

Our study points at the impact of various dimensions of psychological climate affecting extrinsic, intrinsic and social satisfaction of people on the job. One may infer that better introduction to the organization at the time of induction would perhaps help newcomers adjust well to the environment and improve his or her perception of the day-to-day work environment. It is suggested that future research in this area may focus not only on the overall association among the variables but also investigate the dimension that are most well connected with each other. This would help managers generate more practical ideas that would help improve employees' psychological climate and by extension the satisfaction they derive from their job.

REFERENCES

Arbuckle, J.L. and Wothke, W. (1999). *Amos 4.0 User's Guide*. Small Waters Corporation, Chicago IL.

Brown, S.P. and Leigh, T.W. (1996). A new look at psychological climate and its relationship to job involvement, effort, and performance. *Journal of Applied Psychology*, 81: 358-368.

Dieterly, D. and Schneider, B. (1974). The effect of organizational environments and perceived power and climate: A laboratory study. *Organizational Behaviour and Human Performance*, 11: 316-337.

Field, R. and Abelson, M. (1982). A reconceptualization and proposed model. *Human Relations*, 35: 181-201.

Hair, J.F.H., Anderson, R.E., Tatham, R.L. and Black, W.C. (1998). *Multivariate Data Analysis* (5th Ed.). Engelwood Cliffs, NJ: Prentice Hall.

Hrebiank, L.G. and Alutto, J.A. (1972). Personal and role-related factors in the development of organizational commitment. *Administrative Science Quarterly*, 17: 555-573.

James, L.R., Hater, J.J., Gent, M.J., and Bruni, J.R. (1978). Psychological climate: Implications from cognitive social learning theory and interactional psychology. *Personnel Psychology*, 31: 783-813.

James, L.R., James, L.A., and Ashe, D.K. (1991). The meaning of organizations: The role of cognition and values. In B. Schneider (Ed.), *Organizational climate and culture* (pp. 40-84). San Francisco: Jossey-Bass.

Jones, A.P. and James, L.R. (1979). Psychological climate: Dimensions and relationships of individual and aggregated work environment perceptions. *Organizational Behaviour and Human Performance*, 23: 201-250.

Joyce, W.F. and Slocum, J.W. Jr. (1984). Collective climate: Agreement as a basis for defining aggregate climates in organizations. *Academy of Management Journal*, 27: 721-742.

Koch, J.T. and Steers, R.M. (1978). Job attachment, satisfaction and turnover among public sector employees. *Journal of Vocational Behaviour*, 12: 119-128.

Lawler III, E.E. and Hall, D.T. (1970). Relationship of job characteristic to job involvement, satisfaction and intrinsic motivation. *Journal of Applied Psychology*, 54: 305-312.

Lawler, E.E., Hall, D.T., and Oldham, G.R. (1974). Organizational climate: Relationship to organizational structure, process and performance. *Organizational Behaviour and Performance*, 11(1): 138-155.

Leigh, J.H., Lucas, G.H., Jr. and Woodman, R.W. (1988). Effects of perceived organizational factors on role stress-job attitude relationships. *Journal of Management*, 14(1): 41-58.

Litwin, G. and Stringer, R. (1968). Motivation and organizational climate. Boston: Harvard University Press.

Meyer, J.P. and Allen, N.J. (1997). *Commitment in the workplace: Theory, research and application*. Thousand Oaks, California: Sage Publications.

Morris, J.H. and Koch, J.L. (1979). Impacts of role perceptions on organizational commitment, job involvement and psychosomatic illness among three vocational groupings. *Journal of Vocational Behaviour*, 15, 88-101.

Parker, C.P., Baltes, B.B., Young, S.Y., Huff, J.W., Altmann, R.A., LaCost, H.A., and Roberts, J.E. (2003). Relationships between psychological climate perceptions and work outcomes: A meta-analytic review. *Journal of Organizational Behaviour*, 24(4): 389-417.

Payne, R.L. and Pugh, D.S. (1976). Organizational structure and climate. In M.D. Dunnette (Ed.), *Handbook of industrial and organizational psychology* (pp. 1125-1173). Chicago: Rand-McNally.

Ruh, R.A., White, J. and Wood, R.R. (1975). Job involvement, values, personal background, participation in decision making, and job attitudes. *Academy of Management Journal*. 18(2): 300-312.

Schnake, M.E. (1983). An empirical assessment of the effects of affective response in the measurement of organizational climate. *Personnel Psychology*, 36: 791-807.

Sinha, J.B.P. (1997). Human resources in work cultures. *Indian Journal of Industrial Relations*, 33(2): 147-167.

Sinha, J.B.P. (1999). Confluence of cultural and multinational influences: A new paradigm for organizational behaviour. *Indian Journal of Industrial Relations*, 35(1): 27-42.

Sinha, J.B.P. (2000). Integrative indigenous management in India: Practices and prospects. *Indian Journal of Industrial Relations*, 35(4): 439-460.

Sinha, J.B.P. (2001). Evolving perspectives on Indian organization and leadership. *Indian Journal of Industrial Relations*, 36(4): 428-443.

Sinha, J.B.P. and Singh, S. (1995). Employees satisfaction and its organizational predictors. *Indian Journal of Industrial Relations*, 31(2): 135-152.

Steers, R.M. (1977). Antecedents and outcomes of organizational commitment. *Administrative Science Quarterly*, 22: 46-56.

Welsch, H.P., and La Van, H. (1981). Interrelationships between organizational commitment and job characteristics, job satisfaction, professional behaviour, and organizational climate. *Human Relations*, 34(12): 1079-1089.

CHAPTER TWELVE

The Impact of Emotional Intelligence on Self-Rated Performance and Self-Efficacy Perception

Ajay K Jain

INTRODUCTION

The study examines the predictive ability of emotional intelligence (EI) in predicting the self-rated performance and self-efficacy perception. The literature shows that self-rated performance and self-efficacy are conceptualized as the part of self-management perception and practices in organizations which helps in increasing the discipline and attendance at work (e.g., Castaneda, Kolenko, & Aldag; 1999; Latham & Frayne, 1989). Self-rated performance and self-efficacy perception are taken as dependent variables within the assumptions of positive psychology. Positive psychology is a movement started by Seligman and Csikszentmihalyi (2000). At micro level of analysis, the movement focuses on the study and application of positively oriented human resource strengths, and psychological capacities that can be measured, developed, and effectively managed for performance improvement in today's workplace (Luthans, 2002). Overall EI, self-rated performance and self-efficacy perception can be considered as part of self-development process in organizational context that helps in increasing one's ability in managing relationships with the psychosocial environment of the person.

EMOTIONS IN ORGANIZATIONS

The study of emotions at the work setting has a long history (Brief & Weiss,

2002). However, organizational behaviour researchers have neglected the study of emotions at workplace in traditional management and organizational behaviour literature. The inattention to the emotional sub-context of organization is largely due to the long standing view that people, who are ruled primarily by their emotions, were considered negative and irrational. Meanwhile the effects of negative emotions (anger, anxiety, depression etc.) on work behaviour were particularly addressed in literature. Only a few writers worked on positive emotions, like joy at work (Munsterberg, 1912) and zest (Hersey, 1951). In post-1990s era, psychologists have begun to pay greater attention to positive emotions, like fun at work (Abramis, 1987), mechanisms of pride (Frese, 1990), job enjoyment and happiness (Isen & Baron, 1991; Argyle & Martin, 1991). A mild shift in positive mood can, they contend, improve perception and decision making in face to face bargaining (Carnevale & Isen, 1986), performance appraisal (Brief & Motowidlo, 1986), absenteeism and labour turnover (George, 1991). The benefits of the "feel good" factor are echoed by Harrison (1987) and Peters and Austin (1985), who say that love, empathy, verve, zest and enthusiasm are the *sine qua non* of managerial success and organizational excellence.

The starting point for modern research on emotions in organizations seems to have been the sociologist Hochschild's (1983) seminal book on "Emotional Labour: The Managed Heart". This work inspired Rafaeli and Sutton's (1987) and Sutton and Rafaeli (1988) that focused the attention of management scholar on emotional expression as part of the work role. Subsequently, trait affectivity (George, 1991; George & Brief, 1992), mood effects on behaviour (Isen & Baron, 1991) were highly influential topics in turning scholar's attention to the hotter and more transient side of affective experience at workplace.

EMOTIONAL INTELLIGENCE

The work of Gardner (1983), Goleman (1995, 1998), and Baron (1997) led to the development of the construct of EI at workplace. Mayor and Salovey (1997) defined EI as ability to perceive emotions, to access and generate emotions so as to assist thought, to understand emotions and emotional knowledge and to reflectively regulate emotions so as to promote emotional and intellectual growth. This definition combines the ideas that emotions make thinking more intelligent and that thinking intelligently about emotions. Both connect intelligence and emotions. The concept of EI reflects a good synergy between two spheres of human personality, i.e., cognitive and affective, which were studied in isolation in earlier psychological literature. Goleman defined EI as the capacity for recognizing of our own emotions and of others, for motivating ourselves and for managing emotions well in us and in our relationships. More recently, Goleman (2000) defined EI as the ability to manage ourselves and our relationships effectively, which consists of four fundamental capabilities: Self-awareness, Self-management, Social Awareness, and Social Skills. Goleman's effort has popularized the concept of EI among practitioners and managers.

BarOn (1997) has developed the first paper pencil test to measure the concept of EI. He argued that EI is concerned with understanding oneself and others relating to people, and adapting to and coping with the immediate surroundings, which increases one's ability to be more successful in dealing with one's environmental demands. The BarOn EQ-i is a self-report measure of non-cognitive (emotional, social and personal) intelligence, composed of 133 brief items. BarOn has coined the term "Emotional Quotient". In the present work, we have used the BarOn's EQ-i to measure the concept of EI in Indian work context. In brief, EI can be described as cognitively controlled affective processes in enhancing one's effectiveness and satisfaction with his/her psychosocial environment. Therefore, EI can be considered as part of human development process. Jain (2007) found that EI is more strongly related with self-management perceptions and practices compare to impression management behaviour. It means EI acts in improving positive organizational behaviour in terms of self-management behaviour and reduces the negative organizational behaviour in terms of impression management behaviour. Effective self-management appears to offer potential benefits to individual employees and organizations. In a recent research, Jain and Sinha (2006) have found that self-management is positively related with in-role behaviour and organizational citizenship behaviour.

EI AND OUTCOMES

Scientists in various countries, e.g. India are exploring the relationship of EI with job satisfaction, personal effectiveness, general health, turnover intention, commitment, trust, organizational effectiveness etc. (e.g. Jain & Sinha, 2005; Sinha & Jain, 2004). Other recent Western studies have found EI as an important tool related to positive outcomes such as pro-social behaviour parental warmth, positive family and peer relations (Mayer, Caruso, & Salovey, 1999; Salovey, Mayer, Caruso, & Lopes, 2001). In addition, studies showed that lower EI is related to negative outcomes, including illegal drug and alcohol use, deviant behaviour, and poor relations with friends (Brackette, Mayer, & Warner, in press). The underlying assumption of all these studies is that EI is a powerful tool for people to enhance their intrapersonal and interpersonal effectiveness both at work and at home. Therefore, the present study conceptualized EI as an antecedent variable which may predict the self-management behaviour to promote self-development.

EI, Self-rated Performance and Self-efficacy: Self-rated performance is defined as perception of one's success and satisfaction in his/her current job and is measured by rating about his/her task behaviour. Compare to supervisory rating here, employee himself is thought to be the best judge of his/her performance at workplace. This component is concerned with the evaluation of one's performance in relation to self-set standards and goals. Those who value self-performance perception, administer self-reward contingent on their performing certain classes of responses, which they come to value as an index of personal merit. Such people may set for themselves very explicit standards of achievement, and failure to meet those standards are not considered deserving of self-reward and may even elicit self-punitive responses. They may reward themselves generously on those occasions on which they attain self-imposed standards.

It has been seen that job performance is determined by the technical proficiency (Campbell, McCloy, Oppler, & Sager, 1993). Nevertheless, Goleman (1998) stated that IQ and technical skills are important but emotional intelligence is the *sine qua non* of leadership. Research shows that IQ alone explains little of achievement at work or in life. In this regard, Goleman commented that for performance in all jobs, in every field, emotional competence is twice as important as purely cognitive abilities. For success at highest levels in leadership positions, emotional intelligence accounts for virtually the entire advantage. Ashkansay (2003) showed that interest and knowledge of EI predicted the team performance and individual performance for a group of 144 students. In a study of 358 managers in J&J, Cavalo and Brienza (2002) found that highest performing managers had significantly higher emotional competencies. In study of top management executives, Stein (2002) found that 76 high performing CEO's have rated themselves high on empathy self-regard and assertiveness. Sitarenios (2000) has assessed the EI skills of 622 high, medium and low performers and result showed that high and low performers differ significantly in terms of social responsibility, optimism, independence, self-actualization and emotional self-awareness. Based on above body of literature, it has been thought that EI will enhance one's confidence in his/her ability to accomplish the work and rate himself/herself high on the job.

The other dependent variable taken in this study is Self-efficacy. Self-efficacy is a key concept in Bandura's (1986) Social Cognitive Theory. Bandura defined self-efficacy as one's judgement of how well one can execute courses of action required to deal with prospective situations. Self-efficacy includes one's estimate of one's capacity to perform at a certain level all factors considered (e.g. ability, effort, adaptability, attributions, situational factors etc.). Self-efficacy is measured by how well individual rates his/her confidence in attaining the different levels of performance. Locke, Fredrick, Lee and Bobko (1984) found self-efficacy was positively related to performance, the higher the efficacy leads to higher level of performance. Recent evidence indicates that individual with strong self-efficacy reacted less negatively to the strain created by long work hours and work overload than did those with low level of self-efficacy (Jex & Bliese, 1999).

In difficult situations, it is found that people with low self-efficacy are more likely to lessen their effort or give up altogether while those with high self-efficacy will try harder to master the challenge (Stajkovic & Luthans, 1998; Bandura, 2004). In addition, individuals in high self-efficacy seem to respond to negative feedback with increased efforts and motivation, while those low in self-efficacy are likely to lessen their effort when given negative feedback (Bandura & Cervone, 1986). Based on above evidences, it has been conceptualized that EI will enhance individual's belief in his/her capability and capacity carrying out a job successfully.

A relevant research question for the study is framed like this; does EI, as potential for performance, influence the self-rated performance and self-efficacy perception? Based on the above analysis, one can derive the hypothesis that EI will have a positive influence on the perception of self-rated performance and self-efficacy. The conceptual scheme of the present study is depicted in Figure 12.1.

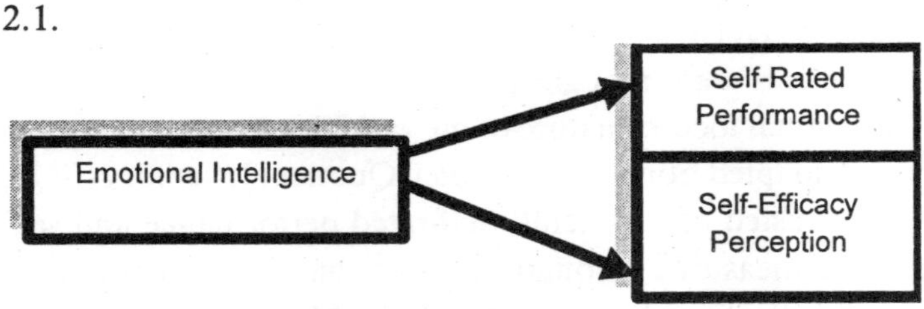

Fig. 12.1: The Conceptual Scheme of the Study

Figure 12.1 is representing EI as independent variable and self-rated performance and self-efficacy perception as dependent variables. It is conjectured that EI will have positive impact on self-rated performance and self-efficacy perception.

METHOD

PARTICIPANTS AND PROCEDURE

The sample consisted of 250 middle-level executives from four plants of two-wheeler (scooter and motorcycle) manufacturing organizations. The organizations, within the private sector, were located in five different cities of north India. The employees were male, in the 25 to 45 year age group, who had spent at least one year in the same organization. Almost all of them were married and had a graduate degree or diploma in engineering. India being a culturally diverse and large country, the data were collected from north Indian organizations to control the cultural differences in work values and physical characteristics of the respondents.

The data were collected by administering questionnaires mainly during office hours with the consent of both the relevant representatives of the employer as well as the respondents. The questionnaires were in English, adapted to suit the target group by slightly modifying the language or the response categories as needed, and were validated in the Indian cultural context. The participants were chosen randomly from each organization and belonged to different departments of the organization. Most of the participants showed their willingness to participate in the study after a short meeting. The data for the study reported in this article were collected as part of the larger study.

MEASURES

Questionnaire measures were used to obtain data on the three variables included in the study, EI, self-rated performance and self-efficacy perception. Self-report measures were thought to be a useful method to collect the data because of individual focused nature of the variables. EI was measured through a questionnaire adapted from the Emotional Quotient Inventory (EQ-i, BarOn, 1997) which consisted of 133-items. Self-rated performance and self-efficacy perception were measured through the questionnaire consisting of 8 items and 4 items respectively and which are borrowed from the work of Castaneda, Kolenko, and Aldag (1999).

The measures used in this study, were borrowed from their original sources and adapted in the Indian work setting by using exploratory factor analysis technique. All survey items were rated on a 5-point Likert type scale ranging from 1 (strongly disagree) to 5 (strongly agree). Results of factor analyses were based on principal axis factoring and oblique rotations of the SPSS-X statistical analysis package programme. A brief description of factors extracted by factor analysis according to the criterion of factor loadings ≥ .35 and Cronbach's alpha reliability coefficient ≥ .70 is as follows.

EMOTIONAL INTELLIGENCE INVENTORY

Using BarOn's (1997) EQ-inventory, the present study has found 21 significant items categorized into five significant factors. These were named as follows: (a) Assertiveness and Positive Self-Concept (α =.74), that is measured through items like "I have a feeling that something is wrong with my mind", "I'm unable to express my ideas to others" etc.; (b) Impulse Control (α = .72), that is measured through items like "It is a problem in controlling my anger", "I have got a bad temper" etc.; (c) Positive Attitude about Life (α =.77) that is measured through items like, "I do not have a good idea what I want to do in my life", "Before something beginning new, I usually feel that I will fail" etc.; (d) Reality Awareness (α =.71), that is measured through items like "I try to continue and develop those things that I enjoy", "Even when upset, I am aware of what is happening to me" etc.; (e) Controlled Problem Solving (α = .71) that is measured through items like "My impulsiveness creates problems", "I am impatient" etc.

The nature of the factor structure of the five obtained factors indicated that the first factor's structure perhaps relates to the EI skill arising out of proper expression of one's ideas and feelings to others with a positive image of one's self. The factor structure of the second factor indicated EI skills through control and regulation of one's negative emotions. The factor structure of the third factor indicates optimistic attitudes about life in general. The factor structure of the fourth factor indicates awareness of one's environment. The factor structure of the fifth factor indicates the implication of EI skills in solving problems by controlling one's negative mood and feelings. Overall, the five factors have some similarity with those found by Goleman (1995), Salovey and Mayer (1990), and BarOn (1997). The majority of the items, however, did not appear to be relevant for measuring EI in our sample of Indian managers, as evident by the fact that out of 133-items only 21 were found to be factor-analytically meaningful. The results of EFA show the significance of context and culture in measuring the validity and reliability of the measure of EI.

SELF-RATED PERFORMANCE AND SELF-EFFICACY PERCEPTION QUESTIONNAIRE

This questionnaire consisted of 12-items culminating in two significant factors. They were named (a) Self-Rated Performance (α =.92), that is measured through items like "I have mastered my job", "I am a high performer" etc.; (b) Self-Efficacy Perception (α =.79) that is measured through items like "it is just not possible to do my job at the level I would like to", "I often have little control over what happens on my job". All 12-items were retained upon factor analysis and reliability testing. In his/her organizational routines, a self-managed individual follows self-managed perceptions and practices to accomplish his/her job.

RESULTS

The conceptual scheme of the study included three major constructs, i.e. EI, self-rated performance and self-efficacy perception. Correlation and regression analysis have been performed to see the relationship of EI with self-rated performance and self-efficacy perception. The results from correlation matrix indicate that five predictors had relatively more strong relationship with self-rated performance compared to self-efficacy perception. Assertiveness and Positive Self-Concept had significant positive correlation with both self-rated performance ($r = .17 < .01$) and self-efficacy perception ($r = .20 < .01$). Rest of the dimensions of EI had insignificant relationship with self-efficacy perception. However, Positive Attitude about Life ($r = .18 < .01$), Reality Awareness ($r = .34 < .01$), and Controlled Problem Solving ($r = .28 < .01$) had significantly positive relationship with Self-Rated Performance.

Step-wise multiple regression analysis was used to determine the strength of association between the five dimensions of EI and self-rated performance and self-efficacy perception. Stepwise option in SPSS-X was used in order to remove the less desirable predictors of dependent variables from the regression equation. Results showed the significant impact of the independent variables on dependent variables in this sample.

Regression analysis showed that EI had predicted self-rated performance and self-efficacy perception positively. The results have confirmed the hypothesis. The significant results of MRA with the criterion variables are as follows: Self-Rated Performance ($F_{(2,247)} = 21.24$, $p \leq .01$) and Self-Efficacy Perception ($F_{(1,248)} = 12.27$, $p \leq .01$).

Reality Awareness dimension of EI was found to be a significant predictor of Self-Rated Performance ($\beta = .25 < .000$; Adjusted $R^2 = .27$) whereas Assertiveness and Positive Self-Concept was found to be a significant predictor of Self-Efficacy Perception ($\beta = .20 < .001$; Adjusted $R^2 = .04$). The predictor variable, i.e. EI was explaining 4 to 27 per cent of variance in criterion variables. As hypothesized, self-rated performance and self-efficacy perception both were significantly predicted by factors of EI. Rest of the dimensions of EI were not retained in the regression equation. It means that Impulse Control, Positive Attitude about Life and Controlled Problem Solving were not found to be the significant predictors of these two criterion variables.

DISCUSSION

The study attempted to examine the strength of association of EI with the self-rated performance and self-efficacy perception. Results have shown significantly positive relationship of EI with both the criterion variables which supports the hypothesis. EI is concerned with effective management of intrapersonal and interpersonal relationships through controlling the negative emotions in self and in others at workplace. It means that managing emotions in cognitively controlled manner acts as a potential for performance which helps in evaluating one's own performance positively. Generally, people who control their anger and negative impulses are perceived effective performers in organizations. Specifically, Reality Awareness dimension of EI was found to be a significant positive predictor of Self-Rated Performance. In an attempt to seek an explanation for these findings, one needs to understand this dimension of EI itself. Reality Awareness is concerned with more precise understanding of one's behaviour and the environment in which she/he works. It helps employee in getting aware of the performance requirements. In order to meet and exceed the performance standards, he/she enhances his/her self-management behaviour to cope up with work pressure. Reality Awareness dimension keeps an employee focused and concentrated to improve his/her performance at work to meet the individual and organizational goals. Reality Awareness helps an employee in two ways. First, it makes them to be aware of their present set of abilities and skills, and secondly, it makes them to build up the future growth on existing abilities. They always seek the opportunities to stretch themselves beyond their limits.

Assertiveness and Positive Self-Concept dimension of EI was found to be the positive predictor of Self-Efficacy Perception. The reason may be that Assertiveness and Positive Self-Concept provides skill and competency to express one's thoughts and feelings positively in an interpersonal encounter and to develop positive self-regard. Positive self-concept helps in overcoming difficult situations and keeping their faith in the abilities intact. Assertiveness makes people to deal effectively with extra workload with a positive frame of mind. Employees with the ability of Assertiveness and Positive Self-Concept are relatively more efficient and complete their work effectively. The feeling of Positive Self-Concept makes them to work hard consistently which bolster self-efficacy perception. These people give positive message to themselves, e.g. I am confident, I am creative, I am friendly etc.

Self-rated performance and self-efficacy perception provides intrinsic motivation to work. Employees always want to keep an eye on how well they are performing and how much they need to improve. EI skills and competency help in getting a realistic idea about how well they do in different circumstances and how much they would be able to improve in their performance.

Overall results showed self-rated performance and self-efficacy perceptions are positively predicted by the dimensions of EI. It may mean that EI is an important ability that provides potential for self-management behaviour which may further lead to higher satisfaction in life and at workplace. Evidence suggests that self-rated performance and self-efficacy perception in itself help executives, managers, and professionals to work under adverse and difficult situations. Self-rated performance and self-efficacy perception is self-rewarding and self-enhancing. It does not matter how much external reward he/she gets. These people are intrinsically motivated at the job that enhances the probability of their future success. They are less likely of being influenced by the negative results in life. The results clearly show that emotionally intelligent employees will have high self-confidence in their abilities and coping skills.

IMPLICATIONS

In recent days, the nature of the organizations and nature of the work and profession have changed drastically. Now organizations are relying more on their employees' commitment, sincerity, hard work, and innovative and creative contributions for the organizational development and transformation and to face the competitive challenges in the context of environmental complexity and uncertainty. To gain the trust and commitment, organizations need to work towards developing the positive human skills like EI and belief in one's self. In this context, some individual level variables like EI can be useful which may act in enhancing self-confidence. The continuous research in the field of EI is showing the powerful impact of EI on organizational behaviour. However, it appears that EI as a multi-factor concept may have different implications in the field of organizational behaviour. The success of future organization will depend on the 'guided usage' of human potential and strength in achieving desired individual and organizational goals, in which EI can be a good source of contribution. EI can provide a competitive advantage to newly emerging organizations in the field of information technology or business process outsourcing, while assuming that all organizations would be able to provide similar kinds of infrastructural facility, like work environment, pay-packages, bonuses, rewards, recognition etc. It is only human strengths which can bring difference in the performance significantly. For example, self-efficacy beliefs for engaging in creative behaviours appear to be critically important in helping individuals to persist in their creative endeavours, especially in the face of difficult or challenging situations (Tierney & Farmer, 2002). Creative self-efficacy is a specific application of Bandura's (1997) conceptualization of self-efficacy as a targeted perception of capacity that involves viewing oneself as being good at creative problem solving and novel idea generation. In the face of the current uncertainty in domestic and international financial markets, along with increasingly intense competition fuelled by globalization, many of the world's most successful companies are adopting a new corporate business model based largely on using individual creativity to facilitate organizational innovation (e.g., McGregor, 2007). The continuous focus in developing the human strengths like EI, self-rated performance and self-efficacy perception can be a good effort in this direction. It will fulfil the aims of positive psychology also.

LIMITATIONS

The future research may be directed to explore the relationship of EI with other individual and organizational level variables for comparison, e.g. employee engagement, people oriented work culture, etc. The research had used the sample from manufacturing industries, in other studies a varied sample from IT or service sector can be a good source of comparison where human skills are much more relevant. Further, it would be noted that the construct of EI as represented through the dimensions in the present study may not be robust enough predictors of variables of interests like self-rated performance and self-efficacy perception. It means the concept of EI has not evolved yet in Indian work context. However, results of the study are indicative of the importance of EI skills in general for the work behaviour within the framework of positive psychology. The findings can be of help in developing the human strength in terms of self-confidence and belief in one's ability.

Acknowledgement: I am thankful to Prof Arvind K Sinha, Prof. of Psychology, IIT, Kanpur, India for his valuable suggestions on this paper.

REFERENCES

Abramis, D.J. (1987). *Fun at work: Does it Matter*? Paper presented at 95th Annual Convention of the American Psychological Association. New York.

Argyle, M. and Martin, M. (1991). The psychological cause of happiness. In F. Stack, M. Argyle and N. Schwartz (Eds.) *Subjective well-being*. Pergamon Press.

Ashkanasy, N.M. (2003). Emotions in organizations: A multilevel perspective. In F. Dansereau and F.J. Yammarino (Eds.), *Research in multi-level issues*, vol. 2: Multi-level issues in organizational behaviour and strategy (pp. 9-54). Oxford, UK: Elsevier Science.

Bandura, A. (1986). *Social foundations of thought and actions: A Social cognitive theory*. Englewood Cliffs, NJ; Prentice Hall.

Bandura, A. (1997). *Self-Efficacy: The exercise of control*. New York: Freeman.

Bandura, A. (2004). Cultivate self-efficacy for personal and organizational effectiveness. In E. Locke (Ed.), *Handbook of principles of organizational behaviour*. Malden, MA: Blackwell.

Bandura, A. and Cervone, D. (1986). *Differential engagement in self reactive influences in cognitively-based motivation. Organizational Behaviour and Human Decision Processes*, 92-113.

BarOn, R. (1997). *The emotional quotient inventory (EQ-i): Technical Manual*. Toronto: Multi Health Systems.

Brackette, M.A., Mayer, J.D., and Warner, R.M. (in press). *Emotional intelligence and its relation to everyday behaviour. Personality and Individual Difference*.

Brief, A.P. and Motowidlo, S.J. (1986). 'Pro-social organizational behaviours', *Academy of Management Review*, 11, 710-725.

Brief, A.P. and Weiss, H.M. (2002). Organizational behaviour: Affect in the workplace. *Annual Business Review*, November-December, 133-141.

Campbell, J.P., McCloy, R.A., Oppler, S.H., and Sager, C.E. (1993). A theory of performance. In N. Schmitt and W.C. Borman (Eds.) *Personnel selection in organization*. (pp. 35-70). San Francisco: Jossey Bass.

Carnvele, P.J.D. and Isen, A.M. (1986). The influence of positive affect and visual access on discovery of integrative solutions in bilateral negotiation. *Journal of Applied Psychology*, 71, 672-678.

Castaneda, M., Kolenko, T.A. and Aldag, R.J. (1999). Self-management perceptions and Practices: A structural Equations Analysis', *Journal of Organizational Behaviour*, 20, 101-120.

Cavallo, K. and Brienza, D. (2002). Emotional competence and leadership excellence at Johnson and Johnson: The emotional intelligence and leadership study. Retrieved on 12th January 2004, www.corpconsultinggroup.com

Frese, M. (1990). Work and emotion. In F. Frey and I. Udis (Eds.) *The image of work.* Bern: Huber.

Gardner, H. (1983). *Frames of mind: The theory of multiple intelligences.* New York: Basic Books.

George, J.M., (1991). State or trait: Effects of positive mood on pro-social behaviour at Work. *Journal of Applied Psychology*, 76, 299-307.

George, J.M. and Brief, A.P., (1992). Feeling good-doing good. A conceptual analysis of the mood at work-organizational spontaneity relationship. *Psychological Bulletin*, 112, 310-329.

Goleman, D. (1995). *Emotional intelligence.* New York, Bantam Books.

Goleman, D. (1998). *Working with emotional intelligence.* New York, Bantam Books.

Goleman, D. (2000). Leadership that gets results. *Harvard Business Review*, March-April, 2000, 78-90.

Harrison, R. (1987). *Organizational culture and quality of service: A strategy for releasing love in the work place.* London: Association for Management Education and Development.

Hersey, R. (1951). *Zest for work.* New York: Harper.

Hochschild, A.R. (1983). *The Managed heart: Commercialization of human feeling.* Berkeley: University of California Press.

Isen, A.M. and Baron, R.A. (1991). Positive affect as a factor in organizational behaviour. *Research in Organizational Behaviour*, 13, 1-53.

Jain, A.K., and Sinha, A.K. (2005). General health in organizations: Relevance of emotional intelligence, trust and organizational support. *International Journal of Stress Management*, 12(3), 257-273.

Jain, A.K. and Sinha, A.K. (2006). Self-management and job performance: In-role and organizational citizenship behaviour, *Psychological Studies*, 51 (1), 19-29.

Jain, A.K. (2007). Comparing the impact of emotional intelligence on self-management and impression management behaviour. In R.K. Pradhan and P. Mathur (Eds.) *Emotional intelligence: Perspectives in organizations.* Delhi: Academic Excellence,

Jex, S.M. and Bliese, P.D. (1999). Efficacy beliefs as a moderator of the impact of work related stressors: A multi level study. *Journal of Applied Psychology*, 349-361.

Latham, G.P. and Frayne, C.A. (1989). Self-management training for Increasing Job Attendance: A Follow-up and a replication. *Journal of Applied Psychology*, 74, 411-416.

Locke, E.A., Frederick, E., Lee, C., and Bobko, P. (1984). The effect of self-efficacy, goals and task performance, *Journal of Applied Psychology*, 69, 241-251.

Luthans, F. (2002). The need for and meaning of positive organizational behaviour. *Journal of Organizational Behaviour*, 23, 695-706.

Mayer, J.D., Caruso, D., and Salovey, P. (1999). Emotional intelligence meets for traditional standards for intelligence. *Intelligence*, 27, 267-298.

Mayer, J.D. and Salovey, P. (1997). What is emotional intelligence? In P. Salovey and D. Sluyter (Ed.) *Emotional development and emotional intelligence: Implication for educators* (pp. 3-31). New York: Basic Books.

McGregor, J. (2007). The world's most innovative companies. *Business Week Online*, May 4, 9.

Munsterberg, H. (1912). *Psychology and business Life*. Leipzing: Barth.

Peters, T. and Austin, N. (1985). *A passion for excellence*. New York: Random House.

Rafaeli, A. and Sutton, R.L. (1987). The expression of emotion as part of the work role. *Academy of Management Review.*

Salovey, P. and Mayer, J.D. (1990). Emotional intelligence. *Cognition and Personality*, 9, 185-211.

Salovey, P., Mayer, J.D., Caruso, D., and Lopes, P.N. (2001). Measuring emotional intelligence as a set of mental abilities with the MSCEIT. In S.J. Lopez, and C.R. Snyder (Eds.) *Handbook of positive psychology assessment*. Washington DC: American Psychological Association.

Seligman, M.E.P. and Csikszentmihalyi, M. (2000). Positive Psychology. *American Psychologist*, 55, 5-14.

Sinha, A.K. and Jain, A.K. (2004). Emotional Intelligence: Imperatives for the organizationally relevant outcomes, *Psychological Studies*, 49 (2-3)

Sitarenios, G. (2000). Emotional intelligence in the prediction of placement success in the company "Business Incentives." Paper presented at conference in Toronto, Canada Multi Health Systems.

Stajkovic, A.D. and Luthans, F. (1998). Self-efficacy and work related performance: A meta-analysis. *Psychological Bulletin*, 240-261.

Stein, S. (2002) on behalf of Innovators Alliance. The EQ factor: Does emotional intelligence make you a better CEO? Retrieved January 7, 2003, from *Multi-Health Systems* Website:. http://eqi.mhs.com/InnovatorsAlliance.htm

Sutton, R.L. and Rafaeli, A. (1988). Untangling the relationship between displayed emotions and organizational sales: The case of convenience. *Academy of Management Journal*, 31, 461-487.

Tierney, P. and Farmer, S.M. (2002), Creative self-efficacy: Its potential antecedents and relationship to creative performance". *Academy of Management Journal*, 45, 1137-1148.

CHAPTER THIRTEEN

EFFECTIVENESS IN THE SECURITY-SERVICE ORGANIZATION: IDENTIFYING CONTRIBUTORS AND CONSEQUENCES

SWETA SRIVASTAVA MALLA

Effectiveness organizations is a central issue for developing societies. The issue of effectiveness in security-service organization becomes all the more important in our country at the moment, which is all set to endorse the path of growth and advancement. This is also the time when country is dealing with the problems of terrorism and hate-crime, which needs to be controlled strictly for the nation to progress further. Hence, the study becomes relevant in the current scenario. In the past few decades, researchers have focused attention on the variable of 'effectiveness' and have tried to explore its dimensions from different perspectives. However, little attention has been paid to effectiveness of the employees occupying a relatively lower position in the organizational hierarchy.

The present study deals with the concept of 'effectiveness' in the context of security-services organizations, owned and run by the government in India, popularly known as the Indian Police. More specifically, an attempt was made here to explore some of the organizational and individual level variables that lead to enhance effectiveness of the security-service personnel. The study also sought to identify some of the consequent variable of effectiveness. The study was planned within the purview of positive psychology, which adopts an open and appreciative perspective regarding human potentials, motives and capacities.

THE VARIABLES IN THE STUDY

Personal Effectiveness: Various definitions have been offered to explain the concept of personal effectiveness. According to Sutton and Ford (1982), personal effectiveness refers to an ability to perform the job effectively. According to Campbell, Dunnette, Lawler, and Weick (1970) the effective manager is one who is an optimizer in utilizing all available and potential resources—material, human, and financial—both, within and without the organization, towards its sustained long term functioning.

Views of Rao (1985) may be taken as representative of conceptualization of effectiveness by Indian scholars. According to Rao the manager who understands his job and job requirements well, is aware of his own and his subordinates' strength and weakness, utilizes his own and his subordinates' strength in performing the tasks, overcome weaknesses and acquire new capabilities through continuous learning on the job, may be considered effective. Therefore, effectiveness depends upon individual's own potential effectiveness, the potential effectiveness of the role, and the organizational climate.

It may be noted that personal effectiveness is an essential component in making a person successful in all aspects of life, including the organizational life. That is why we need effective executives. However, little attention seems to have been paid to effectiveness of the employees occupying a lower position in hierarchy in organizational structure.

Effectiveness on Conceived Roles: In the 20th century personnel selection research had been conducted to choose the right person for the right place to enhance the effectiveness of role behaviour in the organizations. The role behaviour had been linked with knowledge, skills, abilities and other characteristics. It is the effectiveness of role incumbent on these specifics of role behaviour which has been labelled as the effectiveness on conceived roles. Consequently, an individual who is high on the construct of effectiveness on conceived roles may be expected to fulfil these role requirements and obligations to a fuller extent (Boytzis, 1982).

Personally Important Job Accomplishment: For most ordinary mortals the criterion of accomplishment is essentially the external one. From this perspective, an individual's accomplishment would be evaluated primarily from the view point of some agent, agency or institution, other than the individual in question. Nevertheless, some of the theorists have focused in their work on the awareness of a set of feelings and attitudes and a certain sense of who we are (alternatively, who am I?), or the entity known as the self. Constructs related to self or self-concepts are central to the group of humanistic theories, which focus upon the individual's subjective perception of self, the world, and the self within the world.

Such constructs and conceptualizations may be treated as embedded within the humanistic framework. It simply proposes that with the advent of concepts like democracy, dignity of freedom, and free will, people need not necessarily be compelled to measure their success through others' frame of reference. Growth in a holistic sense should imply acquiring a realistic view of what one is and what one ought to be. The basic idea is that one should be free to define his or her own criteria of success and accomplishment and the accomplishment should be evaluated against those criteria. A variant of such notions called the Personally Important Job Accomplishment was included in the present study to bring out that element of a variable popularly known as the personal effectiveness. The variable was purported to assess the extent to which a role incumbent is effective in accomplishment of whatever he or she thinks desirable to accomplish on the job in an effective manner.

Organizational Justice: Issues of justice of fairness are key concern to virtually all individuals. In recent years organizational justice has received considerable research attention (for reviews see Cropanzano & Greenberg, 1997; Greenberg, 1996). It has been found that individuals appraised both what they receive and how they receive it. Greenberg described organizational justice as a literature "grown around attempts to describe the role of fairness as a consideration in the workplace". An organizational justice perspective is concerned with how perceptions of fairness impact on behaviour in organizations.

The study of organizational justice has largely focused on three variables. They are:

Distributive Justice: Distributive justice refers to the fairness of a division or distribution of rewards/resources. Distributive justice has its origin in equity theory (Adams, 1965), which argues that individuals compare their input-output ratios with those of others in order to determine the level of fairness. The word 'distributive' implies that employees perceptions of his type of organizational justice relate to allocation decisions, or 'did I get my fair share of outcome?' Thus, the distributive justice is the perceived fairness of the outcomes or allocation that an individual receives. According to Adams, what people were concerned about was not the absolute level of outcomes *per se* but whether those outcomes were fair. Adams suggested that one way to determine whether an outcome was fair was to calculate the ratio of one's contribution or inputs to one's outcomes and then compare that ratio with that of a comparison with others. He was clear that this process of evaluation was completely subjective.

Procedural Justice: People's perception of justice also involves question of procedural fairness. Every organization has procedures for regulating the distribution of outcomes to receivers. Thibaut and Walkers' (1975) pioneering work suggested that people care at least as much about the procedures used in making allocation decisions as they do about the outcome themselves. According to Leventhal's (1980) conceptualization, there are six rules which, when followed, yield procedures that are considered to be fairer than otherwise would have been the case: (a) *the consistency rule*, stating that allocation procedures should be consistent across persons and over time; (b) *the bias-suppression rule*, stating that personal self-interests of decision makers should be prevented from operating during the allocation process; (c) *the accuracy rule*, referring to the goodness of the information used in allocation process; (d) *the correctability rule*, dealing with the existence of opportunities to change an unfair decisions; (e) *the representativeness rule*, stating that the needs, values, and outlook of all the parties affected by the allocation process should be represented in the process; and (f) *the ethicality rule*, according to which the allocation process must be compatible with fundamental moral and ethical values of the perceiver. Procedural justice is predicted to be related to cognitive, affective, and behavioural reactions towards the organization, such as organizational commitment. Accordingly, when a process leading to a certain outcome is perceived to be unfair, the person's reactions are predicted to be directed at the whole organization, rather than at his/her tasks or the specific outcome in question.

Interactional Justice: Interactional justice pertains to the human side of organizational practice, that is, the way the management is behaving towards the recipient of justice. As such, interactional justice relates to the aspects of the communication process between the source and the recipient of justice, such as politeness, honesty, and respect. Bies and Moag (1986) referred to these aspects of justice as "interactional justice". When considering interactional justice, employees may be asking whether they "were treated differently from similar others" or "whether management adequately explained decisions". Greenberg (1993) suggested that at interactional justice is composed of two facets: interpersonal justice and informational justice. The first labelled interpersonal justice reflects the degree to which people are treated with politeness, dignity, and respect by authorities involved in determining outcomes. The second labelled informational justice focuses on the explanation provided to people that convey information about why procedures used in a certain way or why outcomes were distributed in a certain fashion.

Well-being: Well-being is a complex construct that concerns optimal experience and functioning. The concept of well-being refers to optimal psychological functioning and experience. In part, this reflects the increasing awareness that just as positive affect is not the opposite of negative affect (Cacioppo & Berntson, 1999), well-being too is not the absence of mental illness. Ryan and Deci (2001), in review of the topic, proposed that the study of well-being has witnessed the formation of two relatively distinct, yet overlapping perspectives and paradigms for empirical inquiry into well-being that revolve around two distinct philosophies: hedonic and eudaimonic well-being.

More recently, a debate has come up in this area and that seems to be more related to the present research interest. Keyes, Shmotkin and Ryff (2002) have extended the debate over the issue and proposed two distinct lines of inquiry within the broader domain of well-being, which are referred to as subjective well-being (SWB) and psychological well-being (PWB). According to them, although both approaches assess well-being, they address different features of what it means to be well: SWB involves more global evaluations of affect and life quality, whereas PWB examines perceived thriving *vis-à-vis* the existential challenges of life (e.g., pursuing meaningful goals, growing and developing as a person, establishing quality ties to others). Looking for the key points of convergence among the many formulations, Ryff (1989) suggested a multidimensional model of PWB that distilled six psychological dimensions of thriving. In combination, these dimensions encompass a breadth of wellness that includes positive evaluations of oneself and one's past life (Self-acceptance), a sense of continued growth and development as a person (personal growth), the belief that one's life is purposeful and meaningful (purpose in life), the possession of quality relations with others (positive relations with others), the capacity to manage effectively one's life and surrounding world (environmental mastery) and a sense of self-determination (autonomy).

Internal Motivation: Motivation may be defined as the willingness to exert high level of effort towards organizational goal, conditioned by the individual's ability to satisfy some individual need (Robbins, 2001). De Charms (1968) distinguishes between behaviour that is intrinsically motivated and behaviour that is determined by extrinsic rewards and notes that the introduction of a reinforcer may decrease intrinsic motivation. The most common definition of intrinsic motivation states that behaviour is intrinsically motivated when there is no apparent external reward. This motivation is innate and motivates such things as play, exploration, and the development of cognitive structures.

Further, intrinsically motivated behaviours fall into two general classes. The first class is behaviour that people engage in to seek out optimally challenging situations. These challenges can be thought of as involving an incongruity or discrepancy between a stimulus input and some standard of comparison. The second class is behaviour that aims to conquer the challenge or reduce the incongruity. In other words, people are involved in an ongoing process of seeking and conquering challenges (Deci, 1975). Deci's Cognitive Evaluation Theory states that there are two key determinants of intrinsic motivation. These are feelings of personal control and feelings of competence. Intrinsic motivation is thought to increase as feelings of personal control and competence becomes stronger and to decrease as they become weaker. The competence aspect of Deci's theory of intrinsic motivation seems similar or identical to what Hackman and Oldham (1975) has called internal work motivation. The latter is defined as "the degree to which the employee is self-motivated to perform effectively on the job—that is, the employee experiences positive internal feelings when working effectively on the job and negative internal feelings while doing poorly."

Ego-resilience: The concept of Ego-resilience is essential for psychological health and adjustment. Block and Block (1980) coined the term "Ego-resilience" to the already consisting variable of resilience. Ego-resilience refers to the general capacity for flexible and resourceful adaptation to external and internal stressors. More specifically, Ego-resilience is a personality resource that allows individuals to modify their characteristic level and habitual mode of expression of ego-control so as to most adaptively encounter, function in, and shape their immediate environmental contexts. Block and Block defined Ego-resilience as "resourceful adaptation to changing circumstances and environmental contingencies, analysis of the "goodness of fit" between situational demands, and behavioural possibility, and flexible invocation of the available repertoire of problem solving strategies.

Trust in Leader: The significance of trust in leadership has been recognized by researchers for at least four decades. Over this period of time, the trust that individuals have in their leaders has been an important concept in applied psychology and related discipline. In the present study, trust refers to an individual characteristic or a tendency to expect that leader will not act in a selfish manner and mean what they say and that they will do what they promise to. Furthermore, a willingness to trust stems from positive generalized expectancies associated with the relationships a role incumbent has with his leader.

Antecedents of trust Mayer, Davis, and Schoorman (1995) identified three sets of antecedents or bases for trust which relate to perceptions about the individual to be trusted: competence, integrity, and benevolence. 'Competence' concerns the perceived ability of the trustee, as measured by indicators such as education or credentials, experience, and reliable past role performance. 'Integrity' concerns the degree to which the trustee is considered to perform with honesty, fairness, and consistency of actions and words. 'Benevolence' concerns the extent to which the trustee demonstrates care and consideration for team members, peers, subordinates, and other individuals with whom he or she interacts.

Values: By definition, a value is a conception, explicit or implicit of the desirable which influences the selection of available modes, means and ends of action.

Happiness: Happiness is a common goal towards which people strive, but for many it remains frustratingly out of reach. Psychologists have attempted to define happiness over the past 30 years. Happiness is a pleasant emotional experience, the affective component of subjective well-being (Andrews & Withey, 1976).

Political Interference: Viewing organizations as political entities is not a recent phenomenon. Organizational politics has become an important and popular topic in management literature. Major attempts to define organization politics fall under four heads. They are mentioned below:

1. *Claims against the Resource Sharing Systems*: Political behaviour in an organization has been viewed as actions that make a claim against the organization's resource sharing system. This conflict was thought to be resolved by political processes including coalition formation, bargaining, side payments etc.
2. *Conflict Over Policy Preferences*: Wildavsky (1968) adhered to this view and defined organizational politics as conflict over whose preferences are to prevail in the determination of policy. He also suggested that the budgeting process is a political method of allocating financial resources.
3. *Relationships of Controls and Influence*. Martin and Sims (1974) suggested that politics is concerned with relationships of control or influence. Burns (1961) viewed politics as the exploitation of resources, physical and human, for achievement of more control over others, and thus of safer, more comfortable, or more satisfying terms of individual existence.

4. *Self-serving Behaviour.* A large number of writers have considered politics as behaviour directed towards personal gain. Mintzberg (1985) defined organizational politics as "individual or group behaviour that is informal, ostensibly parochial, typically divisive, and above all, in a technical sense, illegitimate—sanctioned neither by formal authority, accepted ideology, nor certified expertise (although it may exploit anyone of these)". Organizational politics may therefore stem from informal behaviours which are not sanctioned by the organization but which are designed to promote the goals of an individual.

Supervisors' Support: Supervisor support refers to the degree to which employees perceive that supervisors offer to employees the support, encouragement and concern (Burke, Borucki, & Hurley, 1992). The degree of supervisor support may affect employees' performance. For example, an important way in which supervisors facilitate employee performance is by providing key resources, e.g. equipment and training (Guzzo & Gannett, 1988). That is, even if workers know what to do, they may not be able to execute tasks because supervisors have not provided material support. Further, if a service provider perceives supervisors as generally over-critical, he/she may be unwilling to risk some unconventional solution aimed at meeting customer desires, increasing the potential for role conflict. Studies have found that supportive supervision is associated with organizational support, organizational commitment, and job retention (Balfour & Wechsler, 1991; Gerstner & Day, 1997) and that low levels of supervisor support are linked to turnover (Malatesta, 1995; cited in Eisenberger, Stinglhamber, Vandenberghe, Sucharski & Rhoades, 2002).

Organizational Citizenship Behaviour. The current interest in organizational citizenship behaviour can be traced back at least to Katz (1967), who identified the following dimensions of discretionary and spontaneous behaviour that are beyond the explicit role requirement, are (1) cooperating with others, (2) protecting the organization, (3) volunteering constructive ideas, (4) self-training, and (5) maintaining favourable attitude towards the company. This concept was subsequently made more explicit by Smith, Organ, and Near (1983) and was called "organizational citizenship behaviour" (OCB), later defined by Organ (1988) as "individual behaviour that is discretionary, not directly or explicitly recognized by the formal reward system, and that in the aggregate, promotes the effective functioning of the organization". By discretionary, we mean that behaviour is not an enforceable requirement of the role or the job description that is the clearly specifiable terms of the person's employment contract with the organization, the behaviour is rather a matter of personal choice, such that its omission is not gradually understood as punishable.

Organizational Commitment: Organizational commitment (OC) is a well studied concept on management sciences. Organizational commitment reflects the extent to which people identify with, and are involved in their organizations and are unwilling to leave them (Greenberg & Baron, 1999). Mowday, Porter, and Steers (1982) offered a definition of organizational commitment, which has three components. (a) a strong belief in and acceptance of organizational goals and values, (b) a willingness to exert considerable effort on behalf of the organization, and (c) a strong desire to maintain membership in the organization.

In order to explore the nature of relationship, some research questions were identified to facilitate the course of research and data analysis. They are as follows:

1. Which are the variables pertaining to individual level that contribute to Effectiveness?
2. Which are the variables pertaining to organization level that contribute to Effectiveness?
3. Does Effectiveness leads to personally relevant dimensions such as Happiness, Job satisfaction, and Organizational citizenship behaviour?

To recapitulate, the study aimed at making explorations about identifying some important antecedent and consequent variables of "effectiveness". The conceptual scheme used in the study is presented in Figure 13.1.

METHOD

SAMPLE

The sample consisted of 270 male respondents from the lower and middle hierarchical level of Police organization. The respondents, at the time of data collection, were located in four cities situated in the eastern (one city), central (two cities), and western (one city) parts of a large state in north India.

MEASURES

All the measures were translated into Hindi language keeping in view the sample that was predominantly Hindi speaking, and generally not very well versed in English language. Translation of the measures was carried out in

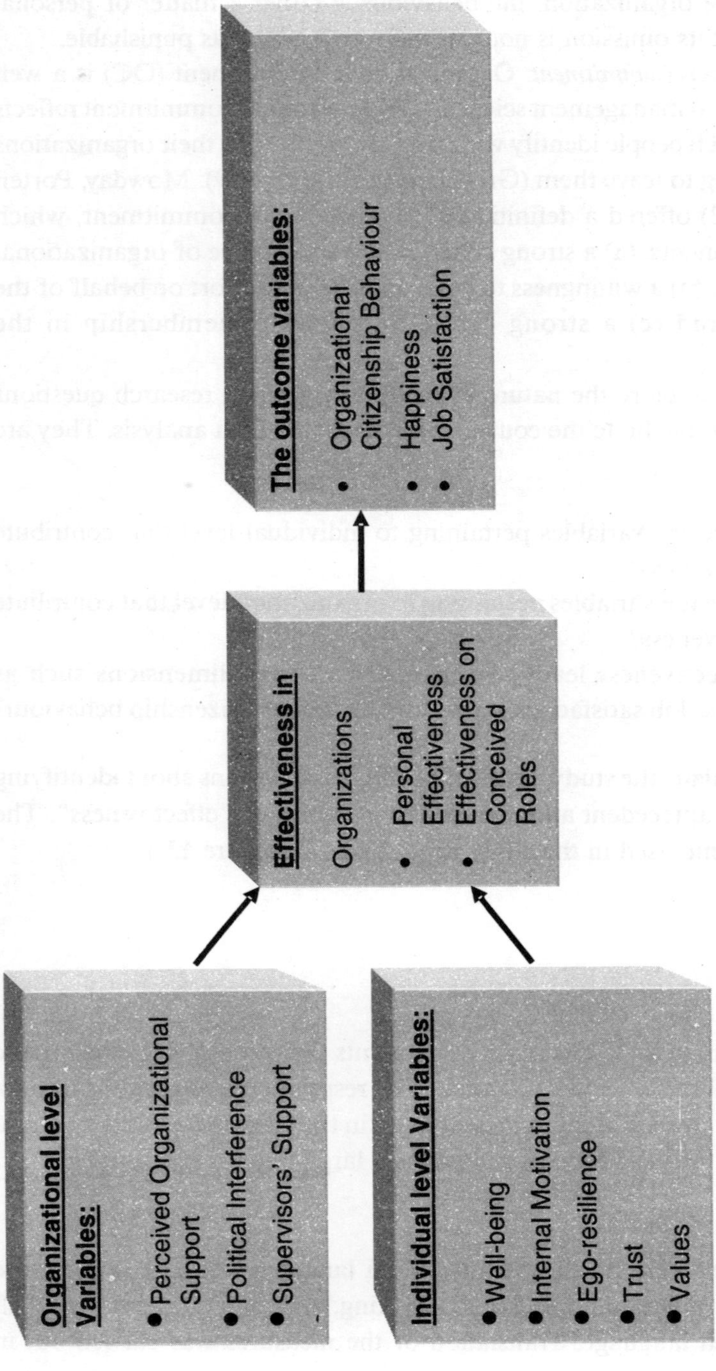

Fig. 13.1: The Conceptual Scheme

two stages, that is, all the measures were first translated to Hindi and then reverse translated again to English. This provided a check for the reliability of translation. Help was sought from a group of five post-graduate students who were reasonably fluent in both the languages, and additionally, also from a senior professor of linguistics to ensure the greater accuracy of the translation. Data were collected on: Organizational Commitment (Mowday, Porter & Steers, 1982; Cronbach α =.73), Well-being (Ryff, 1989; Cronbach α =.76), Personal Values (Hofstede, 2001; Cronbach α =.77), Organizational Values (Hofstede, 2001; Cronbach α =.71), Organizational Justice (Colquitt, 2001; Cronbach α =.78), Perceived Organizational Support (Rhoades, Eisenberger, & Armeli, 2001; Cronbach α =.91), Supervisors' Support (Rhoades, Eisenberger, & Armeli, 2001; Cronbach α =.93), Ego-Resilience (Klohnen, 1996; Cronbach α =.86), Happiness (Andrews & Withey, 1976), Trust in Leader (Dirks, 2000; Cronbach α =.76), Biographical Information, Effectiveness on Conceived Roles (Tsui, 1984; Cronbach α =.85), Job Satisfaction (Cammann, Fichman, Jenkins, & Flesh, 1983; Cronbach α =.84), Personal Effectiveness (Sinha, 1998; Cronbach α =.71), Job Accomplishment (Sutton & Ford, 1982; Cronbach α =.80), Political Interference (Maslyn and Fedor, 1998); Cronbach α =.76), Internal Work Motivation (Hackman & Oldham, 1975; Cronbach α =.74), and Organizational Citizenship Behaviour (Cronbach α =.76). All of these measures were rated on a 5-point scale.

PROCEDURE

The sample would be called a purposive sample in the sense that data could be collected only from those police personnel who could afford to spend an hour at a stretch for this purpose. They were informed about the required time investment on their part before hand. Moreover, officers from the upper hierarchical level could not, due to paucity of time, spend time on such a longish questionnaire. Hence, they were not included in the sample. Structured questionnaires were used for the purpose of data collection.

RESULTS AND DISCUSSION

It would be recalled that the study attempted to identify some of the variables that are important for the maintenance and enhancement of effectiveness among the police service personnel. Another aim of the study was to see how the variable of effectiveness affects some dependent variables. All the questionnaires, except happiness which was a single-item measure, were subjected to factor analysis and only those items were considered which had alpha coefficients more than .70.

Effectiveness was the most important variable in the conceptual scheme for its contribution to the effective functioning of police organization. Consequently, it was considered desirable to locate those variables that make the most impact on this variable. In order to test this concept, several multiple regression analyses were carried out with the dimensions of Effectiveness as criterion variable for certain antecedent variables. The result clearly highlights the importance of as the most significant predictor along with Organizational Commitment, Ego-Resilience, Distributive Justice, Interpersonal Justice, and Political Interference. If managers wish to make an effective workforce, they should be sensitive towards the dimension of Internal Motivation, especially at the entry phase. It makes sense to believe that in a scenario which is considered as not very conducive, supportive or friendly, only those employees would be effective in long run, whose motivation and urge to work comes from within.

Another MRA results which Effectiveness in Preventive/Maintenance Roles was taken as criterion variable and amongst the predictor variables that made the most contribution were identified as Organizational Commitment, Internal Motivation, Distributive Justice, Personal Values regarding working conditions, and Political Interference. This result too, highlights the importance of Internal Motivation. This re-strengthens our stand about Internal Motivation and makes it a special variable from the research and training perspectives.

The result further suggests that along with the intra-psychic variables such as Organizational Commitment and Internal Motivation, the extra-psychic dimensions are also important such as Distributive Justice and Interpersonal Justice. It may be suggested here that managers should also be sensitive towards the distribution of justice in organizations so as to enhance the level of effectiveness of employees. It makes sense to believe that people working at the lower hierarchical levels might get influenced by what they get (Distributive Justice) and how they get (Interpersonal Justice).

However, it is interesting to note that the dimension of well-being, namely Purpose and Development in Life, contributed negatively to the criterion variable. This needs to be explored further. The MRA results, wherein the dimension of Effectiveness in Dealing with Group, Environment and Human Growth Issues was taken as the criterion variable, the major predictors were identified as Internal Motivation, lesser Political Interference, Interactional Justice, Receptive and Empathic Leadership, and Personal Growth and

Satisfying Self-Concept. Here again, in addition to Internal Motivation, factors of workplace environment came out as significant predictors. This suggests that we give only what we get. Hence, interaction with public would largely depend on how employees themselves are treated at their workplace. Whenever organizational effectiveness is dependent upon interaction with public, it is imperative for these organizations to treat their employees well.

Having identified some of the antecedent variables for effectiveness, an attempt was also made to locate some of its consequent variables. The Happiness was taken as the criterion variable and all the five dimensions of effectiveness served as the predictor. The contributing variables were identified as Personally Important Job Accomplishment, Effectiveness in Active Role Implementation, and Effective Dealing with Individuals. It seems when people do their work effectively, especially in not-so-conducive environment, they experience positive emotion such as Happiness. Organizational researchers are working on ways to increase happiness and other positive emotion in employees and this tells us that Effectiveness could be identified as one of such factors.

MRA was also carried out with the dimension of Organizational Citizenship Behaviour as the criterion variable. Major contributing variable was identified as Effectiveness in Active Role Implementation. This also suggests that if organizations care about increasing the citizenship behaviour among its employees, one way could be through increasing employees' effectiveness. On the similar lines, Job Satisfaction was taken as criterion variable for the five dimensions of effectiveness. Significant contributors were identified as Effectiveness in Active Role Implementation, Personally Important Job Accomplishment, and Effective Dealing with Individuals. When individuals are effective, they have a sense of job satisfaction as well, which has been proved to be worthwhile variable for overall organizational functioning.

Since the research endeavour adhered to the multi-dimensional conceptualization of variables (as compared to the uni-dimensional conceptualization), it was considered to be a gainful exercise to look into the relationship between the sets of underlying dimensions constituting a construct canonical correlations (CC) were calculated to gain such insight. CC results indicated that the variables of Happiness, Organizational Citizenship Behaviour, and Job Satisfaction shared significant relationship. This would be taken to mean that high magnitude of effectiveness would also result in the experience of high magnitude of Happiness, Organizational Citizenship Behaviour, and Job Satisfaction. However, the Effectiveness in Active Role

Implementation had negative relationship with Happiness. Looking at the composite picture of the results, it appears that certain individual and organizational level variables are important for Effectiveness. The important individual level variables are Internal Motivation, dimensions of Well-being, Organizational Commitment, and Ego-resilience. The important organizational level variables could be identified as dimensions of Organizational Justice, lesser Political Interference, and Receptive and Empathic Leadership. It was also found that the various dimensions of effectiveness had impact on Happiness, Organizational Citizenship Behaviour, and Job Satisfaction. It may appear to be an interesting phenomenon in the context of police organization which does not seem to be perceived as employee friendly. Still if those employees are chosen that are high on Internal Motivation, some real positive changes may be expected.

Contribution of the Study: The study attempted to look at the organizationally relevant outcome variables for security-service personnel from the perspective of positive psychology. The work could suggest a conceptual scheme to understand the organizational dynamics in a security service organization. The study highlighted and identified the importance of Internal Motivation along with Organizational Justice variable as the ones that contribute most to the Effectiveness of employees. Hence, and researchers and practitioners should focus more on these variables to have a better understanding of the workforce.

Note: Due to paucity of print space, the detailed results are not being reproduced here. They may be obtained from the author on request.

Acknowledgements: Author duly acknowledges the contribution of Prof. Arvind K. Sinha in carrying out this piece of research work. The paper would not have taken its present shape in the absence of Prof. Sinha's guidance and valuable suggestions. The author also acknowledges the fact that the inspiration for this work came from the writings of **Prof. JBP Sinha** who has been studying public sector organizations with a focus on development of the larger society. This piece of research is dedicated to him.

REFERENCES

Adams, J. (1965). Inequity in social exchange. In L. Berkowitz (Ed.), *Advances in experimental social psychology* (Vol. 2, pp. 267-299). San Diego, CA: Academic Press.

Andrews, F.M. and Withey, S.B. (1976). *Social indicators of well-being*. New York: Plenum Press.

Balfour, D.L. and Wechsler, B. (1991). Commitment, performance, and productivity in public organizations. *Public Productivity and Management Review*, 14, 355-367.

Bies, R.J. and Moag, J.F. (1986). Interactional justice: Communication criteria of fairness. In R.J. Lewicki, B.H. Sheppard, and M.H. Bazerman (Eds.), *Research on negotiations in organization* (vol. 1, pp. 43-55). Greenwich, CT: JAI Press.

Block, J.H. and Block, J. (1980). The role of ego-control and ego-resiliency in the organization of behaviour. In W.A. Collins (Ed.), *Minnesota symposia on child psychology* (Vol. 13, pp. 39-101). Hillsdale, NJ: Erlbaum.

Boytzis, P.E. (1982). *The competent manager: A model for effective performance*. New York: John Wiley Sons Inc.

Burke, M.J., Borucki, C.C., and Hurley, A.E. (1992). Reconceptualizing psychological climate in a retail service environment: A Multiple-Stakeholder Perspective. *Journal of Applied Psychology*, 7, 717-729.

Burns, T. (1961). Micropolitics: mechanisms of institutional change. *Administrative Science Quarterly*, 63, 689-718.

Cacioppo, J.T. and Berntson, G.G. (1999). The affect system: Architecture and operating characteristics. *Current Directions in Psychological Science*, 8, 133-137.

Cammann, C., Fichman, M., Jenkins, Jr., D., and Flesh, J.R. (1983). Assessing the attitudes and perceptions of organizational members. In S.E. Seashore, E. Lawler, P.H. Mirvis, and C. Cammann (Eds.). *Assessing organizational change* (pp. 71-138). New York: John Wiley & Sons.

Campbell, J.P. Dunnette, M.D., Lawler, E.E., III., and Weick, K.E. Jr. (1970). *Managerial behaviour, performance and effectiveness*. New York: McGraw-Hill.

Colquitt, J.A. (2001). On the dimensionality of organizational justice: A construct validation of a measure. *Journal of Applied Psychology*. 86, 386-400.

Cropanzano, R. and Greenberg, J. (1997). Progress in organizational justice: tunneling through the maze. In L.T. Robertson and C.L. Cooper (Eds.), *International review of industrial and organizational psychology* (pp. 317-372). New York: Wiley.

De Charms, R. (1968). *Personal causation: The internal affective determinants of behaviour*. New York: Academic Press.

Deci, E.L. (1975). *Intrinsic motivation*. New York: Plenum.

Dirks, K.T. (2000). Trust in leadership and team performance: evidence from NCAA basketball. *Journal of Applied Psychology*. 85, 1004-1012.

Eisenberger, R., Stinglhamber, F., Vandenberghe, C., Sucharski, I.L., Rhoades, L. (2002). Perceived supervisor support: Contributions to perceived organizational support and employee retention. *Journal of Applied Psychology*, 87, 565-573.

Gerstner, C.R. and Day, D.V. (1997). Meta-analytic review of leader-member exchange theory: Correlates and construct issues. *Journal of Applied Psychology*, 82, 827-844.

Greenberg, J. (1993). The social side of fairness: Interpersonal and informational classes of organizational justice. In R. Cropanzano (Ed.), *Justice in the workplace: Approaching fairness in human resource management* (pp. 79-103). Hillsdale, NJ: Lawrence Erlbaum Associates.

Greenberg, J. (1996). *The quest for justice on the job*. New Delhi: Sage Publications India Pvt. Ltd.

Greenberg, J. and Baron, R.A. (1999). *Behaviour in organizations*. (5thed.) New Delhi: Printice-Hall of India Private Limited.

Guzzo, R.A. and Gannett, B.A. (1988). The Nature of Facilitators and Inhibitors of Effective Task Performance. In *Facilitating Work Effectiveness*, F.D. Schoorman and B. Schneider (Eds.), *Lexington*, MA: Lexington Books.

Hackman, R. and Oldham, G.R. (1975). Development of the job diagnostic survey. *Journal of Applied Psychology*, 60, 159-170.

Hofstede, G. (2001). *Culture's consequences*. California: Sage Publications.

Katz, D. (1967). The motivational basis of organizational behaviour. *Behavioural Science*. 9, 131-146.

Keyes, C.L.M., Shmotkin, D., and Ryff, C.D. (2002). Optimizing well-being: The empirical encounter of two traditions. *Journal of Personality and Social Psychology*, 82, 1007-1022.

Klohnen, E.C. (1996). Conceptual analysis and measurement of the construct of ego-resiliency. *Journal of Personality and Social Psychology*, 70, 1067-1079.

Leventhal, G.S. (1980). What should be done with equity theory? New approaches to the study of fairness in social relationships. In K. Gergen, M. Greenberg, and R. Wills (Eds.), Social exchange: *Advances in theory and research* (pp. 27-55). New York: Plenum Press.

Martin, N.H. and Sims, J.H. (1974). Power tactics. In D.A. Kolb, I.M. Rubin, and J.M. Mclntyre (Eds.), *Organizational Psychology: A Book of Readings* (pp. 177-183). Englewood Cliffs, N.J.: Prentice Hall.

Maslyn, J.M. and Fedor, D.B. (1998). Perceptions of politics: does measuring different foci matter. *Journal of Applied Psychology*. 83(4), 645-53.

Mayer, R.C., Davis, J. H; and Schoorman, F.D. (1995). An integrative model of organizational trust. *Academy of Management Review*, 20, 709-34.

Mintzberg, H. (1985). The organization as political arena. *Journal of Management Studies*, 22, 133-154.

Moorman, R.H. and Blakely, G.L. (1995). *Individualism-Collectivism as an individual difference predictor of organizational citizenship behaviour*, 16, 127-142.

Mowday, R., Porter, L., and Steers, R., (1982). *Employee-organization linkages: The psychology of Commitment, absenteeism, and turnover*. New York: Academic Press.

Organ, D.W. (1988). *Organizational citizenship behaviour: The good soldier syndrome*, Lexington, MA Lexington.

Rao, T.V. (1985). Psychological factors in managerial effectiveness. In U. Pareek and D.M. Pestonjee (Eds.) *Behavioural Process in Organizations*, pp. (15-26). New Delhi: Oxford and IBH Publishing Company.

Rhoades, L., Eisenberger, R.; and Armeli, S. (2001). Affective commitment to the organization: The contribution of perceived organizational support. *Journal of Applied Psychology*. 86, 825-836.

Robbins, S. (2001). *Organizational Behaviour.* Prentice Hall of India Private Limited.

Ryan, R.M. and Deci, E.L. (2001). On happiness and human potential: A Review of Research on Hedonic and Eudaimonic Well-Being. *Annual Review of Psychology*, 52, 141-166.

Ryff, C.D. (1989). Happiness is everything, or is it? Explorations on the Meaning of Psychological Well-Being. *Journal of Personality and Social Psychology*, 57(6), 1069-1081.

Sinha, A.K. (1998). A new instrument measuring personal effectiveness. Unpublished manuscript, *Department of Humanities and Social Sciences*, Indian Institute of Technology, Kanpur, India.

Smith, C.A., Organ, D.W., and Near, J.P. (1983). Organizational citizenship behaviour: Its nature and antecedents. *Journal of Applied Psychology*. 68, 653-663.

Sutton, R.I. and Ford, L.H., (1982). Problem solving adequacy in hospital subunits. *Human Relations*, 35, 675-701.

Thibaut, J. and Walker, L. (1975). *Procedural justice: A psychological analysis.* Erlbaum, NJ: Hillsdale.

Tsui A.S. (1984). A role set analysis of managerial reputation. *Organizational Behaviour and Human Performance*, 34: 64-96.

Wildavsky, A. (1968). Budgeting as a political process. In D.L. Sills (Ed.), *The International Encyclopaedia of Social Sciences* (pp. 192-199).

SECTION-3

Social Development

Although individuals constitute a society, social development is more than the sum total of individuals' development. Social institutions make planned effort to create conducive conditions to develop individuals' agentic capabilities, which become instrumental to further social development. Thus, the social development can be conceptualized as a process of capability development and empowerment of the people. People use their empowerment and capabilities in fulfilling their physical, psychological, economic, social and cultural needs. All the six chapters in this section deal with some of these issues pertaining to social development.

In the opening chapter of the section, R. Barry Rubak and Janak Pandey emphasise the need for relevant research in developing countries that has practical applicability. The authors first describe some of the traditional weaknesses of Psychological research in terms of their applied usefulness. Psychology has concentrated more on accumulating knowledge than testing its possible application suggesting solution to policy makers. In the second part of the chapter, they present a conceptual framework for doing research that has some potential to be used in policy formation and also suggest techniques by which it can be made more relevant. It is hoped that the suggested approach might make it more likely that future research on development is useful to decision makers.

The fifteenth chapter, "Self-evolving institutions for sustainable development" by T.N. Sinha and Rajeshwar Mishra, opens with the description of the development scenario in India as extremely induced initiative by government regulated or government crafted institutions. This "trickle-down" framework does not seem to work well. The doles and subsidies have not helped the poor achieve conditions of sustainable development. As soon as the inflow of benefits dry up or the agencies withdraw themselves from the scene, the impact of development reverts back to square one. The authors suggest in order that the development be sustainable, initiative must come from the self-evolving institutions. Such institutions are evolved out of the societal needs, drives, norms and values from the community, and the leadership embedded into the society itself that sharpens the agentic competencies of people and help achieve sustainable development. The chapter is based on the experience of process analysis of evolving institution-building, which has been facilitated by one of the authors.

In the next chapter, Ramadhar Singh describes an interesting crossed social categorization experiment that has important implication for social development in India. Attraction toward target persons categorized by nationality, religion, or gender as well as by all of their pairing was studied in a within participant experimental design. The experiment reveals that the crossed categorization effects are moderated by social status of perceivers and the categories that are crossed with each other. Natural social categories have different meanings for people of different status in India.

The Seventeenth chapter, "Value as a force behind development" by Jyoti Verma, begins with the proposition that individualist values with self-centric core are not a guarantee for socio-economic development of a collectivist country like India. The author takes the stand that the collectivist values of interdependence, sharing of resources, collective goals and norms, duties and obligation etc., have the potential for sustaining collective efforts and activities for development. Special mention is made to familial collectivist value. If this value can be extended beyond the boundary of family, the value can acquire tremendous force and power to initiate a growth and development process at individual, group and societal levels.

In the next chapter, "Individualism-collectivism and development", R.B.N. Sinha poses the question: whether collectivist orientation of Indian culture can be harnessed to facilitate indigenous development of the country? To answer this question, he focuses on the multidimensional facets of development and cultural values. The author takes the position that the dimensions of development and culture co-evolve over a period. Based on an empirical study, the chapter highlights the patterns of relationships between cultural values and development indices.

The last chapter of the section by Purnima Singh opens with the observation that the pace of development over the years has resulted in a fragmented society. Somewhere, we have failed in aligning development with social justice concerns and the process of development has favoured only a small minority of 'haves' in the society. For a more equitable social, order a need to bring social justice concerns to the centre stage of debate and dialogues on development is reiterated. The chapter discusses in details the various facets of social justice and their implication for bringing in a balanced equation between the 'haves' and the 'have-nots'.

CHAPTER FOURTEEN

Policy Relevant Research for Development: A Conceptual Framework and Empirical Approach

R. Barry Ruback and Janak Pandey

One of the major criticisms of academic researchers is that they talk to each other but not to policy makers. For the most part, this gap between research and policy results from a structure that rewards researchers more for publishing in academic journals than for advising government decision makers. And, relatedly, the type of research that is publishable in academic journals is generally not of much use to policy makers.

In this chapter, we present a framework for doing research that has practical utility, that is, has some potential to be used in policy formation. This volume, dedicated to Professor Jai B.P. Sinha, is concerned with development, and we hope that our suggested approach might make it more likely that future research on development is useful to decision makers.

Although we have not conducted research on development *per se*, we have investigated some of the consequences of development in South Asia, including household crowding, urban migration, and reactions to environmental stressors like traffic and air pollution. Here we use our research programme, conducted over the past 21 years, to illustrate our framework for practical research, to point out ways that our research falls short in terms of practical utility, and to suggest techniques by which this research could be made more relevant.

THE PROBLEM OF CROWDING IN INDIA

A social trap exists when individuals act in ways that increase their short-term personal gain, even though their actions produce long-term negative consequences for the larger group (Platt, 1973). Overpopulation is one such social trap. For example, in many developing countries couples seek to maximize the number of children they have, particularly sons, because these offspring when young can help provide income to the family and when older can help to take care of their parents. If every couple decides to maximize their own interests by having many children, then the larger society will suffer if the infrastructure of the country (e.g., water, food, shelter, sewage, and transportation systems) cannot deal with the consequences of these individual maximization decisions.

In many ways, India suffers from the social trap of overpopulation more than do most countries. With more than 1.1 billion people, India is among the most densely populated countries in the world (344 per square kilometre). Further, because India's birth rate is about 2.2 per cent, the problem of overpopulation is certain to get much worse (CIA, 2009).

Given the scope of the overpopulation problem in India, one must wonder whether the social sciences, psychology in particular, can provide policy-makers with any useful information either in the short-term (e.g. helping individuals and groups cope with crowding stressors) or the long-term (e.g. reducing the birth rate). Before addressing this issue, we first consider the need for relevant research in India and other developing countries.

NEED FOR RELEVANT RESEARCH IN DEVELOPING COUNTRIES

There has been abundant evidence of the negative effects of large populations. These problems are of three types (Cone, 1985): (a) aesthetics and the quality of life, (b) health-related problems, and (c) the use of non-renewable resources. Environmental aesthetics refer to behaviours that make the environment more or less pleasant, such as littering, wilderness protection, and urban decay. Health-related problems refer to detrimental effects of pollution, toxic substances, crowding, and noise on physical and mental health. Resource-related problems relate to energy consumption, recycling, overpopulation, and the use of mass-transit.

Psychologists are especially well-trained to investigate health-related problems and stress-related illness (Holtzman, 1987). Crowding, like other environmental stressors (e.g., noise, pollution), appears to produce both physiological and psychological effects in humans.

Although crowding is highest in Asia and Africa, with few exceptions (e.g., Mitchell, 1971), most of the laboratory and field research on crowding has been conducted in North America. Thus, there is some question whether the results generalize to other parts of the world where the effects are of different magnitude and may be qualitatively different. Further, even in North America there have been relatively few experimental investigations of how crowding effects might be alleviated. Even if there were more such studies, because the extent of crowding is generally less in North America than in many parts of the developing world, there would still be a question of whether the results would generalize to situations in other countries.

Moreover, although research on the effects of crowding has been conducted over the past 75 years, most of this work has been aimed at dealing with theoretical problems rather than at suggesting solutions to policy makers. This focus on theory is not unusual among academic researchers, because they are rewarded for conceptual and empirical work rather than for proposing workable social policy solutions.

Given the fact that government and ultimately citizens pay for social science research, at some level social scientists have a duty to conduct research that is relevant and potentially useful to policy makers. In developing countries it is even more important that research has some likelihood of tangible benefit (Jahoda, 1975), because of the number of pressing problems and the limited resources available for dealing with these problems. In these countries, especially, the nature of the problems, the strategies for planning and development, and the order in which the problems should be dealt with require scientific investigation and data-based decisions. Thus, the role of applied psychologists is particularly important in developing nations. It is probably also the case that it is in developing countries that applied psychology most frequently falls short. For this reason, we believe that at least a portion of academic psychologists in developing countries should be involved in practical research, that is, research that can be used directly by decision makers. In that scientific information is only one factor in a policy decision, we need to make sure that it is factually correct and that it addresses the problem directly.

In this chapter we first present a framework for considering the practical utility of psychological research. In this discussion, we describe some of the traditional weaknesses of psychological research in terms of its applied usefulness. In the second part of the chapter, we illustrate the conceptual framework using some of the research on crowding. In particular, we focus on our own crowding research, its strengths and weaknesses in terms of how it might contribute to solving the problems of high-density urban living.

A CONCEPTUAL FRAMEWORK

In this discussion of how crowding research can be made more relevant, we use the framework proposed by Ruback and Innes (1988). We extend their model by considering other relevant factors that determine the usefulness of research.

Practical Research: Ruback and Innes suggested that, in terms of practical applications, research can be considered in terms of two dimensions: (a) whether or not the research investigates the effects of policy variables and (b) whether or not the effects of manipulations are measured by useful dependent variables.

The first of these dimensions concerns what Ruback and Innes called policy variables, which are those factors that can be changed by policy makers. Thus, for example, an arrest for a traffic violation is a policy variable because it is clearly under the control of the police. The police can charge for every traffic violation they see, for no traffic violations at all, or for some but not others.

In contrast to policy variables, non-policy variables are beyond the control of decision makers. Thus, for example, the sex and race of a person are not policy variables, because a decision maker has no control over these factors. Moreover, the use of such non-policy variables in research may often amount to lazy theorizing. Unless there is reason to believe there are inherent biological differences between the sexes or races, then such non-policy variables are merely surrogates for other variables that might have policy implications.

The second dimension of practical research concerns what Ruback and Innes called the utility of the dependent measures. There are numerous variables that could be used to determine whether a manipulation has an effect. However, only some of those variables are of interest to policy makers. For example, the effect of a changed policy for arresting traffic offenders could be measured in terms of whether there are fewer deaths on the road, whether there is an increase in money in the city's coffers because of increased fines, whether the police feel better about their job, whether people have more respect for the police, and whether people believe the roads are safer.

We suggest that some of these variables are of higher utility than are others. That is, city officials are likely to care more about whether there are fewer deaths on the roads than about whether people think the roads are safer. Unfortunately, people's attitudes and beliefs, the factors that psychologists are most likely to use as dependent measures because those are things we care about, are likely to be of little utility to policy makers.

For simplicity, let us consider each of the two dimensions as a dichotomy; that is, no policy variables are manipulated or some policy variables are manipulated and the dependent measures are of either high or low utility. If the two dimensions are combined, then a 2 × 2 matrix with four cells is created (see Figure 14.1).

		Number of Policy Variables Manipulated	
		None	One or More
Utility of the Dependent Measures	Low	Irrelevant and unlikely to be useful I	Potentially useful information about methodology III
	High	Irrelevant but potentially useful politically II	Relevant and potentially useful to policy makers IV

Fig. 14.1: The Relationship Between the Number of Policy Variables Manipulated and the Utility of the Dependent Measures

Quadrant I research involves no policy variables and low utility dependent measures. Most psychological research with college students, such as the juror simulation studies conducted in the United States, falls in this category (see Ebbesen & Konecni, 1982). Or, consider a study of how the air temperature outside affects whether or not people smile. As Mark Twain told us, we can talk about the weather but we cannot do anything about it. Thus, it is a non-policy variable. Further, decision-makers are unlikely to care whether citizens smile or do not smile. Thus, as a dependent variable, it has low utility. This hypothetical research would clearly belong in Quadrant I.

Quadrant II research involves no policy variables, but at least one high utility dependent variable is measured. Research from this Quadrant may be useful politically as suggestive of certain changes, even if no policy variables were directly investigated. However, such research may have indirect policy implications by suggesting possible policy changes that can be investigated experimentally.

For example, studies of differential verbal ability of black and white children as predictors of later job performance would be Quadrant II research. Race is a non-policy variable because it cannot be changed, but job performance is an important measure. Or, if we were to look at the effects of ambient air temperature on rate of crime, we would be conducting Quadrant II research. Although weather cannot be manipulated, crime rate is a high utility dependent measure.

Quadrant III research involves at least one policy variable but only low utility dependent measures. Ruback and Innes argued that much of the research on prison crowding is from Quadrant III, in that although policy variables are investigated (the amount of space per inmate and the number of inmates), most of the dependent variables are irrelevant to decision makers (e.g., perceived control, tolerance of crowding).

In terms of the weather example, a Quadrant III project might look at the effects of installing central air conditioners on how much people smile. That is, there is a manipulation of something policy makers could change, but the dependent measure is of something that is not very important to them.

Quadrant IV research involves at least one policy variable and at least one high utility dependent measure. For example, in the trial courts of the United States, research on whether juror selection procedures tend to produce more findings of guilt is Quadrant IV research. In the weather example, a Quadrant IV research project might investigate the effects of centrally air conditioning large government offices in terms of productivity and interpersonal relationships.

In general, most psychological research falls into Quadrants I and II and occasionally in Quadrant III. Only rarely do psychologists manipulate policy variables, and most of our dependent measures have low practical utility. Our dependent measures, such as psychological characteristics or attitudes, tend to be those most proximal to the treatment and to show a large effect, but they have little policy relevance (St. Pierre, 1985).

In contrast, economics tends to be a very practical discipline because it suggests specific changes that affect important dependent variables (Mark & Shotland, 1985). For example, economists often suggest that the amount of money in circulation should be changed as a way of affecting the interest rate and thereby the rate of inflation. Whether or not the suggestions are justified by empirical evidence, it is clear that economics is lucky enough to be a Quadrant IV discipline. Pettigrew (1985) has suggested that economics is useful because it also has the appearance of mathematical precision and has easily understood outputs.

HOW POLICY VARIABLES MIGHT BE DISCOVERED

If we assume that policy variables should be studied in order to have potentially relevant results, the obvious question is what these variables should be. One possibility is to examine in detail what policy makers do and choose those things that seem reasonably would produce differences. Aside from investigating things that policy makers currently decide, it would also be possible to examine those things that are decided by default. That is, potential policy variables might be those things for which policy makers rely on past procedures and routines but which could be changed.

There are two problems with examining the present procedure, however. First, it is likely to be very restrictive. If we examine only those things that are presently done, we will probably never get to the question of what might be. Second, a hit or miss choosing of possible policy variables is completely a theoretical, and even if differences are found, there will be no explanation for why they occurred.

One approach that overcomes both of these problems relies on the distinction between mediating and moderating variables, a distinction that has recently gained prominence in the psychological literature (Baron & Kenny, 1986). A mediating variable is a variable that is affected by some cause and that, in turn, affects some third variable. The relationship between cause and effect will be diminished if the cause-mediator and mediator-effect relationships are statistically controlled for and will go to zero, assuming there is only one mediating variable and it is reliably measured. In this way, mediators serve as explanations for how the cause produces change in the effect.

In contrast, a moderating variable is some third variable that interacts with a cause to produce one type of effect under one condition and a different type of effect under a second condition. The distinction between mediating variables and moderating variables is important because it has implications for suggesting policy variables that might be fruitfully investigated. In general, a knowledge of mediators may lead to possible improvements in treatment whereas a knowledge of moderators is less likely to be suggestive of improvements (Judd, 1987). A moderator can tell a policy maker when a programme will or will not work. However, it is only a knowledge of mediators that can be suggestive of useful policy changes.

OTHER DIMENSIONS OF PRACTICAL RESEARCH

In addition to policy variables and high utility dependent measures, there are other dimensions that affect the usefulness of research. Here, we discuss two: time perspective and scope of the problem.

Time Perspective: Policy decisions require planning for both the short-term and the long-term. Some problems require immediate intervention, others might require intervention in the near future, and still others might require intervention in the distant future. To use traffic-related examples, a road made impassable by flood damage would require immediate attention, the encroachment of vendors onto a city street might require action in the near future, and the size and layout of the roads needed in the next 20 years would require long-range planning. In sum, one dimension of time is in terms of when an intervention is needed and when the policy decision has to be made.

Time is also important in terms of the effects of policy decisions. Decisions can have immediate effects, intermediate-term effects, and long-term effects. For example, a decision in Delhi to pick up the tonness of garbage that had accumulated in the unplanned sections of the City had immediate effects in removing the waste materials, even if the long-term problem of disease was not solved. An intermediate-term effect might be increasing the electrical grid in three years, following a decision today to expand it. A long-term effect might be stabilizing the population in 25 years.

If we consider these two dimensions of time, when the intervention is needed and when the effects are measured, as dichotomies, then the 2 × 2 matrix in Figure 14.2 illustrates four possible types of research. For example, if people are starving right now, giving them food would have positive short-term effects (i.e., people live) and probable long-term effects (i.e., people are healthier). For the long-term, we might teach the people techniques to grow food more effectively. This teaching might have positive short-term effects (e.g. more self-confidence) and positive long-term effects (e.g. self-sufficiency).

		When a Policy Decision Has to Be Made	
		Now	Future
When the Effects are Measured	Short-Term	A	C
	Long-Term	B	D

Fig. 14.2: Consideration of Time in Terms of When the Intervention is Needed and When Effects are Measured

In this example, the short-term and long-term effects were all positive. It is also possible that they could differ in their direction. For example, cutting timber in the Himalayas gives positive short-term effects (i.e. jobs) but negative long-term effects (e.g. deforestation, soil erosion).

Given that some problems require immediate intervention and others require intervention in the future, and given that some effects appear in the short-term and others appear only in the long-term, research should be in all four cells of the matrix. In practice, however, most academic research falls into Quadrant A: we measure short-term effects of immediate decisions. This occurs not only because the rewards in academics are for quick projects that generate many articles in a short time period but also because policy makers, due to lack of resources, are likely to focus on short-term, stop-gap solutions. Thus, even if researchers wanted to measure long-term effects, it is unlikely that policy makers will be interested in having them measured.

The tendency for policy makers to focus on short-term solutions and short-term effects is probably even more true in developing countries than in more developed countries. Because of a shortage of resources, developing countries are likely to have more problems that require immediate solutions; these countries do not have the luxury of time to deal with the problems. Even if there is time for long-term planning, there are often no resources to implement the plan. Further, because of a shortage of research funds, a long-term commitment to a research project is likely to be absent, with the result that long-term effects are not measured. In summary, we suggest that research is even more likely to come from Quadrant A in Figure 14.2 in developing countries than in more developed countries.

Scope of the Problem: A second aspect of practical research is how the problem under consideration is seen *vis-à-vis* other problems. Thus, for example, overpopulation, although an important problem, cannot be adequately studied without also investigating poverty, illiteracy, welfare and pension systems, religion, environmental degradation, and resource depletion. Policy makers are no more broad minded than academic researchers, but the rewards in academia require researchers to conduct projects of manageable scale. Therefore, these projects are likely to test relatively small questions and to measure effects on some but not all relevant variables. Thus, our research may be dismissed by policy makers because of its limited scope.

PRIOR RESEARCH ON CROWDING

Most of the psychological research on crowding is not very relevant, has limited time perspective, and has limited scope. In the laboratory studies of crowding, there have been manipulations of the amount of space per person and the number of people (spatial and social density) but, for the most part, the dependent variables are of little interest to policy makers. Further, these studies generally involve non-representative subject samples (usually college students) who do not know each other and who interact in short-term crowding situations. Obviously, then, there are real questions about how this research would generalize to long-term crowding situations among people who have some relationship with each other.

In spite of the general limitations of the crowding research, there have been two studies that have clear policy implications. In one, Baum and Davis (1980) found that bisecting a long-corridor dormitory with a lounge area and unlocked swinging doors produced lower ratings of perceived crowding and higher ratings of perceived control, as compared to a similar dormitory where no changes were made.

There has also been some policy-relevant research conducted in prisons in a series of correlational studies by Cox, Paulus, and McCain (1984). Their research suggests that prison inmates living in dormitories feel less crowded if the dormitory is partitioned into cubicles than if the dormitory remains completely open.

Research from the United States suggests that perceived control is a mediator of the relationship between high density conditions and the feeling of being crowded (see e.g. Rodin, 1976; Ruback & Carr, 1984; Ruback, 1986; Stockdale, 1978). There is also some suggestive evidence from India (Ruback & Pandey, 1991). By knowing that perceived control is a mediator of the relationship between external conditions and the feeling of crowding, there is at least the possibility of changing the situation to give people more objective and subjective control so that they can better cope with overcrowded conditions.

SUGGESTED STRATEGY FOR RELEVANT RESEARCH

Relevant research has three prerequisites: (a) a knowledge of findings from basic research on the topic, because such research gives an understanding of basic mechanisms and suggests factors that may be important to policy makers, (b) a commitment to conduct a series of studies in order to be able to understand the unique aspects of the problem in the particular locale, and (c) a willingness to use multiple methodologies to address the topic.

Given these three prerequisites, we think researchers can make their research more relevant and useful to policy makers if they use a two-step research procedure. In the first step, researchers should conduct correlational research to determine if potential policy variables are significantly related to high utility dependent measures, in that statistically significant correlations generally provide clues to mediating factors and causal sequences (Doob, 1968). Creativity is called for in this first step, in the sense that potential policy variables should be broadly considered. There should also be particular focus on what be the mediating variables. Moreover, careful consideration is needed concerning what dependent variables decision makers care about.

If in this first step, potential policy variables are found to be significantly correlated with high utility dependent variables, then the second step of research is required. In this second step, potential policy variables are systematically manipulated to determine if they indeed produce significant changes on the high utility dependent variables.

As part of our two-stage strategy for policy research, we have conducted several studies. In this paper we briefly describe some of our studies, focusing in particular on why we chose to include certain variables and on what policy implications these variables might have for future research and policy.

A RESEARCH PROGRAMME ON THE EFFECTS OF CROWDING

Over the past two decades we have conducted numerous studies on the effects of crowding in South Asia using a multiplistic strategy: multiple methods, multiple dependent measures, multiple populations, and multiple sites. We have used observational, survey, and experimental methodologies. We have used self-report, behavioural, and physiological measures. We have studied adults and children (Pandey, Verma, & Ruback, 2000), males and females (Pandey & Ruback, 1996), religious pilgrims and urban migrants, pedestrians (Ruback, Pandey, & Begum, 1997) and tempo riders (Ruback & Pandey, 1992). Further, we have conducted these studies in rural villages (Ruback & Pandey, 1996), in urban slums (Ruback & Pandey, 2002), at the Magh Mela (Ruback, Pandey, & Kohli, 2008), and on busy streets, and we have tested our ideas in India, Pakistan (Ruback, Pandey, Begum, Tariq, & Kamal, 2004), Bangladesh (Ruback, Begum, Tariq, Kamal, & Pandey, 2002), and Nepal (Pandey, Siddiqui, Udas, & Ruback, 2009).

As a group, our studies have three convergent findings across methods and measures. First, there appear to be consistent gender differences: women respond more negatively than men to crowding inside the home, whereas men respond more negatively to stressors (e.g. traffic, air pollution) outside the home. In large part, these effects are probably due to the fact that women spend so many more hours inside their homes, whereas men spend more time outside their homes. Second, psychological factors matter. In particular, perceptions (e.g. of crowding) mattered more than objective conditions (e.g. objective density). Third, a sense of control over the environment, that outcomes are contingent on behaviour, was linked to better mental health, better physical health, and better interpersonal relations.

Although our research has several methodological advantages over prior research, it has some limitations that restrict its generalizability and its usefulness to policy makers. In terms of direct policy relevance, our correlational studies are what we earlier called Quadrant II research. That is, we did not manipulate any policy variables, but we did include several dependent measures of high utility (e.g., mental well being, physical health). Some of our research suggested that sharing resources with other families, especially toilets and entryways, was related to several negative effects, particularly for women. In subsequent experimental research, these factors could serve as policy variables, and such a study would be what we called Quadrant IV research. Our discovery of potential policy variables came through a scientifically defensible procedure, which we believe is the best way to proceed.

Our studies indicated that perceived control over the environment is, as has been found in North America, an important mediator of the relationship between environmental stressors and psychological reactions. Earlier, we suggested that discovering mediating factors was one way to find possible policy-related variables for future research. The fact that perceived control was an important factor for both men and women and that more objective variables (e.g. density) were relatively unimportant, indicates that psychological constructs have relevance to applied problems. Thus, the fact that perceived control was found to be an important variable suggests that we need to look for potential environmental factors that either increase or decrease the perception of control.

Future research on crowding needs to find other potential policy variables and to confirm those we found here. Then, if these possible policy variables are found to be related to important dependent measures, the next step would be to conduct experiments in which interventions are made and multiple dependent measures are assessed. If there is consistent evidence across the correlational and experimental studies, then we would be confident of our results, and we would be able to make a more convincing case to policy makers.

IMPLICATIONS

Social traps like overpopulation are not amenable to simple solutions. Thus, it should not be surprising that understanding their causes and testing possible solutions will not come through simple, one-shot, cross-sectional studies. Research on problems like crowding requires longitudinal designs, multiple dependent measures, and multiple studies.

At the neighbourhood and city level, research is needed on how people can better cope with the present and future stress of crowding. That is, we need to know what specific environmental interventions might alleviate stress produced by too many people. Our research suggests that perceived control is important. Thus, allowing cities to develop in ways such that people lose control may be particularly damaging.

At the individual level, research is needed that convinces people that it is not in their short- or long-term interest to have many children. For example, our research suggests that having fewer children would probably result in parents having better mental health and better relations with each other. Also, having fewer children would mean more resources (e.g., education, medical care) for those children already in the family.

Social science has concentrated on accumulating knowledge rather than on testing possible applications. Although basic research is crucial for giving us information about basic mechanisms and suggesting possible policy variables, we believe that at least some researchers should be involved in applying knowledge. That is, part of academic research needs to be directed toward producing knowledge that is useful to policy makers. These "appliers of knowledge" should conduct relevant studies that we have herc called practical research. Policy makers would be more likely to read such research, more likely to perceive it as relevant, and more likely to follow it as a basis of change.

SOCIAL REFORM AS NATURAL EXPERIMENTS

It is difficult, if not impossible, to conduct field experiments on many of the issues raised by our research, as they would require changes in things like the poverty level, housing, and water supply. Resources are required to do this kind of research, for both the manipulations and the research itself, and in the developing countries of South Asia, there is simply not enough money to support this kind of research.

However, it is still possible for social scientists to contribute to policy decisions by capitalizing on what Donald Campbell (1969) called natural experiments. Campbell argued that governments make decisions that can be analyzed with little effect on the way the policy is implemented. For example, with limited funds, government can implement a policy (e.g., build a needed road) in some but not all places. By taking frequent measurements in these multiple sites, on some of which a road is built, it would be possible to compare the sites before and after the road is built. Although this quasi-experimental design does not permit the kinds of strong conclusions that can come from true experiments, the information that can be produced can be helpful in ruling out some hypotheses and in suggesting others. But the point is that social scientists should work with policy makers to test, experimentally if possible, quasi-experimentally if not, the utility of programmes.

REFERENCES

Baron, R.M. and Kenny, D.A. (1986). The moderator-mediator variable distinction in social psychological research: Conceptual, strategic, and statistical considerations. *Journal of Personality and Social Psychology*, 51, 1173-1182.

Campbell, D.T. (1969). Reforms as experiments. *American Psychologist*, 24, 409-429.

Central Intelligence Agency. (2009). *World factbook*. https://www.cia.gov/library/publications/the-world-factbook/geos/in.html. Accessed September 18, 2009.

Cox, V.C., Paulus, P.B., and McCain, G. (1984). Prison crowding research: The relevance for prison housing standards and a general approach regarding crowding phenomena. *American Psychologist*, 39, 1148-1160.

Doob, L. (1968). Just a few of the presuppositions and perplexities confronting social psychological research in developing countries. *Journal of Social Issues*, 24, 71-81.

Judd, C.M. (1987). Combing process and outcome evaluation. In M.M. Mark and R.L. Shotland (Eds.), *Multiple methods in programme evaluation*. San Francisco: Jossey-Bass.

Mark, M.M. and Shotland, R.L. (1985). Toward more useful social science. In R.L. Shotland and M.M. Mark (Eds.), *Social science and social policy* (pp. 335-370). Beverly Hills, CA: Sage.

Mitchell, R.E. (1971). Some social implications of high density housing. *American Sociological Review*, 36, 18-29.

Pandey, J. and Ruback, R.B. (1996). Gender differences in reaction to crowding: Studies from South Asia. *International Journal of Psychology*, 31, 4713.

Pandey, J., Siddiqui, R.N., Udas, A.K., and Ruback, R.B. (in press). Residents' reactions to environmental stressors in Kathmandu: A comparison of the inner city versus the outskirts. *Psychological Studies*, 54.

Pandey, J., Verma, M., and Ruback, R.B. (2000). Perceived crowding in Indian classrooms: The effects of age, gender and household density. *Psychology and Developing Societies*, 12, 139-154.

Platt, J. (1973). Social traps. *American Psychologist*, 28, 641-651.

Ruback, R.B., Begum, H.A., Tariq, N., Kamal, A., and Pandey, J. (2002). Reactions to environmental stressors: Gender differences in the slums of Dhaka and Islamabad. *Journal of Cross-Cultural Psychology*, 33, 100-119.

Ruback, R.B. and Innes, C.A. (1988). The relevance and irrelevance of psychological research: The example of prison crowding. *American Psychologist*.

Ruback, R.B. and Pandey, J. (1991). Crowding, perceived control, and relative power: An analysis of households in India. *Journal of Applied Social Psychology*, 21, 315-344.

Ruback, R.B. and Pandey, J. (1992). Very hot and really crowded: Quasi-experimental investigations of Indian "tempos." *Environment and Behaviour*, 24, 527-554.

Ruback, R.B. and Pandey, J. (1996). Gender differences in perceptions of household crowding: Stress, affiliation, and role obligations in rural India. *Journal of Applied Social Psychology*, 26, 417-436.

Ruback, R.B. and Pandey, J. (2002). Mental distress and physical symptoms in the slums of New Delhi: The role of individual, household, and neighbourhood factors. *Journal of Applied Social Psychology*, 32, 2296-2320.

Ruback, R.B., Pandey, J., and Begum, H.A. (1997). Urban stressors in South Asia: Impact on male and female pedestrians in Delhi and Dhaka. *Journal of Cross-Cultural Psychology*, 28, 23-43.

Ruback, R.B., Pandey, J., Begum, H.A., Tariq, N., and Kamal, A. (2004). Motivations for and satisfaction with migration: An analysis of migrants to New Delhi, Dhaka, and Islamabad. *Environment and Behaviour*, 36, 814-838.

Ruback, R.B., Pandey, J., and Kohli, N. (2008). Evaluations of a sacred place: Role and religious belief at the Magh Mela. *Journal of Environmental Psychology*, 28, 174-184.

St. Pierre, R.G. (1985). Are the social sciences able to answer questions about compensatory education programmes? In R.L. Shotland and M.M. Mark (Eds.), *Social science and social policy* (pp. 195-217). Beverly Hills, CA: Sage.

CHAPTER FIFTEEN

SELF-EVOLVING INSTITUTIONS FOR SUSTAINABLE DEVELOPMENT

T.N. SINHA AND RAJESHWAR MISHRA

INTRODUCTION

Let us consider a conversation between a **social worker** and a **rural woman** which goes as follows:

THE SOCIAL WORKER : 'Will you do as I tell you'?

THE WOMAN : 'You good for nothing rogue, why have you come here? You gave us well but no water, a ration card but no grain, go away officer.'

SOCIAL WORKER'S WIFE : 'What a whirl we have got into.'

(*Sinha and Sinha*, 1996)

The above describes the development scenario in India, as elsewhere in the underdeveloped societies, that reflects the disenchantment of the poor with the externally induced development initiatives so far. A superficial analysis might indicate indifference of the development agencies, including the state; a deeper analysis, however, reveals a complex dynamics of dependency created through a number of doles and subsidies based development interventions.

While the empowerment approach of development has focused on **'teaching the man to fish'** as distinct from the relief approach of giving a **'fish hand out'** there is an emerging school of thought going step beyond. To them it is clear that while knowledge of fishing is important; without—(1) free access to water containing fish, (2) the absence of resources to obtain fishing nets, (3) ones own institutional norm to govern fishing right, and (4) freedom to effectively market the fish caught-knowledge of fishing is not enough (Sommer, 2001).

DEVELOPMENT IN PRACTICE: SHIFTING STANCES

Seen in the context of the above the current development practice is dominated by the **'fish hand out'** perspective. Initially, the Government of India assumed full responsibility for addressing all problems by itself. It created centre, state, district, and block level structures directed primarily to planning and/or implementing development schemes. However, the failure of some of its prestigious schemes such as the one directed at the community development (Mehta, 1957) and limited success of many others made it realize that the bureaucratic nature of the government organizations rendered them handicapped in effectively implementing the schemes.

The government officers remained distant, impersonal, rules and procedures bound, insensitive towards the needs of (particularly poor) people, elitist, power oriented, and in fact politicized (Mehta, 1989).

Consequently, the government slowly moved to get NGOs involved in the process of development. Successive Five Year Plans allowed NGOs to supplement government efforts for providing distress relief and social services to disadvantaged groups such as women, scheduled castes and tribes. By the Eighth Five Year Plans period, the government realized the potential of NGOs to go beyond providing distress relief and "make tremendous contributions in bringing about people's participation both in financial terms and through beneficiary support" (The Eighth Five Year Plan, 1992-97: 39). They were called upon to get involved in almost all development related activities. Simultaneously, the government also invited or attracted international organizations such as UNICEF, Oxfam, UNDP, World Bank, WHO, and others to extend, through bi-lateral agreements, a helping hand in development efforts. Now the major private sector players are also being called upon and smaller international agencies are allowed to approach NGOs directly to share some of the development related responsibilities.

While the strategy of the government to address to development challenges evolved from being solely responsible to seeking partnership with development agencies, the design for developing people has not changed radically. It remains **externally determined and supply driven.** Majority of the development agencies—governmental, non-governmental, and international—most often adopt ways and means of reaching various kinds of assistance and relief to people, trying particularly to reach out the poorest of the poor. The approach is to **identify** the targeted poor, estimate the **cost** of giving help, and **deliver** the help in an efficient way, mostly in the areas of health, education, environment, and poverty alleviation. Although, they all employ the rhetoric of self-reliance, people's participation, sustainable development, and so on, their concerns remain how to procure more and more resources and deliver them to the needy. The volume of investment, not necessarily the impact that the investment has created on either improving conditions for development or building recipients' capabilities, has been the basis for estimating the extent of development. The underlying assumptions are that once (a) resources are allocated, (b) required services and products are provided, and (c) regulatory mechanisms are put in place, the people will automatically become developed (Sinha, 2003). This, however, did not bring the required changes as the Millennium Development Goal document comments poverty still haunts millions (MDG, 2000). Jefery Sach (2005) found lives of one billion people in danger because of poverty. India's position on poverty is no better with 2.3 million or 22 per cent of the population still below poverty line (Mukerjee, 2006).

THE ALTERNATIVE STRATEGY: EXPLORING THE FACETS OF HUMAN CAPABILITIES

World Commission Report on Sustainable Development considers development to be sustainable that meets the needs of the present without compromising the ability of future generation to meet their own needs (1987 : 1). This would require that people take charge of their own development and develop capacity for self-regulation to be able to satisfy their present needs and also care for the future. As the people take charge of their own development, they acquire agentic capabilities. Agentic capabilities are central to all other human capabilities. They (agentic capabilities) manifest in self-reflective, self-organizing, and self-regulative mechanisms (Bandura, 1997, 1999) that human being employ that enable them to improve the conditions in which they live and to create new opportunities for further development. Agentic capabilities are constituted of three ingredients: Need for competency, belief in self-efficacy, and proactive orientation to the environment. Keeping people at the centre, White (1959) opines that human beings have a basic need to become competent and keep enhancing their competence that expresses in a variety of ways. Unless they are restricted, they tend to explore the surroundings in which they live, find out different ways of doing things, change what they do not like, behave so as to impress others, achieve success and avoid failure, maximize pleasure and minimize pain, and so on. Their need for competency may or may not be supported by their belief in self-efficacy. That is, they may or may not believe that they have the skills and ability to become competent. Those who do not believe having self-efficacy lack self-confidence and cannot function in a competent way. No matter how strongly they want to succeed, they do not make efforts and remain frustrated and helpless. On the contrary, those, who do believe that they have the skills and abilities, also have self-confidence to function in competent way. They are likely to approach to their environment in proactive way. The same environment that is perceived as formidable and forbidding to those who lack self-efficacy is seen as holding challenges and opportunities to the self-efficacious persons (Tuckman and Sexton, 1992) who turn the odds into the opportunities. The centrality of human being, thus, is crux to sustainable development and must be paid enough attention.

Agentic capabilities are universally valid indicator of human development. Whoever, the poor or the rich, the people of developing or developed countries, are engaged in the process of cultivating capabilities that enable them to solve problems, improve the quality of life, and actualize their potential by transcending their limitations, are developing their agentic capabilities.

In other words, developing conditions in which people live is necessary for, but does not amount to, human development. Human development means developing human capabilities to an optimal level (Kagitcibasi, 2002) by adopting ways and means that enable human beings to take advantages of opportunities created by improved conditions of living and improve them further in order to enhance their capabilities further and further. Development as considered by development economists, for example, Amartya Sen (Dre'ze and Sen, 1996) as freedom of choice and multiplicity of options some one enjoys doing what one values to have similar connotation.

On the contrary, continuing to improve the conditions of living without requiring the people to make efforts to develop their capabilities inculcates excessive dependency in them (Sinha,1992). People consider it a moral responsibility of development agencies to keep them providing the benefits, the magnitude of which depends on how miserable they are or present themselves, but not necessarily on how much efforts they are making on their own. As a result, the people fail to acquire capabilities to solve their problems. The only skills that they cultivate are how to exaggerate the display of their miseries to create a sense of moral compulsions for the agencies to yield maximum benefits to them. Such skills obviously are self-defeating in nature. As soon as the inflow of benefits dries up, people reverse back to square one.

REVISITING DEVELOPMENT: ENHANCING HUMAN COMPETENCIES

In the above section we examined facets of human development. Psychologists such as Bandura (1997, 1999), White (1959) have underlined the need for competency, belief in self-efficacy and proactive orientation as indicators of development. Kagitcibasi (2002) suggests need to have strategy that can help people take maximum advantage of the environment toward enhancing self-growth and competency. Sinha (1992) suggests encouraging people take action to develop their capacities and do not allow them to develop dependency. In sum development should entail:

- Stronger need for competency,
- Belief in self-efficacy, and
- Proactive orientation.

ROLE OF INSTITUTIONS IN ENHANCING HUMAN COMPETENCIES

Bandura (1999) suggested that human agency could be exercised through direct personal agency or through collective agency operating through shared beliefs and efficacy, pooled understandings, group aspirations, incentive systems and collective action. In this context institution, which is part of a larger social system and community, is forward looking, adaptive and proactive part of the community. Institutions as extension of the community vision and aspirations play important role in shaping human competencies.

In the development parlance institutions have been externally crafted or imposed for achieving certain tentative goals although they have had the façade of having institutions for sustainable development. Most of the government regulated or government crafted institutions suffer from being externally determined and not based on the felt need of the community in which its is supposed to be embedded. Cooperatives, self-help groups under the government have norms and procedures prescribed and regulated by the government or any other intermediaries working on behalf of the government (Mishra, 2005). Efficacy of institutions would, therefore, depend on the process of evolution and the facilitators who facilitate them.

SELF-EVOLVING INSTITUTIONS

Mishra (2000, 2001, 2004a, b, c & 2005) has made a differentiation between self-evolving and blueprint paradigm of institutions. Although institutions, by definition, evolve in response to the societal needs and are embedded in social norms and values (Deo, 1990) they tend to be erroneously crafted externally and imposed, as for example government facilitated Self-Help Groups and cooperatives which follow the norms and procedures of the government—which are bureaucratic—rather than representing societal and communitarian needs and aspirations (Mishra, 2005). Self-evolving institutions, on the other hand, evolve out of the societal needs, derive norms and values from the community and have the leadership embedded into the society. Such institutions have high level of adaptability and capacity to respond to several vulnerability faced by the community who are the primary stakeholders. Self-evolving institutions have high level of learning opportunity in the process of their evolution and can thus have, what Bandura (1999) prefers to call pooled understanding, group aspiration, incentive system and collective action. Seen in this context self-evolving institution, which is part of a larger social system and community, is forward looking, adaptive and proactive part of the community. They are extension of the community vision and aspirations. It is postulated that they would play important role in shaping agentic competencies and thus help achieve sustainable development. The following is the schematic presentation of how the link works.

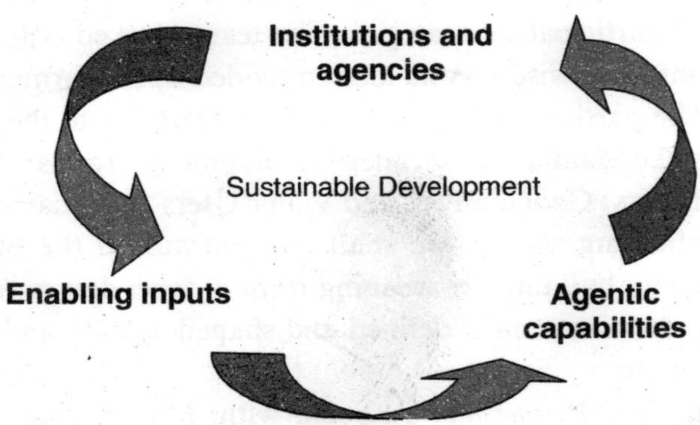

Having examined the conceptual position and proposed link between the institutional evolution and sustainable development an attempt is made, in the following section, to examine and analyze a living case showing how a self-evolving framework can contribute to sustainable development. The case exemplifies the transition from being externally determined to demand-driven development (Sinha, 2003). This is based on process documentation carried over 10 years (1995-2006). To attempt this we shall, first, try to present a background and then the process. In the end we shall present the outcome of the strategy and approach.

THE BACKGROUND

Let us start the story from the beginning. The Netherlands Development Agency and the West Bengal Government, with technical assistance from Euro Consult of the Netherlands, initiated a project in the mid-eighties to explore and create basic infrastructure for irrigation and soil conservation in the three least developed districts of North Bengal with the purpose to increase farmers' production capacity. The implementing agencies of the government had developed a number of irrigation schemes and structures such as tube wells, lift irrigation schemes, and soil conservation. Once the infrastructure was created, the project in the second phase (1988-1993) aimed to improve the use of the irrigation facilities by soliciting community participation and women's involvement through training of the beneficiaries and the extension workers. The project also arranged training for its own staff for improving people's participation. By the end of the second phase, it was realized that the project must bifurcate responsibilities for financial and technical assistance. While the former was left to the government functionaries, the latter was entrusted to a mixed team consisting of Dutch and Indian experts who were called upon to initiate a series of innovations particularly in the pump technology and participative strategies. The team worked with farmers and processed the intuitive wisdom and ideas provided by the farmers—both men and women. The participative approach of the team led to the formation of the institutions like Mahila Dal (Women Development Groups), Mistry (Pump repairing mechanics) Cooperatives, and Water Users' Association of farmers.

In the following section we shall concentrate on the Mahila Dal—evolution, capacity building for weaning from a dependency and externally determined mode to internally defined and shaped agenda and strategy and finally the outcome.

From Subsidy to Partnership: To begin with, Mahila Dals were given a matching amount to save money for a thrift and credit scheme through which they could own and lend pumping sets, take land on lease for agriculture, increase cropping intensity, and engage in other income generating activities. Soon not only the number of Mahila Dals proliferated, but they formed a federation to expand their activities, improve their resources, and gain clout to prevent government functionaries from siphoning off the resources meant for them. When the number of women groups increased, clusters consisting of 10-15 manageable groups evolved with an apex-federation at the helm. The federation helped other women to form their Mahila Dals without any matching grant.

Development of Leadership and Normative Structure: Centre for the Development of Human Initiatives (CDHI) facilitated formation of federation. Through a series of capacity building activities number of women with leadership qualities emerged and assumed greater responsibilities. Growing number of women groups necessitated formation of clusters comprising of 10-15 groups. Interestingly, the clusters are managed by the local women leaders who maintain absolute transparency and accountability. Here, the cluster leaders are compensated for their time by charging a small proportion of money from the financial transactions. Their income is contingent upon how much do they exert and the result they achieve. The arrangements are worked out and determined by the federation represented by the cluster leaders. Thus, normative structure of the federation has evolved and not been imposed from above.

DEALING WITH PERCEIVED INDUCEMENT IN THE ENVIRONMENT

The government sponsored Self-Help Groups (SHGs) of women have substantial subsidies which are available to the member of the groups without considering their efforts. As a result, there is mushroom growth of SHGs but the quality has suffered greatly and the mortality rate is reported to be as high as they are formed. West Bengal has also envisaged formation of federation by Government Order (GO) and the local officials have influenced the selection of officials to the federation. The available indications are that the federation is witnessing sign of conflict and disintegration even before they have been formed. Interestingly, the members of the CDHI facilitated federation, maintained a consistent position and were never enticed by the doles and financial opportunities offered by the government. They have deliberated upon the same and have firmly refused to be drawn into the temporary attraction.

A BUSINESS PLAN OF THEIR OWN

It is often said that the poor women have no planning acumen and capability to plan their business of whatever magnitude they are. From a modest collective fund of Rs. 20,000 the women federation has learned to plan their own activities including financial projections. They have developed sharp business intelligence which always alerts them in case of gaps. Equipped with strict financial norms, the federation has registered a turn over of more than six million Indian rupees and enjoys credible business relationship with one of the reputed nationalized banks. The nationalized banks are competing with each other to have business with the federation.

REFLECTION THROUGH PME

It is not that the federation has not suffered setbacks. There has been couple of occasions when the outstanding amount has been alarming. But continuous participative monitoring and evaluation, which the federation adopts, offered it reliable information and self-corrective opportunities. This helped in reversing the setbacks. Social auditing and peer group pressures have, most often, worked and turnaround strategies evolved on their own using collective wisdom. The reflection has often helped them taking proactive stances to the benefit of the federation.

Social Capital of Formidable Magnitude: The self-evolving process has helped the federation and the members learn from the outcome of their efforts and actions in an environment of objectivity and transparency. A peer group pressure in case of norm violation has never upset their social relationship. As a result, there is a bounding trust and confidence among themselves. This has contributed to valuable social capital which they use to deal with various situations. Government officials and people representatives are often questioned for their decisions which the federation considers as—'not in the interest of the common good'.

THE BALANCE SHEET

From being a modest component of a bilateral project to sporadic credit and thrift programme and then finally graduating into a full-fledged owners' managed women federation—the story is interesting but complex. Women federation has witnessed several twists and turns—members' absenteeism, irregular saving and loan refund, vibrant social mobilization and viable business propositions have defined and scripted the turn around strategy duly facilitated by the local NGO-CDHI. To day, federation has a distinct identity of its own which is acknowledged by the donors, state government (Goswami, 2006) and the PRIs at the local level. The initiative has been observed and analyzed by scholars and professionals. For example, Sinha (2003) found that the women have worked extra hard on their family land and the income that they generated empowered them to undertake a number of agentic activities. Some of these have also been reported to be the following (Chinnakonda, Prasad, Gopal, & Veldhuizen, 2002):

- Increased self-esteem arising out of men's recognition of their contributions,
- Confidence to interact with others such as banks, government functionaries, etc.,
- Capacity to shoulder responsibility in managing irrigation system,
- Increased mobility of movement outside their home for attending meetings and training,
- Ability to negotiate for loans, claiming land titles, and so,
- Involvement in health and education of children, prevention of wife beating and deserting, men's gambling and drinking,
- Confidence to lead and support other women,
- Capability to develop own vision of development, and
- Capacity to manage their federation.

One of the important features of the women federation is its inclusive character where the membership and management responsibilities are evenly distributed among the women cutting across their social positions. By one recent analysis 93 per cent of membership is held by the women belonging to Scheduled Caste (SC). The key positions are held by them as well. The chief functionary of the federation is a SC woman with a modest socio-economic and formal educational background.

WHAT HAS CONTRIBUTED TO THE BUILDING OF THE FEDERATION AND ITS SUCCESS?

Various factors can be attributed to the current status of the federation which have worked in different measures. There is one running theme which should be considered while analyzing the position. The intuitional development has followed a self-evolving process based on Reflective Learning and Action (RLA) which, in effect, means that the partners, in the process of institutional development, have maintained a reflective stance to look back and forth and analyze the situation and then proceed with corrections and improvisation. We used the available tools and methods but had made local adaptation of most of them. This flexibility has helped them consolidate their learning. In terms of concrete inputs, followings need to be considered:

Capacity Building Inputs Including Sensitivity Training: One of the important factors that has contributed to the dependency among the rural people is the perceived benefits through government schemes which are 'effort neutral'. The women in North Bengal were also suffering from this as they are part of the environment and have to go by what the men folk say and do. Our first effort was to wean them away from subsidy mind-set to self-help. Organization of small training programme using emotional appeals brought resources and support from the families and the local PRIs. Small contributions no body would mind. Gradually large number of cases were prepared where people were waiting for subsidies for long time. These cases were shared during the interactions and people were able to see how self-help works better. Small support helping ailing family members, helping children for their education gradually worked better and an environment in favour of self-help got created. This has been very crucial in weaning away the members from subsidy to self-help.

Leadership Development: From the very first day leadership was identified contingent upon performance and quality of initiative. Training sessions never started with what is leadership and types of leadership as we have in the formal class room situations. Training would begin with discussion around who does what and how one does different from the other? What helps one better than the other? Based on the reflections around such questions leadership was identified which often was unanimous. In the West Bengal situation where the political overtones in such programmes run very high, the performance and quality of contribution as indicator of leadership brought a sense of transparency and fair play. As a result, there was implicit emphasis over self-efficacy as the precondition for assuming or getting into leadership position.

Demystifying Democracy: In the current macro-political environment, democracy has the connotation of dominance by physical majority. In one of the impromptu (simulated) electoral exercises, we realized that the prevailing electoral dynamics was often dominated by those who are overtly visible and dominant in their physical and oral presentation. They were not necessarily performers. We had to live with this and allowed the elected leadership to work for some time when she realized that the job was not privileged and there were tasks to be achieved and targets to be met. There were uncomfortable responses from the group and the leadership had difficulty in attending to the demands too. Ultimately change of leadership was suggested not by the members but by the incumbent herself. The democracy contingent upon performance emerged as the preferred theme of governance. And all this happened because there has been environment of openness and transparency.

Group Dynamics: Training in group dynamics followed evolving process as well. The sessions would often be dominated by analysis covering who is where in the social ladder? Who does what? Who benefits and why and so forth? This helped in analyzing social structure and role relationship across class and gender. On the one hand this helped in understanding the current social order, it also helped in articulating how the situation could change.

Training in Achievement Motivation: Why are you what you are? This has been the persistent question in all the training exercise which was combined with encouraging examples and cases from different parts which were brought and presented to be discussed. 'You can make the changes possible (From Parvo naa to Parvo—the Bengali equivalence) in your situation' has been the ultimate message and this worked well. As part of this, several activities like innovation awards, quiz, rural fairs and interactive sessions with the government officials, bankers and people in the academics were organized which all showed the need for efficacy as a necessary condition for improving ones situation.

Institutional Analysis and OD: Through the continued Participative Monitoring and Evaluation (PME) exercises carried out at the group level, it has been possible to have clear understanding of the health of the groups and need for special interventions. Regular OD and institutional analysis are organized in which the vision, mission, normative structure and achievements are reflected upon and analyzed. This helps in identifying gaps and also what possibly could be done to bridge the gap. On a number of occasions, OD has helped turning around various compelling situations.

Business Development Plans (BDP): Until C.K. Prahalad (2006) saw business at the bottom of the pyramid (larger population of rural people at the bottom), BDP has been considered a matter requiring great acumen which common people do not, possibly, have. The women federation has been alive to this as according to its guiding principle the smallest of economic enterprise would work better if it has followed a systematic business plan. Every small loan which comes to the board for approval has a business plan including inflow and outflow of the financial resources. This has helped them tracking their income and expenditure and at the same time in planning how to up-scale or downsize.

Gradual Withdrawal with Mutual Consent: Women federation has been facilitated and supported by the NGO-CDHI. It has always been the intention to phase out and gradually withdraw from the key decision making. The same has been emphasized time and again and followed. Now, the federation has a board of its own, an independent legal registration, bank account and a set of employees. Many of the NGO's employees are now the employees of the federation which take care of their salary and perks. The cardinal principle of benefits contingent upon performance is applicable here again. The independent agreement with the bank and the necessity to survive keeps the employees on their toes.

IN SUM

The self-evolving institution building process has been able to create agentic capabilities among the partners and the managers who have high level of compatibility of their efforts with the core vision of the federation. Today, the federation is very high on self-efficacy, need for competency and performance and proactive stances which, perhaps, have been shaped by the strategies and processes adopted by the federation.

Note: Thanks are acknowledged to Prof. Jai B.P. Sinha for his visit to CDHI and his comments on the functioning of the women federation in Jalpaiguri. We have extensively referred to his paper 'An Approach to Human Development' where he has cited the example of women federation.

REFERENCES

Bandura, A. (1997). *Self-efficacy: The exercise of control.* New York: Freemen.

Bandura, A. (1999). Social cognitive theory: An agentic perspective. *Asian Journal of Social Psychology*, 21, 1, 21.

Chinakonda, D., Prasad, N., Gopal, K.S. and Velduizen, L.van (2002). Water management: Thematic Review of North Bengal Terai Development Project. *Mimeographed*, November 4.

Deo, J.M. (1990) *Institution Building: A processual analysis of a voluntary organization.* Unpublished Ph.D. thesis, Patna University, Patna.

Drèze, J. and Sen, A. (1996). *India: Economic Development and Social Opportunity*. Delhi: Oxford University Press.

Goswami, R. (2006). *Her comments at the innovation award for the UBTMS*, held in Jalpaiguri on the 25th of November.

Jeffery, S. (2005). World poor in danger. *The Time*, March, 14.

Kagitcibasi, C. (2002). Psychology and human competence development. *Applied Psychology: An International Review*, 515-22.

Mehta, B.G. (1957). *Report of the team for the study of community projects and national extension services*. Committee on Plan Projects, Government of India, New Delhi.

Mehta, P. (1989). *Bureaucracy, Organizational Behaviour and Development*. New Delhi: Sage.

Mishra, R. (2000a) *Evolving Institutions for gender integration into natural resources management*, Paper presented at the workshop 'Empowering Rural Women? Policies, Institutions, and Gendered Outcomes in Natural Resources Management' organized by the Institute of Rural Management Anand, (IRMA) Gujarat, September 7-9.

Mishra, R. (2001). *Legacy in Distress: Weaving Community Alliance for Integrated Water Management—A Methodological Perspective* (Co-author), Jalpaiguri, North Bengal Terai Development Project and CDHI.

Mishra, R. (2004a). *Situation analysis of SHG based poverty alleviation strategies*. Sponsored by Panchayat and Rural Development, Government of West Bengal and CARE, West Bengal,

Mishra, R. (2004b). Self-management capacity of SHGs in West Bengal's Jalpaiguri and Cooch Behar, Training strategies, sponsored by CARE, West Bengal.

Mishra, R. (2004c). *Strengthening Human Ecology Bond: BTR Eco-Development Initiatives*, Mimeo, Kolkata: Care, India.

Mishra, R. (2005). Expanding base for self-help based development strategy, *Mimeo*, CDHI.

Mukherjee, A. (2006). Twenty-three crore people still below poverty line, *The Hindu Business Line*, Thursday, June 15.

Prahalad, C.K. (2006). *The future at the bottom of the pyramid*. Pensylvania: Wharton School Publishing.

Sinha, F. and Sinha, S. (1996). *Indifference to Active Participation: Six Case Studies of Natural Resources Development through Social Organizations*. Gurgaon: EDA Rural Systems.

Sinha, J.B.P. (1992). A key address on developing psychology as a policy science: Problems and prospects. In B. Wilpert, H. Motoaki, and J. Misumi (Eds.), *General psychology and environmental psychology:* proceedings of the 22nd International Congress of Applied Psychology (Vol. 2, pp. 403-418). Hove (U.K.) and Hillsdale (USA): Lawrence Erlbaum.

Sinha, J.B.P. (2003). *An approach to human development*. Professor Durganand Memorial lecture delivered in the Psychology Department, Allahabad University, Allahabad on 24th September.

Sommer, J.G. (2001). *Empowering the oppressed: Grassroots Advocacy Movements in India*. New Delhi: Sage Publishers.

Tuckman, B.W. and Sexton, T.L. (1992). Self-believers are self-motivated, self-doubters are not. *Personality and Individual Differences*, 13, 425-428.

White, R.W. (1959). Motivation reconsidered: The concept of competence. *Psychological Review*, 66, 297-333.

World Commission on Environment and Development, (1987). Our Common Future. Geneva: World Commission on Environment and Development.

CHAPTER SIXTEEN

Religious Majority-Minority and Gender Differences in Models of Crossed Categorization Effects: Some Evidence for Social Development

Ramadhar Singh

INTRODUCTION

Without doubt, one of the key figures in the emergence and development of social psychology in India has been Jai B.P. Sinha. It is a privilege to be part of this Festschrift honouring Jai Babu and recognizing his important role in turning social psychology in India into experimental social psychology.

Although I had heard about Jai Babu from my mentors at the University of Bihar, Muzaffarpur, I met him only in October 1965. During my tenure at Patna University (1968-1970), I came in close contact with him. He taught me how to (a) write articles for journals, (b) perform experiments, and (c) read Weiner's (1962) Statistical principles in experimental designs before analyzing the data. I had read about the classic experiments in social psychology (Krech & Crutchfield, 1952). However, it was the reprint of his article (Sinha, 1968) in the Journal of Experimental Social Psychology that led me to become an experimental social psychologist. His early encouragement for doing graduate study in experimental social psychology in the United States, subsequent support for professional development in India, and continuing guidance in what should be studied kept me moving ahead and enjoying the thrills of performing experiments (Singh & Bhargava, 1985, 1986; Singh, Gupta, & Dalal, 1979; Singh, Bohra, & Dalal, 1979; Singh, Yeo, Lin, & Tan, 2007).

Among the developmental issues, I found challenges in justice and fairness (e.g., Singh, 1983, 1997; Singh & Lin, 2011; Tetlock *et al.*, 2007, Tetlock, Self, & Singh, 2010) and prejudice and discrimination (e.g., Singh, Choo, & Poh, 1998; Singh, Sharmini, & Choo, 2004; Singh, Yeoh, Lim, & Lim, 1997). In this chapter, I describe one experiment that has some implications for social development in India, an area (Sinha, 1981) in which Jai Babu has made significant and enduring contributions.

CROSS CATEGORIZATION

In crossed social categorization experiments, out-group (O) and in-group (I) by one categorization (e.g., nationality) are paired with O and I by another categorization (e.g., religion). Such crossings generate four targets, namely, double out-group (OO), out-group by the first but in-group by the second categorization (OI), in-group by the first but out-group by the second categorization (IO), and double in-group (II). Models of crossed categorization effects are often identified from responses to these four target persons (see, e.g., Crisp & Hewstone, 1999, for a narrative review; Migdal, Hewstone, & Mullen, 1998; Urban & Miller, 1998, for a review and meta-analysis).

The available evidence argues for five models. When crossed categorization altogether eliminates the distinction between O and I (e.g., Deschamps & Doise, 1978), the operative model is supposed to be of equivalence (OO = OI = IO = II). Responding to only one of the two categories (OO = OI < IO = II or OO < OI = IO < II) constitutes the model of category dominance (e.g., Hagendoorn & Henke, 1991). When both categories affect evaluation independent of each other, the additive model emerges (e.g., Singh *et al.*, 1997). With two equally important categories, therefore, evaluations of OO and II lie at the two extremes but of OI and IO fall in the middle (OO < OI = IO < II) (e.g., Hewstone, Islam, & Judd, 1993). In conjunctive model, one level of either category takes on all the weight. Such weight for O leads to social exclusion (OO = OI = IO < II) (Vanbeselaere, 1987) but for I promotes social inclusion (OO < OI = IO = II) (e.g., Vanbeselaere, 1991). In the hierarchical ordering model, the secondary category is weighted more at one than other level of the primary category (e.g., Brewer, Ho, Lee, & Miller, 1987). Depending upon whether the secondary category is weighted more at O or I by the primary category, semi-exclusion (OO = IO < OI < II) (Singh & Goh, 2006) or semi-inclusion (OO < OI < IO = II) (Van Oudenhoven, Judd, Hewstone, 2000) model can hold.

Hagendoorn and Henke (1991) varied religion (Muslim *versus* Hindu) and class (lower *versus* upper) of the participants as well as of the target persons in India. The original expectation was to eliminate the differences between perceptions of the religious groups by classifying the participants according to their class (i.e., monthly income). However, lower class Hindus did not show the typical response of a minority group (i.e., out-group bias), nor did Muslims show the typical response of a majority group (i.e., the additive model). That led the authors to conclude that religion implies status in India: "Hindus have an elevated status as a majority group and Muslims are not only a numerical but also a social minority" (p. 257).

Since religion and class of the participants jointly placed them at the different strata of Indian society, it was natural for Hagendoorn and Henke (1991) to yield evidence for as heterogeneous models as they did. To promote a positive social identity, the lower class Muslims might have equated themselves with the superior groups (Singh *et al.*, 1998). Consequently, the equivalence model held with them. In contrast, the upper class Muslims live in fear of being assimilated with the majority Hindus (A.K. Singh, 1988). To affirm their social identity, therefore, they responded to categorization by religion alone. Evidence for the semi-exclusion form of the hierarchical ordering model with the lower class, high caste Hindus suggests that they responded more strongly to O than I by religion, also an out-group fear (Ng, 1981). Only the upper class, high caste Hindus followed the additive model. Clearly, those of the highest social status used both categories; those of the lowest status used none; and those falling in the middle were driven by out-group fear.

The present author hypothesized that social status of the perceivers determines which of the multiple social categories they will use in judging others. This hypothesis came from the suggestion that "… the type of categorizations people use in a given social context are not only the result of the need optimally to categorize the social world… but also of the personal and social needs of the perceivers themselves" (Hagendoorn & Henke, 1991: 258). The author tested this hypothesis with the majority Hindus and the minority Muslims in India, the same participant population as in Hagendoorn and Henke. His choice for this participant population was also guided by the findings from the neighbouring Bangladesh (Hewstone *et al.*, 1993) that nationality was less important than religion to the minority Hindus, and that religion was more important to the minority Hindus than to the majority Muslims.

Subsequent to Hagendoorn and Henke (1991) and Hewstone *et al.* (1993), only four studies employed natural categories of nationality and race (Singh *et al.*, 1997), nationality, religion, and employment (Van Oudenhoven *et al.*, 2000), race and gender (Crisp & Hewstone, 2001), and religion and gender (Crisp, Hewstone, & Cairns, 2001). All these studies had participants from only the in-group according to all the categories manipulated. Moreover, they employed a between-participants design. It was not possible, therefore, to provide any evidence for the convergent validity of the model identified or shed any light on the merit of the hypothesis.

In Singh and Goh (2006), Chinese men and women in Singapore indicated their attraction towards work groups formed according to race and gender of two members. Participants also indicated their preference for one over the other member of the work groups as a colleague. In both tasks, responses by women supported the model of category dominance by race. For men, however, attraction towards the groups obeyed the additive model but preference for a member obeyed the semi-exclusion form of the hierarchical ordering model (i.e., the gender category was considered with I but not with O by race categorization). Importantly, men were more attracted toward O than I by gender, a result at odds with the extant models of crossed categorization effects (Crisp & Hewstone, 1999; Migdal *et al.*, 1998; Urban & Miller, 1998). As race and gender of both the members were fully crossed in a four-factor design, evidence on the convergent validity of the model employed by women and by men came from the same pattern in their respective Gender × Race of Member A and Gender × Race of Member B effects.

The moderating effect of gender of the participants on use of gender category just reported was predicted on the grounds that men are generally perceived to hold higher status than women (Stewart & Vassar, 2000; Stewart, Vassar, Sanchez, & David, 2000). So, ignoring the gender category allows women to equate themselves to the higher status men. In contrast, more attraction towards O than I by gender may satisfy men's desires for forming new relationships (Baumeister & Learly, 1995) or for maximizing outcome of the interaction (Gaertner & Insko, 2000). In fact, women respond to man and woman at the group level (i.e., social attraction as O and I) but men at the individual level (i.e., interpersonal attraction) (Singh, 2006).

Based on past findings (Hagendoorn & Henke, 1991; Hewstone *et al.*, 1993; Singh, 2006; Singh & Goh, 2006), the present author varied social status of the participants by including men and women from majority Hindu and minority Muslim religious groups. Target persons also differed with regard to the very same gender and religion categories plus nationality. There were four crossed categorization scenarios based on one 3-category (nationality (N) × religion (R) × gender (G)) and three 2-category (N × R, N × G, and R × G) designs. Since evaluations of target persons described by three categories as well as by two of them were taken, there were three tests of how one category was utilized when it was crossed with another. Table 16.1 lists the predicted category usage by participants of four status levels in each of the crossed categorization designs.

Table 16.1: Predicted Category Usage by Participants from the Four Religions by Gender Groups in the Four Crossed Categorization Designs

Crossed Categorization Designs	*Participant Groups*			
	Hindu Men	*Hindu Women*	*Muslim Men*	*Muslim Women*
Nationality (N) × Race (R) × Gender (G)	N, R, G	N, R	R	G
N × R	N, R	N, R	R	None
N × G	N, G	N	G	G
R × G	R, G	R	R	G

Muslims played key role in partition of India, and they continue to have ties with and sympathy for the people of Pakistan (Gupta, 1956). Moreover, doubts about the loyalty of Muslims to India have also been raised from time to time (Gupte, 1989; Madhok, 1981, cited in A.K. Singh, 1988). So, the author expected Muslims to equate O with I by nationality. Such equating of national groups would simplify the first three designs to the R × G, R-only, and G-only ones. From evidence for the model of category dominance by religion with the upper class Muslims (Hagendoorn & Henke, 1991), he expected Muslim men to use religion in the first, second, and fourth designs but gender in the N × G design. Muslim women still move veiled in public places, an obvious basis of self-categorization (Hortacsu, 2000). They are not subjected to civil laws concerning divorce either (Gupte, 1989). These societal practices may invoke perception of the self more as a woman than a Muslim. If so, Muslim women would use the model of category dominance by gender in the first, third, and fourth designs but of equivalence in the second design. The equivalence model in the N × R design was predicted because the lower class Muslims did not discriminate between the target persons formed according to religion and class (Hagendoorn & Henke, 1991).

Category woman stands for lower social status (Stewart & Vassar, 2000; Stewart *et al.*, 2000). To elevate their status to that of men, therefore, Hindu women should equate I with O by gender just as Chinese women did in

Singapore (Singh & Goh, 2006). With them, therefore, the first design would be reduced to the second N × R design and the third and fourth designs to N-only and R-only, respectively. In other words, the additive model should hold in the first two designs but the models of category dominance by nationality and by religion in the respective third and fourth designs. Evidence for the additive model with upper class, high caste Hindus (Hagendoorn & Henke, 1991) led to the prediction that Hindu men should use all the categories given. Moreover, they should show greater attraction toward O than I by gender, as did Chinese men in Singapore (Singh & Goh, 2006).

METHOD

PARTICIPANTS

Thirty Hindu and 30 Muslim college students from Allahabad, Uttar Pradesh, India participated. Each religious group had an equal number of men and women (ns = 15; age range: 18-21 years). Paid participation was in response to an appeal by a Hindu female graduate student of psychology.

TARGET PERSONS AND DESIGNS

Twenty target persons were prepared according to four separate crossed categorization designs. Design 1 was a 2 × 2 × 2 factorial, with Pakistani and Indian as the levels of nationality, Muslim and Hindu as the levels of religion, and Woman and Man as the levels of gender. It generated eight target persons. Designs 2, 3, and 4 were 2 × 2 (N × R, N × G, and R × G) factorials and generated 12 target persons. The levels of the categories were the same as in Design 1.

To disguise the manipulations done, another set of 20 filler persons were prepared. They were of different nationality (e.g., Nepalese, Sri Lankan), religion (e.g., Buddhist, Christian), and marital status (e.g., single, married). Experimental booklets presented the filler along with the target persons in completely randomized orders. Descriptions of 10 of these 40 persons appeared in the first part of the booklet and served as practice examples (Anderson, 1982; Singh & Goh, 2006). Such methodological precautions are necessary in a within-participants design that makes hypotheses transparent and judgements relative.

Counterbalancing the orders of presentation of categories in a description generated three versions of the target persons of Design 1 (N-R-G, R-G-N, and G-N-R). Similar counterbalancing resulted in two versions of target persons of Designs 2 through 4. Such descriptions were given to about equal number of participants from the four status groups.

PROCEDURE

Nearly one year after the demolition of the Babri Mosque in Ayodhya by Hindu fundamentalists (December 6, 1992), a Hindu woman conducted this experiment in small groups of 5 participants at a time. She introduced the experimental task as one of social perception in which several strangers were to be judged on the basis of what they had disclosed about themselves. Written instructions in Hindi informed the participants that the strangers were drawn randomly from a population of delegates to a recent convention of college students from countries forming the South Asian Regional Cooperation (SARC). In one of the sessions of the SARC convention, the delegates had supplied 1 to 3 answers to a "Who am I" survey. Responses of a random sample of 40 delegates were picked up for this study. The task for the participant was to read how the stranger had responded to the "Who am I" survey, and then indicate how much they would enjoy company of that person. This item has been used widely in study of interpersonal attraction (Byrne, 1971; Singh & Ho, 2000; Singh, Ho, Tan, & Bell, 2007).

To make the instructions and the task clearer to the participants, the experimenter conducted a practice session with 10 examples. She urged the participants to read the stranger's self-description, form an impression of that person, and then put a vertical mark along a 100mm horizontal line to indicate how much they would enjoy his or her company. The left and right ends of the scale represented the lowest and highest levels of enjoyment of company, respectively. Participants were encouraged to use the entire scale, for the correct responses were whatever they felt to be right. Responses were anonymous.

After the practice session, the experimenter verbally repeated the main points of the instructions to the participants. She also reminded them that responses were anonymous, and that their true feelings about the target persons were the correct responses to them. Finally, she asked the participants to judge 40 strangers one by one. In each case, the participants wrote the code number of the target person and drew a vertical line on the 100mm horizontal line of the response sheet to indicate their attraction towards him or her. Such measure controls for memory of the previous ratings in a within-participants design (e.g. Singh, 1983, 1996, 1997; Sing & Goh, 2006). The same 40 target persons were rated three times in different randomized orders (i.e., from two other new booklets) to generate more reliable responses (Anderson, 1982). After the third booklet was completed, the experimenter thanked the participants for their cooperation and paid them Indian Rupees 10 as compensation.

SCORING AND CODING

The vertical marks along the 100mm line were measured from the left to their nearest integer. Hence, the scores ranged from 0 (lowest) to 100 (highest). The higher the score, the greater is the attraction towards the target person. Data from all three trials of judgements were coded. The target persons were coded as O or I contingent upon whether they were from categories that excluded or included the participants themselves. For the Indian Hindu male participants, for instance, Pakistani Muslim woman and Indian Hindu man were coded as triple out-group (OOO) and triple in-group (III), respectively. For the Indian Muslim female participants, Pakistani Hindu man and Indian Muslim woman were OOO and III, respectively.

RESULTS

CATEGORY USAGE BY FOUR GROUPS OF THE PARTICIPANTS

The main goal in data analysis was to find out category usage by participants from the four social groups. Therefore, the data of Design 1 of the four groups of participants were subjected to separate 3 × 2 × 2 × 2 (trials of judgements × N × R × G) analyses of variance (ANOVAs) with repeated measurements on all four factors. The data of Designs 2 through 4 were also analyzed by separate 3 × 2 × 2 ANOVAs with repeated measurements on all three factors. Table 16.2 lists F ratios from the N × R × G, N × R, N × G, and N × R designs of the four participant groups.

Table 16.2: Statistically Significant Main Effects in the Four Crossed Categorization Designs of the Four Participants Groups

Crossed Categorization Contexts	*Participant Groups*			
	Hindu Men	*Hindu Women*	*Muslim Men*	*Muslim Women*
Nationality (N) × Race (R) × Gender (G)	N, R, G	N, R	R	G
N × R	N, R	N, R	R	None
N × G	N, G	N	G	G
R × G	R	R	R	R, G

Evidently, Hindu men used all the given categories in the first three designs but only religion in the R × G design. The interaction effects are absent in three designs, and the N × R effect of the second design is not supported by a similar interaction effect in the first design. It can be said, therefore, that Hindu men obeyed the additive model in the first three designs but the model of category dominance by religion in the R × G design.

Results from Hindu women are precisely as predicted. There are main effects of both the nationality and religion categories in the N × R × G and N × R designs but of nationality only and of religion only in the N × G and R × G designs, respectively. Stated simply, Hindu women used nationality and religion categories but ignored gender category. Consequently, their responses to the first two designs support the additive model and those to the third and fourth designs support the model of category dominance. No use of gender category by Hindu women not only confirms the finding from Chinese women in Singapore (Singh & Goh, 2006s) but also extends it from attraction toward work groups and colleagues to attraction toward total strangers.

Results from Muslim men are also as predicted. The main effect of nationality category is virtually absent. The main effect of the religion category is statistically significant in the N × R × G, N × R, and R × G designs. The main effect of gender category is significant in the N × G design only. Clearly, responses of Muslim men support the model of category dominance. They used religion category whenever it was available, as in Hagendoorn and Henke (1991). The gender category was used only when it was crossed with nationality category.

Results from Muslim women confirm our predictions as well. They used gender category in N × R × G, N × G, and R × G designs, but ignored both the religion and nationality categories in the N × R design. The only exception is that there is a main effect of religion in the R × G design. However, the main effect of religion was just significant ($p = .051$), and it is inconsistent with the results from the first two designs. So, we retain the model of category dominance by gender. Evidence for the equivalence model in the N × R design of the present Muslim women and in the Class × Religion design of the lower class Muslims (Hagendoorn & Henke, 1991) jointly indicates that some categories do invoke equality of II with OO and crossed groups on the positive side of the response measure in people of lower social status.

IN-GROUP BIAS, OUT-GROUP BIAS, AND NO BIAS

A statistically significant main effect in ANOVA indicates use of a category but does not specify the nature of bias. Tables 16.3, 16.4, and 16.5, therefore, report mean and standard deviation of attraction toward O and I by the respective category of nationality, religion, and gender.

Table 16.3: Means and Standard Deviations of Attraction Toward Out-group (O) and In-group (I) by Nationality as a Function of the Participant Groups and the Crossed Categorization Designs

Participant Groups		*Crossed Categorization Designs*					
		N × R × G		*N × R*		*N × G*	
		O	*I*	*O*	*I*	*O*	*I*
Hindu Men	M	47.02	64.08	40.36	61.97	31.86	75.16
	SD	33.70	28.36	34.82	26.74	28.56	22.18
Hindu Women	M	31.56	62.14	35.68	60.79	25.62	74.6
	SD	29.49	29.64	28.88	31.63	25.25	26.95
Muslim Men	M	60.91	60.39	63.31	60.82	67.19	67.49
	SD	29.04	29.76	29.17	27.57	27.96	24.4
Muslim Women	M	69.63	74.59	69.23	75.78	64.92	78
	SD	27.27	24.09	30.33	23.98	31.77	23.47

Nationality Category: Table 16.3 shows that Muslim men and women were equally attracted towards O and I by nationality. Importantly, their ratings were on the positive side of the response measure. In contrast, Hindu men and women were more attracted towards I than O by nationality in all the three designs. Compared to the nominal neutral point of the response measure (i.e., 50), moreover, their ratings of I were more positive, an in-group bias, but those of O were more negative, an out-group derogation (Singh *et al.*, 1997). Clearly, nationality served as a category for discrimination by Hindus but not by Muslims as predicted.

Religion Category: Table 16.4 indicates a more positive response to I than O by religion. Hindus, regardless of their gender, showed both the in-group bias and out-group derogation in all the three designs. However, Muslim men made a positive distinction from Hindus but did not derogate them. Although the same tendency is present in Muslim women, the in-group bias by religion was significant in only the R × G design. Taken together, then, these results indicate that religion is a more salient category for Hindus than for Muslims.

Table 16.4: Means and Standard Deviations of Attraction toward Out-group (O) and In-group (I) by Religion as a Function of the Participant Groups and the Crossed Categorization Designs

Participant Groups		Crossed Categorization Designs					
		N × R × G		*N × R*		*R × G*	
		O	*I*	*O*	*I*	*O*	*I*
Hindu Men	M	38.93	72.18	31.52	70.8	37.46	78.57
	SD	29.39	25.87	27.32	25.37	29.6	20.26
Hindu Women	M	35.32	58.39	35.92	60.54	26.86	72.32
	SD	29.62	32.74	29.31	31.43	24.69	26.03
Muslim Men	M	52.5	68.81	55.81	68.32	48.13	65.66
	SD	28.98	27.5	26.92	28.47	28.57	27.87
Muslim Women	M	70.2	74.03	68.42	76.59	65.48	77.58
	SD	25.31	26.23	29.57	24.67	27.81	24.88

Gender Category. Table 16.5 shows that responses to the gender category were truly diverse. First, Muslim women made a positive distinction from men, an in-group bias, but did not derogate them. Second, Muslim men revealed such an in-group bias only when gender was crossed with nationality. Third, Hindu women did not make any difference between O and I by gender. Finally, Hindu men showed an out-group bias: They were more attracted towards O than I by gender. Such an out-group bias was significant in the N × R × G and N × G designs but not in the R × G design.

Equality or irrelevance? Mean attraction responses of Hindu women to O and I by gender fluctuate around 50 in Table 16.5. This central tendency implies that the gender category was irrelevant for Hindu women. They did not pay attention to it at all. However, the prediction of the null effect of gender category was based on the logic that Hindu women equate themselves with the higher status Hindu men to promote a positive social identity (Singh & Goh, 2006). To choose between these two possibilities, the author examined the N × R × G effect in Design 1 of Hindu women.

Although the triple interaction effect was marginally significant, $F(1, 14) = 4.07$, $p < .063$, $MSE = 333.40$, the patterns in Religion × Gender effect across O and I by nationality did favour the equality hypothesis over the irrelevance one. Figure 16.1 presents mean attraction as a function of religion (line parameter) and gender (listed on the horizontal axis) of the target persons. The profiles of the Religion × Gender effects at O and I by nationality are

Table 16.5: Means and Standard Deviations of Attraction toward Out-group (O) and In-group (I) by Gender as a Function of the Participant Groups and the Crossed Categorization Designs

Participant Groups		*Crossed Categorization Designs*					
		N × R × G		*N × R*		*R × G*	
		O	*I*	*O*	*I*	*O*	*I*
Hindu Men	M	62.44	48.67	63.01	43.94	64.62	51.4
	SD	29.26	33.69	29.21	34.76	28.51	35.1
Hindu Women	M	47.58	46.13	46.49	53.73	48.2	50.98
	SD	33.19	33.37	36.28	34.94	35.62	32.38
Muslim Men	M	59.8	61.51	62.33	72.34	55.87	57.92
	SD	27.08	31.54	27.33	24.08	28.93	30.12
Muslim Women	M	67.84	76.38	64.92	78	63.53	79.52
	SD	26.29	24.68	31.77	23.47	30.04	20.87

shown in the left and right graphs, respectively. Obviously, O and I by gender received equal but highest ratings when the target person was II by nationality and religion (see top line of the right graph). This agrees with the hypothesis that ignoring gender category of the double in-group was a strategy of identity-enhancement (Singh & Goh, 2006) among Hindu women.

Second, separation between two lines of the left graph is less at I than O by gender. In contrast, separation between two lines of the right graph is less at O than I by gender. As the left and right graphs represent O and I by nationality, respectively, a simple interpretation of the three-way interaction is possible. Whenever social categorizations by nationality and gender converged (i.e., OO of the leftmost point and II of the rightmost point), social categorization by religion resulted in a sharper discrimination. However, when two social categorizations diverged (i.e., OI and IO of the two middle points), the role of social categorization by religion was diminished. Apparently, Hindu women paid attention to gender category but ignored it only when motivation to equate themselves with the higher status men (III) was operative.

GENDER DIFFERENCES IN WEIGHTING OF OUT-GROUP AND IN-GROUP

Mean attraction of Hindu men and of Hindu women listed in Tables 16.3 and 16.4 disclose an interesting gender difference in responses to the nationality and religion categories. Compared to 50, the magnitude of in-group bias is always higher than that of out-group derogation in men. In contrast, the magnitude of out-group derogation is stronger than that of in-group bias in women.

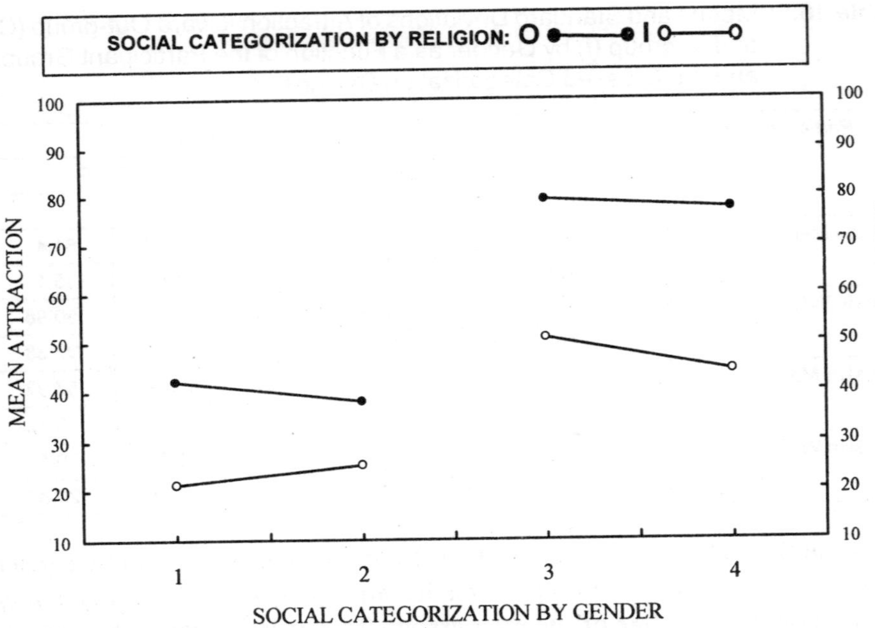

Fig.16.1: Mean attraction as a function of social categorization by religion (line parameter) and social categorization by gender (listed on the horizontal axis) across O (left graph) and I (right graph) by nationality. Data from Design 1 of Hindu women

To capture the foregoing gender differences, the data of N × R × G and N × R designs were analyzed by including gender of the Hindu participants as a between-participants factor in the ANOVAs. The gender of the participants × N × R effect was statistically significant in both the N × R × G and N × R designs, Fs(1, 28) = 4.68 and 6.15, respectively, ps =.03, MSEs = 1258.02 and 786.34. Figure 2 presents mean attraction as a function of nationality (line parameter) and religion (listed on the horizontal axis) of the target persons. The means of Hindu men and Hindu women are shown in the left and right panels; those from their N × R × G and N × R designs are shown in the bottom and top panels.

Two aspects of the results are of interest. First, the bottom and top graphs of men display exactly the same pattern, as do the bottom and top graphs of women. This similarity in patterns across the two designs is important for convergent validation of the model used because the N × R effect was statistically significant in just one case in the separate ANOVAs of the two gender groups (see Table 16.2).

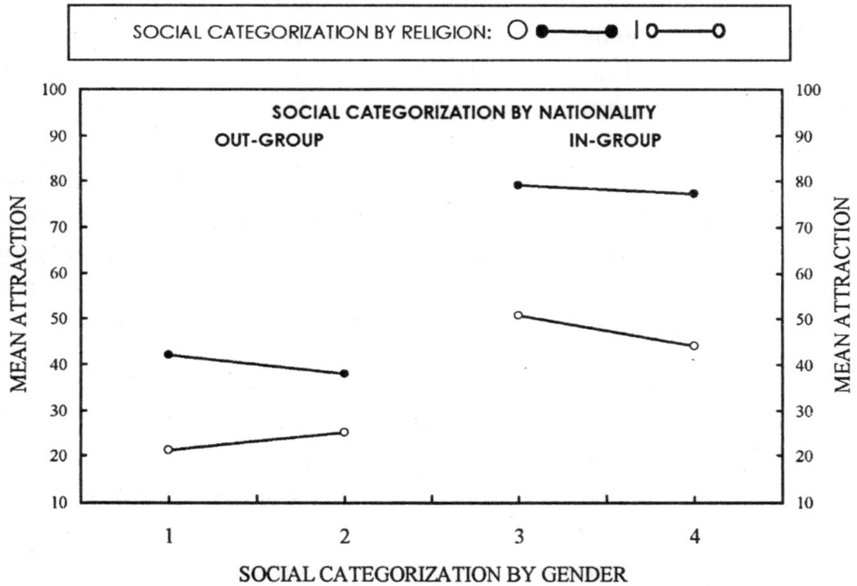

Fig. 16.2: Mean attraction as a function of social categorization by nationality (line parameter) and social categorization by religion (listed on the horizontal axis). Means of Hindu men and Hindu women are shown in the left and right panels; those from their N × R × G and N × R designs are shown in the bottom and top panels

Second, graphs of Hindu men and Hindu women have seemingly different patterns. In case of men, separation between the upper and lower lines is less at I than O by religion; the slope of the upper line representing I by nationality is shallower than that of the lower curve representing O by nationality. Put simply, I took a greater weight than did O. The two curves of women show exactly the opposite: O took a greater weight than did I. These trends in the three-way interaction effect are no doubt suggestive. Nevertheless, they cast doubt on the additive model (Hewstone *et al.*, 1993; Singh *et al.*, 1997) but argue for the semi-inclusion and semi-exclusion models with Hindu men and Hindu women, respectively.

DISCUSSION

SOCIAL STATUS AS A MODERATOR OF CATEGORY USAGE

Social status of people indeed determines which and how many of the multiple categories of others they use. As predicted, Hindu men of higher social status generally used all of the given categories, and they also showed more attraction towards O than I by gender. Hindu women of lower social status than Hindu men used religion and nationality but equated I with O by gender. Clearly, men and women from even the majority group of Hindus differed in category usage.

Similar results came from the minority group of Muslims. Muslim men of higher status by gender but lower status by religion used religion whenever it was available and gender only when it was crossed with nationality. Muslim women of the lowest social status primarily relied on gender of others in judging them. Muslims made no discrimination on the basis of nationality (Gupta, 1956). In fact, they equated O with I by nationality on the positive side of the attraction measure.

Taken as a whole, then, these results confirm the hypothesis that social categories have different meanings for people of different social status in India. Moreover, use of a social category is driven by not only people's need to simplify their social world (Turner, Hogg, Oakes, Reicher, & Wetherell, 1987) but also the relevance it has for their immediate self-definition (Hagendoorn & Henke, 1991).

SOCIAL STATUS AND CATEGORIES AS MODERATORS OF THE MODELS

The models of crossed categorization effects are truly moderated by social status of the perceivers as well as by categories that are crossed with each other. Muslim men, for example, followed the model of category dominance by religion in the N × R × G, N × R, and R × G designs but the model of category dominance by gender in the N × G design. Apparently, the gender category, which was ignored in the first and fourth designs, served as a base for affirming a positive social identity in the N × G design. Muslim women followed the model of category dominance by gender in the N × R × G and N × G designs, the equivalence model in the N × R design, and the additive model in the R × G design. Although the model of category dominance by gender held with them, evidence for the equivalence model in the N × R design and for the additive model in the R × G design indicate that categories themselves also moderate the models of crossed categorization effects (Van Oudenhoven *et al.*, 2000).

Similar moderating effect of categories on the models employed is illustrated by the results from Hindu women. They employed the additive model with the nationality and religion categories presented together but the model of category dominance by nationality and by religion when they were crossed with gender. Such evidence for additive and category dominance models with Hindu women emerged because they equated I with O by gender (Singh & Goh, 2000).

Responses of Hindu men to the nationality and gender categories conformed to the prediction of the additive model but those to the nationality and religion categories to the prediction of the hierarchical ordering model. In the R × G design, they also followed the model of category dominance by religion. In fact, the obtained results for Hindu men and for Muslim women differed from the predicted models in the R × G design only. Perhaps there is something unique about crossing of gender with religion. Besides, Hindu men were more attracted towards O than I by gender (Goh & Singh, 2002). This finding again questions the existing conceptualizations and models of crossed categorization effects (Crisp & Hewstone, 1999; Migdal *et al.*, 1998; Urban & Miller, 1998).

That the models of crossed categorization effects are moderated by the categories themselves is an important addition to the extant literature. This demonstration has been possible because this experiment crossed each of the three categories with another category at least three times. An advantage of such multiple designs is that it provides both the convergent and divergent validation of the models employed. Future work should, therefore, employ our method to check on whether there is genuine category dominance by race in South Africa or the United States, by religion in Northern Ireland or Bangladesh, and by language in Belgium or Quebec of Canada (Hewstone, 1996) or is an outcome of the other category crossed with.

It should be added that results seemingly supportive of an additive model could actually be manifestations of the underlying hierarchical ordering model. Separate ANOVAs for the data of Designs 1 and 2 of Hindu men and women, for example, led to acceptance of the additive model for the nationality and religion categories. Estimates of in-group bias and out-group derogation relative to the nominal neutral point of the response measure, however, indicated that Hindu men had a stronger in-group bias than out-group derogation, and the reverse was true with Hindu women. When the data of Hindu men and women were analyzed together, gender of the participants did moderate the N × R effect (see Figure 2). In other words, responses by Hindu men had a tendency for semi-inclusion (i.e., a greater weighting of I than O); Hindu women had a tendency for the opposite semi-exclusion (i.e., a greater weighting of O than I). On this basis, it is proper to accept the hierarchical ordering model as in Brewer *et al.* (1987) and Hewstone *et al.* (1993, Experiment 2).

MAJORITY-MINORITY DIFFERENCES

The nationality category was important to the majority group of Hindus but not to the minority group of Muslims in India. Whereas the former had both the in-group bias and out-group derogation, the latter equated I with O by nationality. This result differs from that of Hewstone *et al.* (1993) who found nationality to be a weak category for the majority Muslims as well as the minority Hindus in Bangladesh.

Why do Hindus assign more importance to nationality than do Muslims in India or Bangladeshi in general? Following Tajfel and Turner (1986), it can be speculated that Indian Muslims as well as Bangladeshi perceive high permeability of national boundary. They desire to have scope for moving from one country to another. It is estimated that 2 to 15 millions of Bangladeshi nationals reside illegally in India (U.S. Department of State, 1994). Of those living in Delhi, only a minority expressed any hope for going back to Bangladesh (Lin & Paul, 1995). For the Indian Hindus, however, the national boundary is impermeable. It generates a feeling of their significant and mighty position in South Asia. It is unsurprising, therefore, that Indian Hindus give much more importance to nationality than do Muslims or other non-Indians in South Asia.

Similar to the results of Hewstone *et al.* (1993), religion turned out to be more important to Hindus than Muslims of India. This result is of special interest, for Hindus are the majority group in India but the minority group in Bangladesh. Similar responses to the religion category by Hindus of Bangladesh and India indicates that what appeared to be a majority-minority difference in Hewstone *et al.* may actually be the Hindu-Muslim difference, pointing to a revival of the Hindu fundamentalism in South Asia (Malik & Vajpeyi, 1989).

Because the model of category dominance by religion held with the upper class Muslims of India, the less positive evaluation of Hindus than Muslims was considered as 'a communalized response' by Hagendoorn and Henke (1991: 258). Results caution against this interpretation. Muslim men showed in-group bias by religion but did not reject the out-group Hindu. Even in Hagendoorn and Henke, all the four means were on the positive side of their 3-point response measure. Clearly, perceiving others according to only one category—be it religion or gender—is also a way of simultaneously simplifying the social world (Turner *et al.*, 1987) and preserving a positive social identity (A.K. Singh, 1988) among Muslims.

Results further indicate that responses by Hindu men cannot be viewed as communal either. Evidence for the semi-inclusion form of the hierarchical model in their Nationality × Religion effects reflects on their positive orientation to all the groups that share at least one social category. The converging pattern in the Nationality × Religion effect of the present Hindu men matched with that in the Nationality × Employment effect of the majority Dutch in the Netherlands (Van Oudenhoven *et al.*, 2000, Figure 3: 292). Perhaps people of the numerical majority groups are favourably inclined toward assuming the responsibility of carrying similar others with them. Such responsibility appears to have been accepted by the majority Hindus in India (Gupte, 1989).

Hewstone *et al.* (1993, Experiment 2) found evidence for the semi-exclusion form of the hierarchical ordering model in the Nationality × Religion effect in Bangladesh. We found the same with Hindu women of India. As the semi-exclusion form of the hierarchical ordering model implies a disproportionate weight for O than I, it can be said that insecure people of high social status are perhaps afraid of out-groups. As a result, they either reject O or equate I with O. Considered from this angle, Hindu women in India and nationals of Bangladesh may be viewed as still unsure of their identities. Future research should take up this issue.

Models of crossed categorization effects have been receiving so much attention in the literature (Urada, Stentrom, & Miller, 2007) because of the potential that crossed groups initially offered for reducing intergroup bias (Deschanps & Doise, 1978; Hewstone *et al.*, 2002). However, crossing of two categories has not been so successful towards this goal (see, Migdal *et al.*, 1998; Mullen, Migdal, & Hewstone, 2001). The overwhelming evidence for the model of category dominance and some evidence for semi-inclusion and semi-exclusion in the present work raise further doubt on potential of cross categorizations as a bias-reducing intervention. Nevertheless, the high status majority group of Hindu men seem to have assumed the responsibility of carrying some out-groups with them, a healthy sign of social development.

SUMMARY AND CONCLUSION

Attraction towards target persons categorized by nationality, religion, or gender as well as by all of their pairings was studied in a within-participants experiment. The moderating role of the participants' social status in crossed categorization effects was examined by including men and women from the majority Hindu and minority Muslim religious groups in India. As predicted, Muslims ignored categorization by nationality: Responses of men and women displayed category dominance by religion and by gender, respectively. Hindu women ignored categorization by gender, and Hindu men were more attracted toward the out-group than in-group by gender. Responses of Hindu men conformed to the model of social inclusion; those of Hindu women, in contrast, conformed to the model of social exclusion. Obviously, natural social categories have different meanings for people of different status in India, and cross-categorization is of limited value for social harmony and development.

In conclusion, it may be said that the models of crossed categorization effects are indeed moderated by social status of the perceivers and the categories that are crossed with each other. Interestingly, category usage is generally predictable from knowledge of the religious and gender groups of the perceivers.

ACKNOWLEDGEMENTS

This research was supported in part by the National University of Singapore Grants R-107-000-030-112 and R-581-000-049-112 to Ramadhar Singh. The authors thanks Namita Singh for collecting and coding the data; Ajit K. Dalal for coordinating the data gathering; Lydia Tan for entering the data; N. Sriram for his assistance in data analyses; Patrick Lin for preparing the figures; Ajai Singh Gaur for preparing the tables; Ishtiaq Hossain for supplying the literature on Hindu-Muslim and Bangladesh-India relations; and Smita Singh for final reading of this version.

Correspondence concerning this chapter should be addressed to Ramadhar Singh, Organizational Behaviour and Human Resource Management, Indian Institute of Management Bangalore, Bannerghatta Road, Bangalore 560 076, India (e-mail: ramadhar@iimb.ernet.in).

REFERENCES

Anderson, N.H. (1982). *Methods of information integration theory*. New York: Academic Press.

Baumeister, R.F. and Learly, M.R. (1995). The need to belong: Desire for interpersonal attachments as a fundamental human motivation. *Psychological Bulletin*, 117, 497-529.

Brewer, M.B., Ho, H., Lee, J., and Miller, N. (1987). Social identity and social distance among Hong Kong school children. *Personality and Social Psychology Bulletin*, 8, 393-400.

Byrne, D. (1971). *The attraction paradigm*. New York: Academic Press.

Crisp, R.J., and Hewstone, M. (1999). Differential evaluation of crossed category groups: Patterns, processes, and reducing intergroup bias. *Group Processes and Intergroup Relations*, 2, 307-333.

Crisp, R.J., and Hewstone, M. (2000). Crossed categorization and intergroup bias: The moderating roles of intergroup and affective context. *Journal of Experimental Social Psychology*, 36, 357-383.

Crisp, R.J. and Hewstone, M. (2001). Multiple categorization and implicit intergroup bias: Differential category dominance and the positive-negative asymmetry. European *Journal of Social Psychology*, 31, 45-62.

Crisp, R.J., Hewstone, M., and Cairns, E. (2001). Multiple identities in Northern Ireland: Hierarchical ordering in the presentation of group membership. *British Journal of Social Psychology*, 40, 501-514.

Deschamps, J.C., and Doise, W. (1978). Crossed category memberships in intergroup relations. In H. Tajfel (Ed.), *Differentiation between social groups* (pp. 141-158). Cambridge: Cambridge University Press.

Gaertner, L. and Insko, C.A. (2000). Intergroup discrimination in the minimal group paradigm: Categorization, reciprocation, or fear? *Journal of Personality and Social Psychology*, 79,77-94.

Gupta, R. (1956). Caste rankings and intercaste relations among the Muslims of a village in north-western UP. *Eastern Anthropologist*, 10, 30-42.

Gupte, P. (1989). *India: The challenge of change*. London: Methuen.

Hagendoorn, L. and Henke, R. (1991) The effect of multiple category membership on intergroup evaluations in a north Indian context: Class, caste, and religion. *British Journal of Social Psychology*, 30, 247-260.

Hewstone, M. (1996). Contact and categorization: Social psychological interventions to change intergroup relations. In C.N. Macrae, C. Stangor and M. Hewstone (Eds.), *Stereotypes and stereotyping* (pp. 323-368). New York: Guildford Press.

Hewstone, M., Islam, M.R., and Judd, C.M. (1993). Models of crossed categorization and intergroup relations. *Journal of Personality and Social Psychology*, 64, 779-793.

Hortacsu, N. (2000). Intergroup relations in a changing political context: The case of veiled and unveiled university students in Turkey. *European Journal of Social Psychology*, 30, 733-744.

Krech, D., and Crutchfield, R.S. (1952). *Theory and problems in social psychology*. New York: McGraw-Hill.

Lin, S.G., and Paul, M.C. (1995). Bangladeshi migrants in Delhi: Social insecurity, state power, and captive vote banks. *Bulletin of Concerned Asian Scholars*, 27, 3-20.

Madhok, B., (1983). India's Muslim minority-persecuted or pampered? *The Illustrated Weekly of India*, pp. 8-10.

Malik, Y.K., and Vajpeyi, D.K. (1989). The rise of Hindu militancy: India's secular democracy at risk. *Asian Survey*, 29, 308-325.

Migdal, M.J., Hewstone, M., and Mullen, B. (1998). The effects of crossed categorization on intergroup evaluations: A meta-analysis. *British Journal of Social Psychology*, 37, 303-324.

Mullen, B., Migdal, M.J., and Hewstone, M. (2001). Crossed-categorization *vs.* Simple categorization and intergroup evaluations: A meta-analysis. *European Journal of Social Psychology*, 31, 721-736.

Ng, S.H. (1981) Equity theory and the allocation of rewards between groups. *European Journal of Social Psychology*, 11, 439-444.

Singh, A.K. (1988). Intergroup relations and social tensions. In J. Pandey (Ed.), *Psychology in India: The state-of-the-art* (Vol. 2, pp. 159-224). New Delhi: Sage.

Singh, R. (1983). Leadership style and reward allocation: Does least preferred co-worker scale measure task and relation orientation? *Organizational Behaviour and Human Performance*, 32, 178-197.

Singh, R. (1996) Subtractive versus ratio model of "fair" allocation: Can group level analyses be misleading? *Organizational Behaviour and Human Decision Processes*, 68, 123-144.

Singh, R. (1997). Group harmony and interpersonal fairness in reward allocation: On the loci of the moderation effect. *Organizational Behaviour and Human Decision Processes*, 72, 158-183.

Singh, R. (2006). Gender among multiple categories: Social attraction in women but interpersonal attraction in men. In R. Crisp and M. Hewstone (Eds.), *Multiple categories and cross-categorizations: Processes, models, and applications* (pp. 189-208). East Sussex: UK: Psychology Press.

Singh, R; and Bhargava, S. (1985). Motivation, ability, and exam performance: Tests of hypotheses of cultural difference and task difficulty. *Journal of Experimental Social Psychology*, 21, 466-479.

Singh, R; and Bhargava, S. (1986). Constant-weight versus relative-weight averaging in the prediction of exam performance. *Journal of Experimental Social Psychology*, 22, 547-566.

Singh, R., Bohra, K.A., and Dalal, A.K. (1979). Favourableness of leadership situations studied with information integration theory. *European Journal of Social Psychology*, 9, 253-264.

Singh, R., Choo, W.M., and Poh, L.L. (1998). In-group bias and fair-mindedness as strategies of self-presentation in intergroup perception. *Personality and Social Psychology Bulletin*, 24, 147-162.

Singh, R., and Goh, H.Y. (2006). Gender and group versus individual target as moderators of the models of crossed categorization effects. *Psychology and Developing Societies*, 18, 139-166.

Singh, R., Gupta, M., and Dalal, A.K. (1979). Cultural difference in attribution of performance: An integration-theoretical analysis. *Journal of Personality and Social Psychology*, 37, 1342-1351.

Singh, R., and Ho, S.Y. (2000). Attitudes and attraction: A new test of the attraction, repulsion and similarity-dissimilarity asymmetry hypotheses. *British Journal of Social Psychology*, 39, 197-211.

Singh, R., Ho, L.J., Tan, H.L., and Bell, P.A. (2007). Attitudes, personal evaluations, cognitive evaluation, and interpersonal attraction: On the direct, indirect, and reverse-causal effects. *British Journal of Social Psychology*, 46, 19-42.

Singh, R; and Lin, X. (2011). The severity effect on the compensation and imprisonment recommendations: Deterrence as a mediator in Singapore. Asian *Journal of Social Psychology*, in press.

Singh, R., Sharmini, Chew, I. (2004). Intergroup perception as a compromise between in-group bias and fair-mindedness. *Journal of Social Psychology*, 104, 373-387.

Singh, R. Yeo, S.E., Lin, P.K.F., and Tan, L. (2007). Multiple mediators of the attitude similarity-attraction relationship: Dominance of inferred attraction and subtlety of affect. *Basic and Applied Social Psychology*, 29, 61-74

Singh, R., Yeoh, B.S.E., Lim, D.I., and Lim, K.K. (1997). Cross categorization effects in intergroup discrimination: Adding *versus* averaging. *British Journal of Social Psychology*, 36, 121-138.

Sinha, J.B.P. (1968). The n-Ach/n-Cooperation under limited/unlimited resource condition. *Journal of Experimental Social Psychology*, 4, 233-248.

Sinha, J.B.P. (1981). In search of research identity. In J. Pandey (Ed.), *Perspectives on Experimental Social Psychology in India* (pp. 241-252). New Delhi: Concept.

Stewart, T.L., and Vassar, P.M. (2000). The effect of occupational status cues on memory for male and female targets. *Psychology of Women Quarterly*, 24, 161-169.

Stewart, T.L., Vassar, P.M., Sanchez, D.T., and David, S.E. (2000). Attitude toward women's societal roles moderate the effect of gender cues on target individuation. *Journal of Personality and Social Psychology*, 79, 143-157.

Tajfel, H; and Turner, J.C. (1986). The social identity theory of intergroup behaviour. In S. Worchel and W. Austin (Eds.), *Psychology of Intergroup Relations* (pp. 7-24). Chicago: Nelson-Hall.

Tetlock, P.E., Self, W.T., and Singh, R. (2010). The punitiveness paradox: When is external pressure exculpatory—And when a signal just to spread blame? *Journal of Experimental Social Psychology*, in press.

Tetlock, P.E., Visser, P., Singh, R., Polifroini, M. Scott, A., Elson, B., and Mazzocco, P. (2007). People as intuitive prosecutors: The impact of social-control goals on punitiveness and attributions of responsibility. *Journal of Experimental Social Psychology*, 43, 195-209.

Turner, J.C., Hogg, M., Oakes, P., Reicher, S., and Wetherell, M. (1987). *Rediscovering the social group: A self-categorization theory*. Oxford: Basil Blackwell.

Urada, D., Stenstrom, D., and Miller, N. (2007). Crossed categorization beyond the two-group model. *Journal of Personality and Social Psychology*, 92, 649-664.

Urban, L.M., and Miller, N.M. (1998). A meta-analysis of crossed categorization effects. *Journal of Personality and Social Psychology*, 74, 898-908.

U.S. Department of State (1994). *Indian human rights practices*, 1993. http:/ www.cpsr.org/cpsr/privacy/priva...tate_dept_human-rights_guide/India.txt.

Vanbeselaere, N. (1987). The effects of dichotomous and crossed social categorizations upon intergroup discrimination. *European Journal of Social Psychology*, 17, 143-156.

Vanbeselaere, N. (1991). The different effects of simple and crossed categorizations: A result of the category differentiation process or of different category salience? In W. Stroebe and M. Hewstone (Eds.), *European review of social psychology*, (Vol. 2, pp. 247-278). Chichester, England: Wiley.

Van Oudenhoven, J.P., Judd, C.M., and Hewstone, M. (2000). Additive and interactive models of crossed categorization in correlated social categories. *Group Processes and Intergroup Relations*, 3, 285-295.

Winer, B.J. (1962). *Statistical principles in experimental designs*. New York: McGraw-Hill.

CHAPTER SEVENTEEN

VALUES AS A FORCE BEHIND DEVELOPMENT

JYOTI VERMA

INTRODUCTION

Some well known economists, philosophers and social scientists have thought and spoken about values being the force behind individual and societal level development. India has been the birth place of Swami Vivekananada, Mahatma Gandhi, J. Krishnamurti, and Amartya Sen to name just a few, who thought, worried and worked for human well-being and social welfare in their own respective ways and sometimes from within the domains of their profession and personal experiences. These personalities were born as ordinary human beings but were moved by meta values of love compassion and concern for humanity which gave them the courage and conviction to explicate and initiate the process of social change and self-evolvement side by side. Another name is that of Mother Teresa whose *karmbhumi* was India. Mother Teresa's 'self' evolved to the extent of becoming a 'saint' while she served those whom the society had deserted, disowned and purged out of its system. Mother Teresa's life was a living example which showed that when kindness and compassion become the passions of life they acquire tremendous force and power to get translated into acts and social welfare services that are unprecedented.

It appears that the socially conscious individuals and social scientists alike feel concerned that individual well-being and social welfare may not be assured in a complex and plural society replete with harsh social realities as these circumstances present a fertile ground for self-interest values to convert into selfishness. Furthermore, since values present a socio-cultural challenge for development, one wonders whether indigenous values having the potential to defuse the toxicity of self-centric values that hinder or arrest individual well-being and group welfare need to be brought into focus with vengeance. It is argued that values such as austerity, simplicity, satisfaction and familism have the power and integrity to stand against the strong individualist values with self-centric core.

Values refer to the preferences of people in connection with life goals, and distinguish between what is desirable and what is not desirable (Misra and Tripahi, 2004: 158).Values provide stability to the social system and have an impact on social activities, relationships and institutions. Since values have a significant mediating role in changing the definition of development and social change, social sciences have been interested in studying values in conjunction with development. Pareek (1968) proposed that social change is brought about by changes in values of the individual members of society and their values are sustained by relevant motivational patterns.

It is well taken that values pose a great socio-cultural challenge for the development of a society, more so, when development has to be 'centred around man' (Alechina, 1982). However, for the present purpose development shall be treated as an overarching expression without much specification and shall be considered as a package term where well-being, growth and empowerment may be taken as indicators of personal level development while group welfare, corporate social responsibility, and realization of organizational objectives, etc., as indicators of group and organizational level development. Similarly, when used in reference to leadership, development could refer to self-evolvement of the leader and his/her capability to motivate people for realizing group goals and concern for their empowerment and growth.

This is done in full awareness of the fact that development as a concept can be described with maximum possible articulation and indicators of development too can be operationally defined with fineness. However, the liberty is taken with the definition of development as one wants to examine values in conjunction with development in different frames and contexts. It seems that development cannot be conveniently confined to one particular expression or definition under the chosen topic.

D. Sinha and Kao (1988) took up the discussion on values and development in their valuable book 'Social values and development: Asian perspective' in a big way observing that there is need for isolating those values that are functional to development and those that act as impediments. They suggested that through such an analysis, the exact role of values can be understood and they can be utilized for mobilization of human resources for national development (p. 14). Earlier D. Sinha (1969; 1974) had argued that values and needs as mediating variables for development must be understood and explained in the light of the indigenous character of a particular society. At the macro level, the question of a suitable development paradigm or perspective having sensitivity to the values and socio-cultural circumstances specific to a particular country has become increasingly important in Asian context (D. Sinha and Kao, 1988).

Apparently, at the individual level, people would have some guiding principles of life (Schwartz, 1992) and preferences in connection with their life goals. However, often wittingly or unwittingly individuals drive themselves to social pathological conditions in their personal lives and devastating economic conditions for their own group or country. What goes wrong in their guiding principles, choices and preferences is not impossible to analyze and quite often one arrives at the conclusion that there has been shameful disregard of some finer operational values that were important for one's personal well-being or for that matter for the development and welfare of one's society.

Impressed by the spirit of some world thinkers, enlightened personalities and social scientists, the present paper shall make a modest attempt to make the point that some individual level indigenous values and some collectivist values (i.e., familism) may be examined as conducive for personal well-being and group welfare as they seem to hold the latent power to initiate a growth and devolvement process at individual, organizational and group levels. However, these values have been ignored or discarded today apparently for the reason that at their face value they do not seem to be associated with the popular indices of individual affluence and society's economic development. However, first it may be desirable to understand the character of self-centric individualist values.

INDIVIDUALIST VALUES AND THEIR CONSEQUENCE FOR INDIVIDUAL AND SOCIETAL LEVEL DEVELOPMENT

A careful examination of self-centric individualist values like ambition, power, success, achievement and competition, etc., suggest that they are associated with affluence, personal achievement, status and power, etc. However, at the same time the goals of competition, ambition, power, and achievement are often accomplished at the cost of others and may not enhance the individual's well-being or contribute to his/her group's betterment.

The most eye catching and recent incidence is that of the bankers bringing the world economy to shambles because they chose to be selfishly greedy and preferred to behave in a dangerously unethical manner towards their profession.

A recent article by Gurucharan Das (*Times of India,* Sunday, 15th of March, 2009) entitled "Dharma fails on wall street" is worth referring to in this context. Das observes that much has been written on the crisis of the failures of American banks but not enough about its "moral quality". This is exactly what we want to understand. Das contends that "there were many *dharma* failures in this drama" and explains "When American house prices were rising and interest rates were low, even the poor got a chance to get a mortgage and a home. Who could oppose that! Banks combined these mortgages into a collateral debt obligation (CDO), got it rated, and sold it to institutions, who also gained through better returns. When the housing market turned down, the CDOs became toxic."

Das (2009) makes a valid point that "there is very thin line between self-interest and selfishness and the balance of *dharma* tipped the wrong way". Consequently, the undeserving recipient of the loan lied about his ability to repay the loan; the banker who was in any case thinking of short term reward promoted the 'sub-prime' mortgage; the rating agency was dishonest in colluding with the bank while the institution who brought the risky CDO failed in its duty to protect its shareholders and the market was brought to its knee. To add insult to injury, investment bankers who tipped the global economy into a recession, expected bonuses and were shamelessly unremorseful. It was flashed in the media that the Chairman of Merill Lynch spent enormous amount of money to do up his office. Das concludes "Since it is in man's nature to want more, let's learn to live with human imperfection, and seek regulation that not only tames crooks in the market but also rewards *dharma*-like behaviour" (p. 8).

In this backdrop it appears that apparently, self-interest as the prime motivator of human activity has not guaranteed economic development and human welfare happening side by side. Therefore, this shouldn't be surprising that individualist values of self-enhancement and achievement, have contributed only to the prosperity and self-development of the individuals concerned without contributing much to the prosperity and well-being of the society at large. There is empirical evidence suggesting that individualist values like need for achievement leads to selfish behaviour of hording and monopolizing under limited resource conditions (J.B.P. Sinha, 1968). Proposing the main framework for the management model of future, Pareek (1976) talked of macro level shifts in values from elitism to the "whole society emphasis" and from GNP growth to distributive justice.

There is a perspective adopted by economists who prefer to use "Pareto efficiency" as their efficiency goal. Pareto efficiency, or Pareto optimality is a central theory in economics with broad applications in the social sciences besides other disciplines. Thus in a Pareto efficient outcome, we cannot make any person better off without making someone worse off. The biggest criticism of the concept of Pareto efficiency is that it says nothing about equality. Accordingly, the outcome where each individual gets 50 per cent out of a certain total amount and the outcome where one party gets all the money are both Pareto efficient. According to this measure of social welfare, a situation is optimal only if no individuals can be made better off without making someone else worse off.

Competition is another individualist value that has brought less achievement and more despair, depression and pathology at the personal and social levels for the Indian youth in particular. Apparently, parents have been encouraging competition in children of under and above High School age of the kind that seems to be qualitatively closer to the "killer instinct" affecting their formative minds. Competing, however, is culturally detested but for high need for power Indians (McClelland, 1975; J.B.P. Sinha, 1995) it is practiced intensely in a camouflaged form (J.B.P. Sinha, in Press) which turns social relationships into the ground for "game playing" (Eric Berne, 1964) at the interpersonal, social and organizational levels. However, a sensible strategic competition has borne fruits for the business world of Indian finance on the one hand and for 'Team India' in international cricket on the other.

At a deeper level of psychological analysis Krishnamurti (1977) observes that seeking power, whether personal or collective and the desire to be secure, corrupts the mind and brings about its decay. He contends that "It is this self, this constant self-advancement, that makes the mind petty; and though its activity be extensive, though it be preoccupied with politics, science, arts, research or what you will, there is narrowing down of thinking, a shallowness that brings about deterioration, decay" (p. 154). He explicates further that the self, consciously or unconsciously, uses its activity or profession as a means for its own gratification, for the fulfilment of its ambitions, or for the achievement of success in terms of power.

In Krishnamurti's (1977) explication of the process that leads to deterioration of the mind, one is drawn to mark that the mind is engaged continuously in "building the pattern of its own certainty or the security of its own interest; the words, the forms, the expression may vary from culture to culture, but the centre of self-interest remains". In fact, each individual has "Vested interest which he is consciously or unconsciously protecting, watching over, and not allowing anything to disturb" (p. 151). In sum, because what makes the mind to deteriorate is "self-protectiveness and resistance to change", there is neither consideration for the self's own regeneration from decay nor for any change development or revolution.

VALUES FOR HUMAN DEVELOPMENT

India presents a strong case of religious and spiritual personalities, saints and *sanyasis* who denounced the worldly pleasures for themselves but chose the very same mundane world for a higher purpose taking up the roles of selfless social workers, reformers and social change agents. In fact they were able to show how spiritual and humanitarian values can convert religious and spiritual sects into full-fledged institutions of social service on the one hand and turn the personal life of an individual into a gratifying experience on the other. The life and deeds of Swami Vivekanand (1863-1902) is a case in point.

Swamiji felt that the prevalent morality in both individual and social life was mostly based on fear (i.e., fear of the police, fear of public ridicule, fear of God's punishment or fear of *Karma*) and not on the pure and divine nature of the self or *Atman* present in all. Moreover, the current theories of ethics did not explain why a person should be moral and be good to others. Therefore, he based his theory of ethics and principle of morality on the intrinsic purity and oneness of the *Atman* with the 'Supreme Spirit' and argued that by loving and serving the humanity we are actually able to act from the core of our divine self. This was also the concept of a spiritual life for him.

Vivekanand's life is an exceptional example of a young *sanyasi* who initiated the process of social change by motivating youth from modest backgrounds to join him on an extremely difficult but pious mission of reaching out to the poor and deprived masses of India creating opportunities for providing education to children and health services to the needy. He contended that masses needed two kinds of knowledge: secular knowledge to improve their economic condition and spiritual knowledge to infuse in them faith in themselves and strengthen their moral sense. The next question for Swamiji was 'how to spread these two kinds of knowledge among the masses?' Through education was the answer that Swamiji found and perhaps realized that at some point of time individual efforts must turn into forceful collective endeavours taken up by well meaning devoted religious and spiritual institutions. Vivekanand's dream to establish a formal organization for such a purpose saw the day of the light in the years 1897-1898. First, Ramkrishna Mission got formally founded on 1st of May in the year 1897 but it was on 9th of December in the year 1898 that Ramkrishna Math was established on the banks of the Ganges in the village Belur in West Bengal.

Economists and social scientists have contributed in highlighting values as a force behind human development. Nobel laureate world class economists Professor Amartya Sen stirred by "conscience of his profession" thought of 'Welfare economics' which sought to evaluate economic policies in terms of their effect on the well-being of the community and apparently was inspired by social values like justice and equity, majority rule, and the availability of information about individual conditions that inspired researchers to turn their attention to issues of basic welfare, (Sen, 1970). Amratya Sen was seen as a ground-breaker among the late twentieth-century economists for his insistence on discussing issues seen as marginal by most economists. He mounted one of the few major challenges to the economic model that posited self-interest as the prime motivating factor (value) of human activity. In his book, 'Collective choice and social welfare' (1970). Sen examined the idea held by free-market economists that there was no point in the government interfering in public welfare, and the idea held by statists, who believed that the government should intervene on behalf of the people. Sen argued that it was not necessary to come up with a perfect solution to problems of social welfare, but that poorer and less-assertive citizens should not be ignored.

Sen's work in the field of development economics has had considerable influence in the formulation of the Human Development Report, published by the United Nations Development Programme. This annual publication that ranks countries on a variety of economic and social indicators owes much to his contributions among other theorists in the area of economic measurement of poverty and inequality. Such conceptualization of welfare economics is value based and gives a serious thought to as how to conceptualize and evaluate development in the true sense of the term.

Moreover, Amartya Sen gives a thoughtful lead to the question of indicators of development and mentions about indicators that are sensitive enough to capture concrete signs of development in terms of 'capabilities of a society's *citizens*' and desires that *governments* should be measured against these. Let us understand this. Sen talks of citizens' personal choice and freedom towards creating a developed society and points out that this is possible when citizens can use their rights. Rights, he observes, is something that must be provided or cannot be taken away. Sen argues that the concept of 'voting right' is fairly empty because in order for citizens to have a capacity to vote, they first must have "functioning" ranging from the very broad, such as the availability of *education*, to the very specific, such as transportation to the *polls*. He categorically states that only when such barriers are removed can the citizen truly be said to act out of personal choice and freedom towards creating a developed society. Sen contends that in a top-down condition development will always hamper human rights as long as the definition of the terms remain in doubt. Therefore, it is up to the individual society to make the list of minimum capabilities guaranteed by that society. It may be said that in the background of Sen's thought on development there is a deep concern for humanitarian values.

COLLECTIVISM AND DEVELOPMENT

Very briefly, collectivism a dimension of cultural variation "pertains to societies in which people from birth onwards are integrated into strong, cohesive in-groups, which throughout people's life-time continue to protect them in exchange of unquestioning loyalty" (Hofstede, 1991: 51). As a cultural syndrome, collectivism is identified by collective and interdependent view of the self (Markus and Kitayama, 1991); by the priority given to in-group goals over one's personal goals; by the emphasis on relationships rather than to contracts and exchange and lastly, by importance of norms in determining social behaviour.

Triandis (1988a) acknowledged that certain collectivist values are desirable for economic development, and may be adopted by people of developed societies who are predominantly individualists in their cultural orientation. With the example set by some newly industrialized Asian countries, the world has witnessed how nations could develop without giving up their collectivist values.

In the Indian context, the relationship between collectivism and development has so far not been simple and dependable. Ideally speaking collectivist values are supposed to be 'less self-centric' as the self is not placed in the centre of existence or considered the 'unit of survival'. It is rather interdependent and inclined towards 'reaching out' for its collectives. Referring to the Vedantic literature which emerged as the most important psycho-spiritual source of Indian traditional thought, J.B.P. Sinha (forthcoming) talks of cosmic collectivism which presents the most evolved form of collectivist values. Accordingly, "Cosmic collectivism posits that the universe consists of diverse forms and elements. They are compatible as well as conflicting, but are inter-connected and held together by an underlining sense of unity derived from being parts of the same ultimate reality, *Brahman* (p. 3). He quotes from one of the Upanishads to make his point.

> *"This atman is the same in the ant, the same in the elephant, the same in those three worlds...the same in the whole universe"*
>
> [*Brhadaranyaka-Upanisahad*, 1, 3, 22 (dated about 1,000 B.C.].

The spirit of cosmic collectivism is a sure guarantee for a peaceful coexistence which is crucial for the development of a complex and pluralistic society. In reality, however, this has not been the case. Sociologists are of the opinion that the 'spirit of interdependence' forms the basis of Indian collectivism. Groups formed on the basis of neighbourhood, kinship, or functions have served many individual and social interests. Further, religion, occupation, family and civic life prevented dispersion and encouraged the forces of the conjunction of values.

As far as the defining attributes of collectivism goes, collectivism has very strong features for initiating and sustaining collective efforts and activities due to its features of interdependence, sharing of resources, overlap between the individual and collective goals, and significance of norms, duties and obligations as determinants of behaviour (Triandis and Bhawuk, 1997). This is almost prescriptive for development efforts at organizational and societal levels. There are a couple of examples where collectivist value of "familism" has been examined in the context of development (Yang, 1988), and organizational efficiency (Nakane, 1970). In the context of work culture in Indian organizations, J.B.P. Sinha (1990a) observed that alike the Japanese, a blend of organizational principles and traditional social system offers hope for improving work culture in India.

Regretfully, there are more examples of selfish exploitation of collectivist values promoting corruption, violence, and quite often criminalisation of politics and education (Srinivas, 1993). The feature of embeddedness with one's in-group (J.B.P. Sinha, 1990a) has also led to problems like "regression of trust" and "credibility gap" (N.K. Singh & Paul, 1985) and have resulted into caste based group formations in organizations (S.K. Singh, 1986; J.B.P. Sinha, 1990b). Therefore, the picture that we know about the relationship between collectivism and development has a limited use. At best, it helps us understand what constrains and inhibits development efforts at social and organizational levels and why we have not found desirable results from collective values that are almost prescriptive for collective initiatives and efforts for development. On the other hand, optimism lives due to the examples set by some of the newly industrialized countries that developed without giving up their collectivist values.

FAMILISM VALUE

Familism, a cultural value, comprises of strong preference for the unity of the members of a family. It presents most of the identifying features of collectivism besides individual's strong identification with and attachment to his/her nuclear and extended family, strong feelings of loyalty, reciprocity, and solidarity among family members (Triandis, Marin, Betancourt, Lisansky, & Chang, 1982). In this sense familism can be defined as the centrality and priority of family in people's life along with a deep-rooted sense of the individual as embedded in the family (Sabogal, Marin, Otero-Sabogal, Van Oss Marin, & Perez-Stable, 1987). According to the World Value Survey (2005-2007), familism is an universally important value. India is a country with strong familism values and one of the factors of Indian collectivism comprises this value (D. Sinha, 1998a; J.B.P. Sinha, Sinha, Verma & Sinha, 2001).

Familism includes two main types of value orientations: (a) perceived obligations to provide material support to the members of the extended family along with the perception of relatives as behavioural and attitudinal referents (family norms); and (b) reliance on relatives for emotional help and support (family support) (Sabogal, Marin, Otero-Sabogal, Marin, & Perez-Stable, 1987). It is generally accepted that socialization is the source of value transmission and families having strong familism values are likely to be more effective in transmitting guiding principles of life to their future generation. It appears, however, that familism is one value which is fighting for its existence in face of multiple hedonistic influences that seem to work against its survival and transmission. It goes beyond saying that weakening of the 'familism' values is linked in more than one way with the well-being of the individual and his/her becoming a responsible citizen.

There is some evidence in a narrative based study of three generations of women of the same family suggesting strong familism values getting transformed into collectivism of the order where the distinction between the in-group and the out-group became meaningless for the character of the grandmother. The grandmother in this case belonged to the pre-independence era and practiced strong familism values that manifested into continuous selfless service to all the extended family members on the one hand and small thoughtful kind gestures towards the village poor on the other. To quote the author, "In season, mangoes and pickles were free for all, so that the poor could eat their coarse food with them. I am told that she (the grandmother) was extremely generous in giving grains to anybody who asked for them—Free from her home grainery that was not even kept locked. Grandmother never made any distinction between her children and those of her sister-in-law. Her blouse was always stained by the oily heads of the family infants who kept on being born at regular intervals to one or the other daugthers-in-law and whom she carried close to her breast" (pp. 154-155). The example suggests that familism values can get transformed into spirited and encompassing collectivism. It is, therefore, important to examine whether and how familism values get extended beyond the boundaries of the family and be used to erase the sharp distinction that Indians make between 'own' and 'other' (J.B.P. Sinha, 1978; 1979; 1980; 1982a). If this can happen, collectivism could become a value for assuring peaceful coexistence.

INDIGENOUS LEADERSHIP MODELS BASED ON FAMILISM VALUES

Indigenous leadership models that are envisaged to believe and practice familism values are available. *Karta* is one such concept comprising characteristics and role of the Head of the family of an Indian extended family. It is contended that a leader in the role of a *Karta* alike the Head of the family becomes a father figure, nurturing, warm, affectionate, caring, dependable, sacrificing and yet demanding, authoritative and strict disciplinarian who could evoke feelings of security, trust and dependability in creating a familial culture in the organization. As a *Karta* the leader nurtures, grooms, empowers, guides and protects those who work with him/her by directing, guiding, encouraging, appreciating, reprimanding, and inspiring. Similarly, Nurturant-Task (NT) leader of J.B.P. Sinha (1980) and the concept of Parenting Transformational leader of Singh and Bhandarkar (1990) have striking similarities as in theses models the concern of the leader goes beyond the narrow task concern to the holistic growth of the people which is close to the concern of the head of the family for his/her family members.

AMORAL FAMILISM: A PERSPECTIVE AGAINST THE INTEREST OF THE COMMUNITY

J.B.P. Sinha (in press) makes an apt analysis of the Indian reality to show how amoral familism goes against public interest. Accordingly to him "The poverty and its allied maladies have been so pervasive and extreme that even the not-so-poor Indians in the post-Independence era suffer from a poverty syndrome (Sinha, 2000). The poverty syndrome manifests in a fear of getting poor, becoming failure in face of odds, or running into unanticipated misfortune. Even those, who have enough, fear to lose their fortune; if not they, they are afraid, their children might get poor. Poverty syndrome leads to amoral familism characterized by a compelling concern to favour family and friends at the cost of the community or the public interests (Banfield, 1958). Amoral familist Indians, hence, manifest a strong disposition to acquire and hoard material resources by adopting any—even corrupt—means, pursue narrow family interests, and run after short-term gains. They believe that the most effective way to do so is to acquire, consolidate, and enhance power that does not only enable them to accumulate more wealth, establish network with resourceful people for supporting in cornering material gains, but also immune them from being censured for their dubious activities" (p. 8).

It makes sense to understand how collectivist values and familism value in particular could be transformed into a force which initiates and promotes welfare of the collectives outside the boundary of the family. In the same vain it is desirable to understand how some individual level indigenous values might be related to personal well-being of the individuals on the one hand and the group's welfare on the other.

INDIGENOUS VALUES FOR INDIVIDUAL WELL-BEING AND GROUP WELFARE

Projected by the mass media, consumerism has over shadowed Indian values like austerity, simplicity, satisfaction, duty, obligation and humility on the one hand, and an appreciation for a life which is by and large wholesome, simple, modest, non-pretentious, but perhaps restful on the other. If one looks a little closely, these values are development oriented because they are basically non-self-centric at the core and have no toxic effect for others. Furthermore, these values are cost-effective disfavouring spending resources (money, time and energy) in futile activities for bolstering the self or 'showing off'. They are cost-effective also because they visualise well-being and development of the individual self, in conjunction with the economic and social development of the society at large. It is argued that austerity, simplicity, satisfaction, and humility as operative values create an environment for the natural dissolution of consumerist, self-promoting and materialistic values for the reason that perhaps both cannot coexist.

An in-depth examination of these values which are rather Gandhian in spirit will reveal that they have the inherent potential and integrity to stand against the mindless market driven economy and consumerism values because in their character there is 'no demand' for more than what is really needed and an aware "non-chalant" towards the market strategy that first creates 'need' for things that are not required and then forces the consumer to spend on something which is valueless (or adds no value) to their lives. Similarly, these indigenous values hold a natural flare for looking at those 'who have less' and experience a sense of obligation for sharing and extending the self towards others. All the above mentioned values and values such as kindness and humility can transform into self gratifying experiences through service.

The indicators of self-development in this context may be of 'experiential' kind which is likely to manifest into welfare oriented practices irrespective of the fact that they may not have a direct relationship with material affluence of the individual concerned.

A developing society needs to harness, conserve and invest material and human resources for reaching development objectives. For this purpose, it seems necessary to revoke a value orientation which can put a check on wasteful human activity and value less expenditure. Some of our traditional indigenous values seem to be relevant even today for this purpose and are worth examining. Austerity/self-restraint, simplicity, satisfaction, duty, obligation and humility are some relevant values in this context.

AUSTERITY/SELF-RESTRAINT

"Self-restraint", as prescribed in the Indian traditional thinking, does not mean forcible denial of worldly pleasures to the self. The traditional view prefers to caution the self against the painful realities of a life which does not have austerity. Austerity is not an outward show of what one renounces and gives up, but is the realized state of the self which is aware of the fiery nature of the world of desires. In a way, self-restraint helps acquire a philosophical and non-chalant attitude towards material affluence and preference for unrestrained hedonism.

Contrary to what has been said about the inverse relationship between the other worldly attitude and realization of economic aspirations, it seems that the other worldly attitude helps acquire self-restraint and austerity. When the self is not all important, and the pursuits to please the self are not important either, then in a situation like this the self prefers to become "minimal" (Kao, and Hong, Ng Sek, 1988). It is observed, that even in its "minimal" status the self is conducive for work behaviour and consequently for economic well-being. Speaking for societies having belief in collectivist values, it has been observed, that whenever the self has shown restraint against its self-centric activities, and preferred to contribute as an embedded part of its group, team, collective, corporation, or nation, there has been development (for detail see Sinha and Kao, 1988).

SIMPLICITY

"Simplicity" is the value having the quality of being oneself without pretensions. Simplicity mirrors the face of a mind which is innocent and does not care to be what it is not. It may be said that simplicity comes only if one has the courage to be honest with oneself. For a simple person, all the external indicators of self-grandeur are psychologically futile. A simple person's behaviour is not costly because there is no expenditure to acquire and possess things not needed, nor there is desire to bolster the self by joining the rat race initiated by social comparison. Indians have a strong tendency of social comparison and "showing off" (Prasad, 1968) which triggers off consumerism and run for accumulating, and acquiring goods that are not necessarily a good buy for money (Srinivas, 1993). The money thus spent, could have been utilized sensibly and productively had simplicity been an operational value. Apparently, a simple lifestyle saves money, time and energy spent in superfluous activities. Furthermore, simplicity makes interpersonal transactions gratifying (as there are no ulterior motives involved) and business transactions fair because there are no hidden agenda involved.

SATISFACTION/CONTENTMENT

It is not fair to say that satisfaction is a forced outcome of the perception that one has to compromise with one's circumstances as it cannot be altered. Satisfaction neither represents a mental state which shows a regretful succumbing to one's situation nor a tendency of "fatalistic submission" (Kapp, 1963; Segal, 1996), as observed by foreigners to explain Indian personality. On the other hand, it is however true, that satisfaction is not an increasing function of the quantity of assets proclaimed and acquired. As a positive attitude, satisfaction refers to a willing acceptance of one's realities. However, such acceptance comes after the realization that there cannot be an end to one's wants, needs, expectations and desires and it helps to say, and feel, that one has enough. Psychologically speaking, satisfaction/contentment is an outcome of the realization that all searches to possess must end. Because, with possession comes conflict and sorrow. The reasons for such conflict and sorrow are: Firstly, "we want to keep on with the pleasure of possessing and avoid the pain of it". Secondly, "there is no such thing as complete possession of anything at any time" (Krishnamurti, 1977: 259-260).

Unfortunately, efforts to resolve dissatisfaction with one's present standard of living, or to improve one's social position by acquiring things of status symbol, have led many to engage themselves into corrupt practices. An action motivated by dissatisfaction with non-serious concerns and taken up with undue pomp and show is unprogressive and a sign of immaturity for the people of a developing country.

DUTY, OBLIGATION AND HUMILITY

As an individual level value, humility comes after the dissolution of the ego. A humble person is not conscious of his/her humility and doesn't proclaim it. Gandhiji considered humility to be an indispensable ingredient of non-violence. Humility has been the guiding principle behind efforts towards uplifting and empowering the weakest of the weak driving saints like Mother Teresa and Baba Ampte.

At the corporate level conceptualization of 'corporate social responsibility' (CSR) took shape out of the spirit of duty, obligation and humility towards the society from where it earns its business. CSR is an extension or reaching out of the corporate houses beyond business returns towards the welfare of the society. Many companies are realizing that aligning CSR activities closely with business objectives is good for their business and, the business decision-making in a growing number of companies is now linked to ethical values, compliance with legal requirements, and with respect for people, communities and environment.

In the year 2007 on 16th of May, the Business World FICCI-SEDF Corporate Social Responsibility award was given away to six Indian companies—namely, Mahindra and Mahindra, Tata Tea, National Thermal Power Corporation, Oil and Natural Gas Corporation and MSPL by our former Finance Minister Mr. P. Chidambaram. On this occasion the President, FICCI-SEDF and co-chairperson, FICCI Committee on CSR and Community Development, Mr. P.M. Sinha recalled that the general understanding of CSR in India is still deeply rooted in the concept of philanthropy and added "CSR is gradually metamorphosing from a mere philosophy to a strong business case for Indian industry. Over the years, the nature of the involvement of business houses with social causes has undergone a sea change. It has moved away from charity and dependence to empowerment and partnership. This is necessary not only for growth of business, but also for " 'inclusive growth' in the country".

From the same platform the Finance Minister emphasized that management, boards of directors and employees of companies must be driven by a refined social conscience and social responsibility and not by short-term gains, while the senior vice-president, FICCI, Mr. Harshpati Singhania said that the award was of great significance to all, especially the corporate sector, as it recognizes the work of business in enhancing the well-being of the society at large. To quote him, "With the concept of CSR getting more relevant and focused, we realize that the companies operating in both global and domestic markets are increasingly required to incorporate the social, economic and environmental concerns into their business while building shareholders' value and taking care of stakeholders' interest. The field of responsible business practice is one of the most dynamic and challenging subjects facing corporate leaders today. Companies are learning that their involvement in finding solutions to the social issues also helps their own businesses in the long run."

Mr. Chidambaram urged the captains of trade and industry to provide employment to 100,000 differently-abled people while mentioning that the Government can do its part by footing the employee state insurance and employee family protection bills for the first three years of employees in this context (http://www.ibtimes.co.in/articles/20080521/corporate-social responsibility-csr-businessworld-ficci-sedf-award.htm).

DUTY AND OBLIGATION: THE OPERATIVE VALUES FOR SOCIALLY RESPONSIBLE LEADERS

Some corporate leaders and well known public figures known for their social consciousness acknowledge 'duty and obligation' as their operative values and source of motivation. It is contended that the duty and obligation attitude of such leaders is sustained by their concern for 'paying back debts' to the society (which brought them up) through carrying out their duties sincerely in the 'mood of obligation' on the one hand and values of 'other orientation' and 'duty consciousnesses' on the other. This is a model of self-development/ self-evolvement because; it helps in shedding away the false pride of being the 'doer' that one picks up during performing one's duties and meeting obligations. This position when replaced by the belief that we are only 'doing our duties' brings about humility in service (Verma, 2007). Two well known women in public life Kiron Shaw Majumdar and Kiran Bedi find themselves moved by the duty and obligation values. In one of her interviews Kiran Bedi had said that she joined police with a will to serve and it was a divine will. She felt that the challenge for her was to give back what she have got and, therefore, she was constantly looking for an expression of return.

As for now, we would like to think of an indigenous value laden conceptualization of leadership. Indian experts have envisaged and worked on such models. It is argued that the value laden conceptualization of leadership creates possibilities for the leader's own self-development and that of the empowerment of the people who become self-motivated to realise the organizational objectives. The concept of 'enlightened leadership' is a case in point where leadership becomes the expression of some deeply held convictions and ideals that are fundamentally development oriented.

ENLIGHTENED LEADERSHIP: AN INDIGENOUS VALUE LADEN CONCEPT

Apparently, the concept of enlightened leadership is marked by a strong undercurrent of super-ordinate values like patriotism, justice, equality, development and social change and corporate leaders who have been admired for turning around their organizations have been people of higher values and integrity (Srinivas, 2000). Therefore, "How leaders view their own self, values, beliefs, and practices and visualize their own development results into a framework to decide to a large extent how they would influence, motivate and enable their subordinates to give their best to the organization" (House, Wright & Aditya, 1997: 85). Further, enlightened leader does not only functions under the impact of higher order values but is also driven by the growth oriented model of motivation experiencing gratification in the process of performing his/her duties sincerely.

Indian experts had begun the conceptualization of enlightened leadership way back progressing through a developmental route which may be traced back to the NT leader of J.B.P. Sinha (1980), towards the altruistic models of leadership (Kanungo and Mendonca, 1996), to the now talked about self-realization motivated, *Chitta Shuddhi* seeker enlightened leader (Chakraborty, 1987; 1993 and the IIM team at Lucknow). It is believed that "strategies dissociated from value based management do not contribute in the long run" (Suresh Krishna, Sundaram Fastners, & Finance, TVS group quoted in Indian Management, December 1997). Enlightened leader (a) creates value, (b) follows a value system which provides a clear reference point for mobilising the right ideas at the right time, and (c) is self-evolving. The 'altruistic model' of Kanungo and Mendonca (1996) recommended practice of unconditional altruism by the leader which resulted into energized and motivated subordinates who performed on their own.

Verma (2008) contends that "The beauty of this conceptualization lies also in the nature of transactions used by the leader for influencing people which progressively gained qualitative refinement before culminating into an inner source of motivation for the leader. Apparently, the objective of leadership became motivating the subordinates to grow into capable individuals in the process of realising organizational objectives" (p. 44). In sum, the conceptualization of indigenous value based leadership presents a different and wholesome perspective for looking at leadership effectiveness and peoples' well-being (i.e., growth and empowerment) which are significant indicators of development in the organizational context and public life.

Finally, it seems desirable to mention about 'work values and committed behaviour' to wrap up the discussion on values as force for development. Since this topic has been attended else where (Verma, 2004: 97-99), only some observations from the work of Indian experts on work values and committed behaviour important for industrial process and economic development shall be referred.

WORK VALUES AND COMMITTED BEHAVIOUR

Work values are an integral part of a nation's ethos necessary for progress. The relationship between work values and development has been viewed in terms of relationship between work values and organizational effectiveness. Rao (1991) defined work values as the degree of worth ascribed to a particular type of work activity or aspect of work. Work according to the Indian approach refers to one's duty and obligation to work, for meeting the needs and obligations of one's relatives, friends and even strangers. Further, there is emphasis on performing work with the *nishkam* spirit or without any concern for the outcome.

Under Indian traditional paradigm, people work not only for material returns but for becoming effectively functional and self-evolved. They also work for the sake of work and the gratification experienced in the process of work. In fact, work becomes the means for finding meaningfulness and happiness in life and the process of self-purification *chitta shuddhi* (Chakraborty, 1987, 1993).

J.B.P. Sinha (1990a) while explicating the relationship between work values and work culture makes the point that when work values are drawn from the periphery and placed in the centrality of life then the employees could possibly see the link between 'work and worthiness' which apparently is a desirable condition for creating a synergetic work culture in the organizations. Verma (2008) in the context of enlightened leadership observes that when work becomes a value by acquiring a central position in life, it starts acting like an inner source of motivation for realising the attributes of the higher self (i.e., love, kindness, compassion, empathy, generosity, judiciousness, in relationships and dutifulness and honesty, in carrying out responsibilities).

It will suffice to say that there is a general consensus, however, that work is not intrinsically valued in India and work as a concept and culture has not been internalised in Indian organizations (J.B.P. Sinha, 1985). McClleland (1975) observes that work is not seen as duty but as a favour done to others and is performed half heartedly. Similarly, certain seminal characteristics of Western organizations that are favourable for work values are grossly ignored by Indian organizations, perhaps because of the indigenous characteristics of Indian society (Ganesh, 1982). In sum, experts contend that work values rooted in the psycho-spiritual tradition and comprising normative prescriptions do not appear to be functional in the prevalent reality of India. Moreover, work appears to be performed for 'own' and must be heavily compensated if performed for 'others' (J.B.P. Sinha, 1985).

Having said the above, it is fit and desirable to close this part by referring to D. Sinha (1991) who highlighted four strategies for ensuring value-work congruence. Accordingly, first strategy termed "replacement total" is rooted in Weberian thought. Second strategy is reinterpretation rather than wholesome replacement of traditional values (J.B.P. Sinha, 1988). Third strategy exemplified by Hofstede (1988) advocates that the model of man as implied by Western theories should also incorporate traditional values of management development in Eastern cultures and the fourth strategy favours realigning work to socio-cultural factors for development process (Tripathi, 1988).

SUMMING UP

Social scientists agree that despite being a socio-cultural challenge for development, values act as a force behind various forms of development. For the present purpose development has been treated as an overarching expression where, well-being, growth and empowerment could be taken as indicators of personal level development while group welfare, corporate social responsibility, and realization of organizational objectives, etc., as indicators of group and organizational level development. The discussion begins with the proposition that individualist values with self-centric core often show disregard for 'moral quality' in day-to-day life and apparently, self-interest as the prime motivator for human activity is not a guarantee for economic development and human welfare. Referring to the modern thinker J. Krishnamurti the point is made that the process behind resistance to change and development is the self's need for constant self-advancement which makes the mind 'petty' and 'deteriorated' to the extent that it can neither think of its own regeneration nor for any outwardly change and development.

At this point, mention is made to values for human development and the spirit behind the 'welfare economics' of the famous economist Amartya

Sen who was inspired by social values like justice, equity and, majority rule and talked of 'welfare economics' seeking evaluation of economic policies in terms of their effect on the well-being of the community. At this juncture contributions of psychologists who tried to relate the well known dimensions of cultural variation (i.e., individualism and collectivism) with development are recalled. It is contended that the defining attributes of collectivism (i.e., interdependence, sharing of resources, overlap between the individual and collective goals, and norms, duties and obligations as determinants of behaviour) have the potential for initiating and sustaining collective efforts and activities for development.

A special mention is made to the collectivist value of familism with the note that the need is to examine how familism values could be extended beyond the boundaries of the family and help erasing the sharp distinction that Indians make between 'own' and 'other'. Further, attention is drawn towards some indigenous leadership models that believe and practice familism values. The concept of amoral familsm gets a reference for the reason that experts observe that poverty syndrome leads to amoral familism characterized by a compelling concern to favour family and friends at the cost of the community or the public interests.

At this point some indigenous values like austerity, simplicity, satisfaction, and humility are brought into focus followed by the argument that these have the potential and integrity to stand against the market driven economy and consumerist values due to the reason that they hold a natural flare for empathizing with those 'who have less' and experience a sense of obligation for sharing and extending the self towards others. Additionally, theses values are non-demanding at core with hardly any toxic effect for others. It is said further, that when the business world is impressed by the indigenous values of duty, obligation and paying back of debt to the society, it gets engaged into value based practice of 'corporate social responsibility' and at the leadership front, corporate leaders who have turned around their organizations have been people with integrity and higher values. There is mention of altruistic models of leadership which are concerned about peoples' growth and empowerment and the conceptualization of leadership marked by strong undercurrents of super-ordinate values like patriotism, justice, equality, development and social change. The discussion reaches its close by the topic of work values and committed behaviour as work values are an integral part of a nation's ethos necessary for progress.

REFERENCES

Alechina, I. (1982). The contribution of United Nations system of formulating development concepts. In: *Different theories and practices to development*. Paris: UNESCO Publications.

Banfield, E.C. (1958). *The moral basis of a backward society*. Glencoe, Illinois: The Free Press.

Berne, E. (1964). *Games people play—The basic hand book of transactional analysis*. New York: Ballantine Books.

Chakraborty, S.K. (1987). *Managerial effectiveness and quality of work life*. New Delhi: Tata McGraw Hill.

Chakraborty, S.K. (1993). *Managerial transformation by values*. Sage Publications.

Das, G. (2009). Dharma fails on Wall Street. *Times of India*, Patna, 15th of March, p. 8.

Ganesh, S.R. (1982). *Quality of life in Indian organizations: An irreverent view*. Ahemdabad: Indian Institute of Management.

Hofstede, G. (1988). McGregor in South East Asia? In D. Sinha, and H.S.R. Kao (Eds.), *Social values and development: Asian perspective* (pp. 304-314). New Delhi: Sage.

Hofstede, G. (1991). *Cultures and organizations: Software of the mind*. London: McGrow Hill.

House, R.J., Wright, N.S., and Aditya, R.N. (1997). Cross-cultural research on organizational leadership: A critical analysis and a proposed theory. In P.C. Early and M. Eraz (Eds.), *Now perspectives on international industrial organizational psychology*, (pp. 535-625). San Francisco: New Lexington Press.

Kao, H.S.R. and Hong, Ng Sek (1988). Minimal 'self' and Chinese work behaviour: Psychology of the grassroot. In D. Sinha, and H.S.R. Kao (Eds.), *Social values and development*: *Asian Perspective* (pp. 254-272). Sage Publications.

Kanungo, R. and Mendonca, M. (1996). *Ethical dimensions of leadership*. Thousands Oaks, California: Sage.

Kapp, W.K. (1963). *Hindu culture, economic development and economic planning in India*. Bombay: Asia Publishing House.

Krishnamurti, J. (1977). *Commentaries on living* (third series) edited by D. Rajgopal. New Delhi: B.I. Publications.

Markus, H. and Kitayama, S. (1991). Culture and self: Implications for cognition, emotion, and motivation. *Psychological Review*, 98, 224-253.

McClelland, D.C. (1975). *Power: The inner experience*. New York: Free Press.

Misra G. and Tripathi, K.N. (2004). Psychological dimensions of poverty and deprivation. In J. Pandey (Ed.), *Psychology in India revisited: Developments in the discipline*, ICSSR Survey Volume 3 (pp. 118-215). Sage.

Nakane, C. (1970). *Japanese society*. Berkley and Los Angeles: University of California Press.

Pareek, U. (1968). Motivational patterns and planned social change. *International Social Science Journal*, 20 (3), 464-473.

Pareek, U. (1976). Management process for the education of the future. In P.S. Sunderam and A.B. Shah (Eds.), *Education or catastrophe?* (pp. 176-193). New Delhi: Vikas.

Prasad, B. (1968). *Socio-economic study of urban middle class*. New Delhi: Sterling Publications.

Rao, T.V. (1991). *Managerial work value scale. The 1991 Annual: Developing Human Resources*, (pp. 163-177).

Sabogal, F., Marin, G., Otero-Sabogal, R., VanOss Marin, B., and Perez-Stable, E.J. (1987). Hispanic familism and acculturation: What changes and what doesn't? *Hispanic Journal of Behavioural Sciences*, 9, 397-412.

Schwartz, S.H. (1992). Universals in content and structure of values: Theoretical advances and empirical tests in twenty countries. In M. Zanna (Ed.), *Advances in Experimental Social Psychology* (Vol. 25). Orlando, FL: Academic.

Segal, R. (1996). *The crisis of India*. New York: New Your Library Publishers.

Sen, A. (1970). *Collective choice and social welfare*. Holden Day: San Francisco.

Singh, S.K. (1986). *Social groups within an organization*. Unpublished Doctoral. dissertation, Patna University, Patna.

Singh, P. and Bhandarkar, A. (1990). *Corporate success and transformational leadership*. New Delhi: Wiley Eastern.

Singh, N.K. and Paul, O. (1985). *Corporate soul: Dynamics of effective management*. New Delhi: Vikas.

Sinha, D. and Kao, H.S.R. (Eds.) (1988). *Social values and development: Asian perspective*. New Delhi: Sage.

Sinha, D. (1969). *Motivation of rural population in developing country*. Bombay Allied Publishers.

Sinha, D. (1974). *Motivation and rural development*. Calcutta: Minerva Associates.

Sinha, J.B.P. (1968). The n-Ach/n-Cooperation under limited/unlimited, resource conditions. *Journal of Experimental Social Psychology*, 4, 233-246.

Sinha, J.B.P. (1978). Power in superior subordinate relationship. *Journal of Social and Economic Studies*, 6, 205-218.

Sinha, J.B.P. (1979). *Power in Indian Organizations*. A.N. Sinha Institute of Social Studies, Patna, India.

Sinha, J.B.P. (1980). *The nurtutrant task leader*. New Delhi: Concept.

Sinha, J.B.P. (1982a).The Hindu (Indian) identity. *Dynamic Psychiatry*, 15 (74-75): 148-160.

Sinha, J.B.P. (1985). Psychic relevance in work in Indian culture. *Dynamic Psychiatry*, 18, 134-141.

Sinha, J.B.P. (1988). Recognizing values for development. In D. Sinha and H.S.R. Kao (Eds.), *Social values and development: Asian perspective* (pp. 275-284). New Delhi: Sage.

Sinha, J.B.P. (1990a). *Work culture in the Indian context*, New Delhi: Sage.

Sinha, J.B.P. (1990b). The salient Indian values and their socio-ecological roots. *Indian Journal of Social Sciences*, 3 (4), 477-488.

Sinha, J.B.P. (1995). *The cultural context of leadership and power*. New Delhi: Sage.

Sinha, J.B.P. (2000). *Patterns of work culture: Cases and strategies for culture building*. New Delhi: Sage.

Sinha, J.B.P., Sinha, T.N., Verma, J. and Sinha, R.B.N. (2001). Collectivism coexisting with individualism: An Indian scenario. *Asian Journal of Social Psychology*, 4, 133-145.

Sinha, J.B.P. (in press). In G. Misra (Ed.), *Discipline of Psychology in the series "The History of Indian Science, Philosophy and Culture"* (General Editor, D.P. Chattopadhyaya).

Srinivas, M.N. (1993). *Economic and Political Weekly*, May 8, 933-937.

Srinivas, M.N. (2000). *Pilgrimage to Indian ethos management: A look at indigenous approaches to organizational development*. Management Centre for Human Values, Indian Institute of Management, Kolkata.

Triandis, H.C. (1988). Collectivism and development. In: D. Sinha, and H.S.R. Kao, (Eds.), *Social values and development: Asian perspectives* (pp. 285-303). New Delhi: Sage.

Triandis, H.C. and Bhawuk, D.P.S. (1997). Culture theory and meaning of relatedness. In P.C. Earley and M. Erez (Eds.), *New perspectives on international industrial/ organizational psychology* (pp. 13-54). San Francisco: New Lexington Press.

Triandis, H.C., Martin, G., Betancourt, H., Lisansky, J., and Chang, B. (1982). Dimensions of familism among Hispanics and Mainstream Navy Recruits. *Technical Report No. 14,* Department of Psychology, University of Illinois, Champaign.

Tripathi, R.C. (1988). Aligning development to values in India. In D. Sinha and H.S.R. Kao (Eds.), *Social values and development: Asian perspectives* (pp. 315-333). New Delhi: Sage.

Verma, J. (1995).Transformation of women's role in India. In J. Valsiner (Ed.), *Comparative cultural perspective*, Vol. 3. Norwood: N.J. Publishing Corporation.

Verma, J. (2004). Social values. In J. Pandey (Ed.), *Psychology in India Revisited*, ICSSR Fourth Survey, Vol. 3 (pp. 69-117). Sage.

Verma, J. (2008). Enlightened leadership and the spiritual angle of motivation. *The Social Engineer*, 2 (3), pp. 44-53.

World And European Values Surveys Four Wave Integrated Data File, 1981-2004, v.20060423, 2006. The World Values Survey Association (www.worldvaluessurvey.org) and European Values Study Foundation (www.europeanvalues.nl).

Yang, C.F. (1988). Familism and development: An examination of the role of family in contemporary China, mainland, Hong-Kong, Taiwan. In: Sinha, D. and Kao, H.S.R. (Eds.), *Social values and development: Asian perspectives* (pp. 93-123) New Delhi: Sage.

CHAPTER EIGHTEEN

Individualism-Collectivism and Development

R.B.N. Sinha

PREVIEW

In the last few decades the prime indicator of national development has changed from economic growth to a much broader framework that also includes social, cultural, spiritual, and overall human development. Culture has been studied using different theoretical perspectives. One dominant perspective is of Hofstede (1980) who uses values as a way to understand culture. A number of scholars have studied relationships between cultural values and national development.

One may begin with Karl Marx (1867/1976) who postulated that the factors of production determines the levels of a country's economic growth that changes the patterns of relationships among people resulting into a particular cultural configuration. Using the above thesis of Marx, Hofstede (1980) supported this approach by correlating economic affluence with individualism implying that the former causes the latter. As a country's wealth increases, its people become both economically and morally independent of each other and grow as autonomous individuals (Hofstede, 2001). Triandis (1984) identified specific individualistic components that cause economic development. It is generally believed that the lack of resources induce a need to depend on each other that inculcates relationship orientation—a hallmark of collectivism. However, Japan, a collectivist culture (Hamaguchi and Kumon, 1982; Vogel, 1979) has been credited with having the second largest economy with collectivistic efforts. In fact, the Pacific Rim countries (Hong Kong, Singapore, Japan, and Korea), sharing Confucian values of collectivism, have registered high rates of economic development (Hofheinz and Calder, 1982). Harmony within the family member, one of the components of collectivism, has been deemed important that led to recent economic development in the Chinese society (Hicks and Redding, 1983; Redding, 1990). A review of relevant literature by Smith and Bond (1998) revealed that "the strength of the relationship between wealth and various indices of individualism varies from study to study, and in some cases... is small" (p. 314).

Another perspective was advanced by Max Weber (1950) who formulated the thesis that Protestant ethic was the spirit behind the rise of Western capitalism. By the same token, Weber attributed the low level of economic development of India to the Hindu religion, which was alleged to consist of the values antithetical to the protestant ethic. Hinduism, according to Weber, does not promote a faster economic growth because of the Hindu's belief that the world is *maya*, that is, unreal rendering any pursuit of material goal is meaningless and hence non-motivating. Weber was probably looking for an evidence to prove that non-protestant values do not facilitate economic growth and hence, selectively ignored those Hindu values that could be conducive to India's economic growth (Sinha, 1995). He has been amply invalidated by the recent evidence where the so-called Hindu rate of growth or the elephant syndrome has accelerated into the second highest rate of economic growth in the world in the new millennium. The evidence again indicates that a culture may have a number of values, some of which could be facilitating while others could be depressing development. Consequently, culture-development relationships are not always clear.

A middle ground is emerging where scholars (e.g., Allen, Ng, Ikeda, Jawan, Sufi, Wilson &Yang, 2007; Inglehart, 1977) believe that both culture and economic development indeed impact each other, but the causal relationships are quite complex because both culture and development have their own dimensions and dynamics, and both are affected by a host of other factors. Culture, for example, is also shaped by its history, philosophy, changing demographics of the people, and inter-cultural encounters. Similarly, economic development is also, for example, influenced by economic policies, new technology, international trade, and global market conditions. Harrison (2006) and Harrison and Huntington (2001) argued that the relationship between cultural values and economic prosperity is mediated by the political system that affects and is affected by culture. Indian culture has shown remarkable continuity from the primordial Hindu psycho-spiritual thoughts and values that have been incorporating Islamic, Western, and recent global influences (Sinha, 2009). Similarly, India's accelerating rate of economic growth is traced to the government major policy shift towards economic liberalization that started in a big way in 1991 and has been gaining momentum since then.

This chapter first delineates the dimensions of culture and national development and then explores the pattern of relationships between the two. It also examines some of the theoretical and practical implications of the relationships.

FACETS OF CULTURE

Tylor (1874) defined culture as "that complex whole which includes knowledge, belief, art, morals, law, customs, and any other capabilities and habits acquired by man as a member of society". Tylor's view is echoed by Herskovitz's (1955) who widely used culture as "the man-made part of the environment". Social scientists have different perspectives on how to conceptualize culture and its complex features. Because of these diverse perspectives, cultures are said to vary on a number of dimensions such as complexity (e.g. Carneiro, 1970; Murdock and Provost, 1973), tight *versus* loose (Pelto, 1968), context bound or context free (Hall, 1966), power distance, uncertainty avoidance, masculinity *versus* femininity and individualism-collectivism (Hofstede, 1980). Of these dimensions, collectivism and individualism are the most researched dimensions having the potential to understand the dynamics of development. Hofstede (1991) defined individualism and collectivism as follows:

> *"Individualism pertains to the societies in which the ties between individuals are close: everyone is expected to look after himself or herself and his or her immediate family. Collectivism as opposite pertains to the societies in which people from birth onwards are integrated into strong, cohesive in-groups, which throughout people's lifetime continue to protect them in exchange for unquestioning loyalty"* (p. 51).

In individualistic culture, people's behaviour is explained more by their personal attitudes than by social norms, whereas the reverse is true in collectivist cultures (Bontempo and Rivero, 1992). Moreover, their success is attributed to internal characteristics of individualistic culture, and to external features of collectivist culture (Kashima and Triandis, 1986). According to Triandis (1988), the majority of people in a collectivist culture are collectivists and most of the people manifest collectivist orientation on a majority of occasions. Triandis has provided a list of the contrasting attributes of people in collectivist and individualist cultures. In a collectivist culture, according to

Triandis, groups are the basic unit of social perception, relationships are more important than individual work, behaviour reflects social norms rather than their own inclinations, success is attributed to the help from others and the blessing of superiors, self is defined in terms of in-group identity, people are expected to change themselves rather than to change the adverse situation that affects their behaviour, and are more concerned about what others think of them than what they want of their needs and desires. Triandis and Bhawuk (1997) also described four characteristics of collectivism. First, collectivists view the self as interdependent on others. Second, the goals of collectivists are compatible with those of the in-group. Third, their social behaviour is determined primarily by norms, duties and obligations. Last, collectivists accord priority to relationship taking the needs of others into account. All these preoccupations with relationships, in-groups, and social harmony are likely to adversely affect individual's endeavour to maximize their economic gains. This was the reason for Hofstede to conclude that capitalist market economy fosters individualism and in turn depends on it (p. 233). In contrast, "the various socialist types of economic order foster collectivism and in turn depend on it in various degree" (p. 233). Triandis (1984) also supported this view when he unveiled his model for economic development for the third world countries in which he included the following:

> *. . . planning, concern for time and for future, willingness to defer gratification, accuracy of keeping appointments, assembling many elements of production into coordinated systems, interpersonal trust, eagerness to cooperate with others on the basis of role rather than familiarity with the other, small power distance, moderate risk taking, self-control, and hard work* (p. 94).

The constructs of individualism and collectivism have been undergoing further refinements and modifications. Triandis (1990, 1995) suggested that there are two types of collectivism, namely horizontal and vertical collectivism. Horizontal collectivism is a blend of collectivism and low power distance showing a sense of oneness with member of the in-group with a reasonable amount of egalitarianism as is reported in, for example, Israel. Vertical collectivism, on the other hand, is a combination of collectivism and high power distance in countries such as India. Further, he distinguished cultural level individualism-collectivism from individual level in terms of idiocentrism-allocentrism respectively; arguing that some people of a collectivist culture may be idiocentric while some from the individualistic culture may be allocentrism. Further, some may be high or low on both allocentrism and idiocentrism. The contention that individuals can be high on both allocentrism and idiocentrism led to conclude that they are independent dimensions rather than two extremes of the same dimension. Furthermore, the distinction between individual and cultural levels of collectivism (allocentrism) and individualism (idiocentrism) created a need to examine their relationships with the facets of development at both individual and collective levels.

McClelland (1971) explained economic growth by the theory of need for achievement. He contended that the countries in which a large majority of people have high need for achievement would develop faster. Need for achievement in individual's striving to maximize their achievement, improve up on previous performance, compete effectively with others and so on. If large numbers of individuals do so, the country is benefited. However, two experiment designed by Sinha (1968) and Sinha and Pandey (1970) showed that higher nAch can cause greater collective wealth only in situations where the resources are plenty and therefore individual's effects culminate in collective gains. In a resource scare situation, nAch can still enable a few to excel by exploiting limited resources at the cost of others.

COLLECTIVISM AND INDIVIDUALISM OF THE INDIAN CULTURE

Indian culture is by and large considered to be collectivist (Bond, 1988; J.B.P. Sinha and Verma, 1987; Triandis, 1995; Triandis and Bhawuk, 1997; Verma and Triandis, 1998). In contrast to Western "individuals", Indians are "dividuals" (Marriott, 1976). In fact, Indians can be identified with reference to their collectives and in-groups. D. Sinha and Tripathy (1994) argued that India as a case of "co-existence of dichotomies" where one sees "individualism in collectivism culture". Further, Tripathy (1988) added that in "Indian society individualism and collectivism act like figure and ground depending on the situations one rises from figure while the other recedes into the background"(p. 323). The findings of the recent studies (Sinha, Sinha, Verma and Sinha, 2001; Sinha, Vohra, Singhal, Sinha, and Ushashree, 2002; Sinha, 2004, 2008) showed that Indians are both collectivists as well as individualists. They evoke either of the two or both orientation depending on the nature of the situations. Maintaining relationship becomes an on going and sustained preoccupations of Indians. As a result, they construe a situation and attach meaning to it in a more complex way than the people in the West. They are much more sensitive to the long term effects of their behaviour and guided by the consequences. Therefore, they make a distinction between intention and behaviour. In other words, they may behave in one way with having congruent and incongruent intentions. Because of this complex way of conceptualizing a situation and reacting to it, Indians are found to manifest the following five combinations of behaviour and intentions:

- Collectivists behaviour with collectivist intention (CC)
- Individualist behaviour with individualist intention (II)
- Collectivist behaviour with individualist intention or followed by individualist behaviour (CI)
- Individualist behaviour with collectivist intention or followed by collectivist behaviour (IC)
- A mix of collectivist and individualist intention and behaviour (C&I)

Which of the five ways is evoked as a modal combination of responses/ intentions depends on the nature of situation. Sinha, Sinha, Verma and Sinha (2001) reported that family as a place and family members as an in-group induce Indians to resort to CC responses. However, compelling personal needs and goals, if juxtaposed to the interest of family or friends, were found to induce a shift towards individualist behaviour or intention resulting into various combinations of collectivist and individualist behaviour or intentions (C&I, IC, and CI) depending on the urgency (i.e., time constrains) and quality of relationships. Sinha and his associates also confirmed that economic affluence and infrastructural facilities cause a shift towards combining individualism in the response combinations. It was reported (Mishra, 1994) that the urban compared to the rural, more educated compare to less educated and younger compare to older people are relatively more individualist, although the differences were not significant. Mishra did not distinguish collectivist and individualist behaviours and intentions. Therefore, he could not get a clearer picture of how urbanization, income, education and age cause a shift towards individualism. Kagitcibasi (1997) reported that collectivists start to behave differently when they get affluent. With economic development, collectivists manifest greater independence in economic matters while still retaining their emotional interdependence. Individualists, however, generally prefer to remain independent both economically and emotionally. In sum, collectivism and individualism are reported to have a number of facets, some of which might be related to economic development.

DIMENSIONS OF NATIONAL DEVELOPMENT

In the last five-six decades or so, the concept of development has gone under change and is still evolving. To begin with, development was mainly defined in terms of economic growth. Of course, economic prosperity is a major index of a country's development. It has been measured in terms of gross domestic and national products and per capita income, and so on reflecting the standards of living of the people of a country. However, economic development does not constitute the whole domain of national development. Amartya Sen (1984, 1985, and 1989) argued that material affluence indeed played an important role in facilitating human development but it is only a part of the means to achieve human development that encompasses more than economic affluence. Sen emphasized on the importance of non-economic factors such as, enhancement of human capabilities that has enlarged development debate and opened space to other social science discipline to contribute in understanding of development. D. Sinha (1965, 1969) was the first one to draw the attention towards the limitations of Western models by emphasizing the psychological factors involved in rural development. Sinha (1984) observed that economic growth has a curvilinear relationship with quality of life. Further, the statistics of gross domestic product or the per capita income does not reveal the degree of disparity in the distribution of wealth within a country, as the per capita income may be high while a sizeable percentage of population may remain below the poverty line with a very poor quality of life. Chakrovarty (1986) also pointed out that pure economic approach to development has serious limitations and this could be easily understood by the fact that about the first thirty years of economic development in India made the poor poorer.

ECONOMIC DEVELOPMENT

Economic theorists often differ on the issue of economic growth and economic development. Economic growth implies a sustained increase in percapita GNP, whereas economic development also involves changes in economic structure, accompanied by changes in institutions at the economic, political, and the social levels. Economic growth may be necessary, but it is not a sufficient condition for a country's economic development. Dealing with the economic development of societies, Kunkel (1970) concludes that "the major problem of economic development is not the alteration of character, values or attitudes, but the change of those selected aspects of man's social environment which are relevant to the learning of new behaviour patterns" (p. 76). Further, economically developed countries are often deficient in social development as reflected in anomie, alienation, crime etc.

SOCIAL DEVELOPMENT

The expression of 'Social development' was introduced in 1960 in UN Reports. In 1962, The Economic and Social Council of UN recommended an integration of both aspects of development. In societal development, human aspects are coming to the fore, reflected in levels of literacy and schooling, gender equity, health, empowerment, and so on, together constituting what is called human development at a macro level (United Nations Development Programme, 1997). The acceleration of economic growth was no longer the only factor to be considered; it was specified that social changes should also be accelerated in such a way to improve the condition of the mass of the population. Galtung is quoted stating "Development is the development of the people...it should not be considered in terms of the production of goods and services, their distribution, the creation of institution, structural transformation, cultural development or ecological balance. All these things may be indispensable 'social' means or conditions but development as such is that of man, of the member of a society" (Alechina, 1982: 13). According to the Human Development Report (1990) "The real wealth of a nation is its people. And the purpose of development is to create an enabling environment for people to enjoy long, healthy and creative lives". Kamin (1988) stresses about societal development and notes "the three components of societal development, economic, political and socio-cultural-psychological are interpenetrable". His important comment is that "the uniqueness of the particular cultural group is to be referred more to the intrinsic cultural nature of the people that should be understood and utilized to motivate development. This uniqueness when neglected often creates hurdles in the process of change and development". The universal model of development cannot ensure societal development because of cultural uniqueness and variation in social-cultural dimensions (J.B.P. Sinha, 1990).

More recently, Indian psychologists (Das and Jain, 1999) have also shown their interest in societal development. Societal development concerns to women's mental health, organizational development, rural development, language learning and nutrition etc. It denotes more collective arrangements for the fulfilment of not only physical needs but also psychological, social, and cultural needs (Sharma, 1995). According to Pareek (1988), creation of sense of power in individuals and collectives in a society and its use by them in solving their problem may be termed as societal development. It implies four characteristics in individuals and collectives: which is internality, pro-activity, creativity and extension motivation.

HUMAN DEVELOPMENT

The Human Development Index (HDI), developed by Pakistani economist Mahbub ul Haq, Sir Richard Jolly with the help from Gustav Rains of Yale University and Lord Meghnad Desai of London School of Economics, is an index to rank countries by level of "human development". It usually implies whether a country is a developed, developing or underdeveloped country. It combines normalized measures of life expectancy, literacy, educational attainment and GDP per capita for countries worldwide. The HDI combines three basic dimensions:

- Life expectancy at birth (population health and longevity)
- Knowledge and education (measured by adult literacy rate)
- Standard of living (as measured by the natural logarithm of gross domestic product per capita)

However, HDI has been criticized on a number of grounds such as failure to include any ecological considerations, focusing exclusively on national performance ranking and not paying much attention to development from a global perspective. The United Nations Development Programme (UNDP) operationalized human development of a country in terms of its literacy rate, life expectancy at birth, and per capita GDP. The three indicators reflect a country's development and constitute the basic condition for human development. The Human Development Report, 2002 defines human development as follows:

> *"Human development is about people, about expanding their choices to lead lives they value . . . Fundamental to enlarging human choice is building human capabilities; the range of things that people can do or be. The most basic capabilities for human development are leading a long and healthy life, being educated, having access to the resources needed for a decent standard of living and being able to participate in the life of one's community"* (p. 13).

Human development essentially is the capabilities. The most central of which is the agentic capability. Agentic capabilities manifest in self-reflecting, self-organizing and self-regulative mechanism (Bandura, 1999: 21) that human beings employ in order to improve the condition in which they live and to create new opportunity for human development (Sinha, 2003). According to Sinha, agentic capabilities are constituted of three ingredients: need for competency, believe in self-efficacy and proactive orientation to the environment. Thus, agentic capabilities are instrumental for socio-economic growth which further fuel human development.

UNESCO report stressed, "Science and technology may serve as catalysts to speed up development, but they must acquire an endogenous character based on knowledge of local conditions and thus respecting the national identity" (UNESCO document 104EX/51, paras, 29-30).

ENDOGENOUS DEVELOPMENT

The central idea of endogenous development is that the source and strength of development lies within the country concerned. It emphasizes development based on felt needs and aspirations of the people, their traditional values, native culture and intrinsic characteristics of the society. In other words, endogenous development emphasizes that every society must seek its own type of development in accordance with features of its culture and pattern of thought and action. So development evolves change in the entire society, its economy, socio-culture, human and psychological well-being. "When a country develops endogenously, its way of life should be based on respect of its traditional values, for the authenticity of its culture and the creative aptitudes of its people" (Alechina, 1982: 19). In fact, development involves change in the whole society—it's economic, socio-cultural, political and physical structures, as well as the value system and the way of life of the people (Alexander, 1993).

INTERFACES OF CULTURE AND DEVELOPMENT

The exposition of the various dimensions of cultural orientations in terms of the shades of collectivism and individualism as well as national development leads to entertain a possibility of the presence of a complex pattern of relationships in which only some of the dimensions may be correlated meaningfully. It is imperative to unpack the dimensions and relate them empirically to find out what is related to what in order to improve our understanding of the interfaces of culture and development. Furthermore, such an attempt has to be made at both individuals' and collectives' levels in order to be sure the pattern of relationships holds across micro to relatively more macro levels. The study that follows was such an attempt.

SUPPORTIVE RESEARCH

To test the hypothesis related to linkages between indices of development and cultural dimensions of individualism and collectivism, an interview schedule was employed by Sinha (2007) on 240 respondents of eight villages selected from Uttar Pradesh and Bihar. The responses from the house heads were analyzed at individual and village levels. The measures were the following:

Cultural Dimension: Forty-seven items measuring collectivistic and individualistic orientations were developed out of the literature review. Care was taken to word them so, that the items were relevant to rural settings. The five point Likert type scale ranging from Strongly Disagree (1), Disagree (2), Undecided (3), Agree (4), to Strongly Agree (5) was employed to solicit responses. Two examples of the items were the following:

- I am with my family whether they are right or wrong.
- I am a man of independent thought.

Achievement and Aspirations: The second measure pertained to the respondents' perception of the achievements and aspirations of the respondents' family and their village with regard to five common indices (e.g., economic condition, reputation and prestige, education, health care, and harmony) and an additional indicator, law and order, in the village. Cantril's (1965) ladder scale having 10 rungs ranging from Worse Possible (1) to Best Possible (10) was employed. Respondents were asked to locate their family and village, first, as they stood at the time of the interview (Present Status), then as they were 5 years back (Past Status), and finally at the point they were anticipated to reach 5 years from now (Future Status). The achievement index was derived for each of the indices by subtracting the Past from the Present. The aspiration index was computed by subtracting the Present from the Future. Thus, each house head had achievement and aspiration scores for economic condition, reputation and prestige, educational levels, health care facilities, and harmony of the family and, in addition law and order condition in the village.

Infrastructure of the village: The schedule also had items seeking information about infrastructural adequacy of the village in terms of water supply, electricity, schools and colleges, primary health centre, post office, road connections to towns, telephone, distance from Block and District headquarters, etc. The indices of infrastructural adequacy of the villages were weighted and then summed up and averaged to determine the level of the villages.

RESPONDENTS' PERCEPTIONS

The data for assessing cultural dimensions were factor analyzed using the

Principal Component Analysis with varimax rotation. On the criteria that the Eigen value should not be less than 2 and the factor must have acceptable reliability (alpha coefficient >.60), four factors, i.e. Self-reliance that helps the family, Utilitarian individualism, Pure collectivism, and Familial collectivism were found to be acceptable.

Self-reliance that helps the family signifies that the respondents want to remain self-reliant by engaging in various kind of work and simultaneously tend to maintain family relationship even at the cost of bearing losses. They can make any sacrifice for the interest of their family. They believe that a person is recognized by his family, that success of family is their success, and the prestige of the village is their prestige. They prioritize being rational over sentimental. They aspire to excel in whatever they do, value independence of mind, but believe that only the family members can be trusted during a crisis. Thus, the factor has a core of an individualistic value that is put to the service of the family.

Utilitarian individualism suggests that villagers help others only when they see their own interest being served in collective efforts. Otherwise, they tend to pull each other down. They neither agree on a common leader, nor do they trust each other. They lack understanding of each other. They do talk about the need to work for the development of the village, but do not take initiative. Those who have settled elsewhere no longer feel concerned about the problems of the village. The core of this factor is still individualistic that manifests in collectivist behaviour only when their individualistic purpose is served.

Pure collectivism signifies that villagers work collectively on the occasions of religious and marriage ceremonies even at the cost of their own time and interests. They are always ready to help each other and work collectively for the development of the village. They listen to their elders' advice, resolve disputes by themselves and feel proud of their village. This is a purely collectivistic dimension.

Familial collectivism depicted a profile according to which villagers are strongly embedded in their family irrespective of whether the family members are right or wrong. They believe that only the family members can help and protect each others. Others do not care. Hence, they support only family members and form a strong bond in order to do whatever they want to do without caring for others. In other words, the villages consist of familial collectives that are instrumental to the impressive improvement of the families that culminate into the development of the villages also.

RELATIONSHIPS AMONG CULTURAL DIMENSIONS

Despite rotations that aimed to derive orthogonal factors, the four factors were found to be correlated. There was only one factor that tapped pure collectivism and one that reflected individualism, which also took the route of collective behaviour if it was perceived to serve individualistic interests. Naturally, the two—utilitarian individualism and pure collectivism—were negatively correlated. Of the remaining two, self-reliance that helps the family presented a blend where the respondents valued to stand on their own feet, but then put themselves in the service of the family. Family indeed emerged as a focal concern in expressing itself in making purely collective efforts, harvesting the assets of respondents' self-reliance, as well as excluding other villagers as out groups as unworthy of trusts and hence undependable. Hence, these three—Self-reliance that helps the family, Pure collectivism, and Familial collectivism—were positively correlated. A strong presence of familial collectivism in the Indian culture has been noticed earlier also (Sinha and Verma, 1987). Similarly, Indians, compared to Canadians, are also reported to value self-reliance (Aycan, Kanungo, and Sinha, 1999) that probably enhances their agentic self-esteem, but is yielded to the benefits of the family. In sum, the structure of the four factors and the pattern of relationships support the theoretical proposition in the sense that the constructs of collectivism and individualism are much more complex in reality than envisaged by Hofstede (1980).

ACHIEVEMENT AND ASPIRATIONS OF FAMILIES AND VILLAGES

The five indices of achievement and aspirations are economic condition, prestige, education, health, and harmony. They were found significantly inter-related within each at both the family and village levels, except that the respondents' aspirations regarding the harmony in the family were unrelated to their aspirations regarding the education and health of the family members. There was a reason for that. In one of the villages, east Champaran district of Bihar (Prasauni Kisun), a young man was nurtured by the whole family with a good deal of sacrifices. But when he got higher education and a good job, he deserted the family leaving a bitter feeling. However, the finding was robust. Educational achievements and aspirations of the family members were the most robust factors for their self-reliance that was put to the service of the families. On the other hand, utilitarian individualism was detrimental to the educational achievement, health, and harmony in the family. Sinha (2009) analyzed village level achievements and aspirations in all six areas: Economic condition, prestige and reputation of the village in the locality, education of the villagers, their health status, harmony, and law and order condition. The significant inter-correlations in both achievements and aspirations at both village and family levels raise a doubt whether the respondents hold a holistic view of development or a response set was operating affecting a generalized view of the levels of development. Interestingly, families' achievement in economic condition and health status were negatively correlated with their aspirations suggesting that aspirations ran high, although the achievements were meager. On the other hand families' education, harmony, and prestige manifested continuity from the past to the future. Achievements and aspirations at the village level were more strongly correlated, probably because of a generalized orientation that was also marked the perceptions for indices of achievement and aspirations within each.

The village level differences in the infrastructural adequacy were the first hand knowledge, and hence were used to see whether villages differed in the salience of cultural dimensions. Utilitarian individualism and purely collectivism did not differ significantly suggesting that the pure form of neither collectivism nor individualism impact or are impacted by the levels of development. Only, self-reliance that helps the family and familial collectivism mattered, the former was positively and the latter negatively correlated with the levels of development. In other words, the more developed were the villages the greater was the emphasis among the respondents to attain higher levels of self-reliance that can be employed to help the families to improve their level of development. However, the less developed villages were fragmented into familial collectives where the inter-family relationships were negative and distrustful. As a result, the villages could not harvest the developmental benefits of the family. The villages, which were less developed in terms of infrastructural adequacy, were the ones that had higher mean scores of economic indicator of achievement. On the surface, it sounds paradoxical. However, Sinha reported that those were the villages inhabited by schedule and other backward castes which recently had received a number of economic packages grants, benefits, and jobs by both State and Central governments pushing up their levels of the economic development. They were the villages that enjoyed greater harmony. In the higher castes villages, it was the individuals' education and the family level efforts that were the main drivers of development. However, they did not necessarily have high levels of harmony in the village.

CONCLUSIONS

Development indeed was found to have many facets so were the dimensions of culture. Indicators of development in terms of infrastructural adequacy and perceived economic achievement were differentially distributed in the villages particularly because they were different routes through villages developed materially because of their caste structure. Lower castes villages improved their economic condition through governmental interventions while the higher castes villages developed primarily through raising educational levels that probably enlarged their access to more resources. Education emerged as the most potent factor for self-reliance that was put to the service of family. Indices of development in terms of achievements in different socio-economic areas were interrelated both at the family and the village levels implying that, although they were distinctly different conceptually, the villagers took a holistic view of their development. The cultural values too defy a simplistic classification in terms of pure individualism and pure collectivism. Individualism was utilitarian in manifesting selfish as well as collectivistic behaviour if the latter served the former. Similarly, collectivism was familial rather than societal in its concern. Utilitarian individualism was detrimental to families' achievement, health, and harmony.

Acknowledgement: Thanks are acknowledged to Professor J.B.P. Sinha for his valuable guidance during the General Fellowship (F.No. 3-15/01/G/Fel) of the Indian Council of Social Sciences (ICSSR), New Delhi (India) on the basis of which this chapter has been written.

REFERENCES

Alechina, I. (1982). *The contribution of the United Nations System to formulating development concepts. Different theories and practices of development.* p. 13.

Alexander, K.C. (1993). Dimensions and indicators of development. *Journal of Rural Development.* 12 (3), 257-267.

Allen, M.W., Ng, S.H., Ikeda, K., Jawan, J.A., Sufi, A.H., Wilson, M. and Yang, K.S. (2007). Two decades of change in cultural values and economic development in eight East Asian and Pacific island nations. *Journal of Cross-Cultural Psychology*, 38, 247-269.

Aycan, Z., Kanungo, R.N., and Sinha, J.B.P. (1999). Organizational culture and human resource management practices: The model of culture fit. *Journal of Cross-Cultural Psychology*, 30, 501-526.

Bandura, A. (1999). Social cognitive theory: Agentic perspective. *Asian Journal of Social Psychology*, 2, 21-42.

Bond, M.H. (1988). *The Cross-cultural challenge to social psychology*. Newbury Park, California: Sage.

Bontempo, R. and Rivera, J.C. (1992). *Cultural variation in cognition: The role of self-concept in the attitude-behaviour link*. Paper presented at the August meeting of the Academy of Management. Las Vegas Nevada.

Cantril, H. (1965). *The pattern of human concerns*. New Brunswick, NJ: Rutgers University Press.

Carneiro, R.L. (1970). Scale analysis, evolutionary sequences, and the ratings of cultures. In R. Naroll and R. Cohen (Eds.), *A Handbook of Method in Cultural Anthropology*. New York: California University Press.

Chakrovarty, S. (1986). *Planning and policy making in India*. UNESCO paper No. 34, Paris.

Das, U.N. and Jain, U. (1999). *Perspectives on Psychology and Social Development*. New Delhi: Concept Publishing Company Pvt. Ltd.

Hall, E.T. (1966). *The hidden dimension*. Garden City, New York: Doubleday.

Hamaguchi, E. and Kumon, S. (1982). *Nihonteki Shudan Shugi (Collectivism in Japanese style)* (pp. 1-26), Tokyo: Yuhikau (Japanese).

Harrison, L.E. (2006). *The central liberal truth: How politics can change a culture and save it from itself.* Oxford: Oxford University Press.

Harrison, L.E. and Huntington, S.P. (2001). *Culture matters: How values shape political progress*. New York: Basic Books.

Herskovits, M.J. (1955). *Cultural anthropology*, New York, Knopf.

Hicks, G.L. and Redding, S.G. (1983). The Story of the East Asian "economic miracle": Part one. Economic theory be damned! *Euro-Asia Business Review*, 2(3), 24-32.

Hofheinz, R. Jr. and Cadler, K.E. (1982). *The East Asia Edge:* New York: Basic Books.

Hofstede, G.H. (1980). *Culture's consequences: International differences in work related values*. Beverly Hills, CA: Sage.

Hofstede, G.H. (1991). *Culture and organization: Software of mind*. London: McGraw Hill.

Hofstede, G.H. (2001). *Culture's consequences: Comparing values, behaviours, institutions, and organizations across nations* (2nd Ed.) Thousand Oaks, CA: Sage.

Human Development Reports, United Nations Development Programme (UNDP). New York: Oxford University Press, 1990, 2002, and 2004.

Inglehart, R. (1977). *The salient revolution: Changing values and political styles*. Princeton, NJ: Princeton University Press.

Kagitcibasi, C. (1997). Individualism and collectivism. In J.W. Berry, M.H. Segall, and C. Kagitcibasi (Eds.), *Handbook of cross-cultural psychology* (pp. 1-49). Boston: Allyn and Bacon.

Kamin, S. (1988). The value system and its implication for development in Thailand. In Sinha, D. and Kao, H.S.R. (Ed.) *Social values and development: Asian Perspectives*, 15, 15-174. New Delhi: Sage.

Kashima, Y. and Triandis, H.C. (1986). The self-serving bias in attributions as a coping strategy: A cross-cultural study. *Journal of Cross-Cultural Psychology*, 17, 83-98.

Kunkel, J.W. (1970). *Society and economic growth: A behavioural perspective of social change*. New York: Oxford University Press.

Marriott, K. (1976). *Hindu transaction and meeting: Diversity of exchange and symbolic behaviour*, Philadelphia: ISHI Publishers.

Marx, K. (1867/1976). *Capital* (Volume 1). Harmondworth (republished by Penguin).

McClelland, D.C. (1961). *The achieving society*. New York: Van Nostrand.

Mishra, R.C. (1994). Individualist and collectivist orientations across generations. In U. Kim, H.C. Triandis, C., Kagitcibasi, S.C. Choi, and G. Yoon (Ed.). *Individualism and collectivism: Theory, method, and application* (pp. 225-238). Thousand Oaks: Sage.

Murdock, P. and Provost, C. (1973). Measurement of cultural complexity. *Ethnography*, 12, 379-392.

Pareek, U. (1988). Motivation analysis of organizations: Climate (MAO-C). In. J.W. Pfeiffer (Eds). *The Annual: Developing human resources* (pp 160-180). San Diego: University Associates.

Pelto, P.J. (1968). The difference between "tight" and "loose" societies. *Transaction*, 37-40.

Redding, S.G. (1990). *The Spirit of Chinese Capitalism*. Berlin: Walter de Gruyter.

Sen, A. (1984). *Resources, values and development*. Oxford: Basil Blackwell and Cambridge, MA: Harvard University Press.

Sen, A. (1985). *Commodities and capabilities*. Amsterdam: North Holland.

Sen, A. (1989). Development as capability expansion. *Journal of Developmental Planning*, 19, 41-58.

Sharma, S.L. (1995). The concept of social development and the Indian experience. In R.C. Singh and Gadkar (Ed.), *Social development and justice in India*. New Delhi, Radiant Publishers.

Sinha, D. (1965). The integration of modern psychology with the Indian thought. *Journal of Humanistic Psychology*, 5, 6-17.

Sinha, D. (1969). *Indian villages in transition: A motivated analysis*: New Delhi: Associated Publishing House.

Sinha, D. and Tripathi, R.C. (1994). Individualism in a collectivist culture: A case of coexistence of opposites. In U. Kim, H.C. Triandis, C. Kagitcibasi, S.C. Choi, and G. Yoon (Eds.) *Individualism and collectivism: Theory, method, and application* (pp. 123-136). Thousand Oaks: Sage.

Sinha, J.B.P. (1968). The nAch/n Cooperation under limited/unlimited resource conditions. *Journal of Experimental Social Psychology*, 4, 233-248.

Sinha, J.B.P. (1984). Towards a partnership for relevant research in the third world. *International Journal of Psychology*, 19, 169-177.

Sinha, J.B.P. (1990). Role of psychology in national development. In G. Mishra (Ed), *Applied social psychology in India* (pp. 171-199) New Delhi: Sage Publications.

Sinha, J.B.P. (1995). Socio-cultural factors of organizational behaviour in India. In Kwang-Kuo Hawang (Ed.), *Easternization: Socio-cultural impact on productivity* (pp. 97-126). Tokyo: Asian Productivity Organization.

Sinha, J.B.P. (2003). Trends towards indigenization of psychology in India. In K.S. Yang, K.K. Hwang, P. Pederson and I. Diabo (Eds.), *Progress in Asian psychology: conceptual and empirical contributions* (pp. 11-28). Westport and London: Praeger.

Sinha, J.B.P. (2009). The shifting mindset of Indians. In G. Misra (Ed.), in the series *"The History of Indian Science, Philosophy and Culture"* (General Editor, D.P. Chattopadhyaya).

Sinha, J.B.P. and Pandey, J. (1970). Strategies of high nAch persons. *Psychologia*, 13, 210-216.

Sinha, J.B.P., Sinha, T.N., Verma, J. and Sinha, R.B.N. (2001). Collectivism coexisting with individualism: An Indian scenario. *Asian Journal of Social Psychology*, 4, 133-145.

Sinha, J.B.P. and Verma, J. (1987). Structure of collectivism. In C. Kagitcibasi (Ed.) *Growth and progress in cross-cultural psychology* (pp. 123-129). Lisse, The Netherlands: Swets & Zetilinger.

Sinha, J.B.P., Vohra, N., Singhal, S., Sinha, R.B.N. and Ushashree, S. (2002). Normative predictions of collectivist-individualist intentions and behaviour of Indians. *International Journal of Psychology*, 37(5), 309-319.

Sinha, R.B.N. (2004). Choice of the combinations of collectivist and individualist behaviour and intention as a function of generation gap. *Psychological Studies*, 49(1), 14-19.

Sinha, R.B.N. (2007). *Collectivism and endogenous development.* Research project submitted in Indian Council of Social Science Research, New Delhi.

Sinha, R.B.N. (2008). Rashtriya Vikash: Ek Samuhwadi Drishtikoan. *Perspectives in Psychological Researches*, 31(1), 241-247.

Sinha, R.B.N. (2009). Role of culture in rural development. *Social Engineer*, 12(1-2), 51-64.

Smith, P.B. and Bond, B.H. (1998). *Social psychology across cultures*. London: Prentice Hall.

Triandis, H.C. (1984). Toward a psychological theory of economic growth. *International Journal of Psychology*, 19, 79-96.

Triandis, H.C. (1988). Collectivism v. individualism: A reconceptualization of a basic concept in cross-cultural social psychology. In G.K. Verma and C. Bagley (Eds). *Cross-Cultural studies of personality, attitudes and cognition* (pp. 60-95). New York: Macmillan.

Triandis, H.C. (1990). Cross-Cultural Studies of individualism and collectivism. In J. Berman (Ed.), *Nebraska Symposium on Motivation*, 1989 (pp. 41-133). Lincoln: University of Nebraska Press.

Triandis, H.C. (1995). *Individualism and collectivism*. Boulder, CO: West View Press.

Triandis, H.C. and Bhawuk, D.P.S. (1997) Culture theory and the meaning of relatedness. In P. Christopher Earley and M. Erez (Eds.) *New perspectives on international industrial / organizational psychology* (pp. 13-52). San Francisco: The New Lexington Press.

Tripathi, R.C. (1988). Aligning development to values in India. In D. Sinha and H.S.R. Kao (Eds.), *Social values and development: Asian Perspectives*. New Delhi: Sage.

Tylor, E.B. (1874). *Primitive culture: Researches into the development of mythology, philosophy, religion, language, art, and customs*. London: J. Murray.

Verma, J. and Triandis, H.C. (1998). The measurement of collectivism in India. Paper presented at the meeting of the International Association of Cross-cultural Psychology, Bellingham, WA, August.

Vogel, E.F. (1979). *Japan as number one: Lessons for America*. Cambridge, Ma: Harvard University Press.

Weber, M. (1950). *Protestant ethnic and the spirit of capitalism*. New York: Scribner.

CHAPTER NINETEEN

Aligning Development with Social Justice

Purnima Singh

INTRODUCTION

Social and economic developments are the major imperatives of any democratic and civil society. After independence, India displayed commitment to the twin goals of social and economic development, together with ensuring equality, freedom and justice to all. To achieve this, planned development as a strategy was adopted leading to significant gains on the economic and industrial fronts and raising the socio-economic profile of people. But at the same time several complexities in the social structure were also induced. This has not happened only in India, it has happened in other places moving towards development. The question arises: Why has development lead to complexities in societies? What kind of social structure has it created? The answers to these questions are not so simple. Several strands of thinking are there. One proposition is that this may happen when development is not consonant with values and cultural system. Dube (1987) had argued that development leads to new equations which may result in socio-political problems. "The emergence of counter cultures, disharmonies and imbalances are the obvious results of the process of development"(p. 16). Thus, what we have today as a consequence of development is a fragmented society, vast inequalities, poverty, oppression, marginalization and exclusion of a large segment of the population.

The focus today is on inclusive development. Inclusion is about society changing to accommodate differences, and to combat discrimination. It sees society as the problem, not the person. To achieve inclusion, a twin track approach is needed: (1) Focus on the society to remove the barriers that exclude. (mainstreaming) and (2) Focus on the group of persons who are excluded, to build their capacity and support them to lobby for their inclusion.

This paper argues that these complexities resulting from development have occurred because somewhere we have failed to align development with social justice concerns. Similar sentiments are also voiced in the recent World Development Report (2006) which argues for bringing equity at the centre stage of the development discourse. Equity in the report is defined as consisting of two basic principles—equal opportunity and avoidance of absolute deprivation. The report argues that both are necessary to foster the twin goals of economic growth and empowering the poor which are the aim of the development agenda. This line of thinking is now reflected in many statements and initiatives coming from the government. Although there are debates centring on issues of parity and priority, perhaps everyone would agree that there is a need to have more inclusive policies focusing on the disadvantaged and marginalized groups so as to make economic growth process and social development more equitable.

The relationship between justice and development is very well captured by an example from the World Development Report (2006). The Report begins with an illustration of two children born on the same day, in two different backgrounds: One—a girl, belonging to a poor black family from rural background and mother having no formal education. The other—a white male, born in a wealthy urban family and has an educated mother. On the day of their birth, both children were born in families which were vastly disparate in terms of their family circumstances, race, and economic status. Taking into consideration the statistics, the report demonstrates how these predetermined background variables will make a big difference to the life they will lead in future. Thus, the opportunities the two have to reach their full human potential are very different right from the beginning. These differences in opportunity available to the two will translate into different capabilities to contribute to nation's development as well as to share the fruits of development. The report unfolds how at each stage of life both are likely to have different opportunities and this may influence their potential and contribution for national development. Without going into the details of this analysis, all of us would agree that these inequalities are unfair.

One can identify many such differences in life chances across various social groups which are disgustingly unfair. The aim of the paper is not to present a model of development but to highlight that justice concerns are important and should be addressed while discussing and designing development related policies.

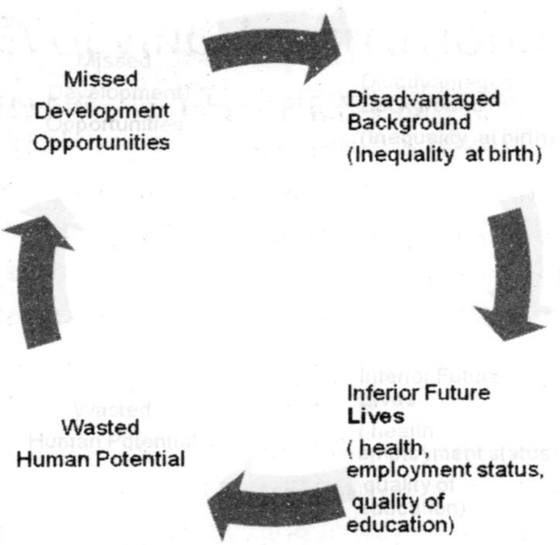

Fig. 19.1: Showing relationship between inequality and development. (Based on the analysis presented in the World Development Report, 2006)

THE DEVELOPMENT DIALOGUE

In the last three decades, the development dialogue has had four different impetuses that have influenced development planning. These are emphases on economic growth and market forces, human development, recognizing the role of institutions and empowerment. Much has been written about the role of markets and their role in economic activities and also that this model of development had its own drawbacks (Shukla, 1987). This led to an emphasis on human development as the key to development process. The emphasis has been on extension of skills, health and capacity building of all people. The stress has been on expansion of human capital. Then came the realization that in order to achieve this, institutions play a vital role and therefore, role of institutions in development was recognized. This marks the third strand of development discourse. As a result there was emphasis on good governance, combating corruption and support for various forms of reforms. The fourth impetus of development has been empowering the people for whom development is intended to be. People should have voice in the development process and should be able to participate in the processes affecting them. Bystydzienski (1992) refers to empowerment as a process by which oppressed persons gain some control over their lives by taking part with others in the development of activities and structures that allow people increased involvement in matters which affect them directly.

These four development impetuses are complimentary and support each other. It is well known that markets and reforms help in expanding opportunities for people and thus help in reducing inequality. Similarly, processes that promote social justice can promote economic growth and empower the people. When justice is not promoted or denied to people, it may result in feelings of marginalization, exclusion and in a more extreme form lead to what Deutsch (2005) calls oppression. The role of psychology in promoting national development had been advocated by Sinha (1984). He, tracing the evolving meaning of development, emphasized the role of psychologists in the development dialogue. He posited that the socio-cultural features of traditional societies played an important role in the developmental process.

SOCIAL JUSTICE: MEANING AND FACETS

Social justice has been a much elusive goal over the years and also one which is heavily politicized. Despite this, it is argued that the goal of social justice is to provide to all a level playing field so as to ensure fair chances to all to develop their skills and talents, become productive and contribute to national development. "It is a yardstick against which we measure everything from the world economic and social order to the events of everyday life" (Sanders & Hamilton, 2001). Empirical research over the years has attempted to answer why justice is important, as well as identify various facets of justice. Research has identified three main facets of justice/injustice—distributive, procedural and retributive. These three facets of justice are also important facets of social justice as denial or aberrations in the three facets result in injustice and lead to feelings of marginalization, exclusion and oppression which in turn has consequences for development. A brief description of the three facets follows:

DISTRIBUTIVE JUSTICE

Prior to the mid-1980s and early 1990s the focus of justice research was on identifying the various principles of justice and to delineate the conditions under which they are applicable. Early theories derived from the notions of cognitive dissonance and social exchange and delved into various principles of justice. Vast amount of research conducted has established that there are multiple justice principles not one, and thus the earlier debate of "one just way" of allocation of resources is now no more acceptable. It is also now well established that historical, political, religious and over all cultural contexts vary widely within and across societies and determine both the world view of people as well as the norms of justice. Further, norms of justice may differ from culture to culture, depending on the meaning of giving, taking away, being needy, and being meritorious. Research demonstrates that differences in allocation norms across cultures are a consequence of the different social realities faced by these cultures. Cultures with high incidence of poverty and slower pace of development may divert more resources in programmes aimed at alleviating poverty and ushering growth and development, in comparison to cultures, which are affluent and more developed. Thus, one prediction that has been well supported by research is that in scarce resource cultures there is less preference for the meritorious when positive resources are to be allocated. Earlier studies in this area in India (Berman, Murphy-Berman & Singh, 1985; Krishnan, 1987; Murphy-Berman, Berman, Singh, Pachauri & Kumar, 1984) indicated greater preference for need or equality and weak-merit preference among Indians. Krishnan (1998) examined the possible effects of situational and resource variables on the relative preference for equality and need. In three allocation scenarios, respondents indicated their own preference, perceived other's preference and perceived fairness of own preference. In the case of own preference, relative salience of equality and need rules over the other rules was demonstrated. Own and other preference were found to be positively and significantly correlated, but they did not indicate the same allocation rule preference pattern. Krishnan (2000) re-examined the strong need weak merit preference in judgements of reward allocation. Results showed that need and merit preferences depended not only on the nature of the resources, but also on the allocation-recipient relationship. Moreover, respondents perceived the greatest unfairness under the merit violation condition.

Other studies have shown that preference for justice principles may vary from context to context. A series of studies have examined the role of caste in allocation judgements. Singh and Pandey (1994) ascertained the role of allocator's caste, the allocation context, and the recipient's need-performance variations. The expected caste differences in allocation preferences were not found in this study. In another study, Pandey and Singh (1997) examined the role of the allocator's caste and context of allocation on relative preference for specific allocation norms, namely, merit, caste, need, socio-economic status of one's family, connections with politicians and with officials, 'source' or right backing, and money. The findings supported the hypothesized effect of allocator's caste on allocation norm preferences. Both these studies also examined the role of the context of allocation on these decisions. Three contexts included in both the studies were: admission to a course, job recruitment and award of a scholarship. Merit was found to be more important for admission and job recruitment, whereas need more important for award of a scholarship. These results corroborate earlier findings that the context is important in allocation judgements.

Krishnan (2001) explored whether social disadvantage matters in justice perceptions and allocation rule preferences. It was assumed that because of their lower status in the society the disadvantaged would feel relatively deprived. In a rural sample categorized as disadvantaged and non-disadvantaged based on caste, the meaning of justice/injustice and extent of prevalence of justice in the Indian society were ascertained. No significant differences were found in the perceptions between the two groups, which implied that perhaps disadvantage did not matter. Both groups conceptualised justice in terms of ethical entitlement, legality and welfare related themes, and injustice in terms of violation of these themes. In addition, it was reported that allocation rule preferences were influenced by resource and situational characteristics including the allocation alternatives available to the respondents. However, in a study comparing a sample of scheduled caste and upper caste respondents, Singh (2004) did find differences in the meaning of social justice given by the two groups. The scheduled caste respondents emphasized equality, need for greater support from the government, measures to bring them at par with others in society, treating them with dignity and respect as salient to bringing about social justice. The upper caste respondents emphasized preference for merit, treatment of all citizens as equals; need to reduce social and economic disparities as important in bringing about social justice. However, one needs to acknowledge that when perceptions of the disadvantaged are considered, criteria of disadvantage other than caste also play a role. Krishnan, Varma and Pandey (2009) investigated the effect of allocator-recipient relationship and internal/external locus of merit and need on both reward and punishment allocation in a distributive context, involving a meritorious and a needy recipient. Between merit, need and equality, subjects showed a clear equality orientation, in both allocation rule preference and perceived fairness of a given allocation.

These studies have shown that different social groups differ in the meaning of justice; however, they have not looked at consequences of distributive injustice. In a stimulating essay, Deutsch (2005) suggests a link between various types of distributive injustices and oppression. Although he does not elaborate a link between injustice, marginalization and development, it is strongly felt that there are linkages between the three. Deutsch considers the distribution of four types of capital-consumption, investment, skill and social and how injustices related to them could result in oppression. Consumption capital is referred to as standard of living having a direct link with income. This may include food, water, housing clothing, health care, education and other services available to people. The social reality is that there are vast differences among different groups in the society in terms of standard of living. Women and various disadvantaged groups suffer and their survival rates as well as contributions to development and taking advantage of development benefits are not only different but at times lower. This is reflected in matters of education, health, and opportunities to develop talents and realize one's potentials. These differences are further fuelled by scarcity of resources which may make people take "tragic choices". Such choices involve questions like how much of a scarce goodwill be made available? Who shall get how much? Many times such questions and their answers are not based on the real needs of people but are based on political manoeuverings and priorities, which make these decisions even more difficult. Often in such situations "social worth" of the recipients needs to the considered. What is the worth or value of the person to the society? How much and in what way individual can contribute to the society? These questions are very difficult to answer. These issues become important when scarce resources, take for example, health care benefits are allocated. Mechanic (1989) reviewing research on health care noted that in U.S. (the same situation would be in other countries also) health care allocations often face painful choices, whether to allocate health care resources to the elderly or younger children. Kuhse and Singer (1988) reported that age of the person especially how much the person would be living is an important factor in deciding how health care money is spent. Health care resources are scarce in all societies. Health care resources involve services provided by physicians, hospitals etc. Since health care resources are scarce, debates concerning what is fair become important. When we look at health care resources in our country, the picture seems to be too grim. Our booming population forces us as a nation to provide health care for too many. Given the spiraling health care costs and health insurance for all a distant reality, the issue of allocation of health care resources is an important one.

Skitka and Tetlock (1992) suggested that in the distribution of public resources (e.g. health care or welfare) allocators appraise the adequacy of the resource pool available and the causes of claimants' needs. When resources are scarce, individuals engage in attribution analysis to assess the source of need and to determine to what extent available resources would help in comforting the need. Results of a third party allocation study showed that when resources were scarce, allocators are more likely to deny claims for those who were responsible for their condition. Claimants whose needs were internally caused and controllable were likely to receive resources only if their need was high and they would be able to use the resources efficiently. Under conditions of high scarcity, subjects provided aid to claimants who were not responsible for their problems but were needy and also had a high chance of success.

Another capital, Deutsch (2005) considers is investment capital which he defines as what people use to create more capital. Income is related to consumption capital and also wealth which in turn is related to investment capital. Vast disparities in wealth are visible in our country. The top five per cent people possess a huge share of wealth and asset base while for the majority it is a big dream. The poor over the years have become poorer and the rich richer.

In terms of skill capital again disparities are inevitable. Deutsch (2005) defines skill capital as "specialized knowledge, social and work skills as well as the various forms of intelligence and credentials that are developed as a result of education and training and experiences in one's family, community and work settings." Who would have this skill capital more? Certainly the rich, the educated, the urbanites and those who have access to opportunities more. The women, the minority, and the disadvantage certainly score lower on this having being denied opportunities over the years. "The most important source of skill capital in today's society is located in the elite universities that provide the credentials for the privileged class" (Perrucci & Wysong, 1999: 14). This statement holds true for the Indian context also. Students from elite management, engineering and medical institutes and good universities are in great demand and rule the job market. The disadvantaged, poor, rural have comparatively fewer chances, although there are always exceptions, to get access to these institutions and acquire the qualifications which have high market value. Thus, they remain at the periphery and are unable to take advantage of the development benefits.

There are also injustices in terms of social capital. One is not going into the various definitions of social capital but stick to the definition provided by Deutsch (2005). He defines it as the network of social ties which can provide information and access to jobs and to the means of acquiring other types of capital as well as emotional and financial support. Deustch sees it as the linkage one has or does not have with organizational power, prestige and opportunities. One's social capital is influenced by family's caste, class, religion, gender, etc. Again one is subjected to a vast array of injustices depending upon one's background which influence one's social capital. Disparities in these various capitals across social group's results in various forms of inequalities, people and groups slowly become a part of the *inequality trap.* The notion of inequality trap may be clear by taking example of women who are certainly a part of the inequality trap. If a woman is born in a poor disadvantaged family, she may not get good education, chances of getting a good job are low and because of poverty her daughter also does not get good education. The same story gets repeated. "An inequality trap may prevent generations of women from getting educated, restrict their participation in the labour market, and reduce their ability to make free informed choices and to realize their potential as individuals. This reinforces gender differences in power that tend to persist over time" (World Development Report, 2006: 21).

PROCEDURAL JUSTICE

An extensive body of research has shown that fairness of the procedures that determine people's outcomes are important. Empirical research has demonstrated that people react to unfairness of procedures in a wide variety of settings (Thibaut & Walker, 1975; Tyler & Lind, 1992). Research has also demonstrated that procedural justice judgements have an important influence on reactions to social policies, evaluation of authorities and rules (Tyler & Lind, 1992). Fair procedures have a psychological importance as they support the assumption that they may give rise to fair outcomes in future. When procedural injustice is perceived, there is less commitment to authorities, organizations and rules. Research has shown that when people have a voice, i.e. they are able to share their views or tell their story they find the situation as fair. These procedures are supposed to be fair because they increase the individuals control over the process and increase one's influence on the decision. Tyler and Lind (2001) in their group value model of procedural justice hold that procedural fairness has symbolic and psychological importance for individuals as it conveys feelings of inclusion in society and upholds the belief that institution holds the person in high regard. According to this model three factors determine the belief that the procedures are fair—neutrality, trust and status recognition which means treating one with dignity, politeness and respect. Some researchers treat the last factor as a separate facet of justice called interactional justice; an issue which is debatable and will not be considered here.

Leventhal (1980) delineated six procedural justice rules—(1) consistency (across people and over time); (2) bias suppression (avoiding self-interest of ideological preconceptions, i.e. personal bias); (3) accuracy (using good accurate information and informed opinions); (4) correctability (having appeal mechanisms); (5) representativeness (having one's concerns, values and outlook considered at all phases of the process); and (6) ethicality (compatibility with fundamental moral and ethical values). Keeping these rules in mind one can question the procedural fairness of our system: Is the system fair? Do people for whom policies are made often have a voice in framing them? Are the judiciary and the police fair to everyone? A few recent well publicized cases are sufficient to disprove this notion of procedural fairness. The high and the mighty people and groups with more capital (consumption, investment, skill and social) have greater access to the judicial, political and administrative system and have voice in matters that affect the society. Who listens to the poor and the disadvantaged? When the poor and the marginalized have no voice, the privileged tend to dominate institutions, have access to land and control labour and market forces. A study on inequalities in governance in four slums of Delhi shows how the privileged, better off and better educated have greater access to bureaucracy and the decisions of the policy makers do not represent the slum interests and thus interventions planned do not help those in need (Jha, Rao & Woolcock, forthcoming). It is true that in most contexts the majority, the elite, the rich and powerful lay down the rules and the minority and the marginalized follow those rules, seldom questioning them. Although in recent times we see these being challenged: but these voices are few.

RETRIBUTIVE JUSTICE

All groups, organizations and societies have rules and norms that regulate behaviour of its members. Often we see that these rules are broken—a realm for retributive justice which focuses on people's concern for rule breaking behaviour. Retribution is the most basic and most pervasive justice reaction associated with human life (Vidmar, 2001). Punishment is warranted as a response to a past event of injustice or wrong-doing. It acts to reinforce the rules that have been broken and balance the scales of justice. Retribution involves making the actor suffer to compensate the victim who's suffering he/she caused. Retributive justice matters because such reactions are at the core of many conflicts and resultant violence. Hogan and Emler (1981) argued that "retribution is also and perhaps more frequently an issue in the minutiae of our everyday formal dealings with one another. Even in the most trivial details of their encounters, people cannot ignore the claims of retributive justice" (p. 133). Despite their arguments concerning pervasiveness of retributive reactions, more than two decades ago, systematic research in this area is not visible even today.

The concepts of retributive justice and corrective justice are often confused to emphasize the same thing. Coleman (1992) argues that retribution is concerned with punishment and corrective justice is concerned with compensation and analysis of how to bring about the *status quo*. The focus of retributive justice is on the wrong-doer and corrective justice on the victim. Societies have institutions which look into various forms of violations and social prohibitions. But do these institutions fulfil the goals for which they are made? In a recent study Singh (2006 a) found that retribution was rated as a response when institutions failed to provide justice. When institutions such as judiciary and police failed to provide justice, or there was a lapse on their part, victims were more likely to resort to settling scores or using tit for tat tactics. In this study, scenarios were presented where for a wrong doing, the offender was either punished or no punishment was given due to some lapse on the part of the institutional mechanisms provided to ensure justice. When institutional mechanisms were effective in delivering justice, retribution was not rated as a response; however, failure on the part of institutional mechanisms led to greater preference for retributive responses. The role of institutions in promoting justice is highlighted by this study. Institutions thus play a vital role in development.

Another issue is that are all people treated equally by the institutions and the criminal justice system? The answer to this question is not very difficult. Why does a celebrity receive all the facilities in the jail but an ordinary poor person languish, although both were sentenced for a similar crime? Is law equal for all? Our experience over the years has shown vast inequalities in the justice system. What we need is a more equitable justice system. The problem is that these systems generally support the interests of the elite and the powerful and they are often inaccessible to the common man.

Although our Constitution gives to each citizen certain equality rights and freedom from being discriminated, the reality is different. It is high time that the law, the legislature, the executive and other institutions need not only to incorporate these rights and freedom into their thinking but also start practicing it. Although, one would agree that it is easier said than done because when attempts are made to protect one group, another group is likely to loose something, it is certainly not a win-win situation all the time.

INJUSTICE, MARGINALIZATION AND DEVELOPMENT: AN ETERNAL TRIANGLE

How do these various injustices relate to development? What happens when people find distributive, procedural and retributive injustices? Injustice, marginalization and development form an eternal triangle whose three corners pose a challenge for all societies including India.

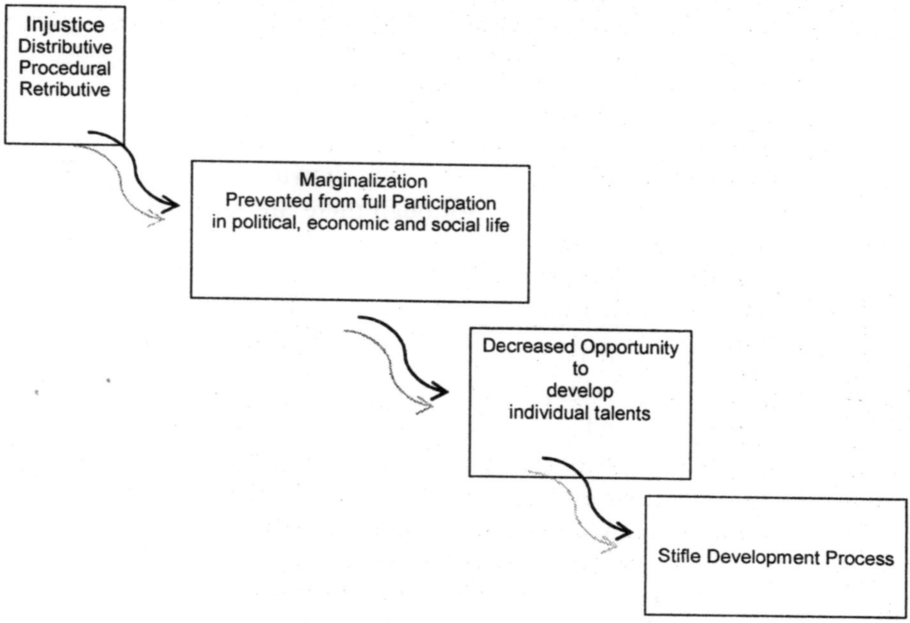

Fig. 19.2: Trajectory of Injustice, Marginalization and Development

Various forms of injustices and inequalities create a situation where people start with very disparate endowments in life. People, because of predetermined characteristics in life like caste, gender, religion, region etc., are faced with very different opportunities in life. They thus differ in schooling they get, education, health status, economic and social mobility, and capacity to influence social and political institutions affecting them. These various types of disadvantages are generally interlinked. Disadvantage in one dimension is reinforced by disadvantage in other dimensions. For example, earlier discussed injustices related to consumption, investment, skill and social capitals are interlinked. Low income and wealth, low consumption and investment capital. Similarly, low income and wealth, low opportunities for skill enhancement and social capital. Social inequalities may mar individual and group potential. A study by Hoff and Pandey (2004) shows how children's performance differs when their caste is made salient. This experiment was done in a number of different villages. Children from different castes were required to perform simple exercises such as solving a maze. Monetary incentives contingent on performance were introduced. The interesting result was that low caste children performed on par with high caste children when their caste was not publicly announced by the experimenter but significantly worse when their caste was made public. This experiment is an interesting reflection of our society. It shows how some of the social stereotypes are internalized and may lead to a loss of potential.

One can see a link between the various forms of injustices. Studies conducted in the organizational context have shown a correlation between distributive and procedural justice. Although there are no empirical studies linking these two with retributive injustice, one can see a logical relationship. In a recent study (Singh, 2006 b) significant correlations were obtained among the two forms of injustice—distributive and procedural. Respondents were asked to evaluate the judicial system, the police and their employers. They were all employed and belonged to economically disadvantaged (monthly income below Rs. 5000) and economically advantaged (monthly income above Rs. 25,000). They were then given questions related to the three facets of justice. 88 per cent of respondents rated the judicial system as unfair; 80 per cent rated the police as unfair and 59 per cent rated their employers as unfair. Results further showed that women rated the police and their employers as unfair; men rated all three as unfair. The economically advantaged rated the judicial system and police as unfair; but rated their employers as fair. The correlation between distributive and procedural justice was .68.

This study further explored the relationship between injustice and marginalization. Table 19.1 shows the correlations between the two facets of injustice and marginalization. Significant correlations were obtained between different facets of injustice and marginalization. Higher perception of injustice was related with marginalization.

Figure 19.2 further shows that marginalization results in decreased participation in political, economic and social life. A general apathy develops towards developmental initiatives. There is a feeling that one is not going to make a difference to the system. When one is not participating, opportunities themselves tend to decrease. Lack of opportunities further decreases chances to develop one's talents and skills. This gets reflected in employment, income and assets one has. As such there is no say in the collective institutions and different programmes from the government. As a result institutions turn out to be unequal and these unequal institutions further increase inequality. There is no sense of agency. "Agency refers to people's capacity to transform or reproduce societal institutions" (*World Development Report,* 2006: 48). When

Table 19.1: Showing Relationship between Two Facets of in Justice and Marginalization

Facets of injustice	*Marginalization (r)*
Distributive	.46 **
Procedural	.39**

one just tends to accept things, without any effort to bring about change, the disadvantages may continue. "From inequality in agency come inequalities in power, voice and self confidence" (*World Development Report*, 2006). The marginalized remain as recipient rather than having a say in the process of development and hence rather than stimulating the process tend to throttle the process. Thus, the dynamics of injustice, development and marginalization is a challenge and can be overcome by aligning social justice with development.

REFERENCES

Berman, J., Murphy-Berman V., and Singh, P. (1985). Cross-cultural similarities and differences in perception of fairness. *Journal of Cross-Cultural Psychology*, 16, 55-67.

Bystydzienski, J. (1992). *Women transforming politics: Worldwide strategies for empowerment*. Indianapolis: Indiana University Press.

Coleman, J.L. (1992). *Risks and wrongs*. London: Cambridge University Press.

Deutsch, M. (2005). *Forms of oppression. Beyond Intractability*. (Eds.). G. Burgess and H. Burgess. Conflict Research Consortium, University of Colorado, Boulder.

Dube, S.C. (1987). Social and psychological implications of development. In K.S. Shukla (Eds.). *The other side of development*. New Delhi: Sage.

Hoff, K. and Pandey, P. (2004). *Belief systems and durable inequalities: An experimental investigation of Indian caste*. Washington D.C.: World Bank Policy Research Working Paper Series 3351.

Hogan, R. and Emler, N. (1981). Retributive justice. In M. Lerner (Ed.). *The justice motive in social behaviour*. New York: Plenum Press (pp. 125-143).

Jha, S., Rao, V. and Woolcock, M. (Forthcoming). *Governance in the gullies: Democratic resposiveness and community leadership in Delhi's slums.* World Development.

Krishnan, L. (1987). Equality and equity in reward allocation in an Indian setting. *Psychological Studies,* 32,97-103.

Krishnan, L. (1998). Allocator/recipient role and resource as determinants of allocation rule preference. *Psychological Studies,* 43 (1 and 2), 21-29.

Krishnan, L. (2000). Resource, relationship and scarcity in reward allocation in India. *Psychologia,* 43, 275-285.

Krishnan, L. (2001). Justice perception and allocation rule preferences: Does social disadvantage matter? *Psychology and Developing Societies,* 13(2), 194-219.

Krishnan, L., Varma, P. and Pandey, V. (2009) Reward and Punishment Allocation in the Indian Culture. Paper accepted for publication in *Psychology and Developing Societies,* 21(1).

Kuhse, H. and Singer, P. (1988). Age and the allocation of medical resources. *Journal of Medicine and Philosophy,* 13, 101-116.

Leventhal, G.S. (1980). What should be done with equity theory? New approaches to the study of fairness in social relationships. In K. Gergen, M. Greenberg and R. Willis. (Eds.) *Social Exchange.* (pp. 27-55). New York: Plenum.

Mechanic, D. (1989). *Painful choices: Research and essays on health care.* New Brunswick, N.J.: Tansaction Publishers.

Murphy-Berman, V. Berman, J.J., Singh, P., Pauchauri, A. and Kumar, P. (1984). Factors affecting allocation to needy and meritorious recipients: A cross-cultural comparison. *Journal of Personality and Social Psychology,* 46, 1267-1272.

Pandey, J. and Singh, P. (1997). Allocation criterion as a function of situational factors and caste. *Basic and Applied Social Psychology,* 19, 121-132.

Perruci, R. and Wysong, E. (1999). *The new society. Lanham:* Rowman Littlefield.

Sanders, J. and Hamilton, V.L. (2001). *Handbook of justice research in law.* New York: Plenum Publishers.

Shukla, K.S. (1987). *The other side of development.* New Delhi: Sage.

Singh, P. and Pandey, J. (1994). Distributive decisions as a function of recipients' need-performance variations and caste of the allocator. In Fons van de Vijver (Ed.), *Proceedings of the Eleventh International Association of Cross-Cultural Psychology* (pp. 330-338). Lisse: Swets & Zeitlinger.

Singh, P. (2004). *Understanding the meaning of social justice.* Unpublished manuscript, Department of Psychology, University of Allahabad, Allahabad.

Singh, P. (2006 a). *Institutional failure and retribution.* Unpublished manuscript. IIT, Delhi.

Singh, P. (2006 b). *Injustice and marginalization.* Unpublished manuscript IIT, Delhi.

Sinha, J.B.P. (1984). Towards partnership for relevant research in the third world. *International Journal of Psychology,* 19, 1-4, 169-177.

Skitka, L.J. and Tetlock, P.E. (1992). Allocating scarce resources: A contingency model of distributive justice. *Journal of Experimental Social Psychology,* 28, 257-265.

Thibaut, J. and Walker, L. (1975). *Procedural justice: A psychological analysis.* Hillsdale, N.J. Erlbaum.

Tyler, T.R. and Lind, E.A. (1992). A relational model of authority in groups. In M. Zanna (Ed.). *Advances in experimental social psychology*. (pp. 115-191). New York: Academic Press.

Tyler, T.R. and Lind, E.A. (2001). Procedural Justice. In J. Sanders and V.L. Hamilton (Eds.) *Handbook of justice research in law*. New York: Plenum Publishers.

Vidmar, N. (2001). Retribution and revenge. In J. Sanders and V.L. Hamilton (Eds.) *Handbook of justice research in law*. New York: Plenum Publishers.

World Development Report (2006). *Equity and development*. The World Bank and Oxford University Press.

SECTION-4

PROF. JAI B.P. SINHA: AS KNOWN TO US

The nostalgic reminiscence of Professor Jai B.P. Sinha as a brilliant scholar, outstanding human being, and a role model for his close-in-contact students or academicians in similar category probably does not fully capture the vastly rich nuances of his wonderful presence, especially the way he has existed in the eyes and minds of his colleagues, associates, and friends. This idea prompted the editors to think of requesting some of his teachers, colleagues, friends, and those who could not contribute to this volume in form of articles/ chapters, for a brief note narrating their association and personal experiences with him. The outcome has been rather revealing of his yet marvellous qualities and personally rewarding to the compilers of this volume. This section presents some such notes reflecting his scholarly yet uniquely unassuming personality and superb facets of his human content.

I. J.B.P. Sinha at the L.S. College, Muzaffarpur

Azimur Rahman*

Thanks for your kind letter dated 7.9.2009 asking me to contribute "note, message or remembrance" in respect of Professor J.B.P. Sinha to be included in the felicitation volume going to be published by his professional colleagues and students. It is a matter of immense pleasure for me to learn that this volume is to come out soon. This has been long overdue but, at the same time, I am of firm opinion that no felicitation volume, how-so-ever inclusive and comprehensive it may be, can successfully reflect the great impact of the writing, research, approach, attitude and spirit of Prof. J.B.P. Sinha on the growth of modern Psychology in India and aboard. I wish a great success to you and your esteemed team engaged in this great academic endeavour.

As for my association with Prof. J.B.P. Sinha, it was for a very short period from December 1954 to the end of 1958. During the period this great Professor was just Jai Jee, a student of 3rd year Psychology Honours in the L.S. College and I was the youngest teacher joining the Department. The difference between me, the teacher and Jai Jee, the student is only of four years. A fresher from Patna College was teaching Jai Jee, a simple, sober, serious, sincere, inquisitive, all-attentive, fully receptive and appropriately responsive student. Jai Jee got the first class first position in Psychology Honours in 1956.

My interaction with Jai Jee became stronger, continuous, productive and more meaningful when he took admission in M.A. classes in L.S. College. My Model teacher was Prof. M.Z. Abedin who welcomed all queries from his students and had on-the-spot solution for them. To be a teacher like him is just an imagination but I did have a desire to tread into his foot-steps and in the pursuit Jai Jee played an immense role. A teacher in formation was facing Jai Jee, a student full of very pertinent question, sometimes getting solution and frequently receiving time petition. I still remember very vividly the amount of labour I had to put in to satisfy Jai Jee.

I have been publicly confessing all these years that *students like Jai Jee can shape an average but sincere teacher into an appreciably good teacher*. The M.A. session ended with Jai Jee getting first class first position in 1958 having delivered more benefits to me than what he received from me.

* Retired Professor and Ex-Head, Deptt. of Psychology, L.S. College, Muzaffarpur, (Bihar) He has been a classroom teacher of J.B.P. Sinha in his college.

We may not be meeting but Jai Jee, I am sure, must be recollecting the sweet memories of those days off and on. I, for myself, feel glorified to have been in the role of teacher of this great Psychologist in the mid-fifties of the last century.

II. A Teacher's Assessment

SALOMON RETTIG*

This is Prof. Salomon Rettig, Hunter College-CUNY. Jai B.P. Sinha was one of my earliest Ph.D. students at The Ohio State University. He was a brilliant student then and remained a top quality psychologist ever since. I have invited him to teach at my University a number of times (Hunter College) and remember that students flocked to his lectures. Jai has also been a very personal and caring friend throughout the years, including during my stay at the A.N. Sinha Institute of Social Studies in Patna, years ago. Jai is indeed an outstanding human being in all respects, including but not confined to the field of psychology. As chair of my department I wanted him to join our faculty but he always decided to return to India despite my wishes. I missed him greatly and wish him the best.

* Former Professor, Deptt. of Psychology, Ohio State University, and Hunter College, City University of New York (CUNY), USA. He has been a teacher of J.B.P. Sinha during his Graduate (Ph.D.) studies.

III. Jai Sinha: A Central Player in Organizational Psychology

HARRY C. TRIANDIS*

Jai B.P. Sinha has made very many contributions to psychology, especially industrial and organizational psychology. Among his contributions is an examination of the dimension of cultural differences that has been labelled individualism and collectivism. We collaborated in some studies of this dimension (see Triandis *et al.*, 1993: 186). After our collaboration he published Sinha (1997) which also included this dimension, and he continues to study it (Sinha *et al.*, 2002). This dimension has since become very popular in cross-cultural psychology. About 100 publications a year, published in the main psychological journals, use this dimension. The major study of culture and leadership by Robert House and hundred and seventy other investigators, from 62 cultures which tested 27 hypotheses that linked culture to interesting outcomes, with data from 17,300 managers in 951 organizations used two measures of this dimension. The recent announcement of the International Congress of Scientific Psychology that will take place in Beijing in 2004 has a special category for sessions that will include studies of this dimension. Outside psychology also there are discussions about the conditions of the world that use this dimension, though usually they do not use the particular labels. For example, Friedman (2000) has celebrated the increased globalization of the world in terms that suggest that individualism is "taking over" most cultures. By contrast, Huntington (1996) has argued that the world is divided along civilization lines, an argument that reflects collectivism. Barber (2001) has discussed the contrast between McWorld and *Jihad*. McWorld is the ideology of Hollywood, which is the prototype of individualism. *Jihad* is the ideology of in group *versus* out group, which is one of the salient characteristics of collectivism. Barber argues that McWorld transforms everybody to consumers, without power to control the market.

The work that Jai and I did involve an examination of what is the substance of this dimension, how does it emerge, and what are its consequences for societal functioning. At this time, when Jai's work is celebrated, it is good to remember that he has been a central player in organizational psychology, linking India to it, and in world psychology. I am sending to him my warm congratulations and best wishes.

* Professor Emeritus (Psychology) at the University of Illinois, Urbana-Champaign, USA & former President of the International Association for Cross-Cultural Psychology has been professional associate of Prof. J.B.P. Sinha.

IV. Jai B.P. Sinha: Visionary of Behaviour in Cultural Matrix

H.S. ASTHANA*

It is a great pleasure to join the students, friends and admirers of Professor J.B.P. Sinha to felicitate him as he enters his 75th year by writing for the **Festschrift** being brought out in his honour. I have known Professor Sinha for almost five decades now from the time he was working at Ranchi and Patna Universities and at A.N. Sinha Institute of Social Studies at Patna.

With a brilliant academic background, the several distinguished positions he has held, the recognition accorded to him, the honours bestowed upon him, the contribution he has made to the discipline through papers and books, in brief, his almost four decades of academic work, he would be the envy of many distinguished psychologists. His work in the field of organizational behaviour, specially its rootedness in cultural matrix has been a major contribution. More specifically, his concept of nurturant task leader circulated in psychological lexicon etches out in bold relief the leadership concept against the background of social ethos. As a person Professor Sinha is an unassuming person, gentle but firm in his convictions, clear and articulate. He is his own best critic. Interacting with him leaves one with the impression that there is always something fresh to think about. I join his admirers in felicitating Professor Sinha on the occasion and wish him many years of healthy, happy and productive life.

* Former Professor of Psychology and Vice-Chancellor, H.S. Gaur University, Saugar, Madhya Pradesh.

V. Extraordinary Academic Achievement

SACHIDANAND*

Jai Ballabh has a uniformly brilliant record as a student. He obtained his doctorate in Psychology from the Ohio State University in 1965. After teaching in the Ranchi University for some time, he joined the A.N. Sinha Institute of Social Studies at Patna as Professor of Psychology and served there for thirty years till his retirement in 1996. In between he taught at the Hunter College, City University of New York, Wake Forest University and Mcgill University as a visiting faculty.

He had important position in academic fields. He was a member of the Executive committee of the Indian Council of Social Science Research (ICSSR), New Delhi. He was also one of the National Fellows of this Council, a coveted honour for any social scientist in this country. He served as national Lecturer of the U.G.C. as well as member of its Psychology Panel. At the international level, he served as member of the Executive Committee of the International Association of Applied Psychology and the International Association of Cross-Cultural Psychology for many years. He was also Fulbright Senior Fellow at the University of Illinois.

He was a member of the editorial board of many national and international research journals and from time to time chaired many international symposia held abroad and delivered Keynote and invited lectures on Psychology and National development, work culture, social value and norms, leadership, etc.

He has published ten books and about 150 research papers in national and international journals dealing with styles of leadership, work culture, productivity, dependence proneness, management, industrial relations, alternative models of development, organizational behaviour, and cultural context of health, Hindu identity and national character and some aspects of research methodology.

He has contributed to multi-disciplinary research and collaborated with me in working on Sarvoday and Development. He organized and encouraged such studies under auspices of the Friday Club. Its main participants were

---

* A Senior colleague of J.B.P. Sinha, He has been an Ex-Vice-Chancellor of Ranchi University, and Ex-Director of A.N. Sinha Institute of Social Studies, Patna (Bihar).

Prof. Surendra Gopal, a historian, Prof. Kapil Muni Tiwari, a socio-linguist and Prof. Hetukar Jha, a sociologist. All of them joined to produce a book entitle 'Social Structure and Alignment' in 1985.

Under his inspirations and guidance a research institute under the name of 'Association for Social Engineering Research and Training' (ASSERT) was set up. Besides taking up research on various problems, it publishes a bi-annual journal, 'The Social Engineer' with a sub-title 'journal of international perspective on development'. The institute provides services in testing, counselling, training and project work. It also sculpted two scales. One of these has been designed on leadership style/behaviour by Dr. Sinha.

Through sustained labour and devotion to academic pursuits, he endeared himself to both to the top leaders of his discipline as well as to those who wanted to learn from him. He turned raw entrants in the discipline into efficient scholars who helped him build up ASSERT and sustain it overtime. His contribution in the field of applied and cross-cultural psychology, organizational behaviour and other field received recognition in India and abroad. Academic honours came to him without seeking.

By his amiable nature Jai Ballabh attracts people and easily makes friends. He does not impose his views on others. He is always helpful and patient. He carries his scholarship lightly and does not flaunt it. He refrains from interfering in other people's concerns. He has an exhaustible fund of goodwill. He does not love power or authority of any kind. Nobody can cast as person on him related to anything. His style of life is decent and dignified but not ostentatious. My own relationship with him is characterized by overwhelming friendliness. Our families have been very close for almost half a century. We have shared joys and sorrows. This affinity grew up as we share the same values and believe in the same vision of a good life. I pray to God to give him a long life so that he could continue to enrich the world of scholarship and scatter it among young social scientists.

VI. A Close Family Friend

RADHA DEVI*

Since the mid-sixties Jai Ballabh Sinha has been a regular visitor to the Department of Psychology, Allahabad University and most of the time he stayed with us at our house, Malviya Road. He attended a number of national and international conferences with Late Prof Sinha. They always found occasions to spend a lot of time together. I know Jai Ballabh quite well for the over 45 years. His family has became part of our extended joint family. He was a great support when Prof. Sinha was hospitalized during the 1974 International Congress of Applied Psychology, in Montreal. Later, in 1982 Prof. D. Sinha joined as the Director of A.N. Sinha Institute. Jai Ballabh was a great support in planning and development of the Institute which celebrated its Silver Jubilee and Mrs. Indira Gandhi visited the institute as the chief guest of the function. After our return to Allahabad we have been in continuous contact and his last visit with his wife Mrs. Geeta Sinha to Allahabad was in December 2007 when we travelled to IIT Kanpur to attend the annual convention of the National Academy of Psychology. It is always a great pleasure to be with Jai Ballabh and Geeta. I love them. It is great this felicitation volume is recording some of his attributes and work. My blessings are for him and his family.

* W/o Late Prof. Durganand Sinha is the chairperson of Prof. Durganand Sinha Trust for Social Sciences. The Trust Organizes Prof. Durganand Sinha memorial lecture and the best doctoral thesis award during the annual convention of the National Academy of Psychology, India.

VII. Professor Jai B.P. Sinha as I Know

RABINDRA N KANUNGO*

It is my pleasure to send this note for the felicitation volume to honour Professor Jai B.P. Sinha. To me, Professor Sinha is my dear friend and colleague 'Jai'. I have been associated with Jai for over quarter of a century, and I can't narrate all the good times we had together both in personal and professional life. However, I am highlighting a few of my experience with Jai. Although I met Jai in a number of international conferences, I became more intimately familiar with him in 1984. I was invited to Patna by Professor Durganand Sinha to give a series of talks at the A.N. Sinha Institute of Social Studies. There I met Jai who was on the faculty and we developed close friendship. For me he was a perfect host showing me around Patna and entertaining me at his residence. I cannot forget the generous hospitality shown to me by Jai and his wife Geeta.

But it was not his personal charm alone that was the basis of our friendship. As we know from psychological research that friendship develops when people are like each other. My research interests are very much similar to Jai's interests. Both of us are interested in indigenous management of organizations, in cross-cultural management, in power and leadership in organizations, and in social development in developing countries. I found Jai's contribution in each of these areas very significant and path breaking. I learned a lot from Jai's work with its focus on India. I really admire his innovative conceptualization of organizational problems and their contextual application for Indian organization. In my opinion, Jai is second to none in this regard. Being impressed by his work, I invited Jai to join me at Mcgill University as a visiting professor for a year. During his tenure at McGill, I even learned more from Jai through our regular almost daily discussions on topics of mutual interest.

He convinced me of the need for 'cultural' as opposed to 'cross-cultural' studies. As a consequence, we jointly published a number of papers. He persuaded me to get more involved in social development research and advocacy. By then, Jai was already a front runner in this area, and he inspired me to follow his path.

---

* Professor Emeritus, Faculty of Management, McGill University, Montrial Canada. He has been professional associate of Prof. J.B.P. Sinha.

Overall, Jai's scholarly works are highly regarded among international scholars. He has profoundly influenced the thinking of the next generation of students of organizational behaviour. He is still continuing his efforts to advance our knowledge and understanding of managerial behaviour in Indian organizations and I do not know if he will ever stop. I am proud of him, and feel fortunate that I came across such a person as Jai during my professional career. I wish him good health and a long productive life.

VIII. My Appreciation to Jai

Michael Harris Bond*

This distinguished, elegant, Indian gentleman also happens to be a scholar of the first water who has contributed mightily to the re-centring of the psychological enterprise away from its innocently ethnocentric American origins. He has reminded the discipline of organizational psychology through empirical demonstration, through trenchant theoretical elaborations, through sustained presentations to international audiences that leadership is more than it is narrowly considered to be in Mainstream imaginations, that we need to broaden our appreciation for the complex dynamics surrounding the question of "how things get done in organizations". Jai Sinha's work has inspired the work of other scholars outside the Mainstream to re-consider the standard operation assumptions promulgated by the American publication juggernaut, so that we now have an empirical and theoretical base capable of sustaining a discipline of cross-cultural management and an *International Journal of Cross-cultural Management.* Amazing! Thank you, Jai, for the sacrifices, the energy and the intellectual resources that you have mobilized to make this future a reality!

* Professor Emeritus, Department of Psychology, Sino Building, Chung Chi College, The Chinese University of Hong Kong. He has been professional associate of Prof. J.B.P. Sinha.

IX. J.B.P. Sinha as I Know Him

YPE H. POORTINGA*

JBP Sinha represents for me a researcher who has made a convincing case for indigenous psychology. The distance between stating that humans are all the same psychologically or that they are vastly different is often small; it is mainly a matter of emphasis. On this celebratory occasion I will try to avoid giving offense to any colleagues impressed with the uniqueness of the Indian psyche and not mention examples of "typically Indian" notions that to me appear readily understandable within the context of the farming community in the northern Netherlands where I grew up. It was colder in my village than in most of India and once the Second World War was over people became affluent to a level hardly found in India. I became a good long distance skater and acquired many other practices and beliefs rarely found in India, but during a five weeks stay in the hills of Orissa with a local family I was impressed with how recognizable things were against the background of my own youth.

This introduction may help to put in perspective my appreciation for JBP's conceptualization of *nurturant-task leadership*. When he elaborated this in his book of 1980 the dominant literature specified two dimensions, concern for productivity and concern for people. The second dimension was from autocratic (bad!) to participative (good!). Nurturant-task leaders were said to occupy an intermediate position, well away from the democratic pole that JBP portrayed as perhaps the ideal, but as unrealistic in the circumstances prevailing in India. Nurturant-task leadership tried to strike a balance between a common framework of leadership and the specific cultural context in which leadership has to be realized. It was a concept with little cultural overload and recognizable for outsiders, while at the same time it had wide-ranging consequences in terms of everyday interactions between a manager and subordinates. JBPs latest book on culture and organizational behaviour, published in 2008, ranges much beyond leadership, but even then it may seem remarkable how few pages have been assigned to nurturant leadership, now named the *nurturant task-participative* (NT-P) model of leadership. In my interpretation there is an evident reason: JBP does not need to argue for this

* Professor Emeritus, Tilberg University, Neitherland and former President of International Association for Cross-Cultural Psychology.

model anymore. Theories have shifted from transactional to transformational styles of leadership; they have moved towards a position that JBP advocated already 30 years ago. What at the time was an exceptional, even a courageous, viewpoint in international organizational research in the meantime has become respectable.

From the 1970s through the 1990s JBP's path has crossed with mine on several occasions in international associations. We also met quite a few times in research meetings for a project initiated by Richard de Ridder on cross-cultural analysis of norm violations and intergroup relations. In my personal memories of JBP three characteristics stand out: his sound thinking and arguing; the agreeable and effective manner in which he can state his opinions; and his hospitality. This may be the occasion to put on record my appreciation for the hospitality that I received during my visits to Patna, for the informative discussions we have had, and for what I have learned from my highly esteemed colleague JBP.

X. JBP Sinha in International Meetings

JOHN BERRY*

Throughout his career, JBP has been a leader in the examination of the interaction between cultural settings and human behaviour. I remember our interactions over the years, mainly at IACCP and IAAP meetings, where he could be relied upon to utter the appropriate words of wisdom with his wry sense of humour and a knowing look in his eyes. His calming voice on matters great and small contributed greatly to the development and operation of these organisations, and to the intellectual debates taking place within them. His past level of activity in the field leads me to believe that he is not really retiring, but merely shifting into the reflective mode that is appropriate to his stature.

With best wishes, John Berry

* Professor Emeritus, Psychology Queens University Canada and past President of the International Association for Cross-Cultural Psychology.

XI. Remembering a Friend

Ron Greene*

It's safe to say I owe my entire professional career to Jai, for without his help I would never have obtained my Ph.D. from Ohio State University here we met as graduate students many years ago. Newly arrived from India, I noticed him wondering around aimlessly, and decided to take him under my wing, hoping at least for an exotic meal. I got that meal and much more, a lifetime of cherished friendship with a brilliant scholar and one of the most interesting men I've ever known.

After several weeks of guidance from me, Jai became completely at home in his new surroundings in Columbus Ohio, and then the tables were reversed. Between the two of us, he was the much stronger academically, and I began to rely on him for guidance in my course and research. He went out off his way many times to give me a little boost or shove when I needed it, but he did himself when it became apparent I was floundering in a required statistics course. Jai had already taken the course and as usual was at the top the class with his usual "A." Although he was busy with many other things, Jai insisted on sitting with me through another quarter of statistics so he could tutor in the evening on the day's work. Even with his help I barely made a passing score, so I know without him I would have ended up a rug salesman in my father's store. It would have made my father happy but I would have been miserable.

One more story, Jai is also responsible for my marriage. Rica and I had been together for several years but she had vigorously resisted my endless proposals of marriage. Nothing I could say could convince her. It just so happened we were planning a trip to Patna to see Jai. In the middle of discussing plans she jokingly mentioned that she might change her mind about marriage if she could have an elephant at our marriage. She thought this impossible and would end my nagging. We both had a laugh, but I decided to write Jai to see if there was any way he could acquire an elephant, and if he could arrange a ceremony for us.

---

* Practicing Clinical Psychologist, currently at Greenbrae, California, USA. He has been a friend of JBP Sinha since his Graduate studies days at the Ohio State University.

He responded that he could and he would. When I told this to Rica her jaw dropped, but figured a deal was a deal and agreed at last to be my bride. Jai arranged a beautifully modified Hindu ceremony and party on the grounds of the A.N. Sinha Institute campus, and we had hundreds of curious well-wishers to share this special time with us. So you see Jai is not only responsible for seeing to it that I became a psychologist, but also that I was able to marry the woman who has brought great joy to my life all these years. What better friend could a man ever have?

XII. Professor Jai B.P. Sinha as I Came to Know Him

Gajendra K. Verma*

I have known Jai Ballabh Sinha as a friend, professional colleague and as an international scholar in the field of social psychology for over three decades. I first met him at the A.N. Sinha Institute of Social Studies, Patna, Bihar and subsequently at international conferences on cross-cultural psychology, even though I knew of him previously through his scholarly reputation in India, and through his publications in international journals.

I have had the pleasure of drawing on and citing his published work in some of my own research work. Professor Sinha is widely respected in the community of social psychologists particularly in the field of cross-cultural psychology, not only in India but in North America and Europe as well. I am delighted to say that he has been widely known as an Indian scholar with depth of knowledge and understanding of the field. He has a reputation for scholarly excellence in the field of cross-cultural psychology.

Professor Sinha is the kind of scholar who believes in "learning, re-learning and un-learning" in the light of new research evidence and conceptualization. He has mastered the art of unravelling the complex strands of individual and social characteristics which are the matrix of the discipline of social psychology. His academic career, writings and publications are indicative of the depth and breadth of his knowledge and commitment in his chosen academic field. He is exemplar of the mature scholar, ageing but not old, still in his 'seventies', active in a number of productive fields. In this he has set an example for the present and the future generations.

* Professor Emeritus, Formerly Dean, Research and Graduate School and Sarah Fielden Professor of Education, University of Manchester, United Kingdom. He is a friend associated with JBP Sinha.

XIII. The Torch Bearer of Psychology in India

R.C. Tripathi*

There are some persons you come to know even before you have met them. In Kalidas's famous play there is one such reference when King Dushyanta sees the kid Bharata for the first time and feels naturally driven towards him. He says that such feelings get aroused only if one had an affectionate relationship with each other in many previous birth cycles. My feelings for Jai Ballabh ji are very similar to Dushyanta's feeling. I feel that he is a 'suhrid' with whom I have a 'janma-jamantar' sambandh.

It was some time in 1966 when I was a young lecturer at Allahabad University that I first heard about him from Professor Durganand Sinha who had returned from a Selection Committee meeting at A.N. Sinha Institute of Social Studies. He was all praise for this young scholar he had appointed as a Professor and held him out as someone we could all learn. He narrated the story of his appointment and followed it up with a gentle admonition that 'I hope you guys too will do some good publishing'! His praise for him never stopped and it only increased our curiosity to meet the man.

I was to meet him much later in person in the Department at Allahabad. Our paths by then had converged almost totally. This was after I returned from the United States obtaining my degree in Organizational Behaviour. JBP had trained as an Experimental Social Psychologist, but had by now started veering towards studying Organizational Behaviour. He held on to his commitment of doing 'socially meaningful research' which for him meant on pressing problems of the country. In this way, his attempt was to use *emic* level concepts. His belief was that psychological problems cannot be understood if they ignored the social and cultural context. So, Indian work organizations as well as leadership within these organizations were to be studied in terms of the Indian cultural context. He saw no discontinuity between the behaviour of members in work organizations with the manner they behaved outside the organizations. Their behaviour was seen as continuous with the way they behaved within their own social communities.

* Ex-Director, G.B. Pant Social Science Institute, and Ex-Head, Deptt. of Psychology, University of Allahabad (UP, India). He has had a long academic and professional association with JBP Sinha.

It did not change because Weber had willed so. The workers who came in socialised the 'organization' rather than the organization socialising them. Yes, the organizations did impose constraints on their behaviours, but organization structure was for ever available for interpolations, *a la* Katz and Kahn. The nurturant task leader, thus, was seen first as nurturant of his subordinates and it was only thereafter that he turned to demanding task performance.

The manner in which social values play out in Indian work organizations has been an abiding theme in JBP Sinha's research. Although, he is not given the credit which is due him, individualism/collectivism research got the fillip it needed because of his contributions in various IACCP conferences. Psychology in India owes a great deal to him for using social values as coordinates to explain and understand the mind set of Indians and how the behaviour of workers in the Indian work organizations needs to be understood within the unique Indian cultural context. His work has influenced the work of a few generations in India. My own academic debt to him is huge because of the close interactions we have had over the years. He always travelled down to Allahabad if he was working on something which was new and we at Allahabad were lucky to hear about it before anyone else did. I had hoped that I shall be able to contribute a paper to his *Fetschrift* developing some of his ideas on scarce resource environment but could not because of certain reasons. I would like to redeem the pledge sometime soon and although, it is a bit unusual, I would like to dedicate this hitherto unpublished paper to you Jaiballabh ji!

XIV. Remembering Friday Group

HETUKAR JHA*

It is difficult to remember now when exactly I met Dr. J.B.P. Sinha first. However, it was, perhaps, in early 1972, that I got a chance of hearing him in a seminar at the A.N.S. Institute of Social Studies, Patna. I remember very well that I was very much impressed by the logic of his argument and his preference for analysis. Soon after the seminar, I went to his chamber (on the first floor of the Institute), introduced myself to him and, then, he asked me to sit and say what was my comment on his paper. There were two or three scholars already sitting around his table and, therefore, our first meeting lasted for only about fifteen minutes. However, I left his room with a feeling that Dr. Sinha is a different kind of intellectual in our academia who could afford time to listen to even young lecturers and students and encourage them to develop sense of precision in thinking.

Gradually, frequency of my visit to the Institute increased and I always found him engaged either in reading or in writing, I must have disturbed his routine of work quite often, but never did I mark any sign of displeasure on his face. In December 1972, on my way back to Patna from Columbus, Ohio, I stayed in New York for day with him. I was disillusioned with the use of American or Western sociological approach for the study of our societies and had decided to devote my time to explore our social reality from the perspective of our own history and tradition. I discussed this with Dr. Sinha who not only supported my view but volunteered wholeheartedly to contribute to this proposal. He also suggested to form a group of scholars who should meet regularly and discuss the different aspects of our society in detail informally. After my return, I discussed this proposal with a number of professors in Patna. But, only Dr. Surendra Gopal of the department of history and Dr. K.M. Tiwary of the department of English appeared to be quite enthusiastic and soon they gave their consent to join this venture. In 1973, Dr. Sinha came back and, then, I informed him about the response of Dr. Gopal and Dr. Tiwary. He became very happy and decided to hold the meeting every Friday in the afternoon in his own chamber.

* Former Professor and Head, Deptt. of Sociology, Patna University, Patna. He has been professionally associated with JBP Sinha.

Thus, we (Dr. Sinha, Dr. Gopal, Dr. Tiwary and myself) began to assemble in his chamber once every week (on Friday) and hold discussion for about two hours on an issue related to our society. The issues were mostly raised by Dr. Sinha. His questions were always quite sharp and precise. With such questions in mind we used to examine the relevant literature and then carry on the discussion that generated more questions. I remember it well that discussion of any issue selected by the Group generally continued for several months. Dr. Sinha always advised us to avoid using our discipline specific jargons. This group gradually began to be called Friday Group and, I think, it was because of the leadership of Dr. Sinha that Friday Group flourished quite visibly for not less than twenty years. We discussed quite a number of issues; all of us together conducted research on violence in three cultural zones of Bihar.

It is really a matter of great pleasure that old students and friends of Dr. Sinha have decided to felicitate him and bring out a volume of research articles in his honour. As I look back, memories of both pleasant and unpleasant experiences crowd in on me. However, following the Sankalpa and Vikalpa processes of our ancient Sankhya Darshan, the determinate perception of the image of Dr. Sinha that emerges in my mind is that of an intellectual for whom the ultimate value lies in learning and generating knowledge more and more. I sincerely pray to Lord to let him remain with us for many decades to come as a source of inspiration for the present generation of students.

XV. Professor Jai B.P. Sinha

VIJOY PRAKASH*

I came to know about the scholarly achievements of Prof. Jai B.P. Sinha, when I was Secretary, Higher Education, Government of Bihar and also as Director of A.N. Sinha Institute of Social Studies, Patna. Although he had left the Institute at that time, he was seen as one of the foundation pillars of research and scholarly activities of the Institute. He was one of the main architects of research edifice of psychology in Bihar. His contributions became the main factor for bringing Bihar on international psychology research map. Even after retiring from A.N. Sinha Institute of Social Studies, his inner passion for research blossomed in the form of development of a forum of psychological research at ASSERT.

I had occasions to interact with him at various workshops organized in the city. I have found him to be a rare breed of scholars totally dedicated to innovation and research. His commitment to task, time management and punctuality is simply exemplary. Even in his seventies his dedication to research and receptivity to new ideas keeps inspiring the future generations. I hope the commemorative issue would pave the way for keeping this inspiration glowing.

* IAS Officer, and currently the Principal Secretary, Govt. of Bihar. He has social and academic associations with J.B.P. Sinha.

XVI. My Recollections of Our Professor Jai B.P. Sinha

SAGAR SHARMA*

I have the honour to recall my long distance association with our highly adored and loved senior colleague Professor Jai B.P. Sinha—presently located in Patna. Prof. Sinha in his mid-seventies continues to be active and contributing to profession. My academic interaction with him dates back to early 1980s, when, on my request, he started mailing his research publications to me at Himachal Pradesh University, Shimla. Simultaneously, I had evaluated a Doctoral thesis of one of his illustrious students (currently a Senior Professor of Psychology)—the topic of that thesis was on "Social Responsibility". His generous act of mailing to me, his published work on Nurturant-Task Leadership Style, Work Culture in Indian context, Indian Psyche, and Contemporary Cultural Orientation of Indian Professors and so on, kept me rather updated with his high quality and a culturally-embedded work as applied to Indian Organizations, including Institutions of higher learning.

Most recently, I had the good fortune of a closer interaction with him at the IIT Kanpur during NAOP (2007) Annual Conference, and listened to his highly illuminating and thought-provoking presentation on "Indian Mindsets and the Condition that EVOKE Them"—that was based on his two studies conducted on samples of Scientists and middle level managers who worked across India. I believe that Professor Sinha's research has stimulated contextually relevant investigations and applications, not only in organizational contexts but also in overall Indian settings. Professor Jai B.P. Sinha's Professional contribution in the growth of Indian Psychology is well-known and respectfully acknowledged by one and all in India and abroad.

With his family, he had also graced our University at Shimla during his visit. I would like to make a special mention of one of his personal attributes. While all of us know about his unending capacity to "nurture" a talent, I think a less number of colleagues know about his high quality humour that is characterised by the elements of surprise and spontaneity without sarcasm. Anyway, I discovered this feature of him at the IIT Kanpur (December 17-19, 2007).

---

* Former Professor and Chair, Psychology Department, H.P. University, Shimla.

To me Professor Jai B.P. Sinha is a complete professional person. May the Almighty God bless him with continued good health and well-being. As he always been a continuously inspiring colleague we wish him a long life for guiding and remaining a role model for all.

XVII. Walking Tall

Ajit Mohanty*

He remained enigmatic in his scholastic simplicity. In an age of obsolescent scholarship, he maintained a level of simplicity in his theorizations. He dealt with complex phenomenon and yet left it at a level simple enough for the average student of psychology to make it a part of his/her daily psychological parlance. His description of the nurturant task leadership or of the *chalta hai* culture sought to explain aspects of profoundly complex organizational and social reality in a manner that makes it almost obvious and impressively lucid. Nevertheless, these simple ideas and concepts were there to etch a permanent place in the literature of psychology. Each of his many ideas could have been turned to a slogan of sorts that often made the management gurus famous and rich. He was the real guru of the gurus; his greatness did not lie in the obscurity of ideas and the superficial attractiveness and catch value of shallow slogans; it rested on the profundity of his thoughts, simplicity of his explanations and the wisdom of his insights. Having read him as a student, I often said to myself "Yes, that is how it is in our own context and experiences. Why didn't I think of this before!" Very few provided such leadership to a discipline and did as much to strengthen the national identity of a profession as did Professor J.B.P. Sinha.

As a student of psychology, I had the image of this great person and academic leader as one beyond reach, too profound, too original and wise. While my short and brief encounters with him as a student at Utkal matched my imaginations of him, I could not but be struck by his simplicity and an aura that was frugal in announcing itself. I always thought that he was great and yet simple. And, at the same time, there was something in him that aroused a sense of reverence and a sense of humility, all simultaneously and deeply. As a young teacher of psychology, I got to understand him a lot better partly because I could watch him closer. For some one aspiring to go abroad for higher studies, I thought he was my hero. Unlike some other tall figures in the discipline, he was not a god to be worshipped from an uninvolved and apathetic distance; he was there, he was real and he could be emulated. I admired his

* Professor, Jakir Hussain Centre of Educational Studies, Jawaharlal Nehru University, New Delhi.

groundedness and his scholarship both joined by an enigmatic simplicity. It is only after my encounters with the Western psychology that I perhaps developed a more effective appreciation of him as a maker of the discipline at least in India. While I was influenced by the western psychology, western scholarship and Western professionalism, I came back with a sense of desperation both because suddenly I became aware of the shallowness of the discipline in my own country and, at the same time, the emptiness of the Western psychology in meeting the challenges of the reality—our own reality. There were not many among the professional psychologists of those days who did not idolize the western psychology as the most progressive know-all, explain-all kind of knowledge—even if they were not only stale by decades but also elusive in making us understand the reality that we know of. Such borrowed knowledge defied our common sense and challenged our emptiness. There were not many who offered insights, which were strangely unconventional and, yet, invitingly simple as did Professor J.B.P. Sinha. Trained and working as a student and researcher in my field of psycholinguistics, I could not have the benefits of his ideas in any direct sense; but I was always deeply conscious of his approach and his refusal to tow the hackneyed lines of the Western psychology. I was definitely emboldened by his forceful, undemonstrative and, yet, daring defiance of the western ideas. He was willing to befriend the west but was also forthright, open and candid in his challenges and in leading many a declaration of revolt from the so called underdeveloped and developing part of the world. While most of our seniors and contemporaries admired the West, idolized, and blindly echoed the Western knowledge, I called them '*Yankee doodlers*', the West admired Professor J.B.P. Sinha and many Western scholars in the international organizations continue to look up to him as a fine scholar and model professional. He hosted many Western stalwarts, befriended them and yet carried the relationship forward not as a blind follower but with his humane critical stance. At A.N. Sinha Institute in Patna, he hosted Professor Triandis and generously invited some of us to participate in his lectures and deliberations. I came back from this encounter deeply and proudly moved and impressed by the manner in which Professor Sinha questioned the foundations of the approach, which had made Professor Triandis so famous. In my early days, there were not many who could do so. Professor J.B.P. Sinha's views and opinions still matter in the global arena of psychology. Our paths did not match; he was as far from psycholinguistics as I was from OB. Nevertheless, there was this strange and deep sense of mutual appreciation that we shared. Whenever we met, he would fondly enquire about my work and take a keen interest in knowing more about the research I was doing. This was not just a formal and superficial expression of goodwill; I realized much later that he was concerned and was watchful of my developments. I was pleasantly surprised when I was invited for a keynote address in the International Congress of Applied Psychology at Madrid in 1994. I still thought then that I had not done enough to attract such international attention. Later, I learnt that Professor J.B.P. Sinha had a say in this recognition and, I am sure, this was one of his many ways of promoting psychology in India in international forum. However, he was never thought of as being parochial in his views and commanded respect by all his colleagues—in India as well as abroad. When the National Academy of Psychology staked its claim to be recognized by the International Union of Psychologists as the representative body from India, it was Professor J.B.P. Sinha whose views were sought for by the International body and his opinions did matter in NAOP's acceptance. His leadership has mattered a lot in shaping psychology in India, in strengthening the national identity of the discipline and in setting a standard for the younger generations to aspire for; I am sure he will continue to inspire by his own example for many more years to come.

Psychology in India is immensely enriched by the august presence of a stalwart like Professor J.B.P. Sinha. Yet, I am not sure, if we have done enough to recognize the greatness of this gem of a human being and scholar. I can only pay, through these inadequate words, my respect to this silent mentor and wish him many more years of active scholarship and happy fruitful life. Psychologists' models are plenty but model psychologists, like this great person still walking, tall are rare.

XVIII. The Pillar of Support

Sudha Rani Sinha*

It is aptly remarked—"*You must first be a believer, if you would be an achiever.*" It was this unflagging belief in himself, the insatiable quest for perfection and the unerring flair for innovation that sums up the professional journey of the renowned psychologist, Prof. J.B.P. Sinha, known widely both in India and rest of the world for his outstanding contribution in the field of psychology. A name synonymous with empathy, compassion and benevolence, Prof. Sinha remains a legendary scholar and academician. Referred the world over for his conceptual and empirical research on Nurturant Task Leadership—a leadership combining task and relationship oriented behaviour with a blend of nurturance, Sinha is an exemplar of this leadership.

'Behind every great man there's a great woman'—Talking cue from this feminist slogan, I thought of unveiling the dynamic persona of our legendary teacher and scholar, Prof. J.B.P. Sinha through the eyes of his wife, Mrs. Geeta Sinha. The transcript is based on the rather informal and very intimate talk that I had with Mrs. Sinha—the woman behind the success of the renowned scholar, Prof. J.B.P. Sinha.

With a relationship spanning over more than half a decade, Mrs. Sinha has been an incredible pillar of strength holding her family together. In hard times, she has never complained, never slowed down, never asked for a thing. Having spent her days and nights caring for her family, continuing her role as a devoted wife and a dedicated mother. Mrs. Sinha's love, commitment, dedication and support are certainly undeniable.

Talking about the early years of her marriage, Mrs. Sinha revealed the ups and downs of her married life. Married at the tender age of twelve, Mrs. Sinha spent the early years of her conjugal life at her mother's place. It was only after Prof. Sinha completed his M.A. and joined his job at Ranchi that both of them started living together. Blessed with a son, after eight years, Mrs. Sinha encouraged him to go and pursue his Ph.D. once he was granted the scholarship. When Sinha left for America, Mrs. Sinha was expecting her second issue. Though it was certainly difficult, Mrs. Sinha never posed a hurdle in her husband's scholarly pursuits and never caused a reason for him to step behind.

---

* Prof. of Psychology, ASSERT Institute of Management Studies (AIMS), Patna.

As a man with strong family values, Prof. Sinha believed in the set of beliefs or morals that help in providing family unity and social interaction as well as providing for a societal view of children's development. Prof. Sinha's undeterring faith in family values is reflected in his relationship towards his parents, his wife, and his children.

A dutiful son, Prof. Sinha has not given them any reason to complain and has maintained a very open and loving relationship with his parents. Son of late Sukdeo Prasad Sinha, a freedom fighter, Sinha's was a rather undemanding childhood, sharing uncomplainingly, his father's attention with the other members of the joint family. A disciplinarian to the core, Prof. Sinha imbibed the quality from his grandfather who showered him with his love, affection and guidance.

Talking about Prof. Sinha as a husband, Mrs. Sinha sums it up in a single word. "perfect." Having spent around fifty years of sharing and togetherness, Mrs. Sinha is simply overwhelmed by his genuine concern and support. Admitting that she had not received very high studies, Mrs. Sinha repeatedly mentioned that her lack of scholarly pursuits was never a botheration for Sinha. He instilled faith in her own self and made her an indispensable part of his social and scholarly gatherings. A man with a strict routine and time table, Mrs. Sinha has meticulously catered to all his demands religiously. Having completely moulded herself in the fashion her husband wanted her to be, Mrs. Sinha has fitted the bill of a perfect life partner herself. Except for the occasional and normal differences that are a part of every marriage, Mrs. Sinha has no memory of any ugly incident in her conjugal life.

As a father, too, Prof. Sinha has emerged as a good parent—a person who is patient, kind, considerate, understanding, and helpful, a good listener, and a disciplinarian at the proper times and provided his children with several life skills, including good decision-making ability, feelings of self-worth and self-control, and good communication skills thus creating a solid foundation for responsible behaviour. Prof. Sinha shared a very friendly relationship with his children spending time with them and being involved in their lives. For Sinha, loving your children meant grounding them, withholding allowance when chores weren't finished and saying no to things they really wanted at times. As a father, he was not too much of a pushover, as children would then grow up lacking discipline. On the other hand, he did not even push them too hard, as they would end up resenting him. Like a good father he knew how to straddle this delicate line.

The mother understands the child at all times. She protects the child whatever happens. The father knows what has to be done so that the child can grow up and become independent. Thus, it was the combined effort of both of them which has nurtured their children, striding successfully on the path to success today. Sinha has proved to be a role model for his children—a son and a daughter and Mrs. Sinha's support and participation in rearing the children is unquestionable.

Great men are impossible without great women. Behind the monuments of masculine genius, whatever their nature, there is always to be seen, hovering like a spiritual presence, the soul of some woman. Whether it is Michelangelo singing the glory of Vittoria Colonna—"*Without wings, I fly with your wings; by your genius I am raised to the skies; in your soul my thought is born*" or Baldassare Castiglione immortalizing Elisabetta Gonzaga—"*Without women nothing is possible, either in military courage, or art, or poetry, or music, or philosophy, or even religion. God is truly seen only through them*", in every case it is the contribution of a woman behind Man's success. It goes without saying that, in the making of Prof. J.B.P. Sinha—the renowned scholar, the dutiful son, the loving husband, and the perfect father, the role of his better half—Mrs. Geeta Sinha is really laudable.

About the Contributors

Arif Hassan a Ph.D. in Psychology from Patna University is a Professor and Deputy Director of the Graduate School of Management at International Islamic University, Malaysia. Earlier Dr. Hassan worked at Magadh University; Patna University, A.N. Sinha Institute of Social Studies, and National University of Educational Planning and Administration, New Delhi. He is a recipient of Fulbright Fellowship and was attached to the University of Pennsylvania. His research publications are in the area of education and human capital development, leadership, justice, change, and cross cultural studies in organizational context. He is the chief editor of IIUM Journal of Case Studies in Management.

Arvind K. Sinha a Ph.D of Patna University is currently a Professor of Psychology at the Department of Humanities and Social Sciences, Indian Institute of Technology, Kanpur. He specializes in Organizational Behaviour and he has authored, co-authored over hundred published articles and conference papers in India and abroad. He has mainly worked in the area of Organizational Behaviour and Social Psychology. He has served on several academic administrative positions. He is currently the Convener of the OB Division, and the President (2009) of the National Academy of Psychology (India).

Ajay K. Jain a Ph.D. from Indian Institute of Technology, Kanpur is presently Associate Professor in Organizational Behaviour at the Management Development Institute, Gurgaon. Earlier he was a Post-doctoral fellow at the Indian School of Business, Hyderabad. He teaches courses on Research Methods, Marketing Research, and Organizational Design and Change. He has published widely in National and International Journals and has presented his papers in National and International Conferences.

Dharm P.S. Bhawuk a B.Tech. from Kharagpur, and an MBA University of Hawaii a Ph.D. from University of Illinois at Urbana-Champaign is currently Professor of Management and Culture and Community Psychology, University of Hawaii. His research interests include cross-cultural training, individualism and collectivism, intercultural sensitivity, diversity in the workplace, indigenous psychology and management. He has published more than 50 book chapters and papers. He is a co-editor of the book *Asian Contributions to Cross-Cultural Psychology* (1996).

Girishwar Misra presently a Prof. of Psychology at Delhi University has earlier served as faculty at Gorakhpur, Allahabad and Bhopal. He founded the Department of Psychology at Bhopal University. He is the Chief Editor of a quarterly journal of Psychological Studies and recently he has edited four volumes of ICSSR sponsored Psychological Research in India. He is a well known cultural, developmental and social Psychologist.

Janak Pandey a Ph.D. of Kansas State University is currently Vice-Chancellor of Central University of Bihar. Earlier served as Vice-Chancellor of Allahabad University, Director, Govind Ballabh Pant Social Science Institute, Allahabad. He has been President of the International Association for Cross-Cultural Psychology. He is a recipient of the Professor V.K.R.V. Rao award, Fulbright and Commonwealth Fellowships. He has published on social influences and social and environmental issues. He edited *Perspectives on Experimental Social Psychology in India* and the six volume of research of psychology in India. The state-of-art based on two rounds ICSSR survey of Psychology research. He has also co-edited Asian contributions to Cross-Cultural Psychology and Handbook of Cross-Cultural Psychology.

J.M. Deo a Ph.D. in Psychology from Patna University is currently a Reader at a Post-Graduate Department of Psychology, College of Commerce Patna, Magadh University. He is a Regional President of IAAP, editor of Social Engineer, a biannual journal of international perspectives on development, and a Consulting Editor of the JIAAP.

Jyoti Verma a Ph.D. in Social Psychology from Patna University recently retired as Prof. of Psychology from Patna University, Patna. She is also one of the founder members of the Association for Social Engineering Research and Training (ASSERT) at Patna. She was a Post Doctoral Fulbright Fellow at the University of Illinois at Urbana Champaing. Dr. Verma has travelled very widely across the world on fellowships, exchange programmes and for participating in international conferences.

She has to her credit around 50 papers in national and international journals. She has served as the member of the executive committee for International Association for Cross-Cultural Psychology.

Kailash B.L. Srivastava a Ph.D. from Indian Institute of Technology, Kanpur is a Professor of Psychology at the Indian Institute of Technology, Kharagpur. Earlier he taught at BITS Pilani, and T.A. Pai Management Institute, Manipal, and also served as visiting faculty in XLRI Jamshedpur, and AIT Bangkok. He has published papers in national and international journals and attended many national and international conferences. He has a board member of Academy of International Business (India chapter), and executive committee member of the National Academy of Psychology, India.

Purnima Singh a D.Phil. from the Centre of Advanced Study, Department of Psychology, University of Allahabad is currently a faculty at IIT Delhi. She has been a Commonwealth Academic Staff Fellow at the University of Bristol, UK. She is a recipient of the Young Scientist Award by the Indian Science Congress Association. She has worked on a number of research projects related to justice, inter-group relations, identity, collective experience and cross-cultural issues. She has been an Associate Editor of Psychology and Developing Societies and Psychological Studies (Springer). At present she is the Treasurer of the National Academy of Psychology, India and Executive of the Asian Association of Social Psychology.

R. Barry Ruback is a Professor of Crime, Law, Justice and Sociology at Pennsylvania State University. He was a Fulbright Fellow, and India-American Fellow, and a Fulbright-Hays Fellow for research in India and was a Fulbright South Asia Regional Scholar for research in India, Pakistan and Bangladesh. He is interested in environmental psychology, psychology and law.

Rajeshwar Mishra a Ph.D. of Patna University served as faculty member of A.N. Sinha Institute of Social Studies and presently he is a faculty of Central University of Bihar. He is a team leader of an Indo-Dutch North Bengal Terai Development Project, Jalpaiguri. He is the founder Secretary of ASSERT. Currently he is Adviser of three institutions in North Bengal which he founded, for example Centre for the Development of Human Initiatives (CDHI), Utter Bengo Teraiahila Samiti (UBTMS), Uttar Benga Mistry Cooperatives.

Ramadhar Singh an M.S. and Ph.D. in Social Psychology from Purdue University earlier served as a Lecturer at Patna University, an Assistant Professor at the Indian Institute of Technology, Kanpur, and a Professor at the Indian Institute of Management, Ahmedbad is currently a Professor of Psychology at the National University of Singapore. Singh is a fellow of the American Psychological Association, Association of Psychological Science, British Psychological Society, Society of Personality and Social Psychology, Singapore Psychological Society, and National Academy of Psychology (India). He has published widely in the international journals of Applied, Developmental and Social psychology. The NUS alumni voted Singh as an Inspiring Mentor in 2009. In 2010, he will join the Indian Institute of Management Bangalore as a Distinguished Professor.

R.B.N. Sinha a Ph.D. in Psychology from Patna University is currently working as Head of the Deptt. of Psychology, B.S. College, Danapur, Patna and life member of ASSERT (Association for Social Engineering, Research and Training). He has been a General Fellow of the Indian Council of Social Science Research (ICSSR), has published over forty research articles in national and international journals. He attended and presented research papers in the 13th World Congress of the World Association for Dynamic Psychiatry (WADP) in Munich (Germany) and 15th International Congress of Applied Psychology (ICAP), Singapore. His current research interests are Cultural and Cross-Cultural Psychology.

Sadanand Singh gained doctorate degrees in Aesthetics at Ranchi University, Hearing and Speech Sciences at the Ohio State University and an Honorary Doctorate of Law from Ohio University. He also served on the faculties of the Ohio State University, Howard University, Ohio University, University of Texas and San Diego State University and as the department chairman at San Diego State University and Howard University as well as being on the Board of Advisors in various committees of Howard, San Diego State, University of California in San Diego, University of Arizona, University of Texas, American Speech, Hearing, and Language Foundation, National Braille Institute, National Institute for the Hard of Hearing and the National Council for the Hearing Impaired. He was honoured with the Second Wilbur Gould Award from The Voice Foundation, the Distinguished Services Award from the Council of Academic Programmes in Communication Sciences and Disorders, the Honours of the American Speech-Hearing Association (ASHA), the

Lyberger Award of the American Academy of Audiology and, in 2009, ASHA's Diversity Champion Award. The nominator statement of this latter award reads: *'Dr. Singh has a great passion for our field and for each individual in our professional community. We owe a great deal to the huge heart of Dr. Singh, not just the American Speech-Language-Hearing Foundation, but all of us, who have received the benefit of his forward-thinking creativity. He is our champion, a leader, and a visionary.'*

Shailendra Singh a Ph.D. from IIT, Kanpur is a Professor of Organizational Behaviour at Indian Institute of Management, Lucknow. He is interested in understanding and enhancing effectiveness of individual and organizational systems both in industrial and social sectors. His research interests include: stress management, emotional intelligence, high performance organizations, mentoring, power and politics, Organizational culture and values, self help groups, health management, and management of education. He has published four books and more than forty papers and in peer reviewed national and international journals. He actively contributes to Management Development Programmes on issues of personal growth and effectiveness.

Soumendu Biswas MBA form EILLM Kolkata and Ph.D. from IIT Kharagpur is currently working with the Xavier Institute of Social Sciences, Ranchi. Earlier he has worked with the cement industry and International School of Business and Media, and IILM Kolkata. He has published 10 papers in journals. He is a member of NAOP India and Indian Society of Training and Development, New Delhi, India. His current research interests include organizational culture, HRM practices and multivariate data analysis with reference to SEM procedures.

Sunita Singh-Sengupta a Ph.D. of Patna University is a Professor of Organizational Behaviour at Faculty of Management Studies, University of Delhi, India. Currently she is a Homi Bhabha Fellow and conducting a global research on "Developing Intra-Psychic Health at Workplace". Prior to this she served Indian Institute of Management, Calcutta as an Associate Professor in the Behavioural Science Group for about ten years. Singh-Sengupta has authored ten books and about three dozen articles in several national and international journal of repute.

Sweta Srivastava Malla a Ph.D. from the Indian Institute of Technology, Kanpur is currently working as Assistant Professor at the Indian Institute of Foreign Trade, New Delhi. She had worked earlier at the Indian Institute of Management, Kozhikode, Calicut, Kerala, and has developed courses in Organizational Theory, and Design, Business Ethics, and Organizational Behaviour, and conducted training courses in Organizational Justice, and Resilience. She has research interests in positive psychology, well-being, and organizational justice paradigms, and has a number of research articles to her credit.

T.N. Sinha first Ph.D. awardees under Prof. J.B.P. Sinha from Patna University, is an honourary Professor of Human Resource Management at Assert Institute of Management Studies, Patna. Recently, Dr. Sinha retired as Professor and Head of the Psychology Department from B.S. College Danapur, Patna (MU). He worked with Prof. Jai B.P. Sinha on a number of research projects and published few research papers jointly with him. He has to his credit around 25 research papers and a number of research reports published in national and international journals of repute. Prof. Sinha has participated in seminars, workshops and conferences in India and abroad and served as Resource person in Training programmes in the field of Education, Health and Management. Prof. Sinha is the founding and life member of Assert and presently serving the organization (ASSERT) as Secretary.

INDEX